To Gary & Diane
Schuller

Supply side
economics is
the antidote to
poverty

[signature]

AN INQUIRY
into the Nature and Causes of the Wealth of States

AN INQUIRY

into the Nature and Causes of the Wealth of States

How Taxes, Energy, and Worker Freedom Change Everything

Dr. Arthur B. Laffer
Stephen Moore
Rex A. Sinquefield
Travis H. Brown

WILEY

Published by John Wiley & Sons, Inc., Hoboken, New Jersey.
Published simultaneously in Canada.

For general information on our other products and services or for technical support, please contact our Customer Care Department within the United States at (800) 762-2974, outside the United States at (317) 572-3993 or fax (317) 572-4002.

Wiley publishes in a variety of print and electronic formats and by print-on-demand. Some material included with standard print versions of this book may not be included in e-books or in print-on-demand. If this book refers to media such as a CD or DVD that is not included in the version you purchased, you may download this material at http://booksupport.wiley.com. For more information about Wiley products, visit www.wiley.com.

Library of Congress Cataloging-in-Publication Data:

ISBN 978-1-118-92122-7 (cloth)
ISBN 978-1-118-92124-1 (ebk)
ISBN 978-1-118-92123-4 (ebk)

Printed in the United States of America

10 9 8 7 6 5 4 3 2 1

We dedicate this book to Professor Colin Campbell of Dartmouth University and his late wife Rosemary Campbell, for their enormous contribution to our understanding of the political economics of states. We especially wish to single out their paper, A Comparative Study of the Fiscal Systems of New Hampshire and Vermont, 1940–1974, *published by the Wheelabrator Foundation in 1976.*

Contents

Prologue

[S]cience needs much more in the way of prior hypothesis and theory than most [researchers are] willing to admit; there is no way to boil down a mass of raw data into a theory unless we are prepared to take a leap of faith by suggesting (and then testing) some generative mechanism for it.

—Philip Ball, *Curiosity*

P rior to diving into the substance of this book, we wish to recognize the enormous contribution to state economics by Dartmouth Professor Colin Campbell. Professor Campbell, now in his 90s, pioneered the analysis of the consequences of different state economic policies and the resulting differences in actual performance metrics. His paper "A Comparative Study of the Fiscal Systems of New Hampshire and Vermont, 1940–1974,"[1] coauthored with his wife Rosemary Campbell, went from policy choices all the way to the provision of public services. For many, many years, both the content of his work and its conclusions were seemingly lost to state policy makers. We intend to rectify this serious oversight.

We also wish to point out our frequent borrowing of context and quotes from the wonderful book, *Curiosity,* by Philip Ball.[2] Nearly every quote at the beginning of each chapter in this book has been drawn from *Curiosity*. If we fail to cite Ball at every instance where appropriate, we beg him please to forgive us. His work is incredible. And, last, we discovered an absolutely superb analysis by Dr. Thomas R. Dye[3] of the nine states that introduced the state income tax, starting with Michigan and

Nebraska in 1967, after having already written our Chapter 1. We started our analysis with West Virginia (1961) followed by Indiana (1963), which were not included by Dye. Dye's conclusions and ours were, as you would suspect, essentially the same.

When it comes to cross-border movements, the study of international economics usually takes as a given that both labor and capital are relatively immobile. By the very definition, international cross-border movements of land don't happen. But, as we all know from reading European and world history, even land changes hands from time to time. There's always the story of the man whose farm was part of a land repatriation from Russia to Poland, reversing the Russian annexation that had occurred after World War II. The farmer was quoted as saying, "Thank God, we won't have to suffer those long Russian winters anymore!"

Within the confines of the specific assumptions, international economics develops and expands the role that incentives have on trade, growth, production, and consumption in both static and dynamic terms, as well as how government policies and natural endowments affect the various economies of the world. International economics has been an anchor tenant for government policies from time immemorial. Trade in goods and services appears to have been an enormously powerful force for the evolution of modern economies from the very first time modern humans appeared on planet Earth. And trade still is an enormously powerful force that attracts a disproportionate amount of attention from governments large and small, near and far.

The United States was built on a clear understanding of the benefits of the free flow of goods, services, and people among the states, of Ricardo's "gains from trade" and Adam Smith's notion of specialization that leads to "comparative advantage." The ideal of total and complete free trade was written into our very foundation papers. The Commerce Clause of the U.S. Constitution has been interpreted to prohibit excessive impediments to the free trade in goods, services, and even labor among the states of the United States.

And under the Privileges and Immunities Clause, people are entitled to migrate and resettle into any state without limitation; they need only abide by the laws and regulations of their new home, just as longtime residents do.[4]

But total uninhibited free trade in goods, services, and labor, as exists among the 50 states of the United States, brings us to an extreme variant of international economics—a corner solution, so to speak. Now the only truly immobile factor of production is land itself. Some forms of fixed capital too may be immobile for the period of their useful lives, but, in due course, even buildings can in a sense slip across state borders, as is witnessed by the decline and fall of Detroit, Michigan, and the expansion and rise of Dallas, Texas. It may take time, but it does happen. Recently we concluded a study on the impact that California's aggressive tax and regulatory policies have had on the extensive infrastructure that Chevron has invested and operates in California.[5] The bottom line of that study was that once the capital is in place and impossible to disassemble and move, the capital itself is helpless to oppose complete expropriation by state government, whether implemented explicitly or implicitly through taxation and regulation.

The economics of the various states of the United States are unique. And the measures of their relative successes and failures are equally unique. In international economics, where populations and labor are essentially immobile, arbitrage across national boundaries occurs through trade in goods and services and through changes in the terms of trade (inflation-adjusted exchange rates). In the case of international economics where populations are immobile, measures of success or failure include income per capita, unemployment, and other measures of the standard of living. When labor is freely and, relatively speaking, costlessly mobile across state boundaries, however, as is the case in the United States, measures such as income per capita or unemployment rates no longer pertain. Any measure of prosperity where the number of people is in the denominator, such as income per capita or the unemployment rate, makes little or no sense when people can move to where income or jobs are located, or the jobs and income can move to where the people are located.

In the case of the 50 U.S. states, increases in income per capita, for example, can occur when a state attracts income over its borders faster than it attracts people or when a state repels people faster than it repels income. While income per capita may increase in both cases, the welfare implications are diametrically opposed. Measures of movement of the factors of production, income, goods, and people are the appropriate metrics for measuring welfare when it comes to each of the 50 states of the United States, not income per capita or unemployment rates.[6] We revisit this principle at several points in the book simply because the point is essential to understanding state economics. Do not use measures standardized by population to evaluate the efficacy of state and local economic policies.

State and local governments have almost unlimited powers to tax, spend, regulate, and oversee as long as their voters choose to permit them to do so and as long as the Commerce Clause of the Constitution and the Privileges and Immunities Clause of the Constitution are not violated. And, with the powerful presence of those clauses, people, goods, and services also have their constitutionally given rights to locate when and where they wish.

Given the trivial differences in language as spoken in the various states, the existence of a common currency, and the fairly similar social customs of the various state populations, as well as the contiguous nature of all save two of our states, in-migration and out-migration are as painless and costless as possible. The economic integration of the 50 states truly is as close to a perfect economic union as can be conceived. As such, the central theme of this book is simply to answer the following and related questions: Do state and local government economic policies redistribute income, or do they redistribute people?

One of the most immoral acts any government can perpetrate on its citizenry is to enact policies that have the effect of destroying the production base from whence all benefits flow.

The chapters of this book are all intended to provide different perspectives on the role played by state and local governments in creating and preserving state prosperity and well-being. Like different vantage points when viewing a sculpture, no one perspective contains the whole truth, but when taken all together, these chapters will comprise a complete rendition of how economic policies impact a state's economy. The mark of genuine science is that its explanations remove the mysteries of policies. Clarity and common sense, supported by direct evidence, are allies of a democratic electorate. Arcane descriptions and excessive complications only dress things up to misdirect the electorate into transferring control to an unworthy elite.

If you look carefully at the differences among the states with respect to taxes, school choice, right-to-work laws, minimum wage, and cultural factors as well, not only does it appear that the blue states are getting bluer, but also that the red states are getting redder. As interesting as the increasing polarization of the states is the drift in the overall spectrum toward red states.

Who could ever have imagined a day when Michigan, the home of the United Auto Workers union and the Teamsters, would become a right-to-work state? And while Wisconsin may not be the headquarters of the auto industry and its unions, it has long been regarded as the political epicenter of the progressive labor movement. With legislation passed under Governor Scott Walker and then unsuccessfully contested by his union-backed naysayers, Wisconsin may not be a right-to-work state in name, but it is a right-to-work state for all practical purposes.

And then, long ago, who could have ever imagined the bankruptcy of Detroit, which in 1950 had a population of 1.8 million mostly prosperous people? Now Detroit has only 680,000 mostly poor people and is the city with the highest violent crime rate in the nation. Politics have consequences, and the two sides of partisan politics, with their wildly different economic visions of what works, have never been as far apart as they are today. To overuse a cliché, America is at a crossroads, and it's not just at the federal level. The battleground is raging in almost every state capital in this nation. Politics, it would seem, bubbles up from the states to the federal level; it doesn't flow down to the states from Washington, D.C.

Chapter 1 is the story of the 11 states that adopted the income tax post-1960. The condition of each state for the five years prior to its adoption of the income tax is contrasted with that state's condition today. Sometimes truth really is stranger than fiction, because each of these 11 states, when compared to the other 39 states, with no exception, declined as a share of population and output. And as shocking as it may seem when compared to the other 39 states, not even one of the 11 states actually increased its share of state and local tax revenues following the adoption of the state income tax.

And, as if 100 percent failure weren't enough, some of the declines were shockingly large, as was the case for Ohio, Michigan, Pennsylvania, and Illinois. Even the poorest of the poor, West Virginia, was made poorer by adopting the insidious income tax. Because some of the states lost people faster than income, however, some of the 11 states reported relative increases in income per capita and tax revenues per capita.

In spite of the fact that a number of the 11 states did have an increase in income and/or tax revenues per capita, the provision of public services in these 11 states generally declined relative to the nation as a whole, putting lie to the claim that tax increases were needed to fund public services.

Chapter 2 takes a rather mundane if not boring topic—the description of much of the data used in this book—and provides those data in an accessible format for the inquisitive reader to peruse. In fact, we succumbed to the temptation ourselves on a number of occasions to point out patterns we observed. We couldn't help but illustrate the performance differences among all states, highlighting the highest and lowest tax rate and tax burden states as well as those infamous 11 states that sought solace in adopting an income tax over the past 50-plus years. You don't have to be a Harvard grad to figure out the result. It may be, as Irving Kristol was fond of saying, that it takes a PhD in economics not to understand the obvious.

Taking oil out of gross state product growth and severance taxes out of tax revenues yields an amazing correlation between individual state growth rates and reductions in tax burdens: The more a state reduces taxes, the faster it grows. The ALEC-Laffer metrics are also clearly related to state performance, but this is laid out in detail in Chapter 8, in a section lifted word for word from an ALEC study entitled "Tax Myths Debunked," by Eric Fruits, PhD, and Randall Pozdena, PhD.[7] Last, we produce in an easily usable tabular form the state migration of adjusted gross income (AGI) data from the Internal Revenue Service. But we refrain from comments here because of the thorough discussion and analysis of these data in Chapter 5. *Bon appétit!*

In Chapter 3, we compare and contrast the performances of select groups of states with respect to a number of policy variables. We are well aware that nature begins with cause and ends with experience, so in our quest to uncover state and local policy prescriptions to make for a better world, we analyze a wide set of key policy variables in their natural extremes. Such sets of extreme policy behavior should, if there are consequences, reveal those consequences in the economic metrics of the state groupings.

For example, taking population growth, net in-migration, employment growth, growth in a state's gross state product, tax revenue growth, and so on, we compare the nine states with no earned income tax to the nine states with the highest earned income tax rates. While we generally stick with percentage changes over the past decade, we make an exception in this chapter and compare the zero earned income tax states to an equal number of the highest earned income tax rate states over the past half century.

We also make these same comparisons with and without oil, as if oil were exclusively a deus ex machina beyond the purview of state lawmakers. State policy, however, does directly impact oil production. By way of example, both Texas and California are endowed with massive reserves of subterranean deposits of oil and gas, and yet California's government has instituted policies that have led to reduced oil production while Texas's government has encouraged increased production. Sticking generally with our groupings, we also compare and contrast corporate taxes (here we used the top and bottom 11 states because of ties) and tax burdens.

In Chapter 4, closely related to Chapter 3, we continue comparisons of state and local policy variables with economic performance metrics. For example, we look at state sales taxes, ALEC-Laffer state outlook rankings, tax progressivity, whether a state has a right-to-work law, state estate taxes, minimum wage differences, and percentages of the labor force unionized.

We believe that it is exceptional cases that best reveal underlying relationships. Or, in the words of William Eamon as quoted in the afore-mentioned book, *Curiosity*, "all the bizarre objects and rarities become urgently relevant to scientific enterprise. They became the vital clues to the underlying mechanisms." And in these two chapters, much is revealed.

The differences in performance between the pro-growth and anti-growth groupings are enormous. The nine zero earned income tax rate states absolutely demolish the highest income tax rate states over the past 10 years and over each and every year of the past 50 years. Better ALEC-Laffer test scores, lower overall tax burdens, more oil, right-to-work legislation, and fewer unions all are strongly associated with more growth in population and greater prosperity. As Larry Wayne Gatlin says, "It ain't rocket surgery."

Chapter 5 mines the recent data releases by the Internal Revenue Service on state-to-state migration of federal tax returns from tax year 1992, which is filing year 1993, to the present. This chapter also drills down on the unique role New Hampshire, with zero income tax and zero sales tax, plays among the old-world statist policies of the other states in New England. This discussion of New Hampshire adds to and updates the wonderful work by Professor Colin Campbell referred to earlier. New Hampshire, in short, is the only ray of hope in an otherwise dismal agglomeration of under-performing states.

The adjusted gross income (AGI) migration data only confirm the overwhelming importance of state economic policies on people's choice of where to live and work. The five worst states (i.e., those with largest net out-migration of tax returns) are New Jersey, New York, Illinois,

Ohio, and Michigan; the five states Connecticut, Wisconsin, Maine, Rhode Island, and Minnesota round out the bottom 10. Is anyone surprised? We aren't.

Zero income tax states far outperform the highest income tax states, as do the lowest tax burden states. It's pretty straightforward. And then there are the right-to-work states versus the forced-union states. It is amazing how much better the right-to-work states are at attracting adjusted gross income and taxpayers. And to cap the analysis off, those 11 states that introduced the income tax over the past 50-plus years are all in the bottom half of net tax returns.

These data are the very data most appropriate for state governments, and their finances and the results couldn't be more definitive.

As part of a comprehensive picture of the effects of state and local taxes, regulations, and spending, Chapter 6 provides a precise statistical analysis of all 50 states over the past 10 years. Using a cross-section time-series least-squares regression analysis, tax rates, tax burdens, oil, and right-to-work legislation are found to be the key independent variables related to population growth and gross state product growth. Surprised? Of course not.

The comprehensive statistical techniques used in this chapter help to corroborate the findings in each of the other chapters. While powerful in and of themselves, the statistical results do nothing save add a whole other layer of confirmation on an already overwhelmingly demonstrated relationship between state and local economic policies and their predicted consequences. Higher tax burdens, higher income tax rates, and higher corporate tax rates all have devastating effects on population and output growth. Right-to-work legislation and oil production, however, have as large positive contributions to individual states' economic well-being as higher tax rates have negative contributions. The picture is clear—crystal clear.

In the realm of the political economy, no battleground could be more grandiose than the clash of ideologies between California and Texas. Two three-term governors are duking it out on the world stage. What could possibly have a greater impact on global opinion?

Here we have the educated, sophisticated, intellectual state of California, where all decisions are either made by government or overseen by government to assure that everything done is for the good of all. And in the other corner we have the wild, unfettered cowboy capitalism of Texas, where government involvement is eschewed and Adam Smith's invisible hand is worshipped.

In Chapter 7, the tax and regulatory differences between Texas and California are enumerated. The tax revenue differences are recorded, government spending is delineated, and, finally, the actual provision of public services, the metrics of economic growth, and the alleviation of want, deprivation, and hardship are exposed for one and all to see. We can think of no other straight-up comparison where the differences are starker or the answers clearer.

California has tax rates that are roughly 65 percent higher than are Texas's tax rates. California has tax revenues that are about 25 percent higher than are Texas's tax revenues. The two states are pretty close to even when it comes to government spending, and by the time they get to the provision of public services, Texas has it all over California.

Texas grows faster, employs more people, and attracts more residents. Texas also has better roads, police protection, fire protection, schools, and prison facilities, as well as less poverty and less need for welfare workers. *C'est ça!*

In our quest to improve public finances in individual states, our purpose is not just to cut taxes and spending, but also to make taxes and spending more efficacious. When it comes to a state's fiscal decisions, or any other government entity's for that matter, there are three considerations. The first consideration is the total size of state and local taxes and spending. Taxes and spending, as a whole, matter—and matter a lot.

Second, it also matters how a state collects the taxes it collects. Generically, the ideal would be to collect taxes in the least damaging fashion in order to garner the requisite revenues to run government at all levels.

And third, how governments in a state spend what they spend also matters enormously. On a conceptual level, the place a government hopes to find itself would be where each dollar spent is on the most beneficial projects. What people don't want is a scenario where only people who do work are taxed and only people who don't work are subsidized. The results won't be attractive.

The ideal spending and tax code for a state would be one where the damage done by the last dollar of tax collected is just a smidgeon less than the benefit provided by the last dollar spent. Then the government should stop spending and taxing dead in its tracks and let the markets solve the rest of the wants and needs of its citizenry.

The final chapter of this book—Chapter 8—is a point-by-point rebuttal of the counterarguments made by our critics. At the outset, to explain migration patterns for people and income among the 50 states, we highlight the role played by self-interest, and we also note that our own self-interest and the self-interest of our critics helps to explain some of our and their comments. And, true to form, no matter how overwhelming our logic and evidence may be, we hold out little hope that the beneficiaries of government largesse who work in tax-exempt organizations would be able to overcome their own perceived self-interest and join with us to design a better future for one and all. It's really true that to someone whose only tool is a hammer the whole world does look like a nail. Many of our critics rebut arguments they know to be true in order to curry favor with their political benefactors.

The purpose to which we intend our research to be put is as a practical guide to state and local officials to better govern and to provide prosperity and quality of life to those governed. In the words of Robert Boyle, as quoted in *Curiosity*:

> I shall not dare to think my self a true naturalist till my skill can make my garden yield better herbs and flowers, or my orchard better fruit, or my field better corn, or my dairy better cheese, than theirs that are strangers to physiology.

To us, a small truth is preferable to a great falsehood, and yet others would seem to prefer complex error to simple truth. State economics isn't all that profound. Just follow the money. To understand the practical workings of a state, you need not be a learned professor. Nor do you need to become mired in the rhetorical swamps of classical disputation. Your experience and common sense should serve you well even in the face of scholarly disapproval. We wrote this book, in part, to set you free to see for yourself just how the world does work.

The truth really should be what we harvest from the bountiful provisions of data afforded us by 50 states over as many years. Knowledge is power.

CHAPTER 1

The Fall from Grace

The Story of States 11 and the Income Tax Adopted

The mark of genuine science is that its explanations take the mystery out of things. Imposture dresses things up to seem more wonderful than they would be without the dress.

—Philip Ball, *Curiosity*

Foremost among the economic policies available to state and sometimes even local governments is the income tax. Today, 41 out of 50 states collect income taxes on so-called earned income. Of the nine states that have chosen not to tax earned income, two tax what is called unearned income. Thus, there are really only seven states where income of any sort is not taxed at either the state or local level. But this wasn't always the case.

The Implementation of an Income Tax— A Terrible Mistake

Immediately prior to 1960, there were 19 states where earned income was not taxed and 31 states where it was. Between 1960 and the present,

11 of those 19 states adopted an income tax, and one lone state—Alaska—got rid of its income tax.

The story of the 11 states that adopted an income tax summarizes the object lesson of this book. Here's their unabridged story:

The 11 states that adopted a state income tax in the past half century encompass a wide cross section of American life, but do not include any states from the South or Far West. As it so happens, there are only three states in the South without an earned income tax—Tennessee, Florida, and Texas—and there are four states in the Far West without income taxes—Nevada, Wyoming, Washington, and Alaska. The other two states without earned income taxes are South Dakota and New Hampshire.

The 11 states that deserted the no-income-tax team are Maine, Rhode Island, Connecticut, New Jersey, Pennsylvania, West Virginia, Ohio, Indiana, Illinois, Michigan, and Nebraska. At the time the income tax was adopted, each of these states believed the economic damage done by the income tax would be minimal and that the increase in public services would be considerable. They were dead wrong!

Table 1.1 shows exactly what happened to the primary economic metrics of the 11 states once they adopted an earned income tax. Because these states adopted income taxes in different years, we use the four years preceding the actual implementation of the income tax and the year of implementation itself as their pre–income tax era. We then compare their pre–income tax era to the most recent year's performance.

Comparing the 11 states to all 50 states introduces a measurement bias, in that the 11 states are double counted; that is, they would be part of the 11 as well as the 50. A preferable measure, and the one we've chosen to use in this chapter for evaluation purposes, is to compare the 11 states that adopted the income tax to the 39 remaining states. While comparing the 11 states to all 50 states creates a bias in the magnitudes, the conclusions would be minimally affected because the directions of change all remain the same. Qualitatively, whether comparing the 11 states to all 50 states or only to the 39 remaining states, the results are basically the same. Quantitatively, they are significantly different.

TABLE 1.1

Metrics of the 11 States That Adopted an Income Tax Post-1960 versus the Percentage of 39 Remaining States*

States	First Year of Tax	Maximum Tax Rate*		Shares of 39 Remaining States								
				Population			GSP			Total State and Local Tax Revenue		
		Initial	Current	5 Years Before	2012	% Change	5 Years Before	2012	% Change	5 Years Before	2011	% Change
Connecticut	1991	1.50%	6.70%	1.81%	1.49%	(18)	2.39%	1.92%	(20)	2.35%	2.25%	(4)
New Jersey	1976	2.50	8.97	4.94	3.68	(26)	5.38	4.25	(21)	5.40	5.25	(3)
Ohio	1972	3.50	5.93	7.59	4.79	(37)	8.03	4.27	(47)	6.07	4.46	(27)
Rhode Island	1971	5.25	5.99	0.68	0.44	(36)	0.64	0.43	(33)	0.65	0.50	(22)
Pennsylvania	1971	2.30	3.07	8.51	5.29	(38)	8.49	5.03	(41)	7.66	5.51	(28)
Maine	1969	6.00	7.95	0.74	0.55	(25)	0.58	0.45	(23)	0.60	0.60	(0.2)
Illinois	1969	2.50	5.00	8.08	5.34	(34)	9.82	5.82	(41)	7.77	5.89	(24)
Nebraska	1968	2.60	6.84	1.10	0.77	(30)	1.03	0.83	(19)	0.93	0.77	(17)
Michigan	1967	2.00	4.25	6.33	4.10	(35)	7.86	3.35	(57)	6.62	3.57	(46)
Indiana†	1963	2.00	3.40	3.80	2.71	(29)	3.81	2.36	(38)	3.37	2.29	(32)
West Virginia†	1961	5.40‡	6.50	1.54	0.77	(50)	1.19	0.63	(47)	1.09	0.69	(37)

*State tax rate only (i.e., does not include any additional local taxes).

†Due to data limitations, shares of personal income have been substituted for Indiana and West Virginia's shares of GSP.

‡Statutory rate was 6.0% of U.S. tax liability applied to a top U.S. rate of 91%.

Source: U.S. Census Bureau, Bureau of Economic Analysis, Laffer Associates.

3

That Giant Sucking Sound Is People, Output, and Tax Revenue Fleeing Income Taxes

In Table 1.1, we list each of the 11 states that has adopted an income tax over the past 50-plus years and, for each state, the year in which the income tax was adopted, the highest income tax rate when the tax was adopted, the current highest income tax rate, the percentage of each state's population to the total population of the 39 states in the five years prior to and including the year of adopting the income tax, the percentage of each state's population to the total of the 39 states in 2012, the percentage of the total of the 39-state gross domestic product (or gross state product [GSP]) for each of the 11 states in the five years preceding and including the adoption year of the income tax, the percentage of total 39-state GSP in 2012 for each of the 11 states, total state and local tax revenues as a share of the total of the 39 states' state and local taxes in the five years prior to adopting an income tax, and, finally, each state's share of total 39-state state and local taxes in 2011.[1] Pay close attention. The results are dramatic.

Economic Malaise

In terms of population, every single one of the 11 states that introduced the income tax over the past 50-plus years declined in relation to the total of the 39 remaining states. West Virginia, the first state in the modern era to adopt the income tax, reduced its share of the population of the 39 remaining states by a full 50 percent. West Virginia went from a population of 1.83 million in 1961 to 1.86 million in 2012. While no other of the 11 states was able to match West Virginia's precipitous decline in relative population, each and every one of the 11 states reduced its percentage of the remaining 39 states. Especially hard-hit were the industrial giants Pennsylvania, Ohio, Michigan, and Illinois.

Compared to the 39 remaining states since the inception of the income tax, Pennsylvania's population has fallen by 38 percent, Ohio's population by 37 percent, Michigan's population by 35 percent, and Illinois's population by 34 percent.

The whole reason for adopting an income tax by each of the 11 states was, of course, to increase tax revenues. But not one state of the 11 experienced a rise in revenues relative to the other 39 states. It makes you wonder just how much consideration the politicians in these 11 states gave to the welfare of their citizens. It's clear what many of the citizens thought—they left.

In terms of state gross domestic product, each state that introduced an income tax since 1960 has also declined as a share of the 39 remaining states. The differences vary in size, but the change in each state's GSP relative to the remaining 39 states' GSP is universally negative. Michigan's results are especially devastating, with a fall in GSP of 57 percent relative to the 39 remaining states.

Table 1.2 really says it all when it comes to the economic consequences of adopting an income tax. We have listed all 50 states' population growth over the past decade from highest to lowest. Just look at the highlighted rankings of those 11 states that have adopted an income tax since 1960. Each of those 11 states is in the bottom half of the U.S. rankings; nine are in the worst 13 states, and three are the worst three states.

The long-term debilitating consequences of adopting an income tax just keep on getting worse. Like a bad case of poison ivy, the state income tax is the gift that just keeps on giving.

But as dramatic as these results are, they don't tell the whole story by any means. The human condition is more than just dollars and cents.

Misleading Measures

As if primed to corroborate our earlier admonition to avoid measures such as average income (income per capita), while each of the 11 states declined as a share of the 39 remaining states in both population and income, five of the 11 states experienced increases in income per capita relative to the rest of the nation, and six had declines in income per

TABLE 1.2

Ten-Year Population Growth by State: Percentage Change, 2002 to 2012 (ranked highest to lowest)

Rank	State	% Change	Rank	State	% Change
1	Nevada	26.92	26	Maryland	8.16
2	Utah	22.82	27	Alabama	7.63
3	Arizona	21.44	28	Nebraska	7.36
4	Texas	20.14	29	Minnesota	7.18
5	Idaho	19.05	30	Kentucky	7.10
6	North Carolina	17.13	31	Kansas	6.35
7	Georgia	16.59	32	Indiana	6.20
8	Florida	15.75	33	Missouri	6.12
9	Colorado	15.53	34	Wisconsin	5.16
10	Wyoming	15.28	35	Iowa	4.77
11	South Carolina	14.99	36	Mississippi	4.42
12	Washington	13.96	37	New Hampshire	4.07
13	Alaska	13.87	38	Connecticut	3.80
14	Delaware	13.76	39	New Jersey	3.65
15	New Mexico	12.41	40	Massachusetts	3.57
16	Virginia	12.34	41	Pennsylvania	3.51
17	Hawaii	12.32	42	Illinois	2.79
18	Tennessee	11.39	43	West Virginia	2.77
19	Oregon	10.98	44	Maine	2.56
20	Montana	10.25	45	Louisiana	2.33
21	South Dakota	9.65	46	New York	2.26
22	North Dakota	9.63	47	Vermont	1.72
23	Oklahoma	9.34	48	Ohio	1.20
24	California	9.09	49	Michigan	−1.32
25	Arkansas	8.99	50	Rhode Island	−1.47

Source: U.S. Census Bureau.

capita. While each of these 11 states was a loser in the competition of all states, six were bigger losers in changes in GSP than they were in population, and five were bigger losers in changes in population than they were in changes in GSP.

Our critics point to the fact that almost half of the 11 states that adopted an income tax since 1960 had increases in average income (i.e., income per capita relative to the rest of the nation) as proof positive that adopting an income tax has no measureable effect on the prosperity of a state. We know better. They're all losers!

To see just how far off track so-called experts can be, just take a look at the following quote by Professor Mickey Hepner, Dean of the University of Central Oklahoma's College of Business, in a debate with Dr. Laffer:

> Now, I'll be honest with you, as an economist I am a floored and shocked that I would ever hear an economist say that average income is not a viable measure or a valid measure for a state's well-being, which I heard just a few minutes ago.[2]

And of course the reason Professor Hepner is "floored and shocked" is simply because he has a hard time grasping the concept that income and people are equally mobile among the states. Sometimes low-performance states repel population faster than they repel income, and income per capita rises. And sometimes low-performance states repel income faster than they repel population, and income per capita falls. In either case, the simple fact is that in both cases these are low-performance states.

Ohio

One of the authors of this book is a Buckeye through and through, tracing most of his family to their northeastern Ohio roots in the very early 1800s. On one of his recent family visits to Cleveland's Lakeview Cemetery, he surveyed the Cleveland where he had been raised. Today, Ohio in general and Cleveland specifically are hollowed-out, crushed shadows of their former selves. The only enterprises prospering are tax-exempt entities such as the Cleveland Clinic and Cleveland State University. In Youngstown, where he was born, a city ordinance requiring abandoned houses to be torn down and grass planted where they once stood has transformed Youngstown from a thriving steel town into an abandoned farm.

Legend has it that in years past, the then mayor of Youngstown blurted out, referring to the river that runs through Youngstown, "The Mahoning River is for jobs, not for fishes." Today, both jobs and fishes are gone.

To see just how bad Ohio's performance over the past 20 or so years has been, we have listed and plotted in Table 1.3 the number of federal

TABLE 1.3

Net In-Migrant Returns as a Percentage of Gross Returns (Returns In ÷ Returns Out)
(ranked highest to lowest)

92/93	93/94	94/95	95/96	96/97	97/98	98/99	99/00	00/01	01/02	02/03	03/04	04/05	05/06	06/07	07/08	08/09	09/10
ID	NV	NV	NV	NV	NV	NV	NV	NV	FL	NV	NV	AZ	AZ	SC	SC	TX	TX
NV	AZ	AZ	AZ	AZ	AZ	AZ	AZ	FL	NV	FL	FL	FL	TX	NC	NC	SC	DC
CO	ID	NC	NC	NC	NC	CO	GA	AZ	AZ	AZ	AZ	NV	NC	NV	TX	NC	CO
OR	GA	GA	GA	FL	FL	GA	FL	CO	OR	ME	DE	ID	GA	AZ	CO	CO	OK
AZ	NC	OR	OR	GA	GA	NC	CO	GA	ME	DE	NC	NC	SC	GA	OR	WY	LA
MT	CO	TN	TN	CO	CO	SC	NC	NC	DE	SC	ID	SC	ID	TN	AZ	WA	SC
WA	TN	ID	FL	TN	SC	FL	NH	NH	NC	ID	SC	TN	FL	TX	WA	DC	ND
GA	FL	FL	NH	DE	DE	DE	DE	OR	GA	OR	GA	DE	AL	ID	GA	OK	NC
UT	OR	CO	AL	ID	ID	NC	SC	DE	SC	GA	GA	OR	DE	OR	UT	OR	AK
NC	UT	ID	TX	UT	TX	ID	SC	GA	NH	VA	TN	TN	CO	UT	TN	LA	WV
TN	MT	AR	TN	TN	TN	TN	VA	SC	MD	GA	MT	GA	UT	WY	NV	TN	NM
FL	NM	WA	DE	DE	DE	OR	TN	NH	TX	TN	VA	FL	MT	CO	ID	WV	VA
AR	AR	SC	WA	WA	WA	VA	ID	ME	CO	NC	ME	AL	WA	WA	WY	AL	SD
NM	WA	UT	ID	ID	ID	TX	ID	TX	VA	MT	AR	WA	AR	MT	MT	AR	FL
AL	DE	DE	NH	NH	NH	WA	MN	VA	NM	NH	NM	MT	DE	DE	DE	AZ	KY
DE	NM	NM	KY	KY	KY	ME	TX	ID	TN	NM	WA	AL	CO	LA	AL	GA	TN
TX	DE	NH	AL	AR	AL	MN	AR	MD	ID	WA	HI	TX	UT	AL	LA	DE	AZ
MN	MS	TX	MO	VA	VA	KY	OR	RI	RI	KY	AL	NM	MT	KY	AR	UT	DE
KY	KY	MO	KY	KY	AR	AR	RI	WA	WA	AR	KY	KY	NM	AR	KY	NM	AR
WV	AL	MT	AR	AR	MS	MS	CA	NM	NM	HI	VA	VA	WY	OK	SD	ND	OR
MO	MO	NM	VA	VA	OK	MO	MN	WY	WY	WV	TX	CO	KY	NM	WV	KY	AL
SC	SC	MS	MS	MS	MO	MD	VT	KY	KY	TX	MS	HI	OK	FL	OK	SD	WA
MS	SD	AL	OK	OK	KS	VT	KY	KY	KY	RI	SD	MO	HI	WV	DC	VA	GA
VA	NH	MN	AL	KS	CA	MA	WI	AR	WV	WA	WY	NH	WV	SD	MS	MT	MT

Source: Internal Revenue Service, Laffer Associates

tax returns moving into Ohio less the number of federal tax returns leaving Ohio as a share of the sum of both. The state of Ohio has gone from very bad to even worse. In the tax/file year 2009/2010, Ohio is second from the bottom, only to be subordinated by Michigan.

The Story of New Jersey—A Colorful Example of Opportunity Wasted

In 1965, New Jersey had neither an income tax nor a sales tax. It was one of the fastest-growing states in the nation, and people were moving from everywhere into New Jersey. To top it off, New Jersey à la 1965 was on sound budgetary footing. Then, in 1966, New Jersey adopted the sales tax, and in 1976 the income tax. Fast-forward.

In 2009, Jon Corzine was New Jersey's governor, and the state had been through years of tax increases, welfare expansion, and regulatory overreach. New Jersey had the third highest property taxes in the nation, the fifth highest personal income tax rates, the third most progressive tax structure, and one of the highest corporate tax rates in the nation. People were leaving the state in droves, and the budget was deeply in the red.

As we did for Ohio in Table 1.3, we have calculated the net federal income tax returns moving into New Jersey divided by the sum of both inflows and outflows. New Jersey sort of hovers at the bottom of the barrel, ending up in 2009/2010 as fifth from the bottom.

Lower Tax Revenue

When people learn that high tax rates are so often associated with budget deficits, while low tax rates accompany fiscal solvency, they ask, "How is that possible?" The only answer is: You can't balance a budget on the backs of the unemployed or collect tax revenues from people who leave your state. High tax rates are a double-edged sword. You collect more, of course, per dollar of income, but you get less income. Each and every one of the 11 states that imposed an income tax saw a decline in its share of the total of the remaining 39 states' state and local tax revenues. Michigan, for example, had total tax revenues fall from 6.62 percent of the remaining 39 states to 3.57 percent.

What also turns out to be a fascinating regularity arising out of the experiences had by these 11 states is that the decline in gross state product (GSP) relative to the remaining 39 states has been greater in each and every case than the decline in tax revenues relative to the 39 remaining states. Higher taxes kill prosperity and often don't even produce more tax revenues.

There's a curve relating tax rates to tax revenues. And there's a corollary to that curve, which postulates that the longer the tax is in place, the greater will be the fall in income relative to what it would have been, and the more likely a tax rate increase will lead to revenue declines relative to what they would have been. The sensitivity of either income or tax revenues to tax changes depends on the ease and expense by which people are able to find available alternatives to their previous actions.

The obvious fact that a state with no taxes will have no public services does not mean that higher tax rates mean more public services. Think about it for a second. If zero taxes means zero public services, what do 100 percent taxes do for public services? Nothing! And as if to hammer the point home, it appears highly likely that in today's world, given enough time, higher tax rates reduce a state's ability to provide quality public services for one and all.

The Rhetoric Surrounding Tax Revenue and the Decline in Public Services

While many a state has had a negative experience with the primary metrics of economic performance following adoption of the income tax, as we have shown, there are other reasons for adopting an income tax. Many people describe a trade-off between economic growth and the quality of life, where introducing an income tax may slow growth, but it's worth it in terms of the quality of life that enhanced public services will have on the state's residents. And this is exactly the so-called logic used to convince state residents that they would benefit from an income tax. Almost never do you find a ballot measure with a tax increase that doesn't have a dedicated purpose for the funds raised.

The logic goes something like this: Introducing an income tax may slow growth, but it does raise state and local tax revenues, which allow the branches of government closest to the people to provide additional services that the people want and need. Therefore, the growth-focused people may not like an income tax, but the quality-of-life-focused people appreciate a new revenue source dedicated to schools, roads, police protection, hospitals, higher income supplements for the most disadvantaged, and so on. Our favorite quote exemplifying this logic comes once again from Dean Mickey Hepner, arguing against an income tax rate cut in Oklahoma in a debate put on by the State Chamber of Commerce of Oklahoma:

> But we could also cut government spending, and this is a concern to me. As an educator, I know that what really matters for business vocation is the ability of us to train the workforce, the ability of us to provide the necessary services that the companies need. It's hard for me to imagine a successful economy that's populated with unhealthy, uneducated individuals who often have to travel down dirt roads populated with criminals.[3]

Dean Hepner's quote does encapsulate a mind-set of trade-offs between growth and quality of life. And, as facetious as his statement is, it is equally wrong, wrong, wrong. Higher tax rates don't provide more and better public services, but they do create the very poverty that necessitates higher welfare spending.

The Case of the Disappearing Tax Revenue

Before we dig further into measures of the provision of public services in each of the 11 states, we need to have a rough overview of the change in the fiscal constraints each of these states faced after they introduced the personal income tax. What is very clear is that each of the 11 states that adopted a state income tax had projected much higher tax revenues, which didn't even come close to materializing. Each of these states also forecast a significant mitigation of fiscal constraints, which did not happen. But what they didn't forecast was how these fiscal constraints would ease. To the extent that the

fiscal constraints eased, it owed far more to declines in population and reductions in public services than to increases in tax receipts.

The first predicted effect when an income tax is introduced assumes
nothing else changes and tax revenues both absolutely and per capita
increase pari passu. Without supply-side responses, income would be the
same, governments would collect more of it, and the private sector would
have less left over. And that would be that. More for the government
would mean guaranteed mitigation of fiscal pressures. Most politicians and
all but a very few economists stop their analysis right here.

But we all should know the story doesn't stop at static tax revenue increases. Some people and businesses react to higher tax rates by moving to
lower-tax jurisdictions to reduce their tax burden, some by changing the
composition of their income to reduce their tax burden, some by changing
the timing of income to change their tax burden, and, last, some by changing the volume of their income. Once an income tax is adopted, all sorts of
parts start moving, but all with one objective in mind—to reduce the static
tax burden of the newly initiated hike in tax rates. It's pretty straightforward.

And then there are the economic consequences of an income tax. All
of these machinations and goings-on ultimately result in changes in population, changes in participation rates, changes in employment rates, changes in
output, changes in the distribution of income, and changes in tax revenues.
In the context of the United States as a whole, all of these changes are easily
placed in a state context relative to other states. As an example, let's look at
Connecticut, the most recent state to introduce an income tax.

Connecticut

In 1991, under Governor Lowell P. Weiker Jr., Connecticut adopted an
income tax with the highest tax rate set at 1.5 percent; it now stands
at 6.7 percent. By 2012 Connecticut's population had fallen from the
five-year average preceding the adoption of the income tax of 1.81
percent of the remaining 39 states to 1.49 percent in the latest year.
In percentage terms, this is a relative decline of 18 percent. Connecticut's
tax revenues also fell from 2.35 percent of the remaining 39 states' state
and local tax revenues to 2.25 percent in 2011, or by 4 percent.[4]

Connecticut, like the other 10 states that adopted an income tax, has also driven a lot of people from their residences in Connecticut to other destinations. These out-migrants have been pushed out of Connecticut to fend for themselves in other states in exchange for the promise of higher welfare and nonwelfare public service inputs in Connecticut. Those ex-residents of Connecticut also fled the state to enjoy their free-and-clear after-tax income. If "revealed preferences" mean anything, these expatriate Connecticut residents prefer their new domiciles' taxes and provisions of public services to those in Connecticut.

As we described earlier for Ohio and New Jersey and as is shown in Table 1.3, we have calculated the net inflow of tax returns into Connecticut as a share of both inflows and outflows of federal tax returns. Connecticut in the years immediately after the introduction of an income tax had a huge out-migration of tax returns. Things got a little better around 2000/2001, but then sank again. It was never as high as the 20th worst state and usually ranked in the bottom 10.

Additionally, when Connecticut's share of the total U.S. population falls, other states' shares of U.S. population have to increase. Where those expatriate Connecticut residents ultimately settle down is also the place where they take their incomes and skills. The expatriates will have a corresponding impact on their destination states just as their departure had on Connecticut. In this case, what's bad for the goose is actually good for the gander.

In Table 1.3 we have displayed, for each of the 50 states plus D.C. and for each year of available Internal Revenue Service (IRS) migration data, the number of net in-migrant tax returns in a given state as a share of the gross number of migrant tax returns for that same state. We have ranked each column by highest to lowest net in-migrant returns as a share of gross migrant returns, thus showing the magnitude and direction of how tax returns have migrated into or out of a state over time. We have then plotted Connecticut, Ohio, and New Jersey for each year to demonstrate just how many tax returns Connecticut, Ohio, and New Jersey have lost each year due to citizens voting with their feet. You'd have to look far and wide to find three bigger losers than these three states.

The stakes have been wagered, and the game is on in the never-ending competition among the 50 states. The one thing we can feel good about is that as long as people are free to choose, this competition will inure to the betterment of all. Connecticut, along with Ohio and New Jersey, is one big loser of a state.

The exodus of relative population from the 11 states that have introduced an income tax has created political changes for their state of origin as it has solved economic challenges for the emigrants. People who have left a state may be financially better off because they don't have to pay that state's income taxes anymore. Unfortunately, they no longer vote in that state and therefore have abandoned those who are left behind to the vagaries of the political process. Assuming those who left the introduced income tax state were generally more opposed to the income tax than those who remained, the tax-increasing politicians would feel emboldened. As long as population falls faster than tax revenues, and tax revenues per capita rise for the remaining population—who do vote—there's an ever-increasing incentive for elected officials to continue this antisocial behavior. It's called political predation—but it can't last forever. It soon morphs into a race to the bottom. Too many politicians, like too many wolves, soon deplete their food source (tax base) and the game ends. In the words of New York City Mayor Michael Bloomberg:

> The more a city spends on wages and benefits for employees over what the marketplace determines is necessary for recruitment, retention, and experience, the less a city can invest in benefits for all residents.
>
> The less it invests in things that benefit all residents, the less attractive a place it is to live [in] and visit. And suddenly, the virtuous cycle I mentioned a moment ago comes grinding to a halt—or worse, goes spinning in reverse.[5]

To summarize the results for all 11 states that have introduced an income tax over the past 50-plus years, each and every one of those states lost tax revenues relative to the 39 remaining states, and each state's gross state product share of the remaining 39 states shrank. Tax burdens rose in each state, and each state's economy underperformed.

No Bang for the Buck—How Costly Tax Increases Fail to Result in Better Provision of Public Services

As we discuss what sort of public service improvements the states have attempted to buy with their anti-growth new income tax, we will be using two conceptually different measures of success for their provision of public services. Where possible, we use outside objective measures to gauge the levels and changes in the levels of public services provided in our 11-state group. Where these objective outside measures are lacking, we use the markedly inferior alternative measure of the increase in inputs, such as full-time equivalent employees per 10,000 of population.

Education Results for the 11 States That Adopted the Income Tax

For example, the U.S. Department of Education evaluates the quality of K–12 education for each state by administering uniform tests across all states in a wide range of subjects and has done so for years and years. There are several revisions of and exclusions to these data from time to time, as we will note. The primary tests are in reading and math. In Table 1.4, we list the national rankings of each of the 11 states from the date of testing closest to when that state introduced its income tax to the most recent date. Judge for yourself whether you think the imposition of the income tax was worth it when it comes to education.

Of the 10 states that introduced an income tax over the past 50-plus years for which we have data (we don't have fourth grade reading or fourth grade math data for Illinois), three increased their fourth grade reading score rankings by a small amount, four fell by a small amount, and three fell in the rankings by over 2 percent. Nothing to write home about here, and hardly poster children for the benefits of initiating an income tax. Performance got worse, not better.

In fourth grade math, three of the states improved, seven got worse, and, of the seven that got worse, four virtually collapsed after adopting an income tax. This is what is meant by dumbing-down.

TABLE 1.4

NAEP Scores* (ranked from biggest improvement to least improvement)

4th Grade Reading	Ratio to U.S., 1992	Ratio to U.S., 2013	% Change
Connecticut	1.03	1.04	0.85
Ohio	1.01	1.01	0.27
Rhode Island	1.01	1.01	0.13
Pennsylvania	1.03	1.03	−0.13
New Jersey	1.04	1.04	−0.14
Indiana	1.03	1.02	−0.81
Nebraska	1.03	1.01	−1.73
Michigan	1.01	0.99	−2.05
West Virginia	1.00	0.97	−3.04
Maine	1.06	1.02	−3.50
Illinois[†]	N/A	0.99	N/A

4th Grade Math	Ratio to U.S., 1992	Ratio to U.S., 2013	% Change
Indiana	1.01	1.03	1.93
Ohio	1.00	1.02	1.75
Rhode Island	0.99	1.00	1.55
West Virginia	0.98	0.98	−0.03
Pennsylvania	1.03	1.01	−1.41
New Jersey	1.04	1.02	−1.50
Nebraska	1.03	1.01	−2.20
Michigan	1.01	0.98	−2.39
Connecticut	1.04	1.01	−2.72
Maine	1.06	1.02	−3.81
Illinois[†]	N/A	0.99	N/A

8th Grade Math	Ratio to U.S., 1990	Ratio to U.S., 2013	% Change
New Jersey	1.03	1.04	1.32
Ohio	1.01	1.02	1.22
Illinois	1.00	1.00	0.91
Rhode Island	0.99	1.00	0.82
Pennsylvania	1.02	1.02	0.35
Indiana	1.02	1.01	−0.63
West Virginia	0.98	0.97	−1.03
Michigan	1.01	0.99	−2.22
Connecticut	1.03	1.01	−2.45
Maine[‡]	1.04	1.02	−2.49
Nebraska	1.05	1.01	−4.57

*While the NAEP is now frequently and widely administered across the United States, this is the case only as of late. For this reason, we weren't able to take the data back any further than 1990. We have selected these grade levels (fourth and eighth grade) and subjects (math and reading) because they provide the greatest amount of available data.
†According to the Department of Education, 1992 NAEP scores for fourth grade math and reading in Illinois are "Not Available."
‡According to the Department of Education, 1990 NAEP scores for eighth grade math are "Not Available." We have substituted Maine's 1992 (the next available date) ratio to the U.S. in its stead.

Source: U.S. Department of Education National Assessment of Educational Progress, Laffer Associates.

For eighth grade mathematics scores, the story isn't any better—of the 11 states, seven states' scores fell relative to the United States as a whole. The most astounding change was that of Nebraska, which fell 4.57 percent! Five of the 11 states' rankings rose, with New Jersey's 1.3 percent increase as the largest. Again, there is nothing here to write home about.

As you can readily see from the educational test scores, if anything, those states that adopted an income tax have performed more poorly after the tax was adopted. Whatever the specifics, there is no case to be made that student test scores improved. The income tax was a failure for education.

Health and Hospital Services

Our next category of services is the category of health and hospital employees. Because we haven't been able to find an acceptable state-by-state objective measure of the quality of health and hospital services, we have developed a measure of health and hospital public service inputs, which is the number of full-time equivalent employees (FTEEs) per 10,000 of population.

Let's take a careful look at health and hospital personnel per 10,000 of population relative to the nation before the state's income tax was adopted to the present for the 11 states. In Table 1.5, we show

TABLE 1.5

Health and Hospital FTEEs per 10,000 Population
(ranked from largest increase to smallest increase)

State	Year of Tax Introduction	Ratio to U.S. in Year of Tax Introduction	Ratio to U.S. in 2011	% Change
Ohio	1972	0.72	0.90	23.9
Nebraska	1968	0.98	1.19	21.6
Indiana	1963	1.00	1.08	8.5
West Virginia	1961	0.76	0.76	0.7
New Jersey	1976	0.75	0.71	−4.6
Michigan	1967	1.07	0.91	−15.7
Connecticut	1991	0.88	0.72	−17.7
Maine	1969	0.59	0.41	−31.2
Illinois	1969	0.88	0.55	−37.5
Pennsylvania	1971	0.71	0.34	−51.4
Rhode Island	1971	0.84	0.39	−53.9

Source: U.S. Census Bureau, Laffer Associates.

health and hospital personnel per 10,000 population before the adoption of the income tax and today. Only four states of the 11 actually had more health and hospital personnel per 10,000 of population following the imposition of the income tax relative to the United States as a whole, and seven had less. Four of those seven had huge drops in their FTEEs in hospital and health services relative to the nation as a whole. Again, the newly adopted income tax states failed their citizens.

Police Protection

The official Federal Bureau of Investigation (FBI) measures of violent crimes (Table 1.6) and property crimes (Table 1.7) do not show any systematic changes in relative rankings for the states that adopted an income tax. In terms of the violent crime rate (again, all of these metrics are relative to the United States as a whole), only three of the 11 states managed to reduce their violent crime rate, whereas the violent crime rate increased in each of the other eight states. As for the

TABLE 1.6				
Violent Crime Rate (ranked from largest reduction in crime rate to least reduction in crime rate)				
State	**Year of Tax Introduction**	**Ratio to U.S. in Year of Tax Introduction**	**Ratio to U.S. in 2012**	**% Change**
Michigan	1967	1.54	1.17	−24
Illinois	1969	1.36	1.07	−21
New Jersey	1976	0.85	0.75	−12
Connecticut	1991	0.71	0.73	3
Ohio	1972	0.75	0.77	4
Rhode Island	1971	0.56	0.65	16
Pennsylvania	1971	0.68	0.90	33
Nebraska	1968	0.49	0.67	37
Maine	1969	0.23	0.32	39
Indiana	1963	0.61	0.89	46
West Virginia	1961	0.40	0.82	105

Source: FBI Uniform Crime Reporting Statistics, Laffer Associates.

TABLE 1.7			
Property Crime Rate (ranked from largest reduction in crime rate to least reduction in crime rate)			
State	**Year of Tax Introduction**	**Ratio to U.S. in Year of Tax Introduction**	**Ratio to U.S. in 2012**	**% Change**
Michigan	1967	1.34	0.89	−34
New Jersey	1976	1.04	0.72	−31
Rhode Island	1971	1.22	0.90	−26
Connecticut	1991	0.94	0.75	−20
Illinois	1969	0.90	0.90	0
Indiana	1963	0.97	1.06	9
Ohio	1972	0.88	1.09	24
Pennsylvania	1971	0.61	0.76	24
Nebraska	1968	0.74	0.96	31
Maine	1969	0.56	0.88	58
West Virginia	1961	0.34	0.83	141

Source: FBI Uniform Crime Reporting Statistics, Laffer Associates.

property crime rate, four of the 11 states showed a reduction in the rate of property crimes, one of the 11 states (Illinois) was unchanged, and six of the 11 states showed an increase in property crime rates. It's a crime what the adoption of the income tax has done to the citizens of those states.

Welfare

When it comes to poverty relative to the nation as a whole, only three of the 11 states actually showed reductions in their state poverty rates (see Table 1.8). The other eight states had increases in their relative poverty rates and, of those eight states, four showed very large increases in poverty.

If one of our quality-of-life measures is less poverty, as it should be for any civilized people, then the official measures of poverty weigh against adopting a personal income tax. Given what the income tax does to output, employment, and tax revenues, we really shouldn't be surprised by this result. Whoever heard of a state being taxed into prosperity? Now we know it's the reverse.

TABLE 1.8						
Poverty Rate (ranked from biggest improvement to least improvement)						
		Ratio of State Poverty Rate to U.S. Poverty Rate in Year of Tax Introduction or First Year Before Tax			**Ratio of State Poverty Rate to U.S. Poverty Rate in 2012**	
State	**Year of Tax Introduction**	**1959**	**1969**	**1991**	**2012**	**% Change**
West Virginia	1961	1.57			1.12	−29
Nebraska	1968	1.01			0.82	−19
Maine	1969		1.00		0.86	−14
New Jersey	1976		0.60		0.62	5
Rhode Island	1971		0.81		0.91	13
Illinois	1969		0.75		0.84	13
Connecticut	1991			0.60	0.69	14
Pennsylvania	1971		0.78		0.93	19
Michigan	1967	0.72			0.91	27
Indiana	1963	0.79			1.01	28
Ohio	1972	0.73			1.03	41

Source: U.S. Census Bureau, Laffer Associates.

Highways

As a pièce de résistance, we took the Reason Foundation's overall 50-state performance rank from its annual report on the performance of state highway systems for the 11 states that introduced an income tax in the past 50-plus years (see Table 1.9).

As fate would have it, five of the 11 states improved their relative rankings, and six states' rankings fell. And to make matters worse, those six states that declined individually in their rankings declined by more than those five states where rankings improved.

It's hard to see an improvement in public services from the imposition of an income tax from these data. In fact, it's hard to see an improvement in anything from these data. The adoption of the income tax led to (1) population exodus, (2) income exodus, (3) less tax revenue, (4) more poverty, and (5) reduced public services. Thanks but no thanks, income tax.

TABLE 1.9

State Highway System (ranked from biggest improvement in overall performance rank to least improvement in overall performance rank)

State	Rank in 1984	Rank in 1990	Rank in 2009	Change in Rank from Previous Period to 2009
Michigan	44		30	▲ 14
Ohio	31		25	▲ 6
Illinois	38		34	▲ 4
New Jersey	50		46	▲ 4
Connecticut		46	44	▲ 2
Rhode Island	46		49	▼ 3
Nebraska	2		6	▼ 4
West Virginia	26		32	▼ 6
Indiana	13		22	▼ 9
Pennsylvania	28		39	▼ 11
Maine	12		29	▼ 17

Source: Reason Foundation Annual Highway Report.

CHAPTER 2

Economic Metrics

Data cannot be meaningfully collected without a prior hypothesis simply because there is too much of it.

—Philip Ball, *Curiosity*

This chapter is descriptive by nature, placing each state in a number of rankings among all states. In the first section of this chapter, we rank each state by its primary economic metrics such as decadal growth in population, labor force, employment, and output. In the second part of the chapter, we also rank the states by their 10-year state finance performances.

Because we are generally of the opinion that everything happens for a reason and that high among those reasons are economic policy differences among the states, in the third section of this chapter, we also rank all states by the ALEC-Laffer criteria and by what we consider to be the most important state and local policy variables. These rankings include the Tax Foundation's measure of total tax burden.

In the final section, we rank each and every state by the annual net migration flows of tax returns from the 1992/1993 tax/file year to the 2009/2010 tax/file year and total adjusted gross income (AGI) over the entire 1992–2011 period as reported by the U.S. Internal Revenue Service (IRS).

While descriptive by nature, the chapter also offers a number of observations in each of the sections on state performances as we proceed.

Primary Economic Metrics

Each state's economic performance starts with population, and from population moves on to the state's labor force, and then from the labor force on to employment and from employment to output. In terms of each of these measures of economic performance, we use the percentage change over the most recent 10-year period. The various state economies can display a great deal of variability. We all are well aware that many factors contribute to the well-being of a state's economy, but we believe that high on that list of causes are state and local economic policies that have considerable impact on a state's performance.[1]

State and local governments can enact policies that either attract or repel interstate migration; policies can also impact how many of their residents choose to join the labor force and how many members of the labor force actually get jobs. State and local policies can also influence the types of jobs a state has and how productive those jobs are. This process starts with population and ends with total output. State and local policies affect each and every step of the process from beginning to end.

State and local government policies are not the only factors influencing the process that starts with population and ends with total state output. In fact, state policies may not in every instance be the most important influences on the organization of labor, capital, and technology to create output. Over the past decade, for example, North Dakota, Wyoming, and Alaska have registered the fastest growth in total output of the 50 states due in large measure to their recent development of oil fields and the fact that those states have small economic bases that reflect any given change in oil production as a larger percentage change in total state output.

When it comes to oil, coal, and other extractive products, we have to be careful to ascertain how much of the added value is a result of good state and local policies and how much is merely the fortuitous location of underground deposits. Even given the latest developments in the research of psi effects, it seems to us malarkey that North Dakota's or anyone else's governor and legislature could have retroactively engineered ancient deposits of flora and fauna in their state. But you can never be sure. According to Dean Mickey Hepner, the clairvoyance of politicians can be awesome. State policies are also important, however, even when it comes to oil, and differences in state policies can reasonably be expected to have measurably different impacts on state results.

In Table 2.1 we list the objective metrics of each of the 50 U.S. states over the past 10 years. Column 1 ranks each state's population growth over the past decade from the state with the greatest population growth to the least. Column 2 again ranks each state from highest to lowest, this time in terms of its state's labor force participation rate's decadal change.

The third column combines Column 1, growth in a state's population, and Column 2, the percentage change in a state's labor force participation rate, and is the percentage growth in the state's labor force over the past decade.[2] Again, labor force growth is ranked from highest to lowest.

Column 4 is the 10-year percentage change in each state's employment rate (1 minus the unemployment rate) which, when added to each state's growth in labor force, Column 3, results in the percentage change in each state's total employment over the past decade, Column 5. As is the case with the other columns, each of these columns is ranked by state from the highest (top) to the lowest (bottom).[3]

With Column 5 being decadal employment growth, Column 6 is the ranking of nominal output per worker growth of each state over the past decade. When Columns 5 and 6 are added together,[4] the result is total nominal income growth for each state over the past decade, Column 7. Again we rank each state from the state with the greatest growth in nominal output to the state with the least growth in nominal income from top to bottom.

Column 8 is Column 7 less Column 1[5] and is the decadal growth in nominal income per capita. Column 9 is closely related to Column 4 and is the 2012 end-of-year unemployment rate for each state, again ranked from best (lowest) to worst (highest).

If you allow yourself a little bit of time to peruse the table, you'll be able to start seeing lots of patterns among the states. We'll point out a number of them ourselves, but the data are fascinating per se.

TABLE 2.1

Percentage Change, 2002–2012

Rank	Column 1 Population		Column 2 Labor Force Participation Rate		Column 3 Labor Force		Column 4 Employment Rate		Column 5 Employed		Column 6 Productivity*		Column 7 Gross State Product		Column 8 Gross State Product per Capita		Column 9 (Percentage, Dec-2012) Unemployment Rate	
1	NV	26.9%	ND	0.9%	NV	21.9%	ND	0.4%	TX	16.1%	ND	97.7%	ND	125.1%	ND	105.4%	ND	3.2%
2	UT	22.8%	RI	-0.8%	TX	16.6%	AK	0.1%	NV	15.0%	WY	78.0%	WY	99.5%	WY	73.0%	NE	3.8%
3	AZ	21.4%	NJ	-1.4%	FL	15.3%	UT	0.0%	UT	14.6%	LA	69.7%	AK	79.5%	LA	70.8%	SD	4.3%
4	TX	20.1%	KY	-1.5%	UT	14.5%	NE	-0.2%	ND	13.9%	AK	60.7%	TX	78.5%	AK	57.6%	WY	4.9%
5	ID	19.1%	PA	-1.8%	WY	13.5%	OK	-0.4%	WY	12.1%	MT	58.7%	UT	74.9%	MT	54.2%	VT	4.9%
6	NC	17.1%	NE	-1.9%	ND	13.4%	TX	-0.4%	FL	11.7%	OR	58.1%	LA	74.8%	WV	51.6%	IA	5.0%
7	GA	16.6%	LA	-1.9%	AZ	13.3%	LA	-0.6%	AK	11.7%	WV	56.5%	MT	70.0%	NE	51.1%	OK	5.1%
8	FL	15.7%	IL	-2.1%	ID	13.2%	KS	-0.6%	ID	11.2%	IA	56.1%	OR	66.2%	OR	49.7%	HI	5.1%
9	CO	15.5%	CT	-2.1%	VA	12.4%	WA	-0.9%	WA	11.1%	HI	54.1%	OK	62.9%	OK	49.0%	MN	5.4%
10	WY	15.3%	NY	-2.4%	CO	12.3%	VT	-1.0%	AZ	10.6%	TX	53.8%	NE	62.2%	TX	48.6%	UT	5.4%
11	SC	15.0%	KS	-2.6%	NC	12.2%	NH	-1.0%	VA	10.4%	OK	52.8%	HI	61.8%	IA	47.6%	KS	5.5%
12	WA	14.0%	MD	-2.6%	WA	12.1%	SD	-1.1%	CO	9.5%	UT	52.6%	NV	61.4%	HI	44.1%	LA	5.6%
13	AK	13.9%	VT	-2.6%	SC	11.6%	MN	-1.2%	NC	8.8%	NE	52.4%	WA	58.5%	NY	43.4%	VA	5.6%
14	DE	13.8%	ME	-2.6%	AK	11.5%	OR	-1.2%	SC	7.9%	IN	48.9%	WV	55.8%	KS	42.5%	MT	5.6%
15	NM	12.4%	WV	-2.9%	GA	10.6%	WY	-1.3%	MT	7.1%	DE	47.0%	IA	54.6%	UT	42.4%	NH	5.7%
16	VA	12.3%	VA	-3.0%	MD	9.1%	IA	-1.3%	OK	6.7%	MS	46.4%	ID	54.4%	MD	42.1%	TX	6.2%
17	HI	12.3%	FL	-3.1%	MT	8.8%	NM	-1.4%	MD	6.5%	AL	46.3%	SD	53.8%	SD	40.3%	ID	6.3%
18	TN	11.4%	WY	-3.3%	TN	8.6%	WV	-1.5%	NE	6.5%	KS	45.9%	MD	53.7%	MS	39.8%	NM	6.6%

#	St	%	#	St	%	#	St	%	#	St	%	#	St	%	#	St	%	#	St	%	#	St	%	#	St	%
19	OR	11.0%	19	OK	−3.3%	19	NM	7.4%	19	MA	−1.5%	19	SD	5.9%	19	NY	45.8%	19	VA	53.3%	19	WA	39.1%	19	MO	6.6%
20	MT	10.3%	20	AR	−3.3%	20	SD	7.1%	20	OH	−1.5%	20	NM	5.8%	20	SD	45.2%	Avg.†		51.7%	Avg.†		38.8%	20	AK	6.6%
21	SD	9.6%	21	SD	−3.4%	21	OK	7.1%	21	MT	−1.6%	21	GA	5.7%	Avg.†		44.8%	20	KS	51.6%	20	VT	36.9%	21	MD	6.7%
22	ND	9.6%	22	MT	−3.9%	22	HI	7.0%	22	WI	−1.7%	22	TN	5.5%	21	MD	44.4%	21	DE	51.1%	21	PA	36.9%	22	MA	6.7%
23	OK	9.3%	23	TN	−3.9%	Avg.†		6.9%	23	ID	−1.7%	23	OR	5.1%	22	MN	43.5%	22	NC	50.9%	22	VA	36.4%	23	WI	6.7%
Avg.†		9.3%	24	MS	−4.1%	23	NE	6.7%	24	VA	−1.8%	24	HI	5.0%	23	WA	42.6%	23	AZ	50.7%	23	MN	36.4%	24	OH	6.7%
24	CA	9.1%	25	WA	−4.1%	24	CA	6.6%	25	MO	−1.8%	Avg.†		4.6%	24	NM	41.9%	24	NM	50.2%	24	AL	36.2%	25	AL	6.8%
25	AR	9.0%	26	CO	−4.1%	25	AR	6.6%	26	HI	−1.9%	25	AR	4.4%	25	AR	41.5%	25	AR	47.7%	25	IL	35.9%	Avg.†		7.0%
26	MD	8.2%	27	NH	−4.2%	26	OR	6.5%	27	AL	−2.0%	26	KS	3.9%	26	CA	41.1%	26	CO	46.9%	26	RI	35.6%	26	DE	7.1%
27	AL	7.6%	Avg.†		−4.5%	27	KY	6.4%	28	AR	−2.1%	27	KY	3.6%	27	NV	40.4%	27	AL	46.6%	27	AR	35.5%	27	AR	7.1%
28	NE	7.4%	28	TX	−4.7%	28	DE	6.3%	Avg.†		−2.1%	28	NH	3.2%	28	MA	40.1%	28	NY	46.6%	28	MA	35.2%	28	ME	7.2%
29	MN	7.2%	29	MA	−4.8%	29	CT	5.6%	29	AZ	−2.4%	29	LA	3.0%	29	RI	39.9%	29	MN	46.2%	29	IN	34.8%	29	WV	7.4%
30	KY	7.1%	30	OH	−5.0%	30	NJ	5.1%	30	NY	−2.4%	30	DE	2.8%	30	PA	39.2%	30	MS	46.0%	30	NM	33.6%	30	WA	7.5%
31	KS	6.4%	31	SC	−5.5%	31	KS	4.6%	31	PA	−2.4%	31	CA	2.3%	31	ID	38.8%	31	FL	45.0%	31	KY	33.4%	31	CO	7.5%
32	IN	6.2%	32	IA	−5.6%	32	PA	4.3%	32	MD	−2.4%	32	VT	2.0%	32	VA	38.8%	32	CA	44.4%	32	NH	33.0%	32	TN	7.6%
33	MO	6.1%	33	NC	−5.9%	33	NH	4.3%	33	CO	−2.5%	33	MN	1.9%	33	IL	38.8%	33	TN	43.5%	33	DE	32.8%	33	AZ	7.9%
34	WI	5.2%	34	MN	−5.9%	34	ME	3.8%	34	IL	−2.5%	34	PA	1.8%	34	NC	38.7%	34	IN	43.1%	34	CA	32.4%	34	FL	7.9%
35	IA	4.8%	35	CA	−6.0%	35	LA	3.6%	35	MS	−2.6%	35	CT	1.3%	35	WI	38.5%	35	KY	42.8%	35	ME	30.8%	35	PA	7.9%
36	MS	4.4%	36	AK	−6.0%	36	IL	3.2%	36	KY	−2.6%	36	NJ	1.0%	36	KY	37.9%	36	PA	41.7%	36	CT	30.8%	36	KY	8.0%
37	NH	4.1%	37	WI	−6.1%	37	NY	3.1%	37	TN	−2.9%	37	IL	0.6%	37	MO	36.8%	37	SC	41.7%	37	WI	30.7%	37	NY	8.2%

(continued)

27

TABLE 2.1 (Continued)

Percentage Change, 2002–2012

	Column 1 Population		Column 2 Labor Force Participation Rate		Column 3 Labor Force		Column 4 Employment Rate		Column 5 Employed		Column 6 Productivity*		Column 7 Gross State Product		Column 8 Gross State Product per Capita		Percentage, Dec-2012 — Column 9 Unemployment Rate	
38	CT	3.8%	GA	-6.1%	VT	3.1%	NC	-3.1%	NY	0.6%	VT	36.5%	MA	40.0%	NJ	30.0%	CT	8.2%
39	NJ	3.6%	ID	-6.3%	MN	3.1%	ME	-3.1%	ME	0.5%	AZ	36.3%	IL	39.7%	ID	29.7%	OR	8.3%
40	MA	3.6%	NV	-6.4%	MS	2.4%	MI	-3.1%	AL	0.2%	TN	36.0%	VT	39.3%	NC	28.8%	IN	8.3%
41	PA	3.5%	UT	-6.5%	AL	2.3%	FL	-3.1%	MA	-0.1%	NH	34.2%	NH	38.4%	TN	28.8%	SC	8.6%
42	IL	2.8%	OR	-6.5%	MA	1.5%	DE	-3.3%	MS	-0.3%	CO	34.1%	GA	38.1%	CO	27.2%	IL	8.6%
43	WV	2.8%	AL	-7.1%	RI	1.2%	SC	-3.3%	WV	-0.4%	CT	34.1%	WI	37.5%	NV	27.2%	GA	8.7%
44	ME	2.6%	NM	-7.3%	WV	1.1%	IN	-3.4%	WI	-0.7%	ME	33.4%	CT	35.8%	MO	26.9%	MS	8.9%
45	LA	2.3%	MO	-7.5%	WI	1.0%	NJ	-3.9%	IA	-1.0%	NJ	33.4%	NJ	34.8%	OH	26.5%	MI	8.9%
46	NY	2.3%	AZ	-7.9%	IA	0.4%	CA	-4.0%	MO	-1.6%	OH	32.0%	MO	34.7%	FL	25.3%	NC	9.4%
47	VT	1.7%	IN	-7.9%	MO	0.2%	CT	-4.2%	OH	-3.1%	SC	31.3%	ME	34.2%	AZ	24.1%	NJ	9.5%
48	OH	1.2%	HI	-8.2%	IN	-0.5%	GA	-4.4%	IN	-3.9%	GA	30.6%	RI	33.6%	SC	23.2%	CA	9.8%
49	MI	-1.3%	DE	-9.5%	OH	-1.5%	RI	-5.6%	RI	-4.5%	FL	29.8%	OH	28.0%	GA	18.4%	NV	9.8%
50	RI	-1.5%	MI	-9.5%	MI	-7.6%	NV	-5.7%	MI	-10.4%	MI	27.1%	MI	13.8%	MI	15.4%	RI	9.9%

* Productivity is gross state product per employed worker.
† "Avg." is an equal-weighted average of the 50 states.

Source: Bureau of Labor Statistics, Bureau of Economic Analysis.

Table 2.1 is fascinating in part because it contains so much relevant information in a format that facilitates easy comparisons of states. The table literally allows state-by-state comparisons for the most critical metrics. But our focus in this chapter is not on just any generic bilateral comparison. Our hope is to provide a framework to uncover the effects the many various state policies have on economic metrics and from these results to infer a more general guide to achieving economic prosperity.

Science needs much more in the way of prior hypothesis and theory than most researchers are willing to admit: There is no way to boil down a mass of raw data into a theory unless we are prepared to take a leap of faith by suggesting (and then testing) some generative mechanism for it.

The powerful influence the overall U.S. economy has on state economies is rarely so clearly demonstrated as it has been during the past decade. The decade began rather innocently in 2002 but ended with the aftermath of the Great Recession. Over this 10-year period the U.S. unemployment rate rose from 5.8 percent in 2002 to 8.1 percent in 2012. Forty-seven of the 50 states witnessed an increase in their unemployment rates. The point here is simply that the many states of the nation have far more in common with each other than there are differences. We focus, however, on their differences and not on their similarities.

A quick observation from Table 2.1 is the absolutely dismal performance of Michigan. Over the past decade, Michigan has had the lowest labor force participation rate growth, lowest labor force growth, lowest employment growth, lowest productivity growth, lowest output growth, and lowest growth in output per capita in the nation. As of December 2012, Michigan also had the sixth highest unemployment rate. Given all that we read in the news about the bankruptcy of Detroit, the plight of Michigan as a state makes Detroit's bankruptcy more understandable. Michigan has been the poster boy of what not to do.

Nevada is also quite amazing but in the opposite direction. Nevada had the highest population growth and labor force growth of all 50 states. Because the end of this decade was consumed by the aftermath of the Great Recession, Nevada was hard-hit as a result of its earlier successes. Therefore, employment growth in Nevada was second

highest in the nation and output growth was 12th highest. Combining
the highest population growth with the 12th highest output growth
put Nevada as the eighth lowest growth in output per capita. But, as of
December 2012, Nevada had the second highest unemployment rate
in the country. From our perspective, the resultant poor output per
capita and unemployment rate numbers are a direct result of Nevada's
spectacular growth and good policies. You can't lose jobs if you never
created them.

A similar story but not quite as extreme is that of Florida over the
past decade. Florida had high population growth, labor force growth,
and employment growth, yet much reduced output growth. As a consequence, Florida had low, low, low growth in output per capita and a high
ending unemployment rate. The amazing growth machine that is and
was Florida looks much worse in a slowdown. But all things considered,
Florida too was a superstar of the past decade.

The three fastest-growing states in gross state output—North Dakota,
Wyoming, and Alaska—were modest performers in population growth.
This discrepancy, if anything, reflects the powerful influence oil has
had on relative growth rates in output vis-à-vis growth in population.
High gross state product (GSP) and low population sensitivity to oil are
also found in our econometric chapter, Chapter 6. Really high output
growth due to oil and more modest population growth put these states
at the very high end of output per capita growth.

What really caught our eye, however, were three observations
from Table 2.2. First, in spite of all that's going on in the states, eight
of the nine zero personal income tax (PIT) states were in the top
half of decadal population growth, while six of the nine highest income tax rate states were in the bottom half of population growth (see
Column B1). Second, all 11 of the states that adopted an income tax
over the past 50-plus years were in the bottom half of decadal population growth (see Column B2). And last, eight of the nine highest tax
burden states were in the bottom half of population growth and a
majority of the nine lowest tax burden states were in the top half of
population growth (see Column B3).

TABLE 2.2

Ten-Year Population Growth, Percentage Change, 2002–2012

Rank	B1 9 Highest PIT Rate States / 9 Lowest PIT Rate States		B2 Last 11 States to Introduce a PIT		B3 9 Highest Tax Burden States / 9 Lowest Tax Burden States		Rank
1	Nevada	26.9%	Nevada	26.9%	Nevada	26.9%	1
2	Utah	22.8%	Utah	22.8%	Utah	22.8%	2
3	Arizona	21.4%	Arizona	21.4%	Arizona	21.4%	3
4	Texas	20.1%	Texas	20.1%	Texas	20.1%	4
5	Idaho	19.1%	Idaho	19.1%	Idaho	19.1%	5
6	North Carolina	17.1%	North Carolina	17.1%	North Carolina	17.1%	6
7	Georgia	16.6%	Georgia	16.6%	Georgia	16.6%	7
8	Florida	15.7%	Florida	15.7%	Florida	15.7%	8
9	Colorado	15.5%	Colorado	15.5%	Colorado	15.5%	9
10	Wyoming	15.3%	Wyoming	15.3%	Wyoming	15.3%	10
11	South Carolina	15.0%	South Carolina	15.0%	South Carolina	15.0%	11
12	Washington	14.0%	Washington	14.0%	Washington	14.0%	12
13	Alaska	13.9%	Alaska	13.9%	Alaska	13.9%	13
14	Delaware	13.8%	Delaware	13.8%	Delaware	13.8%	14
15	New Mexico	12.4%	New Mexico	12.4%	New Mexico	12.4%	15
16	Virginia	12.3%	Virginia	12.3%	Virginia	12.3%	16
17	Hawaii	12.3%	Hawaii	12.3%	Hawaii	12.3%	17
18	Tennessee	11.4%	Tennessee	11.4%	Tennessee	11.4%	18
19	Oregon	11.0%	Oregon	11.0%	Oregon	11.0%	19
20	Montana	10.3%	Montana	10.3%	Montana	10.3%	20
21	South Dakota	9.6%	South Dakota	9.6%	South Dakota	9.6%	21
22	North Dakota	9.6%	North Dakota	9.6%	North Dakota	9.6%	22
23	Oklahoma	9.3%	Oklahoma	9.3%	Oklahoma	9.3%	23
24	California	9.1%	California	9.1%	California	9.1%	24
25	Arkansas	9.0%	Arkansas	9.0%	Arkansas	9.0%	25
26	Maryland	8.2%	Maryland	8.2%	Maryland	8.2%	26
27	Alabama	7.6%	Alabama	7.6%	Alabama	7.6%	27
28	Nebraska	7.4%	Nebraska	7.4%	Nebraska	7.4%	28
29	Minnesota	7.2%	Minnesota	7.2%	Minnesota	7.2%	29
30	Kentucky	7.1%	Kentucky	7.1%	Kentucky	7.1%	30
31	Kansas	6.4%	Kansas	6.4%	Kansas	6.4%	31
32	Indiana	6.2%	Indiana	6.2%	Indiana	6.2%	32
33	Missouri	6.1%	Missouri	6.1%	Missouri	6.1%	33
34	Wisconsin	5.2%	Wisconsin	5.2%	Wisconsin	5.2%	34
35	Iowa	4.8%	Iowa	4.8%	Iowa	4.8%	35
36	Mississippi	4.4%	Mississippi	4.4%	Mississippi	4.4%	36
37	New Hampshire	4.1%	New Hampshire	4.1%	New Hampshire	4.1%	37
38	Connecticut	3.8%	Connecticut	3.8%	Connecticut	3.8%	38
39	New Jersey	3.6%	New Jersey	3.6%	New Jersey	3.6%	39
40	Massachusetts	3.6%	Massachusetts	3.6%	Massachusetts	3.6%	40

	TABLE 2.2						
	(Continued)						
	B1				**B3**		
Rank	9 Highest PIT Rate States		**B2**		9 Highest Tax Burden States		Rank
	9 Lowest PIT Rate States		Last 11 States to Introduce a PIT		9 Lowest Tax Burden States		
41	Pennsylvania	3.5%	Pennsylvania	3.5%	Pennsylvania	3.5%	41
42	Illinois	2.8%	Illinois	2.8%	Illinois	2.8%	42
43	West Virginia	2.8%	West Virginia	2.8%	West Virginia	2.8%	43
44	Maine	2.6%	Maine	2.6%	Maine	2.6%	44
45	Louisiana	2.3%	Louisiana	2.3%	Louisiana	2.3%	45
46	New York	2.3%	New York	2.3%	New York	2.3%	46
47	Vermont	1.7%	Vermont	1.7%	Vermont	1.7%	47
48	Ohio	1.2%	Ohio	1.2%	Ohio	1.2%	48
49	Michigan	–1.3%	Michigan	–1.3%	Michigan	–1.3%	49
50	Rhode Island	–1.5%	Rhode Island	–1.5%	Rhode Island	–1.5%	50

Source: Bureau of Economic Analysis.

Tax Revenue Performance of All States over the Past Decade

Moving now from population, labor force, and output measures, we cross over into state and local government finances. Just as a state can't tax its way into prosperity, it also can't balance its budget on the backs of people who don't work. To run a state, state and local governments need tax revenues—lots of tax revenues. To get those tax revenues into the state's coffers, a state needs a viable tax base that the government can tax, and a tax rate to do the heavy lifting. The interesting twist here is that the size of the tax base and the tax rate itself are integrally related to each other.

In Table 2.3, the first column shows the 10-year growth in nominal gross state product over the period 2001 to 2011. Column 7 in Table 2.1 was also the 10-year growth in nominal income but reported for the more recent period 2002 to 2012. Delays in the reporting of fiscal data are the reason we use the period 2001 to 2011 in Table 2.3. We felt it more important that all data covered the same fiscal period rather than being the most recent. Column 1 of Table 2.3, which represents the nominal growth in a state's gross state product, is the tax base for both state and local governments.

TABLE 2.3

Percentage Change, 2001–2011

Column 1 Gross State Product			Column 2 State and Local Tax Revenue as a % of Gross State Product			Column 3 State and Local Tax Revenue			Column 4 State and Local Tax Revenue per Capita			Column 5 2012 Fiscal Condition Index Score*			Column 6 As of 11/4/2013 S&P General Obligation Credit Rating†		
1	ND	109.1%	1	LA	-16.4%	1	AK	232.8%	1	AK	191.4%	1	AK	8.80	1	AK	AAA
2	WY	103.7%	2	OK	-12.2%	2	ND	169.3%	2	ND	151.4%	2	SD	2.79	1	DE	AAA
3	AK	84.7%	3	UT	-11.5%	3	WY	121.1%	3	WY	92.8%	3	ND	2.75	1	FL	AAA
4	TX	73.2%	4	ID	-8.8%	4	NV	66.7%	4	NY	61.2%	4	NE	2.53	1	GA	AAA
5	LA	72.3%	5	OR	-8.7%	5	NY	64.7%	5	VT	59.8%	5	WY	2.23	1	IN	AAA
6	UT	72.0%	6	SD	-8.7%	6	VT	63.5%	6	NJ	51.5%	6	FL	1.99	1	IA	AAA
7	MT	68.7%	7	NE	-6.0%	7	TX	63.3%	7	WV	50.3%	7	OH	1.71	1	MD	AAA
8	OR	68.0%	8	TX	-5.7%	8	MT	61.0%	8	IA	47.4%	8	TN	1.71	1	MO	AAA
9	SD	65.3%	9	MT	-4.6%	9	AR	60.8%	9	AR	47.3%	9	MT	1.66	1	NE	AAA
10	HI	64.6%	10	HI	-4.3%	10	CO	60.7%	10	NH	47.2%	10	AL	1.25	1	NC	AAA
11	NV	63.7%	11	WA	-4.2%	11	HI	57.6%	11	MT	46.3%	11	UT	1.03	1	TX	AAA
12	NE	61.3%	12	VA	-3.9%	12	NJ	57.6%	12	RI	45.3%	12	OK	0.93	1	UT	AAA
13	OK	60.7%	13	GA	-3.9%	Avg.†		56.5%	13	PA	45.1%	13	ID	0.70	1	VA	AAA
14	ID	57.0%	14	KY	-3.8%	13	AZ	56.1%	14	MA	44.8%	14	MO	0.60	1	WY	AAA
15	MD	56.0%	15	MD	-2.5%	14	WV	54.7%	Avg.†		43.0%	15	IN	0.53	15	ID	AA+
16	IA	55.2%	16	AL	-2.4%	15	NH	54.5%	15	KS	42.0%	16	NV	0.49	15	KS	AA+
17	WA	55.0%	17	IN	-2.3%	16	IA	54.1%	16	CT	41.6%	17	WI	0.12	15	MA	AA+
18	VA	54.8%	18	NM	-1.9%	17	CA	54.0%	17	NE	41.6%	18	IA	0.09	15	MN	AA+
19	WV	53.8%	19	MO	-0.9%	18	DE	53.5%	18	IL	41.2%	Avg.†		0.00	15	NM	AA+
20	NM	52.8%	20	IA	-0.7%	19	OR	53.3%	19	LA	41.0%	19	MS	-0.14	15	ND	AA+
Avg.†		51.7%	21	WI	-0.2%	20	NC	53.2%	20	CA	40.9%	20	TX	-0.18	15	OH	AA+
			22	ME	0.0%										15	OK	AA+
			23	KS	0.0%										15	OR	AA+

(continued)

TABLE 2.3 (Continued)

Column 1 — Gross State Product	Column 2 — State and Local Tax Revenue as a % of Gross State Product	Column 3 — State and Local Tax Revenue	Column 4 — State and Local Tax Revenue per Capita	Column 5 — Fiscal Condition Index Score* (2012)	Column 6 — S&P General Obligation Credit Rating† (As of 11/4/2013)
21 KS 50.8%		21 UT 52.2%	21 HI 40.2%	21 SC −0.19	15 SC AA+
22 AZ 50.6%		22 MD 52.2%	22 MD 40.1%	22 NH −0.21	15 SD AA+
23 AR 49.9%	24 OH 0.1%	23 NE 51.6%	23 CO 39.0%	23 WA −0.23	15 TN AA+
24 NC 49.4%	25 MS 0.2%	24 SD 50.9%	24 SD 38.9%	24 CO −0.24	15 VT AA+
25 AL 48.6%	26 WV 0.6%	25 KS 50.8%	25 MS 38.5%	25 VA −0.28	15 WA AA+
26 DE 47.5%	27 SC 1.3%	26 FL 50.3%	26 OR 37.5%	26 NM −0.34	29 AL AA
27 FL 47.4%	28 MN 1.5%	27 PA 50.3%	27 MN 36.5%	27 KS −0.40	29 AR AA
28 CO 46.3%	29 MI 1.8%	28 TN 50.2%	28 TX 35.8%	28 GA −0.45	29 CO AA
29 NY 44.5%	30 NV 1.8%	29 NM 49.8%	29 TN 35.0%	29 AR −0.47	29 CT AA
30 KY 44.4%	31 FL 2.0%	30 MA 49.5%	30 AL 34.9%	30 MI −0.51	29 HI AA
31 MS 44.3%	32 NC 2.5%	31 VA 48.8%	31 DE 34.5%	31 AZ −0.51	29 LA AA
32 MN 44.3%	Avg.† 2.9%	32 WA 48.6%	32 ME 33.1%	32 OR −0.57	29 ME AA
33 TN 43.5%	33 AZ 3.6%	33 CT 47.9%	33 VA 32.2%	33 NC −0.57	29 MS AA
34 PA 42.9%	34 DE 4.1%	34 MN 46.5%	34 NM 32.0%	34 LA −0.60	29 MT AA
35 CA 42.5%	35 RI 4.3%	35 IL 45.4%	35 IN 30.6%	35 MN −0.87	29 NV AA
36 IN 42.2%	36 TN 4.6%	36 AL 45.1%	36 WI 30.5%	36 ME −1.00	29 NH AA
37 NH 41.7%	37 PA 5.2%	37 MS 44.6%	37 WA 30.3%	37 DE −1.14	29 NY AA
38 VT 41.1%	38 IL 5.7%	38 RI 44.4%	38 NC 30.3%	38 VT −1.17	29 PA AA
39 SC 40.6%	39 AR 7.3%	39 LA 44.0%	39 KY 29.4%	39 RI −1.18	29 RI AA
40 RI 38.4%	40 CA 8.1%	40 ID 43.1%	40 OK 29.2%	40 KY −1.26	29 WV AA

Rank	State	Value	Rank	State	Value	Rank	State	Value	Rank	State	Value	Rank	State	Score	Rank	State	Rating
41	WI	38.0%	41	WY	8.5%	41	SC	42.5%	41	FL	28.9%	41	WV	-1.30	29	WI	AA
42	IL	37.6%	42	MA	8.7%	42	OK	41.0%	42	NV	28.6%	42	PA	-1.31	45	AZ	AA-
43	ME	37.5%	43	NH	9.0%	43	KY	38.9%	43	AZ	27.2%	43	HI	-1.46	45	KY	AA-
44	MA	37.5%	44	CO	9.9%	44	IN	38.8%	44	OH	26.5%	44	MD	-1.59	45	MI	AA-
45	GA	36.9%	45	CT	10.4%	45	WI	37.8%	45	MO	25.3%	45	NY	-1.78	45	NJ	AA-
46	NJ	35.1%	46	NY	13.9%	46	ME	37.5%	46	SC	23.9%	46	CA	-2.01	49	CA	A
47	MO	34.6%	47	VT	15.9%	47	MO	33.4%	47	UT	23.5%	47	MA	-2.23	50	IL	A-
48	CT	34.0%	48	NJ	16.6%	48	GA	31.6%	48	ID	19.3%	48	IL	-2.42			
49	OH	28.1%	49	ND	28.8%	49	OH	28.2%	49	MI	17.5%	49	CT	-2.48			
50	MI	14.1%	50	AK	80.2%	50	MI	16.1%	50	GA	12.4%	50	NJ	-2.81			

* Fiscal Condition Index Score is a ranking from the Mercatus Center. It ranks states according to cash, budget, long-run, and service-level solvency metrics.

† Ratings are S&P credit ratings as of 11/4/2013.

‡ "Avg." is an equal-weighted average of the 50 states.

Source: Bureau of Economic Analysis, U.S. Census Bureau, Mercatus Center, Standard & Poor's.

Column 2 of Table 2.3 is a highly aggregated measure of the decadal change in a state's average tax rate—total state and local tax revenues divided by gross state product. Column 3 is what we all are looking for after all is said and done—it's the percentage change in total state and local tax revenues over the decade 2001 to 2011 (Column 3 is the sum of Columns 1 and 2).[6] This number reported in Column 3 represents the wherewithal for state and local governments in a state to carry out their appointed obligations to the citizens of that state.

Column 4 of Table 2.3 is a combination of Column 1 of Table 2.1 and Column 3 of Table 2.3 and is the percentage increase in total tax revenues per person in the state.[7] Column 4 of Table 2.3 really provides a metric of how one state can change what it provides the average citizen versus any other state.

We also include two additional columns in Table 2.3, Columns 5 and 6. Column 5 is a comprehensive composite measure of each state's fiscal condition for the fiscal year 2012 as developed by Sarah Arnett of the Mercatus Center at George Mason University.[8]

Sarah Arnett based her measure of fiscal condition on a lengthy academic tradition of measures of a state's solvency ranking in each and every state, from best to worst. This measure of fiscal condition includes measures of (1) cash solvency or the ability of a state to meet its near-term liquidity needs; (2) budget solvency which entails a matching of the state's ability to generate enough revenues over a budget cycle to meet the expenditure obligations the state faces; (3) long-run solvency which measures revenue and expenditure sources and obligations far into the future, including pension benefits, political will, capital replacement, and other such long-term considerations; and finally (4) service-level solvency, which is a more subjective measure as to whether a state can generate the revenues to provide the services that are needed by residents of the state. Those four measures of solvency are then weighted individually and aggregated into one single measure of a state's fiscal condition—Column 5.

Column 6 is the latest bond ratings by Standard & Poor's for each state.

An obvious observation to be drawn from the data displayed in Table 2.3 is the extraordinarily powerful impact oil has both on gross state product growth and on state and local tax revenue growth. But once you get over the oil connection, another counterintuitive (to many people but not to us) observation rears its powerful form. Those states with the highest growth rates in output tend to be those states where taxes as a share of gross state product actually shrink or grow less rapidly, and the slowest-growing states in terms of output have the fastest-growing taxes relative to output. If this isn't the essence of supply-side economics, we don't know what is.

In Figure 2.1 we have plotted each state's growth in total output less oil production over the past decade against growth in each state's tax revenues without severance taxes as a share of total state output. The correlation is amazing.

The relative change in tax revenues without severance taxes as a share of state output is a damn good proxy for the change in a state's overall relative tax burden. If ever an argument for the benefits of tax cuts existed, this is it.

The ALEC-Laffer State Rankings

In the six editions of *Rich States, Poor States*, we analyze all sorts of state and local economic policies, from A to Z.[9] Each edition contains a number of narratives, as well, that vary from year to year depending upon political initiatives and concrete results. But the one evergreen segment of the book is the actual rankings of the various states. We rank each state not only by its actual past economic performance, but also by its economic outlook based on the actual policies implemented by each state's state and local policy makers. In other words, we look at both what has been and what we expect will be (see Chapter 8, section on the probity of the ALEC-Laffer measures).

In *Rich States, Poor States*, the overall rank for each state is composed of a combination of some 15 policy and policy-like variables. These are: (1) the highest state and local marginal personal income tax rate on earned income in a specific city within each state; (2) the

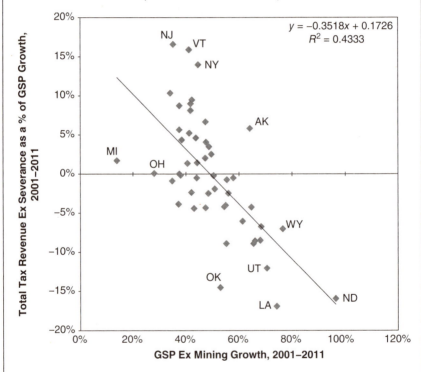

FIGURE 2.1

Ten–Year Percentage Change in Total Tax Revenues ex Severance Taxes as a Percentage of GSP versus 10–Year Percentage Change in GSP ex Mining (2001 to 2011)

Source: U.S. Census Bureau, Bureau of Economic Analysis, Laffer Associates.

highest marginal corporate income tax rate in the same specific city as used in (1); (3) the actual progressivity of the personal income tax (e.g., the change in the tax rate between incomes of $50,000 and $100,000); (4) the state burden of property taxes measured as total property taxes as a share of state personal income; (5) the state burden of sales taxes, again measured as total state and local sales taxes as a share of state personal income; (6) the remaining state and local tax burden as a share of personal income; (7) whether the state does (yes) or doesn't (no) have an estate tax; (8) recently legislated state tax changes over the past two years; (9) state and local debt service as a share of total tax revenue; (10) the number of public employees per 10,000 of population; (11) the quality of the state's legal system as measured by the U.S. Chamber of Commerce State Liability Systems Ranking; (12) workers' compensation costs per $100 of wages; (13) the state's minimum wage; (14) whether the state is (yes) or is not (no) a right-to-work state; and finally (15) how many tax and/or expenditure limits are in effect in the state.

In this book, as shown in Table 2.4, we have selected the overall state rankings; the top personal income tax rate; the top corporate income tax rate; the sum of property, sales, and remaining tax burdens; whether the state has an estate tax; and whether the state is a right-to-work (RTW) state as our six key ALEC-Laffer criteria. We have also included as a seventh item the Tax Foundation's measure of total tax burden for each state. This last measure as well as the sum of property, sales, and remaining tax burden are less current than are the other measures due to data release lags.

The ALEC-Laffer measures of prospective economic performance have been subjected to intense scrutiny and criticism. Therefore, we spare the readers any observations on these data at this juncture because of the very detailed analysis contained in Chapter 8.

Internal Revenue Service Tax Migration Data

The U.S. Internal Revenue Service (IRS) has been keeping track of tax returns by filer from time immemorial. Since the tax year of 1992, however, which is the filing year of 1993, the IRS has been reporting these data by state and county in collective groups so as not to reveal any single tax return data. We can trace groups of filers by filing location since filing year 1993 for income earned in 1992. We not only know where they filed one year and the preceding year, but we also know the number of dependents, types of income, and, most important of all,

TABLE 2.4

Selected ALEC-Laffer Ranking Variables and Tax Foundation Tax Burden

i.		ii.			iii.			iv.			v.		vi.		vii.		
	Overall		Top Personal Income			Top Corporate Income			Sum of Property, Sales, and Remaining Tax			Estate or Inheritance		RTW?		Tax Burden (Tax Foundation) as a Share of Personal Income	
State	Rank	State	Tax Rate	Rank	State	Tax Rate	Rank	State	Burdens	Rank	State	Tax?	State	RTW?	State	Income	Rank
UT	1	AK	0.00%	1	NV	0.0%	1	OR	$57.62	1	AK	No	AL	Yes	AK	7.0%	1
ND	2	FL	0.00%	1	SD	0.0%	1	MD	$62.43	2	AL	No	AR	Yes	SD	7.6%	2
SD	3	NV	0.00%	1	WY	0.0%	1	VA	$62.77	3	AR	No	AZ	Yes	TN	7.7%	3
WY	4	SD	0.00%	1	TX	2.7%	4	KY	$63.32	4	AZ	No	FL	Yes	LA	7.8%	4
VA	5	TX	0.00%	1	AL	4.2%	5	OK	$64.08	5	CA	No	GA	Yes	WY	7.8%	5
AZ	6	WA	0.00%	1	CO	4.6%	6	AL	$64.29	6	CO	No	IA	Yes	TX	7.9%	6
ID	7	WY	0.00%	1	MS	5.0%	7	MT	$64.82	7	FL	No	ID	Yes	NH	8.1%	7
GA	8	NH	0.00%	1	SC	5.0%	8	ID	$65.41	8	GA	No	IN*	Yes	AL	8.2%	8
FL	9	TN	0.00%	1	UT	5.0%	8	MO	$65.68	9	ID	No	KS	Yes	NV	8.2%	9
MS	10	LA	3.62%	10	ND	5.2%	8	MA	$65.79	10	IN†	No	LA	Yes	SC	8.4%	10
KS	11	ND	3.99%	11	LA	5.2%	11	UT	$67.58	11	KS	No	MS	Yes	AZ	8.4%	11
TX	12	AL	4.02%	12	FL	5.5%	12	GA	$68.26	12	LA	No	NC	Yes	NM	8.4%	12
NV	13	AZ	4.54%	13	GA	6.0%	13	NC	$68.49	13	MI	No	ND	Yes	MT	8.6%	13
IN	14	CO	4.63%	14	KY	6.0%	14	SC	$70.74	14	MO	No	NE	Yes	MS	8.7%	14
WI	15	KS	4.90%	15	OK	6.0%	14	AK	$71.21	15	MS	No	NV	Yes	OK	8.7%	15
CO	16	NM	4.90%	15	MO	6.2%	14	ND	$71.68	16	MT	No	OK	Yes	ND	8.9%	16
AL	17	IL	5.00%	17	HI	6.4%	17	WV	$72.18	17	NC†	No	SC	Yes	MO	9.0%	17
TN	18	MS	5.00%	17	AR	6.5%	18	NM	$72.37	18	ND	No	SD	Yes	GA	9.0%	18

OK	19	UT	5.00%	17	TN	6.5%	19	DE	$72.91	19	NH	No	TN	Yes	CO	9.1%	19
MI	20	IN	5.02%	20	MT	6.8%	19	OH	$73.40	20	NM	No	TX	Yes	DE	9.2%	20
AK	21	MA	5.25%	21	NC	6.9%	21	PA	$74.45	21	NV	No	UT	Yes	VA	9.3%	21
NC	22	OK	5.25%	21	AZ	7.0%	22	AR	$75.19	22	OH†	No	VA	Yes	UT	9.3%	22
MO	23	IA	5.42%	23	KS	7.0%	23	KS	$76.62	23	OK	No	WY	Yes	WA	9.3%	23
AR	24	VA	5.75%	24	WV	7.0%	24	CA	$77.17	24	SC	No	AK	No	FL	9.3%	24
IA	25	RI	5.99%	25	ID	7.4%	24	CO	$77.37	25	SD	No	CA	No	KY	9.4%	25
OH	26	GA	6.00%	26	VA	7.6%	26	LA	$77.69	26	TX	No	CO	No	ID	9.4%	26
NH	27	WV	6.50%	27	NM	7.6%	27	MN	$78.28	27	UT	No	CT	No	IA	9.6%	27
LA	28	MI	6.65%	28	NE	7.8%	28	NH	$78.32	28	VA	No	DE	No	IN	9.6%	28
MA	29	CT	6.70%	29	WI	7.9%	29	AZ	$78.75	29	WI	No	HI	No	KS	9.7%	29
DE	30	NE	6.84%	30	WA	8.0%	30	CT	$78.90	30	WV	No	IL	No	NE	9.7%	30
SC	31	MT	6.90%	31	IN	8.0%	31	TN	$79.25	31	WY	No	KY	No	OH	9.7%	31
WV	32	PA	7.00%	32	MA	8.0%	32	IA	$79.48	32	CT	Yes	MA	No	WV	9.7%	32
NM	33	MO	7.00%	33	MI	8.0%	32	IN	$80.03	33	DE	Yes	MD	No	MI	9.8%	33
PA	34	AR	7.00%	34	MD	8.3%	32	MS	$80.43	34	HI	Yes	ME	No	NC	9.9%	34
MD	35	SC	7.00%	34	NH	8.5%	35	NE	$80.94	35	IA	Yes	MI*	No	OR	10.0%	35
WA	36	ID	7.40%	36	VT	8.5%	36	SD	$81.39	36	IL	Yes	MN	No	AR	10.0%	36
NE	37	NC	7.75%	37	CA	8.8%	36	IL	$83.12	37	KY	Yes	MO	No	HI	10.1%	37
KY	38	WI	7.75%	37	ME	8.9%	38	WI	$83.90	38	MA	Yes	MT	No	VT	10.1%	38
NJ	39	MN	7.85%	39	CT	9.0%	39	WA	$86.90	39	MD	Yes	NH	No	MD	10.2%	39
HI	40	ME	7.95%	40	NJ	9.0%	40	TX	$87.46	40	ME	Yes	NJ	No	IL	10.2%	40
ME	41	DE	8.00%	41	RI	9.0%	40	RI	$87.47	41	MN	Yes	NM	No	PA	10.2%	41
MT	42	KY	8.20%	42	AK	9.4%	40	MI	$87.84	42	NE	Yes	NY	No	ME	10.3%	42
CT	43	OH	8.43%	43	IL	9.5%	43	NJ	$88.76	43	NJ	Yes	OH	No	MA	10.4%	43
OR	44	MD	8.95%	44	MN	9.8%	44	ME	$90.51	44	NY	Yes	OR	No	MN	10.8%	44

(continued)

TABLE 2.4 (Continued)

i. Overall		ii. Top Personal Income			iii. Top Corporate Income			iv. Sum of Property, Sales, and Remaining Tax			v. Estate or Inheritance		vi.		vii. Tax Burden (Tax Foundation) as a Share of Personal		
State	Rank	State	Tax Rate	Rank	State	Tax Rate	Rank	State	Burdens	Rank	State	Tax?	State	RTW?	State	Income	Rank
RI	45	VT	8.95%	44	IA	9.9%	45	HI	$91.37	45	OR	Yes	PA	No	RI	10.9%	45
MN	46	NJ	9.97%	46	DE	10.5%	46	NY	$91.49	46	PA	Yes	RI	No	WI	11.1%	46
CA	47	OR	10.61%	47	OR	11.3%	47	FL	$91.81	47	RI	Yes	VT	No	CA	11.2%	47
IL	48	HI	11.00%	48	PA	17.1%	48	VT	$97.51	48	TN†	Yes	WA	No	CT	12.3%	48
NY	49	NY	12.70%	49	NY	17.2%	49	NV	$104.12	49	VT	Yes	WI	No	NJ	12.4%	49
VT	50	CA	13.30%	50	OH†	N/A	N/A	WY	$113.78	50	WA	Yes	WV	No	NY	12.8%	50
As of 2013		As of 2013			As of 2013			As of 2010			As of 1/1/2013		As of 1/1/2013		As of 2010		

* Michigan is now a right-to-work state, but the law did not go into effect until late March 2013 (and has not been counted as having a RTW law for this list). Indiana became a right-to-work state in 2012.

† Ohio repealed its estate tax effective Jan. 1, 2013. Indiana repealed its inheritance tax in May 2013 retroactively to Jan. 1, 2013. North Carolina repealed its estate tax in July 2013 retroactively to Jan. 1, 2013. Tennessee's estate tax is in the process of being phased out, with full elimination on Jan. 1, 2016.

† For more on Ohio's corporate income tax rate, see Chapter 3.

Source: Laffer Associates, Tax Foundation.

adjusted gross income (AGI) in the tax year for which they have filed. The analysis of these data is contained in Chapter 5.

Just so readers are perfectly clear on how the IRS prepares and presents migration data, here is an excerpt from the IRS's migration data methodology flyer:

> This section defines what is meant by tax year, filing or calendar year, and migration year. In most cases, the tax year is the year in which income is actually earned. The year in which an income tax return is filed is the "filing" year, and it is almost always one calendar year after the actual tax year. The residence of a taxpayer, for purposes of the migration data files, is noted at the time the individual income tax return is filed, the filing year. For example, the 2003 migration data report the place of residence for individuals who were filing their tax year 2002 Forms 1040 in calendar year 2003. Furthermore, since the migration data show movement from year to year, the files are expressed in 2-year increments, such as the 2002–2003 migration data. Thus, the file would show actual changes in residence from calendar year 2002 to calendar year 2003. It is important to note that the income information reported on the migration files is for the tax year corresponding to the earlier of the 2 years. In this example, the income data present on the 2002–2003 migration data files would be for tax year 2002.[10]

For example, for the 18 years of tax returns, 1992/1993 to 2009/2010, the total number of returns moving from Texas to California is 300,310, while the number of returns moving from California to Texas over this same time period is 427,607—quite a difference in favor of Texas. Not only did more filers move from California to Texas than from Texas to California, but the average adjusted gross incomes of the filers moving from California to Texas was considerably larger than was the average adjusted gross income of filers moving from Texas to California.

In each and every year the surplus of filers moving to Texas from California was positive.

Now, there are clearly some cautions about the use of these data. Again, to quote the IRS:

[T]he source and design of this dataset present some limitations. As mentioned, those who are not required to file United States Federal income tax returns are not included in this file, and so the data under-represent the poor and the elderly. Also excluded is the small percentage of tax returns filed after late September of the filing year. Most taxpayers whose returns are filed after this date have been granted an extension to file by the IRS. These taxpayers are likely to have complex returns that report relatively high income, and so the migration data set may under-represent the very wealthy, as well.

The matching process also causes some returns to be excluded from the counts. When the current-year tax return is compared to the prior-year tax return, only the Social Security Number of the primary taxpayer is considered. If a secondary filer exists (as in the case of a married couple filing jointly), that Social Security Number is not recorded or compared in creating the migration dataset. If, for example, a husband and wife file a joint return in the prior year, but divorce and file separately in the current year, only the husband's current-year return will have a match with the prior-year return. The now ex-wife's current-year return becomes a non-match and will not be included in the data counts. Other changes in filing status—from joint to married filing separately—will also affect the data.[11]

In Table 2.5, we list the net in-returns (returns moving into each state less the returns moving out of each state) divided by total migrating returns (returns moving in plus returns moving out) for each state in percentage terms. Thus, for the tax year/filing year 1992/1993 the net returns moving into Idaho were almost 20 percent (19.8 percent, to be exact) of the total migrating returns. Using the rounded 20 percent number for Idaho, this would mean that for every 10 returns moving out of Idaho, there were 15 returns moving into Idaho. These data are provided for each state by tax year/filing year from 1992/1993 through 2009/2010. We also provide a cumulative total of all net in-returns as a share of total migrating returns for each state for all 18 years and the all-states total number of in-returns for all 18 years as the bottom row. The states are ranked from the highest percentage of net in-returns to the lowest percentage of net in-returns for each state for each year and the cumulative totals for each state over the entire 1992/1993 through 2009/2010 period.

The bottom line of Table 2.5 is the annual total of all migrating returns (i.e., the sum of all in-returns for each year) from 1992/1993 through 2009/2010. This bottom row of total migrating returns now presents data reflecting the degree to which people are migrating from one state to another by year. As you will easily see, there are large variations in the number of tax filers who migrate from year to year. The volume of migration at first glance appears to be highly sensitive to the state of the overall economy.

In Table 2.6 we list the percentage of net inflow of adjusted gross income (AGI) divided by total state adjusted gross income for each state by tax year/filing year from 1992/1993 through 2009/2010. These data are ranked each and every year by the percentage of AGI in the net in-returns divided by total state AGI from highest to lowest.

The bottom row of this table is the total of all states' in-AGI divided by the total of all states' AGI by year. The final column of this table is total net in-AGI for each state calculated by summing each year's indexed net in-AGI over the period where each year's in-AGI is indexed to the state's average AGI for that year. This column is not the simple summation across all years, but instead represents the time equivalent adjusted AGI indexed summations over all the years.

Thus, Nevada's total state AGI is 36 percent higher today than it would have been had there been no net in-migration of AGI over the 17 years reported in this table. There are a substantial number of assumptions underlying the calculation and interpretation of this number, for sure. This calculation assumes no one stops working or dies, that average in-AGI grows with the state's average AGI, and that there are no indirect effects of state AGI migration such as children working or what have you. While these assumptions if taken literally are stretches, their biases tend to cancel from state to state over time, and therefore the relative rankings should be quite accurate.

The analysis of these data is contained in Chapter 5.

The final table, Table 2.7, is for the nominal summation for the 18 years from 1992/1993 through 2009/2010 focusing on tax return

TABLE 2.5

Net In-Returns as a Percentage of Gross Returns
(Returns In + Returns Out)

92/93	93/94	94/95	95/96	96/97	97/98	98/99	99/00	00/01	01/02
ID 19.8%	NV 29.4%	NV 24.8%	NV 24.6%	NV 26.7%	NV 21.3%	NV 20.1%	NV 20.1%	NV 19.9%	FL 17.7%
NV 19.3%	AZ 23.1%	AZ 23.3%	AZ 19.4%	AZ 18.0%	AZ 16.4%	AZ 15.8%	AZ 14.8%	FL 15.6%	NV 17.6%
CO 18.5%	ID 19.5%	NC 16.8%	NC 16.5%	NC 15.3%	NC 13.5%	CO 13.5%	GA 12.1%	AZ 14.0%	AZ 14.9%
OR 18.4%	GA 18.1%	GA 16.0%	GA 16.4%	FL 15.2%	FL 13.3%	GA 13.3%	FL 11.9%	CO 12.4%	OR 8.9%
AZ 17.2%	NC 16.6%	OR 15.6%	OR 15.9%	GA 13.4%	GA 13.3%	NC 11.4%	CO 10.6%	GA 8.9%	ME 8.5%
MT 16.5%	CO 16.2%	TN 15.1%	TN 13.5%	CO 12.5%	CO 11.4%	SC 10.0%	NC 9.9%	NC 8.1%	DE 8.0%
WA 16.4%	TN 15.5%	ID 14.7%	FL 11.8%	OR 11.6%	SC 10.7%	FL 9.9%	DE 8.0%	NH 7.9%	NC 7.3%
GA 15.4%	FL 15.0%	CO 14.3%	CO 11.2%	SC 10.3%	OR 7.4%	DE 8.2%	NH 7.8%	OR 6.3%	GA 6.8%
UT 14.6%	OR 15.0%	FL 13.6%	ID 9.2%	WA 9.6%	TX 7.3%	NH 6.0%	SC 7.1%	DE 5.1%	SC 6.2%
NC 13.2%	UT 14.7%	MT 11.4%	TN 8.6%	TN 9.3%	TN 6.8%	TN 5.9%	VA 6.6%	WA 4.6%	NH 5.9%
TN 13.0%	MT 12.1%	AR 11.2%	WA 8.4%	ID 6.9%	DE 6.6%	ID 4.9%	ME 6.6%	ME 4.5%	MD 4.8%
FL 12.8%	NM 11.7%	WA 9.5%	SC 7.8%	DE 6.5%	WA 6.4%	OR 4.8%	TN 5.4%	TX 4.2%	TX 4.8%
AR 12.4%	AR 10.7%	UT 8.8%	UT 6.6%	UT 5.7%	ID 4.7%	TX 4.5%	ID 5.1%	SC 4.1%	CO 4.7%
NM 9.2%	WA 9.2%	NM 7.7%	TX 6.2%	TX 5.1%	NH 4.1%	VA 4.1%	MN 3.4%	VA 4.0%	VA 4.2%
AL 9.0%	TX 8.3%	DE 6.5%	NH 6.0%	NH 4.4%	KY 2.0%	WA 3.5%	TX 3.4%	ID 3.2%	TN 4.2%
DE 6.7%	DE 7.6%	MO 5.3%	TX 4.8%	AL 3.9%	AL 1.9%	MN 3.2%	AR 2.3%	MD 3.0%	ID 4.2%
TX 6.4%	MS 6.6%	SC 5.3%	MO 4.7%	MO 3.2%	VA 1.2%	KY 2.1%	OR 1.9%	TN 2.4%	RI 3.9%
MN 6.2%	KY 5.5%	NH 5.1%	MT 4.6%	KY 2.7%	AR 0.8%	ME 1.1%	RI 1.9%	WA 2.4%	WA 3.8%
KY 6.1%	AL 5.3%	TX 4.5%	NM 2.9%	AR 2.2%	MS 0.5%	MO 0.2%	CA 1.8%	CA 1.6%	NM 3.3%
WV 5.7%	MO 5.2%	MS 4.3%	KY 2.8%	VA 1.9%	OK 0.4%	AR -0.7%	WA 1.0%	MN 1.5%	WY 2.7%
MO 4.6%	SC 4.7%	KY 3.8%	MN 2.4%	MS 1.5%	MO -0.4%	MS -0.9%	KY 0.9%	VT 0.5%	KY 1.9%
SC 4.5%	SD 3.9%	AL 2.8%	MS 2.3%	OK 0.7%	KS -0.5%	MD -1.1%	MO 0.9%	MO -0.5%	AK 1.8%
MS 4.4%	NH 3.4%	VA 1.8%	OK 1.7%	MN -1.6%	VT -1.3%	VT -1.9%	MO 0.3%	KY -0.6%	VT 1.4%
VA 4.4%	VA 3.0%	MN 1.8%	AL 1.7%	KS 1.7%	CA -2.2%	MA -2.0%	WI -0.5%	AR -1.1%	WV 1.4%
WI 4.2%	MN 2.9%	IN 1.7%	VT 1.2%	IN -2.3%	MN -2.0%	MT -2.2%	MT -1.0%	DC -1.6%	HI 1.3%
SD 3.9%	WY 2.7%	SD 1.5%	VA 1.1%	NM -2.4%	MD -2.6%	CA -2.2%	CA -1.4%	MO -2.0%	MO 0.6%
IN 2.8%	OK 1.1%	VT 0.8%	IN 0.4%	ME -2.9%	RI -2.6%	MS -2.3%	WI -1.7%	AR -3.1%	AR 0.3%
WY 2.3%	IN 1.0%	WI 0.6%	WI 0.2%	VT -3.2%	VT -3.3%	AL -2.4%	IN -2.8%	AK -3.3%	OK -0.1%
OK 1.6%	WI 0.2%	NE 0.1%	NE -0.7%	MA -3.5%	ME -3.7%	WI -2.4%	AL -4.0%	MA -3.4%	MT -0.2%
AK 1.5%	AK 0.1%	OK -0.1%	ME -1.1%	MT -3.5%	IN -4.1%	DC -3.1%	MT -4.0%	WI -3.4%	WI -2.0%
NH -0.2%	VT 0.1%	WY -0.2%	WV -2.7%	MD -3.5%	AK -4.2%	OK -3.3%	MA -4.2%	UT -5.5%	AL -3.4%
VT -0.2%	WV -0.2%	MD -1.1%	WY -3.4%	AK -4.1%	NM -4.7%	KS -3.6%	UT -4.3%	AL -5.8%	MN -3.4%
KS -1.4%	MD -0.7%	WV -1.7%	MD -3.6%	WI -5.2%	MT -4.9%	IN -3.7%	WY -4.5%	OK -5.9%	CT -3.9%
HI -2.0%	KS -1.7%	KS -3.5%	SD -4.1%	NE -5.8%	WY -5.5%	UT -3.9%	DC -4.7%	SD -5.9%	MS -4.0%
MD -2.1%	NE -2.5%	LA -3.6%	MA -4.1%	CA -6.5%	WI -5.7%	AK -4.8%	NM -5.4%	PA -4.3%	PA -4.3%
NE -2.9%	HI -3.3%	ME -4.5%	MI -4.7%	WY -7.1%	OH -6.2%	SD -6.5%	KS -5.6%	IN -6.4%	UT -4.8%
ND -4.4%	LA -4.7%	ND -4.5%	AK -5.1%	WV -7.8%	RI -7.1%	WV -7.0%	OK -5.7%	MS -6.4%	DC -5.1%
IA -4.4%	ND -5.5%	MI -5.4%	ND -5.4%	LA -8.9%	LA -8.3%	WY -7.1%	CT -6.5%	NM -6.8%	KS -5.4%
PA -4.6%	ME -7.0%	KS -5.7%	MI -6.0%	MI -9.0%	DC -9.0%	NM -7.7%	MI -6.6%	IL -5.9%	SD -5.5%
ME -6.0%	PA -7.6%	OH -6.0%	OH -6.1%	OH -9.4%	NE -9.3%	NE -8.1%	AK -7.4%	NJ -7.2%	IN -5.9%
OH -6.1%	IA -7.8%	MA -7.2%	IA -6.7%	RI -9.8%	IA -9.6%	CT -8.3%	WV -8.1%	KS -8.1%	CA -6.4%
LA -9.8%	MA -8.1%	AK -8.6%	LA -7.8%	SD -9.9%	NJ -10.3%	NJ -8.6%	NJ -8.5%	WV -8.3%	NJ -6.8%
IL -10.7%	OH -8.8%	HI -8.8%	PA -9.4%	IA -10.2%	SD -10.6%	MI -8.6%	PA -9.1%	PA -8.9%	LA -7.9%
NJ -11.5%	NJ -11.2%	PA -9.5%	IL -10.8%	ND -11.5%	OH -10.7%	IA -8.8%	HI -9.5%	MI -10.6%	NE -9.2%
DC -11.9%	IL -12.0%	NJ -10.5%	HI -11.3%	NJ -11.5%	CT -10.9%	OH -9.6%	NE -9.6%	NE -11.0%	MA -9.7%
RI -12.2%	MI -13.3%	IL -10.8%	NJ -12.1%	HI -12.0%	PA -11.1%	LA -9.8%	OH -10.0%	OH -11.6%	OH -10.5%
MA -13.4%	DC -13.6%	CT -14.7%	RI -12.1%	DC -12.1%	MI -11.5%	PA -10.0%	IA -10.6%	IL -12.8%	IA -11.7%
MI -15.2%	RI -15.2%	RI -15.7%	CT -14.6%	IL -13.2%	HI -11.6%	IL -12.1%	IA -13.1%	IA -13.8%	MI -11.9%
CT -18.0%	CT -17.5%	DC -16.1%	DC -15.6%	CT -13.6%	IL -13.4%	HI -15.1%	LA -13.7%	LA -14.7%	ND -12.8%
NY -25.3%	NY -26.4%	CA -24.1%	CA -16.8%	PA -13.7%	ND -13.5%	ND -16.2%	ND -16.8%	NY -17.2%	IL -13.7%
CA -26.1%	CA -29.4%	NY -27.2%	NY -28.0%	NY -27.6%	NY -23.4%	NY -19.0%	NY -17.8%	ND -17.3%	NY -18.2%

	92/93	93/94	94/95	95/96	96/97	97/98	98/99	99/00	00/01	01/02
Total In	2,727,709	2,725,567	2,824,716	2,771,108	2,839,414	2,875,985	2,907,796	2,954,941	2,994,681	2,962,850

Source: Internal Revenue Service, Laffer Associates.

02/03		03/04		04/05		05/06		06/07		07/08		08/09		09/10		Net In-Returns as a % of Gross Returns (Returns In + Returns Out) from 1992/1993 to 2009/2010		
NV	18.9%	NV	25.1%	AZ	24.3%	AZ	23.3%	SC	17.6%	SC	16.6%	TX	14.5%	TX	11.1%	1	NV	18.3%
FL	17.2%	FL	23.1%	FL	21.8%	NV	20.0%	NC	16.8%	NC	16.0%	SC	11.0%	DC	9.8%	2	AZ	16.3%
AZ	15.0%	AZ	19.3%	NV	20.8%	TX	17.6%	NV	15.8%	TX	13.6%	NC	10.6%	CO	8.8%	3	NC	12.5%
ME	11.6%	DE	10.2%	ID	14.1%	NC	17.4%	AZ	15.8%	CO	10.9%	CO	10.5%	OK	7.6%	4	FL	11.9%
DE	11.1%	NC	9.9%	NC	12.6%	GA	17.1%	GA	14.3%	OR	10.4%	WY	10.2%	LA	7.5%	5	GA	11.4%
SC	8.1%	ID	9.8%	SC	12.3%	SC	15.6%	TN	13.1%	AZ	10.2%	WA	8.5%	SC	7.4%	6	CO	9.7%
ID	7.1%	SC	9.8%	TN	11.4%	ID	14.2%	TX	12.7%	WA	9.5%	DC	8.4%	ND	7.3%	7	OR	9.5%
OR	6.3%	GA	9.0%	DE	11.2%	OR	13.2%	ID	12.2%	GA	8.6%	OK	8.3%	NC	6.9%	8	SC	9.4%
VA	5.9%	TN	7.3%	OR	10.1%	TN	12.8%	OR	11.1%	UT	8.5%	OR	7.8%	AK	6.6%	9	TN	8.9%
GA	5.8%	MT	6.7%	GA	9.3%	UT	12.8%	UT	10.3%	TN	8.0%	LA	7.0%	WV	6.5%	10	ID	8.7%
TN	5.8%	VA	6.2%	AR	7.9%	AL	11.0%	WY	9.9%	NV	7.8%	TN	6.6%	NM	6.5%	11	TX	7.4%
NC	5.7%	ME	6.1%	WA	6.2%	WA	10.7%	CO	8.9%	ID	7.6%	WV	5.3%	VA	4.8%	12	DE	7.3%
MT	4.8%	AR	5.7%	MT	5.5%	AR	10.4%	WA	7.7%	WY	7.1%	AL	5.2%	SD	4.5%	13	WA	6.8%
NH	4.4%	NM	5.0%	AL	5.1%	DE	8.8%	MT	7.3%	MT	6.2%	AR	4.4%	FL	4.5%	14	AR	5.2%
NM	3.9%	WA	3.9%	TX	5.1%	CO	8.7%	DE	7.1%	DE	6.2%	AZ	4.0%	KY	4.5%	15	MT	4.0%
KY	3.8%	HI	3.0%	NM	4.9%	UT	7.0%	LA	6.6%	AL	6.1%	GA	4.0%	TN	4.5%	16	KY	3.3%
AR	3.6%	AL	2.8%	KY	4.1%	MT	6.5%	AL	6.3%	LA	4.8%	DE	3.9%	AZ	4.4%	17	VA	3.3%
HI	3.4%	KY	2.7%	VA	4.1%	NM	5.6%	KY	5.8%	AR	4.5%	UT	3.8%	DE	4.4%	18	UT	2.9%
WV	3.0%	TX	2.7%	CO	2.9%	WY	4.7%	AR	5.3%	KY	4.1%	NM	3.8%	AR	4.4%	19	AL	2.8%
TX	2.9%	MS	2.4%	HI	2.9%	OK	4.2%	OK	5.1%	SD	3.5%	ND	3.6%	OR	4.3%	20	NM	2.4%
RI	2.8%	SD	2.4%	MO	1.9%	KY	3.3%	NM	4.9%	WV	2.9%	KY	3.5%	AL	3.2%	21	NH	2.3%
MD	2.6%	NH	2.2%	ME	1.9%	MO	3.1%	FL	3.0%	OK	2.6%	SD	3.4%	WA	3.2%	22	MO	1.8%
MO	1.5%	MO	1.4%	UT	1.7%	HI	1.6%	WV	2.5%	DC	1.8%	VA	3.4%	GA	2.5%	23	OK	0.8%
WA	1.1%	WY	1.3%	NH	1.4%	WV	1.5%	SD	2.0%	MS	0.7%	MT	2.5%	MT	2.4%	24	WY	0.1%
AL	1.0%	OR	1.1%	WV	1.2%	VA	1.4%	MO	1.9%	NM	0.5%	AK	0.9%	UT	1.2%	25	MS	-0.1%
VT	0.7%	WV	0.2%	DC	0.4%	DC	0.8%	MS	0.8%	VA	0.4%	ID	0.0%	MD	0.9%	26	ME	-0.3%
AK	0.5%	AK	0.2%	OK	-0.3%	SD	0.5%	DC	0.5%	IA	-0.1%	MO	-0.2%	NE	0.5%	27	WV	-0.7%
MS	-1.1%	CO	-0.4%	SD	-0.3%	NH	0.4%	VA	0.3%	MO	-1.1%	MA	-0.3%	HI	0.2%	28	SD	-1.3%
OK	-1.4%	MD	-0.9%	WY	-0.4%	AK	-1.3%	ME	0.1%	HI	-1.3%	NV	-0.6%	MO	0.2%	29	MN	-1.4%
PA	-1.5%	VT	-2.3%	DC	-1.9%	IN	-1.7%	MN	-2.4%	FL	-1.9%	IA	-0.7%	IA	-0.7%	30	MD	-1.4%
WY	-1.7%	DC	-2.7%	MD	-1.9%	ME	-1.8%	NH	-2.7%	ND	-1.9%	KS	-1.9%	ID	-0.8%	31	VT	-1.8%
WI	-1.7%	WI	-2.8%	IN	-2.1%	MN	-2.7%	IN	-2.9%	KS	-2.0%	NE	-1.9%	KS	-1.3%	32	AK	-2.1%
CO	-1.9%	OK	-2.8%	VT	-2.8%	PA	-3.7%	PA	-3.5%	IN	-2.7%	MS	-2.0%	MS	-1.5%	33	IN	-2.4%
SD	-2.0%	PA	-3.4%	AK	-3.2%	VT	-4.0%	AK	-3.5%	ME	-3.0%	PA	-2.6%	VT	-2.4%	34	WI	-3.0%
IN	-2.0%	LA	-3.9%	PA	-4.0%	MD	-4.2%	KS	-4.0%	NH	-3.4%	MD	-2.7%	PA	-3.0%	35	KS	-4.1%
CT	-3.3%	ND	-4.0%	WI	-4.4%	IA	-4.9%	IA	-4.9%	AK	-3.4%	FL	-3.1%	MA	-3.0%	36	HI	-4.2%
MN	-4.7%	UT	-4.1%	MN	-5.0%	WI	-5.1%	ND	-4.9%	PA	-4.2%	IN	-4.3%	NV	-3.1%	37	DC	-4.6%
LA	-4.8%	IN	-4.7%	IA	-6.1%	KS	-5.2%	HI	-5.6%	MN	-4.8%	HI	-4.7%	WY	-3.1%	38	NE	-5.5%
NE	-5.0%	MN	-5.4%	LA	-6.1%	NE	-7.9%	WI	-5.8%	NE	-4.9%	CA	-4.8%	CA	-3.3%	39	PA	-6.3%
DC	-5.8%	IA	-6.6%	NE	-6.6%	MS	-8.1%	VT	-6.4%	MA	-5.8%	VT	-5.1%	IN	-4.2%	40	IA	-6.8%
CA	-6.2%	NE	-7.2%	KS	-6.9%	ND	-8.2%	MD	-6.6%	WI	-6.0%	NH	-5.8%	NH	-5.1%	41	ND	-7.3%
KS	-6.6%	RI	-7.4%	ND	-9.1%	IL	-9.8%	IL	-7.6%	MD	-6.6%	MN	-6.2%	CT	-8.2%	42	LA	-7.4%
ND	-6.9%	KS	-8.3%	CT	-9.3%	CT	-10.5%	NE	-7.7%	IL	-7.0%	WI	-6.4%	WI	-8.2%	43	MA	-7.8%
UT	-7.3%	CA	-9.5%	IL	-12.7%	MA	-14.2%	CA	-11.0%	CA	-7.1%	IL	-7.4%	ME	-8.3%	44	RI	-8.3%
NJ	-9.0%	CT	-9.7%	NJ	-13.6%	OH	-14.8%	CT	-11.6%	VT	-7.3%	ME	-7.7%	RI	-8.4%	45	CT	-10.3%
IA	-9.5%	OH	-11.7%	OH	-14.0%	NJ	-15.2%	CA	-14.1%	CT	-9.4%	CT	-8.2%	MN	-8.5%	46	CA	-10.5%
OH	-9.7%	NJ	-11.8%	RI	-14.4%	CA	-15.9%	OH	-14.3%	NY	-11.4%	NY	-8.8%	NJ	-8.9%	47	OH	-10.6%
MI	-11.5%	IL	-14.0%	CA	-15.0%	RI	-16.3%	RI	-14.6%	NJ	-11.9%	NJ	-9.0%	NY	-9.8%	48	NJ	-10.7%
MA	-13.4%	MI	-15.1%	MA	-17.5%	NY	-21.3%	NJ	-14.6%	RI	-13.2%	OH	-12.3%	IL	-10.5%	49	IL	-11.4%
IL	-14.0%	MA	-17.9%	MI	-19.3%	MI	-23.4%	NY	-17.6%	OH	-13.2%	RI	-12.6%	OH	-12.5%	50	MI	-15.2%
NY	-17.1%	NY	-21.9%	NY	-23.2%	LA	-54.6%	MI	-28.5%	MI	-29.8%	MI	-27.0%	MI	-21.7%	51	NY	-20.1%

02/03	03/04	04/05	05/06	06/07	07/08	08/09	09/10
2,871,554	2,885,696	3,006,642	3,185,682	3,100,843	3,169,383	3,026,084	2,836,418

TABLE 2.6

Net In-AGI as a Percentage of AGI
Filed in a Given Year

92/93	93/94	94/95	95/96	96/97	97/98	98/99	99/00	00/01	01/02
NV 3.2%	NV 4.5%	NV 3.8%	NV 3.9%	NV 3.9%	NV 3.7%	NV 3.0%	NV 3.3%	NV 3.4%	NV 2.9%
ID 2.3%	AZ 3.0%	AZ 3.1%	AZ 2.5%	AZ 2.2%	AZ 2.3%	AZ 1.9%	AZ 2.1%	FL 2.2%	FL 2.4%
AZ 2.0%	ID 2.3%	CO 1.9%	FL 1.5%	FL 2.0%	FL 2.0%	FL 1.8%	FL 2.0%	AZ 1.8%	AZ 1.6%
CO 1.8%	FL 1.8%	FL 1.8%	NC 1.3%	CO 1.3%	SC 1.3%	WY 1.7%	CO 1.2%	NH 1.2%	NH 1.1%
FL 1.8%	CO 1.8%	ID 1.7%	CO 1.3%	NC 1.1%	CO 1.2%	CO 1.4%	ID 1.1%	CO 1.1%	WY 1.1%
MT 1.7%	NM 1.6%	MT 1.4%	ID 1.3%	SC 1.1%	NC 1.1%	SC 1.2%	NH 1.1%	ME 1.0%	ID 1.0%
OR 1.5%	MT 1.5%	NC 1.4%	OR 1.2%	GA 1.0%	ID 1.1%	ID 1.1%	SC 1.0%	SC 0.9%	SC 1.0%
WY 1.3%	NC 1.4%	GA 1.3%	GA 1.2%	WY 1.0%	GA 0.8%	NH 1.1%	ME 0.9%	ID 0.8%	ME 0.9%
GA 1.2%	GA 1.3%	OR 1.2%	MT 1.1%	ID 0.9%	WY 0.8%	NC 1.1%	NC 0.8%	VT 0.8%	OR 0.8%
AR 1.2%	OR 1.2%	NM 1.2%	SC 0.9%	WA 0.8%	NH 0.8%	GA 0.8%	WY 0.8%	NC 0.7%	MT 0.7%
NC 1.2%	UT 1.2%	AR 1.2%	TN 0.9%	NH 0.8%	WA 0.6%	VT 0.6%	MT 0.6%	WA 0.6%	VT 0.6%
WA 1.2%	AR 1.1%	TN 1.0%	VT 0.8%	OR 0.7%	MT 0.5%	MT 0.6%	VT 0.6%	DE 0.5%	NC 0.6%
NM 1.1%	TN 1.0%	UT 1.0%	AR 0.7%	TN 0.6%	OR 0.5%	TN 0.5%	GA 0.6%	WY 0.5%	NM 0.5%
UT 1.1%	WY 1.0%	WA 0.9%	WA 0.7%	UT 0.6%	TX 0.5%	ME 0.5%	DE 0.4%	MT 0.4%	DE 0.5%
TN 0.9%	WA 0.7%	SC 0.8%	NH 0.6%	VT 0.5%	VT 0.5%	SC 0.4%	AR 0.4%	OR 0.4%	HI 0.5%
SC 0.8%	SC 0.7%	VT 0.7%	WY 0.5%	ME 0.4%	ME 0.2%	TX 0.3%	TN 0.3%	HI 0.3%	RI 0.4%
SD 0.6%	SD 0.7%	NH 0.6%	UT 0.5%	TX 0.4%	MS 0.2%	WA 0.3%	TX 0.2%	GA 0.3%	CO 0.4%
NH 0.6%	VT 0.6%	MS 0.4%	TX 0.3%	MT 0.3%	AR 0.2%	AR 0.2%	VA 0.2%	RI 0.3%	GA 0.3%
AL 0.6%	NH 0.5%	SD 0.4%	NM 0.3%	MS 0.3%	AL 0.1%	OR 0.2%	MS 0.1%	VA 0.1%	WA 0.3%
VT 0.6%	TX 0.5%	WY 0.3%	MS 0.3%	AR 0.3%	VT 0.1%	VA 0.1%	KY 0.1%	TX 0.1%	TN 0.3%
MS 0.4%	MS 0.5%	TX 0.3%	ME 0.2%	AL 0.2%	DE -0.1%	RI 0.1%	OR 0.1%	CA 0.1%	AR 0.1%
TX 0.4%	AL 0.3%	DE 0.3%	AL 0.2%	KY 0.1%	CA -0.1%	MS 0.1%	SD 0.0%	AR 0.0%	TX 0.1%
WV 0.4%	KY 0.3%	ME 0.2%	SD 0.2%	MO 0.0%	VA -0.1%	DE 0.0%	WA 0.0%	TN 0.0%	VA 0.1%
VA 0.3%	DE 0.3%	MO 0.2%	MO 0.2%	DE 0.0%	KY -0.1%	KY 0.0%	CA -0.1%	SD 0.0%	WV 0.1%
KY 0.3%	WV 0.2%	KY 0.2%	DE 0.2%	OK -0.1%	KS -0.1%	WI -0.1%	WI -0.1%	UT -0.1%	MD 0.0%
MN 0.3%	WI 0.1%	AL 0.1%	KY 0.1%	VA -0.1%	OK -0.2%	CA -0.1%	AL -0.1%	WI -0.2%	AL 0.0%
WI 0.3%	MO 0.1%	WI 0.1%	WI 0.0%	IN -0.2%	WV -0.2%	AL -0.1%	RI -0.2%	MI -0.1%	MS -0.1%
DE 0.2%	IN 0.1%	VA 0.1%	OK 0.0%	WI 0.0%	MA -0.2%	MN -0.3%	MN -0.2%	MD -0.3%	KY -0.1%
IN 0.2%	VA 0.1%	IN 0.1%	IN 0.0%	NM -0.2%	SD -0.3%	MA -0.2%	MA -0.3%	KY -0.2%	SD -0.1%
ME 0.0%	MN 0.0%	MN 0.0%	WV 0.0%	MA -0.2%	IN -0.3%	MO -0.3%	MO -0.3%	AL -0.2%	PA -0.2%
MO 0.0%	KS -0.1%	WV 0.0%	VA 0.0%	SD -0.2%	UT -0.3%	IN -0.3%	MI -0.3%	MN -0.2%	MO -0.2%
PA -0.1%	OK -0.1%	NE 0.0%	MN -0.1%	CA -0.3%	RI -0.3%	MI -0.3%	DC -0.2%	MO -0.2%	OK -0.2%
KS -0.2%	PA -0.2%	OK -0.1%	NE -0.1%	MI -0.3%	WI -0.3%	PA -0.4%	IN -0.3%	MO -0.2%	CT -0.2%
MD -0.2%	MD -0.3%	MI -0.2%	MI -0.2%	KS -0.3%	PA -0.4%	NJ -0.4%	MN -0.3%	MS -0.3%	MN -0.2%
OK -0.3%	LA -0.3%	LA -0.3%	MA -0.2%	MN -0.3%	MN -0.4%	CT -0.4%	UT -0.3%	PA -0.3%	UT -0.3%
IA -0.3%	NE -0.3%	IA -0.3%	OH -0.3%	WV -0.4%	MI -0.4%	MD -0.5%	PA -0.4%	MI -0.4%	AK -0.3%
OH -0.3%	MA -0.3%	KS -0.3%	PA -0.3%	OH -0.5%	MO -0.4%	MI -0.5%	WV -0.4%	AK -0.4%	IN -0.3%
NE -0.4%	OH -0.4%	MA -0.4%	KS -0.4%	PA -0.5%	NM -0.5%	OK -0.5%	OK -0.5%	WV -0.5%	NJ -0.3%
MI -0.5%	IA -0.4%	PA -0.3%	IA -0.4%	MD -0.5%	IA -0.5%	IA -0.5%	CT -0.5%	CT -0.5%	CA -0.3%
NJ -0.5%	MI -0.4%	MD -0.3%	MD -0.5%	NE -0.5%	LA -0.5%	UT -0.5%	KS -0.5%	OK -0.6%	MI -0.4%
HI -0.5%	NJ -0.5%	OH -0.3%	LA -0.5%	IA -0.6%	MD -0.6%	KS -0.5%	HI -0.5%	NJ -0.7%	MA -0.4%
RI -0.6%	ME -0.5%	ND -0.5%	ND -0.5%	LA -0.6%	OH -0.6%	OH -0.6%	NJ -0.6%	OH -0.7%	KS -0.5%
IL -0.6%	ND -0.6%	NJ -0.6%	NJ -0.6%	NE -0.6%	NE -0.6%	NM -0.7%	NM -0.6%	KS -0.8%	OH -0.5%
MA -0.6%	CT -0.6%	CT -0.7%	IL -0.7%	CT -0.6%	CT -0.7%	LA -0.8%	IA -0.8%	NE -0.8%	LA -0.6%
CT -0.6%	HI -0.6%	IL -0.7%	CT -0.7%	IL -0.7%	NE -0.8%	IL -0.8%	IL -0.8%	IA -0.9%	NE -0.6%
LA -0.7%	IL -0.7%	HI -0.9%	CA -0.7%	RI -0.8%	IL -0.9%	NE -0.9%	LA -0.8%	IL -0.9%	IA -0.6%
ND -0.7%	AK -0.8%	CA -1.1%	RI -0.8%	ND -0.9%	AK -1.0%	HI -0.9%	NE -0.8%	LA -0.9%	IL -0.8%
AK -1.0%	RI -0.9%	NY -1.3%	HI -1.0%	HI -0.9%	HI -1.0%	NY -1.0%	NY -0.9%	NY -0.9%	NY -1.0%
CA -1.1%	NY -1.3%	AK -1.3%	AK -1.3%	AK -1.2%	ND -1.0%	ND -1.1%	DC -1.2%	AK -0.9%	ND -1.1%
NY -1.2%	CA -1.3%	RI -1.9%	NY -1.3%	NY -1.4%	NY -1.2%	AK -1.2%	ND -1.2%	KS -0.9%	DC -1.8%
DC -3.7%	DC -3.5%	DC -5.0%	DC -3.4%	DC -3.5%	DC -2.9%	DC -2.0%	AK -1.4%	ND -1.4%	

In-AGI as a % of Total AGI:	92/93	93/94	94/95	95/96	96/97	97/98	98/99	99/00	00/01	01/02
	2.6%	2.6%	2.7%	2.6%	2.6%	2.7%	2.7%	2.7%	2.7%	2.5%

Source: Internal Revenue Service, Laffer Associates.

02/03	03/04	04/05	05/06	06/07	07/08	08/09	09/10		Constant AGI AGI Gained (Lost) Due to Migration from 1992/1993 to 2009/2010 as a Share of 2009 Total AGI Earned in a Given State	
NV 3.1%	NV 3.1%	NV 2.6%	AZ 2.2%	NV 2.0%	SC 1.8%	WY 1.4%	MT 2.1%	1	NV	36.0%
FL 2.0%	FL 2.5%	FL 2.6%	FL 2.0%	SC 1.9%	NC 1.3%	SC 1.4%	FL 1.0%	2	FL	27.7%
AZ 1.6%	AZ 1.9%	AZ 2.5%	SC 1.9%	AZ 1.5%	MT 1.2%	NC 0.8%	SC 1.0%	3	AZ	27.6%
MT 1.5%	MT 1.4%	ID 1.8%	NV 1.9%	NC 1.5%	AZ 1.2%	FL 0.8%	WY 0.7%	4	SC	19.3%
ME 1.2%	SC 1.2%	SC 1.4%	ID 1.9%	FL 1.4%	WY 1.1%	CO 0.7%	AZ 0.6%	5	ID	17.5%
ID 1.0%	ID 1.1%	NC 1.1%	NC 1.4%	MT 1.2%	FL 1.1%	NV 0.6%	NC 0.5%	6	MT	16.7%
NH 1.0%	ME 1.1%	MT 1.0%	WY 1.2%	ID 1.1%	NV 1.0%	MT 0.6%	TX 0.5%	7	NC	16.2%
SC 1.0%	NH 1.0%	OR 0.8%	OR 1.1%	WY 1.0%	CO 1.0%	AZ 0.6%	SD 0.5%	8	CO	14.4%
WY 0.8%	WY 0.8%	NH 0.7%	MT 1.1%	TN 0.9%	TN 0.7%	TX 0.6%	NM 0.5%	9	WY	14.3%
NC 0.5%	NC 0.7%	TN 0.7%	WA 0.9%	CO 0.9%	ID 0.7%	WA 0.5%	TN 0.4%	10	NH	11.3%
DE 0.5%	DE 0.6%	NM 0.6%	TN 0.9%	OR 0.8%	OR 0.7%	TN 0.5%	NV 0.4%	11	OR	10.7%
VT 0.5%	AR 0.5%	WA 0.6%	CO 0.8%	UT 0.8%	SD 0.6%	SD 0.5%	CO 0.3%	12	TN	9.8%
OR 0.4%	HI 0.5%	AR 0.6%	AR 0.8%	WA 0.7%	TX 0.6%	OR 0.5%	DE 0.3%	13	GA	9.4%
RI 0.4%	NM 0.5%	WY 0.6%	NM 0.8%	TX 0.7%	WA 0.6%	AR 0.4%	WA 0.3%	14	WA	8.7%
AR 0.4%	TN 0.4%	DE 0.6%	UT 0.8%	GA 0.7%	UT 0.6%	NM 0.3%	ID 0.3%	15	AR	8.0%
TN 0.4%	SD 0.4%	HI 0.5%	TX 0.7%	SD 0.5%	GA 0.4%	DE 0.3%	OR 0.3%	16	VT	7.0%
HI 0.3%	WA 0.3%	SD 0.4%	GA 0.7%	NM 0.5%	AL 0.3%	AL 0.3%	VA 0.3%	17	ME	6.4%
SD 0.3%	VT 0.3%	CO 0.4%	NH 0.7%	DE 0.5%	DE 0.3%	ID 0.3%	OK 0.2%	18	TX	5.8%
NM 0.3%	VA 0.3%	VT 0.4%	DE 0.5%	AR 0.4%	OK 0.3%	OK 0.2%	AL 0.2%	19	DE	5.4%
VA 0.3%	GA 0.2%	GA 0.3%	AL 0.5%	AL 0.4%	NM 0.2%	UT 0.2%	UT 0.2%	20	NM	5.1%
AL 0.2%	AL 0.2%	TX 0.3%	VT 0.5%	AL 0.4%	ME 0.2%	GA 0.2%	GA 0.2%	21	SD	4.8%
GA 0.2%	MS 0.2%	AL 0.3%	SD 0.4%	ME 0.3%	HI 0.2%	DC 0.2%	KY 0.2%	22	UT	4.0%
KY 0.2%	OR 0.2%	KY 0.2%	ME 0.3%	OK 0.2%	MS 0.1%	NH 0.1%	WV 0.2%	23	AL	3.3%
WA 0.1%	TX 0.2%	MS 0.2%	HI 0.2%	MS 0.1%	VT 0.1%	WV 0.1%	AR 0.1%	24	MS	2.0%
WV 0.1%	KY 0.1%	UT 0.2%	WV 0.2%	KY 0.1%	NH 0.1%	VT 0.1%	ND 0.1%	25	KY	1.4%
TX 0.1%	WV 0.1%	ME 0.2%	OK 0.1%	VT 0.0%	KY 0.1%	VA 0.1%	LA 0.1%	26	VA	1.1%
MS 0.1%	CO 0.1%	WV 0.1%	MO 0.1%	WV 0.0%	OK 0.0%	KY 0.0%	HI 0.0%	27	WV	−0.5%
CT 0.0%	UT 0.0%	VA 0.1%	KY 0.0%	MO −0.1%	WV 0.0%	MS 0.0%	MD 0.0%	28	MO	−1.5%
WI 0.0%	WI −0.1%	MO −0.1%	PA −0.1%	WI −0.2%	MO −0.1%	PA −0.1%	VT 0.0%	29	WI	−1.8%
CO 0.0%	RI −0.1%	PA −0.1%	IA −0.1%	PA −0.2%	IA −0.1%	IA −0.1%	ME −0.1%	30	OK	−2.2%
PA 0.0%	PA −0.1%	OK −0.2%	VA −0.2%	VA −0.2%	PA −0.1%	LA −0.1%	MS 0.0%	31	IN	−3.2%
MO −0.1%	MO −0.2%	IN −0.2%	WI −0.2%	IN −0.3%	WI −0.2%	MO −0.1%	NH −0.1%	32	MN	−3.4%
MD −0.1%	LA −0.3%	WI −0.2%	IN −0.2%	MN −0.3%	VA −0.2%	ND −0.1%	PA −0.1%	33	PA	−3.7%
MI −0.3%	IN −0.3%	IA −0.3%	MN −0.3%	NE −0.3%	LA −0.2%	ME −0.1%	IN −0.1%	34	HI	−3.8%
UT −0.3%	MN −0.3%	CT −0.3%	MS −0.3%	KS −0.3%	MN −0.3%	MA −0.2%	AK −0.1%	35	MD	−6.0%
MN −0.3%	AK −0.3%	MN −0.3%	KS −0.4%	HI −0.4%	IN −0.3%	MN −0.2%	IA −0.1%	36	KS	−6.3%
LA −0.3%	OK −0.3%	KS −0.3%	AK −0.4%	IA −0.4%	CA −0.3%	CA −0.2%	CA −0.1%	37	IA	−6.7%
IN −0.3%	MI −0.4%	NE −0.4%	CT −0.5%	ND −0.4%	MA −0.3%	KS −0.2%	MO −0.1%	38	CA	−7.1%
OK −0.3%	MD −0.4%	LA −0.4%	NE −0.6%	LA −0.5%	IL −0.4%	HI −0.3%	NE −0.2%	39	MA	−7.6%
CA −0.3%	CA −0.4%	MD −0.5%	MD −0.6%	IL −0.5%	NE −0.4%	IN −0.3%	MA −0.2%	40	NE	−7.6%
NE −0.4%	CT −0.4%	OH −0.6%	IL −0.6%	CA −0.6%	ND −0.4%	WI −0.3%	KS −0.2%	41	CT	−8.3%
NJ −0.4%	NE −0.4%	MI −0.6%	DC −0.7%	AK −0.6%	KS −0.5%	NE −0.3%	MN −0.3%	42	RI	−8.9%
OH −0.4%	ND −0.5%	ND −0.6%	CA −0.7%	OH −0.6%	NJ −0.6%	CT −0.3%	CT −0.3%	43	MI	−9.0%
IA −0.4%	KS −0.5%	AK −0.6%	MI −0.7%	MA −0.7%	CT −0.6%	MD −0.4%	WI −0.3%	44	OH	−9.2%
AK −0.6%	NJ −0.5%	CA −0.6%	ND −0.8%	CT −0.7%	AK −0.6%	AK −0.4%	DC −0.4%	45	NJ	−9.6%
KS −0.7%	OH −0.6%	IL −0.8%	OH −0.8%	RI −0.7%	MD −0.6%	IL −0.4%	OH −0.5%	46	LA	−10.0%
ND −0.7%	AK −0.6%	NJ −0.8%	MA −0.8%	MD −0.7%	OH −0.7%	NJ −0.5%	NJ −0.5%	47	ND	−11.3%
MA −0.8%	IL −0.7%	MA −1.0%	NJ −0.8%	NJ −0.8%	NY −0.8%	OH −0.5%	IL −0.5%	48	IL	−11.3%
IL −0.8%	MA −0.9%	RI −1.0%	RI −1.1%	NY −1.0%	DC −0.9%	RI −0.6%	RI −0.6%	49	AK	−12.5%
NY −0.9%	NY −1.1%	NY −1.3%	NY −1.2%	MI −1.0%	RI −1.0%	NY −0.7%	NY −0.7%	50	NY	−17.4%
DC −2.4%	DC −1.7%	DC −1.7%	LA −3.4%	DC −1.2%	MI −1.1%	MI −0.9%	MI −0.8%	51	DC	−32.8%

02/03	03/04	04/05	05/06	06/07	07/08	08/09	09/10
2.4%	2.4%	2.5%	2.6%	2.5%	2.4%	2.2%	2.0%

TABLE 2.7

Aggregate of All Returns Filed in the 18 Years 1992/1993 to 2009/2010

State	Returns				AGI per Return			AGI			
	In-Returns	Out-Returns	Net In-Returns	Net In as a % of (In + Out)	In-AGI per Return ($)	Out-AGI per Return ($)	Premium of In-AGI per Return over Out-AGI per Return	In-AGI ($000s)	Out-AGI ($000s)	Net In-AGI ($000s)	Net In as a % of Total AGI Filed in State Last Year
FL	4,329,910	3,409,588	920,322	11.9	$50,068	$37,570	33.3%	$216,790,077	$128,097,362	$88,692,715	25.6
AZ	1,738,313	1,251,602	486,711	16.3	$42,656	$38,232	11.6%	$74,148,747	$47,851,177	$26,297,570	24.4
NC	2,086,265	1,622,353	463,912	12.5	$41,451	$38,551	7.5%	$86,478,091	$62,543,641	$23,934,450	14.2
TX	3,376,212	2,896,095	480,117	7.7	$43,256	$42,426	2.0%	$146,042,822	$122,869,642	$23,173,180	5.2
NV	1,010,359	702,912	307,447	17.9	$42,565	$36,966	15.1%	$43,005,516	$25,983,751	$17,021,765	33.0
GA	2,100,454	1,675,222	425,232	11.3	$40,133	$42,229	-5.0%	$84,298,271	$70,742,169	$13,556,102	8.0
SC	1,011,431	834,043	177,388	9.6	$42,681	$35,547	20.1%	$43,168,815	$29,647,659	$13,521,156	17.5
CO	1,449,223	1,193,576	255,647	9.7	$43,207	$41,403	4.4%	$62,616,846	$49,418,132	$13,198,714	11.8
WA	1,465,256	1,277,893	187,363	6.8	$42,653	$40,141	6.3%	$62,497,087	$51,296,277	$11,200,810	7.4
TN	1,315,655	1,100,906	214,749	8.9	$38,641	$37,656	2.6%	$50,837,657	$41,455,354	$9,382,303	8.5
OR	903,067	748,464	154,603	9.4	$37,963	$36,942	2.8%	$34,282,936	$27,649,527	$6,633,409	9.2
ID	404,576	339,963	64,613	8.7	$37,368	$33,008	13.2%	$15,118,112	$11,221,576	$3,896,536	15.6
NH	390,458	371,819	18,639	2.4	$49,695	$43,550	14.1%	$19,403,777	$16,192,901	$3,210,876	9.6
AR	554,695	499,982	54,713	5.2	$34,198	$32,245	6.1%	$18,969,565	$16,121,956	$2,847,609	6.3
MT	274,451	253,869	20,582	3.9	$36,327	$29,515	23.1%	$9,970,095	$7,492,934	$2,477,161	13.9
AL	766,451	724,650	41,801	2.8	$37,367	$36,285	3.0%	$28,640,022	$26,293,863	$2,346,159	2.9
UT	493,614	467,860	25,754	2.7	$39,038	$37,765	3.4%	$19,269,618	$17,668,537	$1,601,081	3.3
VA	2,018,368	1,891,501	126,867	3.2	$44,997	$47,193	-4.7%	$90,820,400	$89,265,214	$1,555,186	0.8
WY	203,188	201,795	1,393	0.3	$41,047	$33,681	21.9%	$8,340,274	$6,796,664	$1,543,610	12.2
ME	259,697	260,458	(761)	-0.1	$41,624	$35,901	15.9%	$10,809,697	$9,350,617	$1,459,080	5.7
NM	539,887	515,314	24,573	2.3	$35,873	$34,821	3.0%	$19,367,213	$17,943,978	$1,423,235	4.2
DE	246,441	212,512	33,929	7.4	$45,974	$48,485	-5.2%	$11,329,756	$10,303,548	$1,026,208	5.1
KY	753,553	706,010	47,543	3.3	$35,264	$36,478	-3.3%	$26,573,007	$25,754,019	$818,988	1.1
VT	166,124	172,256	(6,132)	-1.8	$41,572	$35,627	16.7%	$6,906,116	$6,137,017	$769,099	5.7
SD	193,852	198,814	(4,962)	-1.3	$36,568	$32,298	13.2%	$7,088,710	$6,421,280	$667,430	4.1
MS	522,692	525,204	(2,512)	-0.2	$32,635	$31,375	4.0%	$17,058,130	$16,478,306	$579,824	1.4

WV	323,410	328,269	(4,859)	-0.7	$33,181	$33,002	0.5%	$10,730,971	$10,833,483	($102,512)	-0.3
HI	382,512	414,813	(32,301)	-4.1	$35,892	$34,806	3.1%	$13,729,290	$14,437,800	($708,510)	-2.6
OK	696,019	685,819	10,200	0.7	$32,917	$34,841	-5.5%	$22,910,905	$23,894,343	($983,438)	-1.6
ND	161,429	186,754	(25,325)	-7.3	$29,868	$32,279	-7.5%	$4,821,595	$6,028,277	($1,206,682)	-8.0
AK	256,510	267,041	(10,531)	-2.0	$33,159	$37,895	-12.5%	$8,505,611	$10,119,519	($1,613,908)	-9.9
MO	1,079,785	1,043,107	36,678	1.7	$38,034	$40,989	-7.2%	$41,068,301	$42,755,662	($1,687,361)	-1.5
RI	219,184	258,580	(39,396)	-8.2	$43,987	$44,048	-0.1%	$9,641,316	$11,389,960	($1,748,644)	-7.4
WI	750,324	798,132	(47,808)	-3.1	$41,797	$42,160	-0.9%	$31,361,302	$33,649,358	($2,288,056)	-1.8
NE	347,440	388,501	(41,061)	-5.6	$35,489	$38,053	-6.7%	$12,330,183	$14,783,780	($2,453,597)	-6.4
KS	641,076	696,012	(54,936)	-4.1	$38,655	$40,269	-4.0%	$24,780,725	$28,027,754	($3,247,029)	-5.5
IA	498,951	572,018	(73,067)	-6.8	$36,088	$37,506	-3.8%	$18,005,967	$21,454,110	($3,448,143)	-5.4
DC	393,861	429,144	(35,283)	-4.3	$43,410	$48,396	-10.3%	$17,097,386	$20,768,925	($3,671,539)	-21.9
IN	988,225	1,038,388	(50,163)	-2.5	$38,431	$40,387	-4.8%	$37,978,581	$41,937,749	($3,959,168)	-3.2
MN	767,916	790,709	(22,793)	-1.5	$41,865	$45,865	-8.7%	$32,149,124	$36,266,242	($4,117,118)	-3.2
LA	663,618	794,223	(130,605)	-9.0	$33,483	$35,804	-6.5%	$22,219,748	$28,436,292	($6,216,544)	-8.0
CT	621,726	764,219	(142,493)	-10.3	$65,572	$63,084	3.9%	$40,767,581	$48,210,245	($7,442,664)	-7.2
MD	1,283,770	1,321,441	(37,671)	-1.4	$44,329	$48,950	-9.4%	$56,908,353	$64,684,681	($7,776,328)	-5.1
PA	1,618,082	1,831,896	(213,814)	-6.2	$46,766	$45,971	1.7%	$75,670,893	$84,214,770	($8,543,877)	-3.0
MA	1,096,307	1,285,592	(189,285)	-7.9	$48,630	$50,657	-4.0%	$53,313,316	$65,124,732	($11,811,416)	-6.6
MI	993,975	1,354,346	(360,371)	-15.3	$41,897	$43,539	-3.8%	$41,645,055	$58,967,096	($17,322,041)	-9.0
OH	1,354,163	1,677,034	(322,871)	-10.7	$41,170	$44,540	-7.6%	$55,751,296	$74,694,463	($18,943,167)	-8.4
NJ	1,366,147	1,693,947	(327,800)	-10.7	$56,734	$58,156	-2.4%	$77,506,476	$98,512,637	($21,006,161)	-8.4
IL	1,685,281	2,119,438	(434,157)	-11.4	$44,408	$49,296	-9.9%	$74,839,633	$104,480,853	($29,641,220)	-10.1
CA	3,697,622	4,580,090	(882,468)	-10.7	$43,644	$45,146	-3.3%	$161,378,278	$206,774,453	($45,396,175)	-5.9
NY	2,205,544	3,292,895	(1,087,351)	-19.8	$44,784	$50,494	-11.3%	$98,773,291	$166,272,249	($67,498,958)	-15.1
Total:	52,667,069	52,667,069	0	-0.4			Total:	$2,257,716,534	$2,257,716,534	0	91.0

Source: Internal Revenue Service, Laffer Associates.

migration. We list the total number of in-returns, out-returns, net in-returns, and net in-returns as a percentage of total migrating returns in the "Returns" columns. In the "AGI per Return" columns, we have the average AGI per in-return, per out-return, and the percent premium of the average AGI per in-return vis-à-vis the out-return for each and every state. In the "AGI" columns we have the total unadjusted AGI for all in-returns and out-returns, the net in-return AGI, and finally the net in-return AGI as a percentage of total state AGI in the 2009/2010 year. These data are ranked by state from the highest net in-AGI to the lowest.

The Nine Members of the Fellowship of the Ring to Balance Out the Nine Nazgûl[1]

[A]lthough nature begins with the cause and ends with experience, we must follow the opposite course, namely, begin with the experience, and by means of it investigate the cause.

—Philip Ball, *Curiosity*

States provide a special environment in which to evaluate economic performance. Each state is subject to federal policies, and each state exists in a virtually perfect free trade zone with all other states. And yet, each state also has a great deal of autonomy. States are free to enact all sorts of policies on their own, and their political leaders are beholden only to their own electorate. As a result, states are often correctly described as crucibles for policy experiments. Given the great variability of state policies over many years, there exists a huge reservoir of data reflecting past experiments. This reservoir allows us to explore the relative efficacy of a wide variety of state policies. Not only do we have a plethora of state data, but we also have a fascinating interaction of state data with federal data.

This chapter centers on nine tables and charts, each of which ranks groupings of states according to a specific policy metric to allow readers to easily see the relative impacts of state policy choices on state performance outcomes. The tables in this chapter examine state policy choices on tax rates, tax burdens, and an aggregate of state and local policies called the ALEC-Laffer rank. Corresponding to these policy choices are relevant performance metrics ranging from population growth to net domestic in-migration to employment and output growth to state and local tax revenue growth. We also selectively take these measures all the way to the provision of public services.

These policy measures are compared to performance metrics on a one-to-one basis. No attempt is made in this chapter to analyze combinations of policies, save for our policy variable called the ALEC-Laffer rank, which looks at a combination of 15 policy variables. While the conclusions that can be drawn from one-to-one comparisons are limited, they are nonetheless very helpful in allowing us to evaluate just what politicians and the whole gamut of the state governance network have accomplished. The world may be complex and mysterious, but some of the consequences of human action are just begging to be revealed.

In reading this chapter, it is not only healthy to be skeptical; it is vital. In the eyes of public officials, the errors of inaction are rarely as damaging as the errors of action. This was brought to Arthur Laffer's attention when he visited with Missouri Governor Jay Nixon. There's a whole different level of concern and risk aversion when a person is held personally responsible for policies than when that person isn't held personally responsible. But what we would like you to keep in mind, along with a healthy dose of skepticism, is what you would conclude if the results were the exact opposite from what they are. Healthy skepticism should not replace an open mind.

We find population growth to be of particular relevance. Population growth over the past 10 years is displayed first because we cannot think of a better indicator of a state's quality of life and economic desirability than lots and lots of people choosing to move into a state.[2] We also show data for net domestic in-migration, which only counts those who have willingly moved from one state to another (i.e., the change in population that is unaffected by births, deaths, or foreign immigration). To put this in-migration metric on a comparable basis for all states, we have summed 10 years (2003 to 2012) of net in-migration for each state and divided that sum by the state's population in 2008. By looking at in-migration in such a way, we have a number that roughly shows what portion of a specific state's population was gained (if positive) or lost (if negative) from state-to-state migration. It is just about as good a measure of so-called "voting with your feet" as can exist. These people actually packed up their bags and got outta Dodge.

The following tables also show data for nonfarm employment growth, which is simply the percentage change in nonfarm employment over the 10-year period, and gross state product (GSP) growth, also known as state GDP growth. GSP growth is the 10-year percentage change in the size of a state's economy as measured by the Bureau of Economic Analysis.

In the following tables, we have chosen to compare, when possible, the top nine of the 50 states to the bottom nine of the 50 states in terms of policy choices. Comparing the top nine to the bottom nine allows us to see both extremes of the spectrum for each policy choice. To our logic, it's the exceptional cases that prove the rule. Wide disparity in policies should lead to significant differences in results if those policies matter. Adding the more homogeneous and less differentiated center of the distribution into the comparison adds little to policy variations yet adds a lot to noise. Separating signal from noise is far easier when only the extremes are analyzed. Averages have been computed for each group of nine states as well as for all 50 states as a whole.[3] We have chosen the number nine because there are currently nine states without personal earned income taxes, and we have continued this practice where reasonable throughout the rest of the chapter.[4]

An Analysis of the Top Personal Income Tax (PIT) Rates

Table 3.1 compares and contrasts the nine states that are without personal earned income taxes to the nine states with the highest marginal earned income tax rates. The average 10-year population growth of the nine zero earned income tax states was 8.3 percentage points higher than the average of the nine highest income tax rate states, or 14.6 percent and 6.3 percent, respectively. Not one single state in the group of nine highest earned income tax rate states had 10-year population growth as high as the average of the nine zero earned income tax states. New Hampshire was the only zero earned income tax state whose population grew less than the average of the nine highest earned income tax rate states. While New Hampshire does eschew an earned income tax like its other eight colleagues, in many other policy features it is quite different from the zero earned income tax states. For example, New Hampshire taxes dividend and interest income, as does Tennessee, but no other zero earned income tax state does. Likewise, New Hampshire is a forced-union state rather than a right-to-work state, as are only Alaska and Washington State in the group of zero earned income tax states. But more on this later.

In our next metric, net domestic in-migration, the nine zero earned income tax states once again trounce the living bejabbers out of the highest earned income tax rate states. On an equal-weighted basis of the average in-migration over the past 10 years, the zero income tax states *gained* net 3.9 percent of their population solely due to interstate net in-migration, while the nine highest earned income tax rate states *lost* net 2.2 percent of their population due to interstate net in-migration. Nevada is attracting people at an amazing rate. But not only is Nevada an incredibly attractive state in and of itself, but it also happens to be right next to California, which is a true taxaholic. Being next to California also helps explain how Oregon manages to be a very high income tax rate state at the same time it is also a big in-migration magnet. Oregon also has no sales tax.

TABLE 3.1

Nine Zero Earned Income Tax States versus Nine Highest Personal Earned Income Tax (PIT) Rate States (top marginal PIT rate is as of 1/1/2013; performance metrics are 2002 to 2012 unless otherwise noted)

State	Top Marginal PIT Rate*	10-Year Growth					
		Population	Net Domestic In-Migration	Nonfarm Payroll Employment	Personal Income	Gross State Product	State and Local Tax Revenue†
Alaska	0.00%	13.9%	-1.2%	13.8%	60.6%	79.5%	232.8%
Florida	0.00%	15.7%	5.6%	3.4%	53.3%	45.0%	50.3%
Nevada	0.00%	26.9%	10.3%	8.6%	52.0%	61.4%	66.7%
South Dakota	0.00%	9.6%	2.1%	9.7%	70.3%	53.8%	50.9%
Texas	0.00%	20.1%	4.3%	15.5%	72.0%	78.5%	63.3%
Washington	0.00%	14.0%	3.8%	8.0%	56.2%	58.5%	48.6%
Wyoming	0.00%	15.3%	5.3%	16.9%	75.9%	99.5%	121.1%
New Hampshire†	0.00%	4.1%	0.7%	2.4%	39.0%	38.4%	54.5%
Tennessee†	0.00%	11.4%	4.5%	1.9%	49.0%	43.5%	50.2%
Equal-Weighted Average of Nine Zero Earned Income Tax Rate States§	0.00%	14.6%	3.9%	8.9%	58.7%	62.0%	82.0%
50-State Equal-Weighted Average§	5.69%	9.3%	0.9%	4.2%	51.1%	51.7%	56.5%
Equal-Weighted Average of Nine Highest Earned Income Tax Rate States§	10.23%	6.3%	-2.2%	1.7%	46.4%	46.4%	52.2%
Kentucky	8.20%	7.1%	1.8%	2.1%	45.2%	42.8%	38.9%
Ohio	8.43%	1.2%	-3.2%	-5.0%	33.2%	28.0%	28.2%
Maryland	8.95%	8.2%	-2.2%	3.8%	51.6%	53.7%	52.2%
Vermont	8.95%	1.7%	-1.0%	1.3%	45.8%	39.3%	63.5%

(continued)

TABLE 3.1 (*Continued*)

State	Top Marginal PIT Rate*	Population	Net Domestic In-Migration	Nonfarm Payroll Employment	Personal Income	Gross State Product	State and Local Tax Revenue†
				10-Year Growth			
New Jersey	9.97%	3.6%	-5.6%	-2.2%	39.2%	34.8%	57.6%
Oregon	10.61%	11.0%	4.4%	3.3%	44.5%	66.2%	53.3%
Hawaii	11.00%	12.3%	-2.0%	8.8%	63.6%	61.8%	57.6%
New York	12.70%	2.3%	-8.0%	4.0%	50.3%	46.6%	64.7%
California	13.30%	9.1%	-3.9%	-0.4%	44.1%	44.4%	54.0%

*Top marginal PIT rate is the top marginal rate on personal earned income imposed as of 1/1/2013 using the tax rate of each state's largest city as a proxy for the local tax. The deductibility of federal taxes from state tax liability is included where applicable.

†State and local tax revenue is the 10-year growth in state and local tax revenue from the Census Bureau's State and Local Government Finances survey. Because of data release lag, these data are 2001 to 2011.

‡New Hampshire and Tennessee tax interest and dividend income—so-called unearned income—but not ordinary wage income.

§Averages are equal-weighted.

Source: Laffer Associates, U.S. Census Bureau, Bureau of Labor Statistics, Bureau of Economic Analysis.

Data for employment growth tell much the same story as do the data for population and in-migration. Over the past 10 years, the average equal-weighted nonfarm employment growth for the nine zero earned income tax states was 7.2 percentage points higher than the average of the nine highest earned income tax rate states, or 8.9 percent and 1.7 percent, respectively. Here again not one state, not even Oregon, in the group of the nine highest earned income tax rate states performed as well in employment growth as the average employment growth of the nine zero income tax states, although Hawaii came close. But even more to the point, not a single zero earned income tax state performed as poorly in employment growth as the average of the nine highest income tax rate states over the past 10 years. Tennessee did come close, but then again, over this period Tennessee had both an unearned income tax (the Hall Tax) and a gift and estate tax, which has subsequently been repealed (fully effective in 2016).

Table 3.1, like those tables and charts that follow, shows the pervasive nature of the relationship between taxes and performance. While there are exceptions and outliers in both the top nine states and the bottom nine states, there can be no doubt that state and local economic policies matter.

Aggregate state personal income growth is closely related to employment growth, so it shouldn't surprise anyone that the average of the nine zero earned income tax states outperformed the average of the nine highest earned income tax rate states in personal income growth by 12.3 percentage points over the past 10 years. In this category, Hawaii was able to experience personal income growth greater than the nine-state average of the zero earned income tax states. So while it's beyond the scope of this book, further analysis of Oregon and Hawaii could be quite revealing.

Gross state product (GSP), also called state gross domestic product (GDP), is a measure of the value of all the goods and services produced within a state during the year. State GSP is the most commonly used measure of the size of a state's economy. Using the GSP measure, the average of the nine zero earned income tax states' economies grew

62 percent over the past 10 years, while the average of the nine highest earned income tax rate states grew 46.4 percent, resulting in a zero earned income tax state outperformance against the nine highest tax rate states of 15.6 percentage points over the past decade.

And here is where these types of outperformance really make differences. Take California, for example. If California had performed at the average of the nine zero income tax states over the past decade, total employment would have been 9.3 percent higher in 2012 than it was, which means that California would have 1.35 million more people employed than it does. Total gross state product in California would have been 15.6 percent greater in California in 2012 than it was, which in dollar terms is a whopping $216 billion. Jerry Brown would have a budget surplus, the unemployment rate would have been light-years lower, the participation rate higher, the poverty rate lower, and the citizens of California happier and more prosperous. Instead of leaving California in their U-Hauls and United Van Lines trucks, people would be flocking into the Golden State just as they did in the 1980s following the passage of Proposition 13 and Reagan's tax cuts. And Beach Boys songs would be back in vogue. Similar stories could be told for every one of the high tax rate states.

But just as these tables show a way to a brighter future for the high tax rate states, they also stand as an ominous warning to all those states that envision sugarplums if only they could raise tax rates. And that means you, California and Minnesota and Illinois.

Finally, let's look at the 10-year growth of state and local tax revenues. After all, states implement income taxes to gain revenue, not to lose revenue. The following results may shock some readers—the nine zero earned income tax states' state and local tax revenues grew an average of 82.0 percent, while the nine highest income tax rate states' state and local tax revenues grew only 52.2 percent. This means that, over the past 10 years, the average of the zero income tax states outperformed the average of the nine highest income tax rate states in tax revenue growth by a full 29.8 percentage points! To be fair, though, these numbers could be somewhat misleading and thereby they could possibly overstate the advantage of the zero income tax rate states. In the first place, severance taxes (incurred when nonrenewable natural resources are extracted) in two of the zero income tax states are enormous and thereby really impact the averages. Second, those two states with huge growth in severance tax revenues are very small states otherwise, and thus equal weighting of averages makes a huge difference, too. Little states with big percentage swings dominate the averages. But more on this in the next section.

Public Services and the Personal Income Tax

But we all know taxes and economic growth aren't everything, even though they are a lot. Presumably, the highest personal income tax rate states adopted those high tax rates in order to fund exceptional levels of public services for their citizens. And, on the other end of the spectrum, the zero earned income tax states have been faulted time and again for not caring enough for their citizens in general and for those who are less fortunate in particular.

Far and away the most significant public service item for state and local governments is the provision of educational services for children from kindergarten through high school (K–12). In this category, the zero income tax states employ an equal-weighted mean of 305 full-time equivalent employees (FTEEs) for every 10,000 of population, while the nine highest tax rate states employ 299 full-time equivalent employees for every 10,000 of population.

If we had used the median number of full-time equivalent employees by states, the zero income tax rate states would employ 313 versus 284 for the highest tax rate states.

Stated simply, the zero income tax states provide at least as much, if not more, by way of educators than do the highest tax rate states.

Contrary to popular belief, high personal income tax rates do not—I repeat, do not—imply increased levels of the provision of public services. In all categories other than the employment of welfare workers, the nine zero income tax rate states do, if anything, a better job in providing education, police, hospitals, fire, prison, and highway services (585 per 10,000 population) than do the nine highest tax rate states (495 per 10,000 of population).

Using a measure of dollars spent by states is just as misleading a metric of the provision of public services as are tax rates, because dollars spent reflect more the power of state and local unions to negotiate higher wages rather than more or more highly qualified employees. For example, the mean annual pay per full-time equivalent employee is $46,265 for the zero income tax states in 2011 and is $53,010 for the highest tax rate states; the median annual pay is $44,664 and $49,429, respectively.

Why on earth would any state want to tax its residents more and provide them with less in the way of public services in order to pay state employees more? The answer, my friend, has more to do with the politics of state and local government employee unions and the public officials who are their employers spending other people's money.

Test scores as administered by the Department of Education show a slight advantage to the high tax rate states over the zero income tax states in both median and mean test scores. However, it is more than interesting to note that the state with the lowest education test scores of all 18 states is California. California also has the highest income tax rate and the highest poverty rates in the nation and has the second lowest number of full-time equivalent educational employees per 10,000 of population. And just to top the story off, California has the second highest-paid educational employees. Go figure. (See Chapter 7.)

When it comes to other categories of public services, the zero income tax rate states provide more and pay less with one exception. When it comes to the number of full-time equivalent public welfare and housing and community development employees, the highest income tax rate states employ way more full-time equivalent employees than do the nine zero income tax rate states, and the highest income tax rate states pay those public welfare employees considerably higher wages as well.

Given the much slower growth in population, gross state product, payroll employment, and personal income associated with high personal income tax rates, it shouldn't surprise anyone that the nine highest income tax rate states need all of those public welfare employees, especially with poverty levels at 15.1 percent for the highest tax rate states versus 13.9 percent for the zero tax states. It's a vicious cycle.

The Effects of Oil and Severance Taxes

A word of caution for those who quickly dismiss any results due to severance taxes and oil production: Oil is not simply a gift from on high. State policies matter here as much as anywhere. Look at California versus Texas. California arguably has more oil reserves underground than does Texas, yet produces less while Texas produces more. State policies in California are inimical to domestic oil production, while Texas encourages oil production. We'll have a lot more to write about on this topic in the California/Texas chapter (Chapter 7). In Table 3.2, we compare and contrast the 45 states with the least reliance on severance taxes as we did for all 50 states in Table 3.1. Figure 3.1 illustrates the 20 states with the greatest severance tax revenues as a share of total state and local tax revenues over the past decade. As you can see, by the time you have removed the top five oil severance tax states on a per dollar of total state and local tax revenue basis, you're left with a far more representative group of states. It's interesting to note that Texas, while a large severance tax state, still ranks only ninth in the nation because its economy is so large that, as a share of total state and local tax revenues, Texas's severance taxes aren't really all that huge.

Even after removing the two zero earned income tax rate states that enjoy enormous severance taxes from oil extraction and the five highest severance tax states from the average of all states, the average of the seven remaining states without earned income taxes still significantly outperforms the average of all 45 states and the average of the nine highest income tax rate states in total state and local tax revenue growth. In the metrics of population growth and net domestic in-migration over the past 10 years, no individual state in the group of the highest income tax rate states outperforms the average of the seven zero earned income tax states without significant severance tax revenues.

TABLE 3.2

Seven Zero Earned Income Tax Rate States with Minimal Reliance on Severance Taxes versus Nine Highest Earned Personal Income Tax (PIT) Rate States (top marginal PIT rate is as of 1/1/2013; performance metrics are 2002 to 2012 unless otherwise noted)

State	Top Marginal PIT Rate*	Population	Net Domestic In-Migration	Nonfarm Payroll Employment	Personal Income	Gross State Product	State and Local Tax Revenue[†]
				10-Year Growth			
Florida	0.00%	15.7%	5.6%	3.4%	53.3%	45.0%	50.3%
Nevada	0.00%	26.9%	10.3%	8.6%	52.0%	61.4%	66.7%
South Dakota	0.00%	9.6%	2.1%	9.7%	70.3%	53.8%	50.9%
Texas	0.00%	20.1%	4.3%	15.5%	72.0%	78.5%	63.3%
Washington	0.00%	14.0%	3.8%	8.0%	56.2%	58.5%	48.6%
New Hampshire[†]	0.00%	4.1%	0.7%	2.4%	39.0%	38.4%	54.5%
Tennessee[†]	0.00%	11.4%	4.5%	1.9%	49.0%	43.5%	50.2%
Equal-Weighted Average of Seven Zero Earned Income Tax States with Minimal Reliance on Severance Taxes[§]	**0.00%**	**14.6%**	**4.5%**	**7.1%**	**56.0%**	**54.2%**	**54.9%**
Equal-Weighted Average of 45 States with Least Reliance on Severance Taxes[§]	6.01%	9.0%	0.8%	3.0%	48.6%	48.2%	49.1%

Equal-Weighted Average of Nine Highest Earned Income Tax Rate States§

	10.23%	**6.3%**	**-2.2%**	**1.7%**	**46.4%**	**46.4%**	**52.2%**
Kentucky	8.20%	7.1%	1.8%	2.1%	45.2%	42.8%	38.9%
Ohio	8.43%	1.2%	-3.2%	-5.0%	33.2%	28.0%	28.2%
Maryland	8.95%	8.2%	-2.2%	3.8%	51.6%	53.7%	52.2%
Vermont	8.95%	1.7%	-1.0%	1.3%	45.8%	39.3%	63.5%
New Jersey	9.97%	3.6%	-5.6%	-2.2%	39.2%	34.8%	57.6%
Oregon	10.61%	11.0%	4.4%	3.3%	44.5%	66.2%	53.3%
Hawaii	11.00%	12.3%	-2.0%	8.8%	63.6%	61.8%	57.6%
New York	12.70%	2.3%	-8.0%	4.0%	50.3%	46.6%	64.7%
California	13.30%	9.1%	-3.9%	-0.4%	44.1%	44.4%	54.0%

* Top marginal PIT rate is the top marginal rate on personal earned income imposed as of 1/1/2013 using the tax rate of each state's largest city as a proxy for the local tax. The deductibility of federal taxes from state tax liability is included where applicable.

† State and local tax revenue is the 10-year growth in state and local tax revenue from the Census Bureau's State and Local Government Finances survey. Because of data release lag, these data are 2001 to 2011.

‡ New Hampshire and Tennessee tax interest and dividend income—so-called unearned income—but not ordinary wage income.

§ Averages are equal-weighted. AK, WY, ND, NM, and OK—the five states with the greatest reliance on severance tax revenue as a share of total tax revenue over the past decade (see Figure 3.1)—have been removed from the 50-state average in order to further remove any distortions caused by severance tax revenues.

Source: Laffer Associates, U.S. Census Bureau, Bureau of Labor Statistics, Bureau of Economic Analysis.

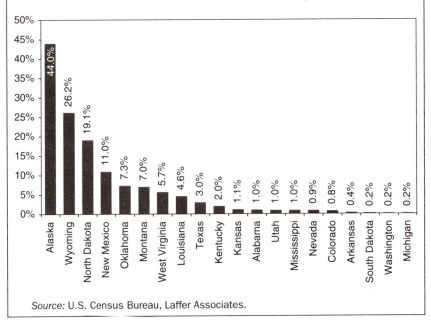

FIGURE 3.1

Twenty States with the Greatest Severance Taxes as a Share of Total State and Local Tax Revenue (average share of state and local tax revenue from severance taxes, 2002 to 2011)

Source: U.S. Census Bureau, Laffer Associates.

The results of the 10-year averages of the seven zero earned income tax states with minimal severance tax revenue versus the nine highest income tax rate states that also had minimal severance tax revenues were: population growth, 14.6 percent versus 6.3 percent; net domestic in-migration, 4.5 percent versus –2.2 percent; nonfarm payroll employment growth, 7.1 percent versus 1.7 percent; personal income growth, 56.0 percent versus 46.4 percent; gross state product growth 54.2 percent versus 46.4 percent; and state and local tax revenue growth, 54.9 percent versus 52.2 percent. Even the average of the seven zero earned income tax states with minimal severance tax reliance significantly beats the 45-state performance averages of all states with minimal severance taxes in every category.

What we implore the reader to consider after reading these two sections of this chapter is what your conclusions would be if the results had been reversed 180 degrees. If every one of the high tax rate states had outperformed the average of the zero income tax states, we, for ourselves, would be begging our critics for lenient terms of surrender.

Yes it's true, as we have shown, that oil production does affect state performance, and conceivably lots of other factors do as well, but the results of Tables 3.1 and 3.2 are incredibly robust. We are hard-pressed not to conclude that it is highly likely that state income tax rates materially, negatively impact state performance. But let's go on. Our case gets even better.

A Longer-Term View of the Data

Another consideration when we juxtapose high and zero income tax states is that the time period under consideration may not be typical for the comparisons and that the results we have found are, in fact, unique to the time period selected. With this in mind, we have extended our tests 50 years back in time.

For each and every year from 1970 to the present, we have compared all of the zero income tax states with an equal number of the highest income tax rate states. As we do regress back in time, remember that the number of zero income tax states increases because 11 states since 1961 have introduced an earned income tax and only one state, Alaska, has gotten rid of it. Also, remember that while we report the results from 1970 on, in truth we are using all of the data generated from 1960 on as a consequence of our choice of a 10-year period to measure the key metrics.

At this juncture, due to data limitations and the risk of being so repetitious that our readers lose interest, we report our results for only the zero and the highest earned income tax rate groupings and their annual difference (see Figure 3.2 and Figure 3.3[5]). The individual state data are readily available for the asking.

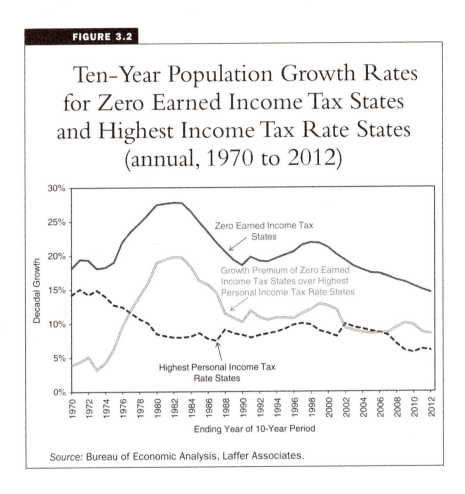

FIGURE 3.2

Ten-Year Population Growth Rates for Zero Earned Income Tax States and Highest Income Tax Rate States (annual, 1970 to 2012)

Source: Bureau of Economic Analysis, Laffer Associates.

What Figure 3.2 and Figure 3.3 show visually is that for each and every single year from 1970 on, the 10-year moving averages illustrate that the zero earned income tax states have outperformed their highest tax rate counterparts—no exceptions.

And in some years, especially in the early 1980s, the differences in performance were far greater than they are today. Again, if you are inclined to dismiss results such as these for whatever reasons, we beg you to imagine what you would conclude if the highest tax rate states had outperformed the zero earned income tax states every single year over this same time period. We can't imagine how the data could be more compelling in demonstrating that state income taxes are deleterious to a state's prosperity.

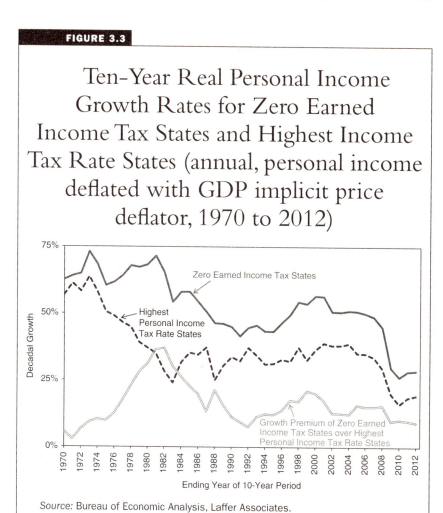

FIGURE 3.3

Ten-Year Real Personal Income Growth Rates for Zero Earned Income Tax States and Highest Income Tax Rate States (annual, personal income deflated with GDP implicit price deflator, 1970 to 2012)

Source: Bureau of Economic Analysis, Laffer Associates.

An Analysis of Corporate Income Taxes

Ohio does not have a corporate tax as other states do. Instead of a corporate income tax (CIT), Ohio has a gross receipts tax of 0.26 percent. Translating a gross receipts tax into a corporate income tax is nothing short of impossible. But our guess is that a gross receipts tax of 0.26 percent would put Ohio in the top half of all corporate tax states and maybe even among the top 11. For the purpose of top and bottom groupings and the 50-state averages of Table 3.3, we'll simply exclude Ohio.

Table 3.3 compares the 11 states with the lowest corporate income tax rates to the 11 states with the highest corporate income tax rates.

TABLE 3.3

Eleven Lowest Corporate Income Tax (CIT) Rate States versus 11 Highest Corporate Income Tax Rate States (top marginal CIT rate is as of 1/1/2013; performance metrics are 2002 to 2012 unless otherwise noted)

State	Top Marginal CIT Rate*	10-Year Growth					
		Population	Net Domestic In-Migration	Nonfarm Payroll Employment	Personal Income	Gross State Product	State & Local Tax Revenue†
Nevada	0.00%	26.9%	10.3%	8.6%	52.0%	61.4%	66.7%
South Dakota	0.00%	9.6%	2.1%	9.7%	70.3%	53.8%	50.9%
Wyoming	0.00%	15.3%	5.3%	16.9%	75.9%	99.5%	121.1%
Texas	2.72%	20.1%	4.3%	15.5%	72.0%	78.5%	63.3%
Alabama	4.23%	7.6%	2.2%	0.0%	48.8%	46.6%	45.1%
Colorado	4.63%	15.5%	4.2%	5.7%	48.4%	46.9%	60.7%
Mississippi	5.00%	4.4%	-1.1%	-2.0%	49.3%	46.0%	44.6%
South Carolina	5.00%	15.0%	7.1%	2.9%	51.3%	41.7%	42.5%
Utah	5.00%	22.8%	2.4%	16.4%	65.0%	74.9%	52.2%
North Dakota	5.15%	9.6%	1.5%	30.3%	109.5%	125.1%	169.3%
Louisiana	5.20%	2.3%	-5.7%	1.6%	56.5%	74.8%	44.0%
Equal-Weighted Average of 11 Lowest Corporate Income Tax Rate States†	**3.36%**	**13.6%**	**3.0%**	**9.6%**	**63.6%**	**68.1%**	**69.1%**
49-State Equal-Weighted Average (50 States ex OH)†	7.25%	9.5%	1.0%	4.4%	51.4%	52.2%	57.1%

Equal-Weighted Average of 11 Highest Corporate Income Tax Rate States†

	11.05%	5.9%	-2.0%	1.9%	45.1%	48.2%	68.2%
Connecticut	9.00%	3.8%	-3.4%	-1.6%	41.4%	35.8%	47.9%
New Jersey	9.00%	3.6%	-5.6%	-2.2%	39.2%	34.8%	57.6%
Rhode Island	9.00%	-1.5%	-6.0%	-3.0%	37.8%	33.6%	44.4%
Alaska	9.40%	13.9%	-1.2%	13.8%	60.6%	79.5%	232.8%
Illinois	9.50%	2.8%	-4.9%	-2.3%	36.3%	39.7%	45.4%
Minnesota	9.80%	7.2%	-1.2%	2.4%	45.4%	46.2%	46.5%
Iowa	9.90%	4.8%	-0.9%	4.2%	53.1%	54.6%	54.1%
Delaware	10.49%	13.8%	5.0%	0.8%	44.0%	51.1%	53.5%
Oregon	11.25%	11.0%	4.4%	3.3%	44.5%	66.2%	53.3%
Pennsylvania	17.07%	3.5%	-0.2%	1.5%	43.6%	41.7%	50.3%
New York	17.16%	2.3%	-8.0%	4.0%	50.3%	46.6%	64.7%

* Top marginal CIT rate is the top marginal rate on corporate income imposed as of 1/1/2013 using the tax rate of each state's largest city as a proxy for the local tax. The deductibility of federal taxes from state tax liability is included where applicable. Ohio has been omitted from the group of the 11 lowest CIT rate states because Ohio's primary business tax is a gross receipts tax rather than a corporate income tax, making it unfit for inclusion in this table.

† State and local tax revenue is the 10-year growth in state and local tax revenue from the Census Bureau's State and Local Government Finances survey. Because of data release lag, these data are 2001 to 2011.

‡ Averages are equal-weighted.

Source: Laffer Associates, U.S. Census Bureau, Bureau of Labor Statistics, Bureau of Economic Analysis.

The reason for choosing the number 11 is rather droll but basically hinges on ties where two or more states have the same highest corporate income tax rate. Eleven just happened to be the next lowest number greater than nine where there were no ties.

The differences in highest corporate income tax rates are quite significant across states, and while variations in deductions, exemptions, exclusions, and income thresholds are also potentially significant, they do tend to reinforce rather than offset each other.

Just looking at population growth differences over the past decade, the highest corporate income tax rate states grew considerably more slowly than did those states with the lowest corporate income tax rates—5.9 percent versus 13.6 percent, respectively. The population growth differences were only slightly larger for the highest and lowest personal income tax rate states. This is doubly impressive when we realize that only four of the 11 lowest corporate income tax rate states overlap with the lowest personal income tax rate states, and only three of the 11 highest corporate income tax states overlap with the nine highest personal earned income tax rate states. There's a lot of new information contained in this table.

With net domestic in-migration, nonfarm payroll employment growth, personal income growth, and gross state product growth, the differences in results are quite similar to the differences found with respect to personal income tax rate extremes. When it comes to state and local tax revenue growth, the differences between the highest and lowest corporate income tax rate states are insignificant.

When looking at the provision of public services in terms of the number of full-time equivalent employees per 10,000 of population, those 11 states with the lowest corporate tax rates do considerably better than do the 11 states with the highest corporate income tax rates save for public welfare and housing and community development employees. Again, the anomaly of public welfare employees probably is a direct consequence of poor economic performance by the high tax states. High tax rates lead to poor performance, and poor performance begets more needy people, and more needy people require more public welfare employees. And in keeping with the results for the personal income tax rate comparisons, the highest corporate tax rate states pay their public employees a lot more than do the lowest corporate tax rate states.

An Analysis of the Overall Tax Burden

In this section of this chapter, we discuss one of the most powerful policy variables—the total state and local tax burden as a share of personal income—and how that policy variable relates to economic performance metrics, in an attempt to evaluate the growth consequences of state and local taxation. This variable plays an important role throughout the entire book. It, more than anything else, represents each state's total tax burden. The tax burden is not a tax rate but is more in line with total tax revenues, and thus spending, per dollar of gross state product. (See Table 3.4.[6])

When viewing state and local governments, there are three overriding considerations: (1) tax rates matter, (2) the total tax burden matters, and, finally, (3) how those governments spend the money also matters. It probably won't surprise you by now that the lowest tax burden states are very similar to the lowest tax rate states and those states that provide the most public services save for welfare. Lower tax rates mean higher growth, lower tax burden, and better public services. It sounds pretty good to us.

While we would like to claim credit for the tax burden measure, in truth it is the Tax Foundation that has developed this measure of the overall tax burden for each and every state.

It appears from these two tables—Table 3.1 and Table 3.4—that seven zero earned income tax states are also part of the nine low tax burden states, but only three of the highest earned income tax rate states are also components of the nine highest tax burden states. Pretty amazing! Washington State and Florida are the two zero earned income tax states that missed the cut for the nine lowest tax burden states and were replaced by Louisiana and Alabama—Roll Tide! The only three overlaps between the nine highest tax burden states and the nine highest earned income tax rate states were New Jersey, New York, and California. Three cheers for the three worst. What this comparison shows is that there are lots of ways to overtax but only a few ways to keep tax burdens low. This variable is crucial, as you'll see later.

TABLE 3.4

Nine States with the Lowest Tax Burden as a Share of Personal Income versus Nine States with the Highest Tax Burden as a Share of Personal Income
(tax burden is as of 2010; performance metrics are 2002 to 2012 unless otherwise noted)

State	Tax Burden as a Share of Personal Income*	10-Year Growth					
		Population	Net Domestic In-Migration	Nonfarm Payroll Employment	Personal Income	Gross State Product	State and Local Tax Revenue†
Alaska	6.97%	13.9%	–1.2%	13.8%	60.6%	79.5%	232.8%
South Dakota	7.58%	9.6%	2.1%	9.7%	70.3%	53.8%	50.9%
Tennessee	7.72%	11.4%	4.5%	1.9%	49.0%	43.5%	50.2%
Louisiana	7.75%	2.3%	–5.7%	1.6%	56.5%	74.8%	44.0%
Wyoming	7.77%	15.3%	5.3%	16.9%	75.9%	99.5%	121.1%
Texas	7.93%	20.1%	4.3%	15.5%	72.0%	78.5%	63.3%
New Hampshire	8.11%	4.1%	0.7%	2.4%	39.0%	38.4%	54.5%
Alabama	8.18%	7.6%	2.2%	0.0%	48.8%	46.6%	45.1%
Nevada	8.24%	26.9%	10.3%	8.6%	52.0%	61.4%	66.7%
Equal-Weighted Average of Nine Lowest Tax Burden States†	**7.81%**	**12.4%**	**2.5%**	**7.8%**	**58.2%**	**64.0%**	**80.9%**
Equal-Weighted Average of Nine Lowest Tax Burden States ex WY and AK†	7.93%	11.7%	2.6%	5.7%	55.4%	56.7%	53.5%
50-State Equal-Weighted Average†	9.46%	9.3%	0.9%	4.2%	51.1%	51.7%	56.5%

Equal-Weighted Average of Nine Highest Tax Burden States[†]	11.34%	4.0%	-3.5%	-0.2%	42.2%	39.2%	48.9%
Maine	10.26%	2.6%	1.0%	-1.5%	40.4%	34.2%	37.5%
Massachusetts	10.43%	3.6%	-3.7%	0.5%	43.0%	40.0%	49.5%
Minnesota	10.79%	7.2%	-1.2%	2.4%	45.4%	46.2%	46.5%
Rhode Island	10.85%	-1.5%	-6.0%	-3.0%	37.8%	33.6%	44.4%
Wisconsin	11.07%	5.2%	-0.7%	0.1%	38.4%	37.5%	37.8%
California	11.23%	9.1%	-3.9%	-0.4%	44.1%	44.4%	54.0%
Connecticut	12.27%	3.8%	-3.4%	-1.6%	41.4%	35.8%	47.9%
New Jersey	12.42%	3.6%	-5.6%	-2.2%	39.2%	34.8%	57.6%
New York	12.77%	2.3%	-8.0%	4.0%	50.3%	46.6%	64.7%

* Tax burden as a share of personal income is calculated by the Tax Foundation and is currently as of 2010.

[†] State and local tax revenue is the 10-year growth in state and local tax revenue from the Census Bureau's State and Local Government Finances survey. Because of data release lag, these data are 2001 to 2011.

[‡] Averages are equal-weighted.

Source: Tax Foundation, Laffer Associates, U.S. Census Bureau, Bureau of Labor Statistics, Bureau of Economic Analysis.

What this table also shows is the enormous sacrifice a state is forced to make for an increase in its tax burden. For whatever growth variable you wish to focus on, the nine lowest tax burden states perform much, much better than do the nine highest tax burden states. It's really amazing. The difference in the average growth of gross state product over the past 10 years, for example, falls only slightly shy of 25 percent. That's incredible. And then, we may ask, for what did these states make this sacrifice?

- The nine lowest tax burden states have more full-time equivalent education employees per 10,000 of population than do the nine highest tax burden states.
- The nine lowest tax burden states are increasing the number of full-time equivalent education employees far faster than are the nine highest tax burden states.
- The nine lowest tax burden states pay the education employees a lot less per full-time equivalent employee than do the nine highest tax burden states—think public-sector teacher unions.
- What's true for education is just as true for all other nonwelfare public service employees—the lowest tax burden states provide more, are increasing their numbers faster, and are paying them less.
- When it comes to welfare employees, the highest tax burden states hire more, pay them more, and are growing at close to the same rate as the nine lowest tax burden states.

It's hard to imagine a greater contrast—low taxes, high growth, plentiful public services, and less welfare versus high taxes, anemic growth, insufficient public services, and lots of public welfare workers (see Table 3.5).

An Analysis of the ALEC-Laffer State Economic Competitiveness Index

The annual *Rich States, Poor States* publication by the American Legislative Exchange Council (ALEC) ranks states according to 15 policy variables, including tax rates, tax burdens, tax progressivity, regulatory policies, fiscal solvency, and labor policies. Table 3.6 compares the nine states

TABLE 3.5				
Provision of Public Services by Tax Burden				
		FTEE per 10,000 Population*		**Average Annual Pay***
	State	**2011**	**% Change 2001–2011**	**2011**
Education	9 Lowest Tax Burden	318.7	3.6	$44,431
	50-State Average	304.6	1.4	$47,236
	9 Highest Tax Burden	287.9	−0.9	$56,366
Other Nonwelfare	9 Lowest Tax Burden	266.6	−2.4	$50,045
	50-State Average	228.3	−5.5	$51,291
	9 Highest Tax Burden	206.7	−10.5	$62,062
Welfare	9 Lowest Tax Burden	20.2	−2.0	$42,832
	50-State Average	19.7	−8.6	$43,912
	9 Highest Tax Burden	25.9	−3.2	$53,887

* Levels are equal-weighted averages within the groups of states.

with the highest ALEC–Laffer rankings to the nine worst-ranked states. Upon examination, the ALEC–Laffer rankings prove themselves to be strong indicators of state performance (see Chapter 8). The average of the nine best-ranked states performed significantly better than both the 50-state average and the average of the nine worst-ranked states in each category examined. The results were as follows for the nine best-ranked states versus the nine worst-ranked states: population growth, 15.8 percent versus 5.2 percent; net domestic in-migration, 4.4 percent versus −2.1 percent; nonfarm payroll employment growth, 11.4 percent versus 1.7 percent; personal income growth, 65.5 percent versus 45.2 percent; gross state product growth, 66.1 percent versus 46.9 percent; and state and local tax revenue growth, 69.3 percent versus 53.4 percent.

TABLE 3.6

Nine Best ALEC-Laffer Ranking States versus Nine Worst ALEC-Laffer Ranking States (ALEC-Laffer rankings are as of 2013; performance metrics are 2002 to 2012 unless otherwise noted)

State	ALEC-Laffer Rank 2013*	Population	Net Domestic In-Migration	Nonfarm Payroll Employment	Personal Income	Gross State Product	State and Local Tax Revenue[†]
				10-Year Growth			
Utah	1	22.8%	2.4%	16.4%	65.0%	74.9%	52.2%
North Dakota	2	9.6%	1.5%	30.3%	109.5%	125.1%	169.3%
South Dakota	3	9.6%	2.1%	9.7%	70.3%	53.8%	50.9%
Wyoming	4	15.3%	5.3%	16.9%	75.9%	99.5%	121.1%
Virginia	5	12.3%	1.8%	6.6%	56.8%	53.3%	48.8%
Arizona	6	21.4%	9.8%	8.6%	59.1%	50.7%	56.1%
Idaho	7	19.1%	6.2%	9.5%	54.3%	54.4%	43.1%
Georgia	8	16.6%	5.1%	1.4%	45.6%	38.1%	31.6%
Florida	9	15.7%	5.6%	3.4%	53.3%	45.0%	50.3%
Equal-Weighted Average of Nine Best ALEC-Laffer Ranking States[†]	**5.00**	**15.8%**	**4.4%**	**11.4%**	**65.5%**	**66.1%**	**69.3%**
50-State Equal-Weighted Average[†]	25.50	9.3%	0.9%	4.2%	51.1%	51.7%	56.5%

Equal-Weighted Average of Nine Worst ALEC-Laffer Ranking States†	46.00	5.2%	-2.1%	1.7%	45.2%	46.9%	53.4%
Montana	42	10.3%	4.7%	11.4%	60.7%	70.0%	61.0%
Connecticut	43	3.8%	-3.4%	-1.6%	41.4%	35.8%	47.9%
Oregon	44	11.0%	4.4%	3.3%	44.5%	66.2%	53.3%
Rhode Island	45	-1.5%	-6.0%	-3.0%	37.8%	33.6%	44.4%
Minnesota	46	7.2%	-1.2%	2.4%	45.4%	46.2%	46.5%
California	47	9.1%	-3.9%	-0.4%	44.1%	44.4%	54.0%
Illinois	48	2.8%	-4.9%	-2.3%	36.3%	39.7%	45.4%
New York	49	2.3%	-8.0%	4.0%	50.3%	46.6%	64.7%
Vermont	50	1.7%	-1.0%	1.3%	45.8%	39.3%	63.5%

* ALEC-Laffer rank as of 2013. For more information on the ALEC-Laffer rankings, see the annual ALEC publication *Rich States, Poor States*, available here: www.alec.org/publications/rich-states-poor-states/.

† State and local tax revenue is the 10-year growth in state and local tax revenue from the Census Bureau's State and Local Government Finances survey. Because of data release lag, these data are 2001 to 2011.

‡ Averages are equal-weighted.

Source: Laffer Associates, U.S. Census Bureau, Bureau of Labor Statistics, Bureau of Economic Analysis.

What is of special interest is comparing the ALEC-Laffer rankings with (1) the nine zero earned income tax rankings versus the nine highest income tax rate states and (2) the nine lowest tax burden states versus the nine highest tax burden states. The ranking criteria and the rankings themselves are very different. For example, only three of the zero earned income tax states are in the top nine ALEC-Laffer rankings, and only four of the lowest ALEC-Laffer ranked states are in the highest income tax rate states.

As was the case for the personal income tax rate, the corporate income tax rate, and the overall tax burden, the highly ranked ALEC-Laffer states also more than match the nine low-ranked states in the provision of public services save for public welfare, housing, and community development employees. And, of course, the nine highest-ranked ALEC-Laffer states also pay annual salaries that are a lot lower than the low-ranked states.

CHAPTER 4

Piling On

Nature is never so wondrous, nor so wondered at, as when she is known.

—Philip Ball, *Curiosity*

This chapter carries out the analysis of the previous chapter, only with a different set of policy variables. We have also included sales taxes, estate taxes, and a measure of property taxes that, much to our surprise, did show some significant degree of negative correlation with economic growth. So much for Henry George.

As the reader will quickly see, the relationship between sales tax burdens and performance measures is very different from all of the other major taxes and their consequences that we reviewed in the previous chapter. States do need to tax something in order to provide public services, and from our criteria, of the major taxes, the sales tax best serves this need. In terms of our research, the sales tax is one of the least damaging taxes.

Juxtaposed to the sales tax, perhaps the most damaging general tax is the estate or inheritance tax per dollar of revenue collected. It collects few revenues and causes significant distortions. High tax rates on small tax bases are to be avoided.

Following closely on the heels of the property tax, estate tax, and the sales tax, the next three topics of this chapter vary greatly in their significance to the economic performance of a state. High on the significance ladder is the issue of right-to-work versus forced-union, followed by percentage of labor force unionized and, last, whether the state has a separate minimum wage above the federal minimum wage. While the percentage of the labor force that is unionized is not exactly a policy variable, it is directly influenced by a number of policy variables, including, of course, whether the state is a right-to-work state. But right-to-work is not alone. In Wisconsin, for example, Governor Scott Walker and his fellow Republicans in both Wisconsin state houses had a very public and very contentious political battle with the state's Democrats over lots of issues, including requiring each union member to approve in writing the use of his or her dues for political purposes.

After Governor Walker won a recall election, he and his legislators were able to successfully pass their agenda. And Wisconsin is on a new journey.

An Analysis of the Property Tax Burden

In this section we compare the nine states with the lowest property tax burdens to the nine states with the highest property tax burdens (see Table 4.1). What we find with regard to property taxes is that very high property tax states tend also to be high overall tax burden states, and they do perform poorly pretty much across the board. The high property tax burden states do not do exceptionally poorly when it comes to home price appreciation versus all states.

Low property tax burden states do perform significantly better than all states when it comes to home price appreciation, but with respect to other metrics are only slightly better than all states.

An Analysis of the Sales Tax Burden

In our quest for completeness, we have also looked at total state and local sales tax burden (see Table 4.2). The sales tax burden is one of the more interesting categories to examine, because the results, while on the surface seem contradictory to the importance of the relationship between tax rates and economic growth, they really confirm the principles of taxation that we examine in this book. For each performance metric from population growth through growth in gross state product,

TABLE 4.1

Nine Lowest Property Tax Burden (% of GSP) States versus Nine Highest Property Tax Burden (% of GSP) States (property tax burden is as of 2011; performance metrics are 2002 to 2012 unless otherwise noted)

State	2011 Property Taxes as a % of GSP*	10-Year Growth							
		Population	Net Domestic In-Migration	Nonfarm Payroll Employment	Personal Income	Gross State Product	State and Local Tax Revenue†	All Transactions Home Prices	Purchase Only Home Prices
Delaware	1.03	13.8%	5.0%	0.8%	44.0%	51.1%	53.5%	30.4%	26.2%
Oklahoma	1.43	9.3%	1.8%	7.2%	62.9%	62.9%	41.0%	27.6%	28.3%
Alabama	1.45	7.6%	2.2%	0.0%	48.8%	46.6%	45.1%	22.0%	19.0%
Louisiana	1.49	2.3%	-5.7%	1.6%	56.5%	74.8%	44.0%	37.7%	36.6%
Arkansas	1.70	9.0%	2.8%	2.7%	56.0%	47.7%	60.8%	23.3%	22.1%
New Mexico	1.72	12.4%	1.3%	5.0%	57.9%	50.2%	49.8%	31.0%	31.0%
Kentucky	1.79	7.1%	1.8%	2.1%	45.2%	42.8%	38.9%	19.3%	18.5%
North Dakota	1.83	9.6%	1.5%	30.3%	109.5%	125.1%	169.3%	58.5%	64.0%
Hawaii	1.89	12.3%	-2.0%	8.8%	63.6%	61.8%	57.6%	66.6%	68.1%
Equal-Weighted Average of Nine Lowest Property Tax Burden States†	**1.59**	**9.3%**	**1.0%**	**6.5%**	**60.5%**	**62.6%**	**62.2%**	**35.1%**	**34.9%**
50-State Equal-Weighted Avg.†	2.84	9.3%	0.9%	4.2%	51.1%	51.7%	56.5%	23.3%	22.3%
Equal-Weighted Average of Nine Highest Property Tax Burden States†	**4.47**	**2.7%**	**-3.1%**	**-0.3%**	**41.0%**	**37.8%**	**50.4%**	**24.0%**	**20.3%**

(continued)

83

TABLE 4.1

(Continued)

State	2011 Property Taxes as a % of GSP*	10-Year Growth							
		Population	Net Domestic In-Migration	Nonfarm Payroll Employment	Personal Income	Gross State Product	State and Local Tax Revenue†	All Transactions Home Prices	Purchase Only Home Prices
Illinois	3.61	2.8%	-4.9%	-2.3%	36.3%	39.7%	45.4%	8.1%	4.2%
Wisconsin	3.88	5.2%	-0.7%	0.1%	38.4%	37.5%	37.8%	15.7%	10.0%
New York	3.88	2.3%	-8.0%	4.0%	50.3%	46.6%	64.7%	33.0%	33.1%
Connecticut	4.09	3.8%	-3.4%	-1.6%	41.4%	35.8%	47.9%	20.7%	17.6%
Maine	4.57	2.6%	1.0%	-1.5%	40.4%	34.2%	37.5%	29.1%	26.2%
Rhode Island	4.60	-1.5%	-6.0%	-3.0%	37.8%	33.6%	44.4%	19.2%	14.5%
New Jersey	5.17	3.6%	-5.6%	-2.2%	39.2%	34.8%	57.6%	28.5%	27.1%
Vermont	5.18	1.7%	-1.0%	1.3%	45.8%	39.3%	63.5%	48.9%	42.8%
New Hampshire	5.24	4.1%	0.7%	2.4%	39.0%	38.4%	54.5%	12.9%	7.2%

*Property tax burden is 2011 "Property Tax" (from the Census Bureau's State and Local Government Finances survey) as a share of 2011 gross state product.

†State and local tax revenue is the 10-year growth in state and local tax revenue from the Census Bureau's State and Local Government Finances survey. Because of data release lag, these data are 2001 to 2011.

‡Averages are equal-weighted.

Source: Laffer Associates, U.S. Census Bureau, Bureau of Labor Statistics, Bureau of Economic Analysis, Federal Housing Finance Agency.

TABLE 4.2

Nine Lowest Sales Tax Burden States versus Nine Highest Sales Tax Burden States (sales tax burden is as of 2011; performance metrics are 2002 to 2012 unless otherwise noted)

State	Sales Tax Burden*	10-Year Growth					
		Population	Net Domestic In-Migration	Nonfarm Payroll Employment	Personal Income	Gross State Product	State and Local Tax Revenue†
New Hampshire	0.00%	4.1%	0.7%	2.4%	39.0%	38.4%	54.5%
Montana	0.00%	10.3%	4.7%	11.4%	60.7%	70.0%	61.0%
Delaware	0.00%	13.8%	5.0%	0.8%	44.0%	51.1%	53.5%
Oregon	0.00%	11.0%	4.4%	3.3%	44.5%	66.2%	53.3%
Alaska	1.04%	13.9%	-1.2%	13.8%	60.6%	79.5%	232.8%
Virginia	1.23%	12.3%	1.8%	6.6%	56.8%	53.3%	48.8%
Vermont	1.31%	1.7%	-1.0%	1.3%	45.8%	39.3%	63.5%
Maryland	1.35%	8.2%	-2.2%	3.8%	51.6%	53.7%	52.2%
Massachusetts	1.42%	3.6%	-3.7%	0.5%	43.0%	40.0%	49.5%
Equal-Weighted Average of Nine Lowest Sales Tax Burden States†	**0.71%**	**8.7%**	**1.0%**	**4.9%**	**49.5%**	**54.6%**	**74.3%**
50-State Equal-Weighted Average†	2.33%	9.3%	0.9%	4.2%	51.1%	51.7%	56.5%
Equal-Weighted Average of Nine Highest Sales Tax Burden States†	**3.86%**	**13.9%**	**3.4%**	**6.9%**	**58.5%**	**60.9%**	**61.6%**
Nevada	3.27%	26.9%	10.3%	8.6%	52.0%	61.4%	66.7%
Tennessee	3.55%	11.4%	4.5%	1.9%	49.0%	43.5%	50.2%
Arizona	3.70%	21.4%	9.8%	8.6%	59.1%	50.7%	56.1%
Arkansas	3.76%	9.0%	2.8%	2.7%	56.0%	47.7%	60.8%

(continued)

TABLE 4.2

(*Continued*)

State	Sales Tax Burden*	Population	10-Year Growth				
			Net Domestic In-Migration	Nonfarm Payroll Employment	Personal Income	Gross State Product	State and Local Tax Revenue[†]
Louisiana	3.78%	2.3%	–5.7%	1.6%	56.5%	74.8%	44.0%
Wyoming	3.94%	15.3%	5.3%	16.9%	75.9%	99.5%	121.1%
New Mexico	4.01%	12.4%	1.3%	5.0%	57.9%	50.2%	49.8%
Hawaii	4.34%	12.3%	–2.0%	8.8%	63.6%	61.8%	57.6%
Washington	4.43%	14.0%	3.8%	8.0%	56.2%	58.5%	48.6%

*Sales tax burden is 2011 "General Sales and Gross Receipts Tax Burden" (from the Census Bureau's State and Local Government Finances survey) as a share of FY2011 personal income.

[†]State and local tax revenue is the 10-year growth in state and local tax revenue from the Census Bureau's State and Local Government Finances survey. Because of data release lag, these data are 2001 to 2011.

[‡]Averages are equal-weighted.

Source: Laffer Associates, U.S. Census Bureau, Bureau of Labor Statistics, Bureau of Economic Analysis.

save state and local tax revenue growth, we have examined we observed that the average of the nine states with the lowest sales tax burdens underperformed the average of the nine states with the highest sales tax burdens. How can this be? And yet it's true.

The results for the 10-year growth of the average of the nine states with the lowest sales tax burdens versus the average of the nine highest sales tax burden states were as follows: population, 8.7 percent for the lowest versus 13.9 percent for the highest; net domestic in-migration, 1.0 percent for the lowest versus 3.4 percent for the highest; nonfarm payroll employment growth, 4.9 percent for the lowest versus 6.9 percent for the highest; personal income growth, 49.5 percent for the lowest versus 58.5 percent for the highest; gross state product growth, 54.6 percent for the lowest versus 60.9 percent for the highest; and, finally, for state and local tax revenue growth, 74.3 percent for the lowest versus 61.6 percent for the highest sales tax burden states. These results for sales taxes are precisely the opposite of what we found for personal income, corporate income, tax burden, ALEC-Laffer ranking, and property taxes.

Given that higher sales tax burdens tend to be less harmful to growth than many other forms of taxation, the sales tax is an interesting and fairly unique candidate for use in replacing more economically damaging taxes.

The principles of taxation would suggest that there are two very different yet key features of a tax system that promote economic growth. First, the total tax burden is in and of itself a critical component of the growth equation. In the words of Henry George:

> The best tax by which the public revenues can be raised is evidently that which will most closely conform to the following conditions:
>
> 1. That it bear as lightly as possible upon production so as least to check the increase of the general fund from which taxes must be paid and the community maintained.[1]

But, while the overall tax burden is critical, so too is the measure of exactly how taxes are collected. Again, in the words of Henry George,

The mode of taxation is, in fact, quite as important as the amount. As a small burden badly placed may distress a horse that could carry with ease a much larger one properly adjusted, so a people may be impoverished and their power of producing wealth destroyed by taxation, which, if levied in another way, could be borne with ease.[2]

In essence, a well-run state wants the lowest tax burden on overall production capable of raising the requisite revenues to fund the appropriate level of government spending, and it also wants to collect those revenues in the least damaging fashion. All taxes are bad for growth, but some are a lot worse than others. What a state should prefer is a low-rate, broad-based flat tax, and a sales tax fits this concept to a T. That is why we observe high sales tax states outperforming low sales tax states. High sales tax states often have less of the more damaging taxes, and low sales tax states often have more of the more damaging taxes.

It's interesting that two of the zero earned income tax rate states—New Hampshire and Alaska—also have no or low sales tax burdens and are members of the lowest overall tax burden states. On the other hand, there are four zero earned income tax rate states—Nevada, Tennessee, Wyoming, and Washington—that are members of the nine highest sales tax burden states. Nevada, Tennessee, Wyoming, and Louisiana, which are also high sales tax burden states, are also among the nine lowest overall tax burden states. This type of diversity is the core reason why we can learn so much from the states. Almost everything that can happen has already happened somewhere at sometime in some state. We must learn from our past experiences.

To repeat, two of the lowest sales tax burden states—New Hampshire and Alaska—are also members of the nine lowest overall tax burden states. Four of the highest sales tax burden states—Nevada, Tennessee, Wyoming, and Louisiana—are members of the nine lowest overall tax burden states.

Estate and Inheritance Taxes

States without estate or inheritance taxes—so-called "death taxes"—dramatically outperform those states with death taxes (Table 4.3). Here's how the average of the 29 states without death taxes stacks up versus the

TABLE 4.3

Twenty-Nine States without Estate or Inheritance Taxes versus 21 States with Estate or Inheritance Taxes (estate or inheritance taxes are as of 1/1/2013; performance metrics are 2002 to 2012 unless otherwise noted)

State	Estate or Inheritance Tax? 1=Yes*	Population	Net Domestic In-Migration	10-Year Growth			
				Nonfarm Payroll Employment	Personal Income	Gross State Product	State and Local Tax Revenue[†]
Equal-Weighted Average of 29 States without Death Taxes[†]	0.00	11.1%	2.0%	5.8%	54.5%	55.4%	60.9%
50-State Equal-Weighted Average[†]	0.42	9.3%	0.9%	4.2%	51.1%	51.7%	56.5%
Equal-Weighted Average of 21 States with Death Taxes[†]	1.00	6.8%	−0.6%	2.0%	46.4%	46.7%	50.4%

* Estate or inheritance tax status as of 1/1/2013 from McGuireWoods LLP. Tennessee is currently in the process of phasing out its estate tax (fully repealed for CY 2016), but, for the purposes of this table, has been counted as having an estate tax. North Carolina has repealed its estate tax retroactively to 1/1/2013, but this law was not in place until July 2013 and, for the purposes of this table, has been counted as having an estate tax.
[†] State and local tax revenue is the 10-year growth in state and local tax revenue from the Census Bureau's State and Local Government Finances survey. Because of data release lag, these data are 2001 to 2011.
[‡] Averages are equal-weighted.

Source: Laffer Associates, McGuireWoods LLP. U.S. Census Bureau, Bureau of Labor Statistics, Bureau of Economic Analysis.

21 states with death taxes in 10-year growth rates: population growth, 11.1 percent to 6.8 percent; net domestic in-migration, 2.0 percent to −0.6 percent; nonfarm payroll employment growth, 5.8 percent to 2.0 percent; personal income growth, 54.5 percent to 46.4 percent; gross state product growth, 55.4 percent to 46.7 percent; and state and local tax revenue growth, 60.9 percent to 50.4 percent.

While the estate tax is small in terms of tax revenue generation in comparison to other state and local taxes, its impact can be deadly (pun intended). The prospect of an estate tax falls on those very people who create the most jobs, consume the most, and generally energize the state's economy the most. These people don't work and save to pay taxes. They work and save for their legacy, their grandchildren, and a better way of life after they are gone.

Because the tax rate is usually high, alternatives are readily available, and the tax base is small, the estate tax fits into the category of the least efficient taxes in a state's arsenal of tax options. Unfortunately, rhetoric surrounding the estate tax often appeals to the worst demons of our nature and is used opportunistically by demagogues to incite class jealousies. Nothing fits the slogan of "tax the rich" more than the estate tax. And yet few taxes actually hurt the poor more.

Right-to-Work Laws

As defined by the National Right to Work Legal Defense Foundation, a right-to-work (RTW) law "guarantees that no person can be compelled, as a condition of employment, to join or not to join, nor to pay dues to a labor union."[3] The differences in performance outcomes between the states that have right-to-work laws and the states without such laws—herein referred to as "forced-union" states—are dramatic (see Table 4.4).

Right-to-work laws are allowed under Section 14(b) of the Taft-Hartley Act of 1947, which was passed in response to the staunchly pro-union Wagner Act of 1935. The Wagner Act allowed employees to self-organize and bargain collectively with immunity from employer interference. The Taft-Hartley Act added some checks and balances, while

Average of 23 Right-to-Work States versus Average of 27 Forced-Union States (right-to-work status is as of 1/1/2013; performance metrics are 2002 to 2012 unless otherwise noted)

State	Forced-Union State? 1=Yes*	10-Year Growth					
		Population	Net Domestic In-Migration	Nonfarm Payroll Employment	Personal Income	Gross State Product	State and Local Tax Revenue[†]
Equal-Weighted Average of the 23 Right-to-Work States[‡]	0.00	12.6%	3.0%	6.8%	58.0%	59.1%	57.8%
50-State Equal-Weighted Avg.[‡]	0.54	9.3%	0.9%	4.2%	51.1%	51.7%	56.5%
Equal-Weighted Avg. of the 27 Forced-Union States[‡]	1.00	6.5%	-0.9%	1.9%	45.2%	45.4%	55.4%

*Right-to-work status is as of 1/1/2013. For this reason, Michigan has been counted as a forced-union state (RTW did not go into effect in Michigan until March 2013).

[†]State and local tax revenue is the 10-year growth in state and local tax revenue from the Census Bureau's State and Local Government Finances survey. Because of data release lag, these data are 2001 to 2011.

[‡]Averages are equal-weighted.

Source: National Right to Work Legal Defense Foundation, Laffer Associates, U.S. Census Bureau, Bureau of Labor Statistics, Bureau of Economic Analysis.

slightly curbing the broad range of powers afforded to unions by the Wagner Act. Specifically, the Taft-Hartley Act allowed states to pass right-to-work laws. By 1948, 11 states had right-to-work laws on their books.

As of the writing of this book, there are 24 states that are right-to-work states, although we don't include Michigan as a right-to-work state in Table 4.4, since its right-to-work law didn't go into effect until March 2013. However, Indiana just preceded Michigan as one of two states that became right-to-work since 2011.

Over the past decade, the average of the 23 right-to-work states grew 12.6 percent in population compared to average population growth of 6.5 percent in forced-union states—a growth differential of 6.1 percentage points. For net domestic in-migration, the RTW states averaged 3.0 percent versus the forced-union states' –0.9 percent. For nonfarm payroll employment growth, the RTW states grew, on average, 6.8 percent versus the forced-union states' 1.9 percent.

The growth differential in personal income over the past 10 years between right-to-work and forced-union states was an enormous 12.8 percentage points in favor of right-to-work states, with the RTW states' personal income growth averaging 58.0 percent to the forced-union states' 45.2 percent. For gross state product growth, the story is much the same, with the RTW states (59.1 percent) outperforming the forced-union states (45.4 percent) by a 10-year growth differential of 13.7 percentage points. The final category, state and local tax revenue growth, showed the average of the 23 RTW states slightly outperforming the forced-union states' average, 57.8 percent versus 55.4 percent.

Even though we know in the real world today all of the state policy variables interact with each other and commingle, it is still highly instructive to view each of the policy variables as standing alone and see how each policy variable by itself correlates with state economic performance. But sometimes contradictions become altogether too delicious to ignore. For example, three of the nine zero earned income tax states are also forced-union states, and the other six are right-to-work states. Who would have thought that two policies born of opposing ideologies could coexist for as long as they have?

The three forced-union states are none other than New Hampshire, Washington State, and Alaska. Each of these three forced-union states grew in population more slowly than the average of all zero earned income tax states. Each had less in-migration than the average of the other zero earned income tax states. In payroll growth, Washington and New Hampshire underperformed the nine-state average whereas Alaska way outperformed. Oil does, in fact, have its privileges. Alaska also outperformed the average of all nine zero earned income tax states in both personal income growth and growth in gross state product. Washington and New Hampshire continued to underperform in both of these categories.

Recently, several states have been debating whether to implement right-to-work laws, and two states—Indiana and Michigan—have successfully passed right-to-work legislation over the past couple of years. Prior to Indiana's passage of right-to-work legislation in 2012, the last state to pass such a law was Oklahoma in 2001, and before that was Idaho all the way back in 1985. If history serves us well as a guide for what will be, Indiana's and Michigan's passage of right-to-work legislation will serve as a boon to those states' anemic economic performance.

While right-to-work legislation per se has been the focal point for most states, Wisconsin under Governor Scott Walker chose a different path, with very similar results. Wisconsin restricted collective bargaining for most public employees and tied wage increases to inflation. Contracts will be limited to one year, and wages will be frozen until a new contract is settled. Collective bargaining requires an annual vote of all members to maintain certification; employers will be prohibited from collecting union dues, and members of collective bargaining will not be required to pay dues. There are fire, police, and state trooper exceptions, but all in all Wisconsin is not the state it used to be.

Labor Force Unionization

In line with whether a state is a right-to-work state or a forced-union state, we also have data on the degree to which each state is actually unionized—that is, the share of the employed labor force who are members of a union (see Table 4.5). While these data overlap the right-to-work/forced-union

TABLE 4.5

Nine States with Least Unionized Workforces versus Nine States with Most Unionized Workforces (unionization rate is as of 2012; performance metrics are 2002 to 2012 unless otherwise noted)

State	Share of Employed with Union Membership*	10-Year Growth					
		Population	Net Domestic In-Migration	Nonfarm Payroll Employment	Personal Income	Gross State Product	State and Local Tax Revenue†
North Carolina	2.93%	17.1%	6.9%	4.0%	52.6%	50.9%	53.2%
Arkansas	3.17%	9.0%	2.8%	2.7%	56.0%	47.7%	60.8%
South Carolina	3.29%	15.0%	7.1%	2.9%	51.3%	41.7%	42.5%
Mississippi	4.29%	4.4%	-1.1%	-2.0%	49.3%	46.0%	44.6%
Georgia	4.36%	16.6%	5.1%	1.4%	45.6%	38.1%	31.6%
Virginia	4.44%	12.3%	1.8%	6.6%	56.8%	53.3%	48.8%
Idaho	4.76%	19.1%	6.2%	9.5%	54.3%	54.4%	43.1%
Tennessee	4.80%	11.4%	4.5%	1.9%	49.0%	43.5%	50.2%
Utah	5.15%	22.8%	2.4%	16.4%	65.0%	74.9%	52.2%
Equal-Weighted Average of Nine States with Lowest Employee Unionization†	**4.13%**	**14.2%**	**4.0%**	**4.8%**	**53.3%**	**50.0%**	**47.4%**
50-State Equal-Weighted Average†	10.37%	9.3%	0.9%	4.2%	51.1%	51.7%	56.5%
Equal-Weighted Avg. of Nine States with Highest Employee Unionization ex AK†	18.34%	6.2%	-2.9%	1.0%	44.7%	45.0%	49.5%

Equal-Weighted Average of Nine States with Highest Employee Unionization†	18.79%	7.0%	-2.7%	2.4%	46.5%	48.8%	69.9%
Oregon	15.76%	11.0%	4.4%	3.3%	44.5%	66.2%	53.3%
New Jersey	16.09%	3.6%	-5.6%	-2.2%	39.2%	34.8%	57.6%
Michigan	16.61%	-1.3%	-5.8%	-10.3%	22.3%	13.8%	16.1%
California	17.15%	9.1%	-3.9%	-0.4%	44.1%	44.4%	54.0%
Rhode Island	17.82%	-1.5%	-6.0%	-3.0%	37.8%	33.6%	44.4%
Washington	18.47%	14.0%	3.8%	8.0%	56.2%	58.5%	48.6%
Hawaii	21.68%	12.3%	-2.0%	8.8%	63.6%	61.8%	57.6%
Alaska	22.38%	13.9%	-1.2%	13.8%	60.6%	79.5%	232.8%
New York	23.15%	2.3%	-8.0%	4.0%	50.3%	46.6%	64.7%

*Share of employed with union membership is the number of employed wage and salary workers who are members of unions as a share of total (public and private) wage and salary employment in the state. Data are as of 2012 and were extracted from Unionstats.com.
†State and local tax revenue is the 10-year growth in state and local tax revenue from the Census Bureau's State and Local Government Finances survey. Because of data release lag, these data are 2001 to 2011.
†Averages are equal-weighted.

Source: Unionstats, Laffer Associates, U.S. Census Bureau, Bureau of Labor Statistics, Bureau of Economic Analysis.

designation, they aren't exactly the same and the results tend to reinforce what we saw in Table 4.4.

Only one state—Michigan—of the most unionized states in the nation is currently a right-to-work state, but Michigan became a right-to-work state only in 2013, so for historical analysis purposes we include Michigan as a forced-union state. But times they are a-changin', and we personally will be waiting on tenterhooks to see how the saga of Saginaw unfolds. Bo Schembechler appears to have the upper hand on "Woody" Hayes.[4]

What is especially interesting, to us at least, is the juxtaposition of zero earned income tax states and unionization. Who would have guessed that two of the four most unionized states in the United States—Washington State and Alaska—are also zero earned income tax states, and only one of the zero earned income tax states (Tennessee) is a member of the nine least unionized states?

While many of the variables we consider are closely related to each other, their differences are far more revealing than are their similarities.

Again, we plead with each and every skeptical reader, do be on your guard for mistakes, tendentious statements, and misleading innuendos, but also keep an open mind and imagine what your opinions would be if the results of these comparisons were the exact opposite of what they actually are. These results are very, very powerful.

State Minimum Wages

Federal law trumps state law. The federal minimum wage, standing at $7.25 per hour in 2013, applies to all states, but some states have their own separate minimum wages that are higher than the federal minimum wage. A high minimum wage creates the classic problem of pricing out workers from the jobs market, especially those marginal low-skilled workers.

Table 4.6 presents the results for the average of the 31 states where the minimum wage equals the federal minimum wage versus the average of the 19 states with higher-than-federal minimum wage policies: population growth, 9.6 percent versus 8.9 percent; net domestic in-migration,

TABLE 4.6

Thirty-One States with Federal Minimum Wage versus 19 States with Minimum Wages above Federal (minimum wages are as of 1/1/2013; performance metrics are 2002 to 2012 unless otherwise noted)

State	State Minimum Wage*	10-Year Growth					
		Population	Net Domestic In-Migration	Nonfarm Payroll Employment	Personal Income	Gross State Product	State and Local Tax Revenue†
Equal-Weighted Average of 31 States with Federal Minimum Wage*	7.25	9.6%	1.0%	5.3%	54.0%	55.3%	55.7%
50-State Equal-Weighted Average‡	7.53	9.3%	0.9%	4.2%	51.1%	51.7%	56.5%
Equal-Weighted Average of 19 States with Minimum Wage Higher than Federal‡	7.99	8.9%	0.6%	2.3%	46.2%	45.9%	57.9%

*States can choose to have a minimum wage or not to have a minimum wage. Since all states are subject to federal law, those states with either minimum wages below the federal level (currently $7.25 per hour) or no state minimum wage at all are subject to the federal minimum wage. In the case that a state has its own minimum wage law above the federal minimum wage, that higher state wage applies. Minimum wage data in this table are as of 1/1/2013 and were extracted from a Department of Labor data set.

†State and local tax revenue is the 10-year growth in state and local tax revenue from the Census Bureau's State and Local Government Finances survey. Because of data release lag, these data are 2001 to 2011.

‡Averages are equal-weighted.

Source: Laffer Associates, Department of Labor, U.S. Census Bureau, Bureau of Labor Statistics, Bureau of Economic Analysis.

1.0 percent versus 0.6 percent; nonfarm payroll employment growth, 5.3 percent versus 2.3 percent; personal income growth, 54.0 percent versus 46.2 percent; gross state product growth, 55.3 percent versus 45.9 percent; and state and local tax revenue growth, 55.7 percent versus 57.9 percent. As you can easily see, the state-by-state variations aren't sufficiently large to create significant differences in the average measures of state performance.

One of the most notable aspects of this comparison is that, on average, the group of 31 states without separate higher minimum wages actually performed better over the past decade in both employment growth—beating the higher-than-federal minimum wage state average by three percentage points—and in personal income growth—beating the higher-than-federal minimum wage state average by 7.8 percentage points. It seems to us that a lack of a separate higher minimum wage is the way to go, as it tends to produce more jobs and more overall income! From both a conceptual level and an empirical perspective, lower minimum wages are better than higher minimum wages. It's far better to have a job at a lower wage than be unemployed at a higher wage.

From a demagogical rhetorical vantage, however, you'll never stop the misleading statements and slogans coming from irresponsible politicians and community organizers. These people are the enablers of a self-destructive dependency state. Just imagine what would happen to the U.S. economy if the minimum wage were, say, $100 per hour indexed to inflation. And to go one step further, imagine what would happen to a single state if it alone legislated a $100 per hour minimum wage indexed to inflation and no other state had a minimum wage over $8 per hour. We think you get the picture.

While the current array of minimum wages really doesn't provide enough variation to uncover the consequences, there are signs that a number of states are considering fairly radical experiments in higher minimum wages. We'll just have to wait and see.

CHAPTER 5

Give unto Caesar

The whole business thing is predicated a lot on the tax laws. . . . It's why we rehearse in Canada and not in the U.S. A lot of our astute moves have been basically keeping up with tax laws, where to go, where not to put it. Whether to sit on it or not. We left England because we'd be paying 98 cents on the dollar. We left, and they lost out. No taxes at all.

—Keith Richards[1]

The book *How Money Walks*,[2] written by one of our authors (Travis H. Brown), examines how millions of Americans moved among the states between the years 1995 and 2010, taking with them more than $2 trillion in adjusted gross income (AGI), what we commonly refer to as "working wealth." Using definitive data mapping of publicly available Internal Revenue Service (IRS) taxpayer data, *How Money Walks* developed a model that shows from where money is leaving and to where it is walking, from state to state and all the way down to the county level. This chapter of this book summarizes, updates, and modifies the findings in *How Money Walks*, including extending our window of IRS data back to 1992/1993.

This book shows how some states, like no income tax Florida, saw tremendous gains ($88.7 billion net inflow of adjusted gross income in an 18-year period), while other states, like New York, experienced crippling losses ($67.5 billion in that same time frame) (see Table 2.7 in Chapter 2). The New York/Florida comparison is one of myriad examples of the undeniable correlation between the migration of wealth away from high-tax states and into low-tax states.

Opponents of pro-growth policy often cry foul, arguing that lower taxes hurt things like education, police, the poor, highways, and so on. While often well-intended, bottom-up policy is and will always be backwards. In contrast, by creating business-friendly environments, proponents of pro-growth policy aren't ignoring a moral imperative, as is often charged; rather, we are upholding it by encouraging a competitive arena in which businesses thrive and expand and create new and better jobs. In such an arena, opportunities abound and the sky is the limit for the men and women who want to make better lives for themselves and their families.

Growth economics is the approach that has made America great, separated Americans from other countries' citizens, and made the United States the envy of the world. And in the future, the line between the haves and the have-nots will be between economic policies of states that commit to growing their economies and lifting people up, and those states that choose to grow government and keep people down by making their citizens dependent on government.

While some states, such as New York and California, appear intent upon sealing their own doom, other big winners, like Texas and Florida, are seizing the opportunity to pull away from the pack. And yet some states appear to have already gone over the cliff, including Michigan and Vermont. Still others remain on the cusp, their fate yet to be determined. The Commonwealth of Pennsylvania is one such state.

The Keystone State sits amid several high-tax states that are all suffering a mass exodus of citizens leaving for more business-friendly climates. Key among the winners are no- and low-tax states like Florida, New Hampshire, Arizona, and Texas (see Table 2.7 in Chapter 2). A quick analysis of wealth migration trends over the past couple of decades makes clear a shifting of the sands that Pennsylvania leaders will do well to study, understand, and address if that state is to avoid the same perils that have befallen some of its neighbors.

In Table 5.1 we show the net migration of tax returns (in-returns minus out-returns divided by total in-returns and out-returns) by state by year for the years 1992/1993 through 2009/2010. These states are ranked each year from the highest percentage of in-returns to the lowest percentage of in-returns (largest percentage of out-returns). Table 5.1 highlights the annual performances of Michigan, Ohio, Illinois, New York, and New Jersey (i.e., the five worst-performing states in the 2009/2010 year). These are not the states Pennsylvania should emulate.

When using out-migration of adjusted gross income (AGI) over the whole period, New York State was the biggest loser of all states. New York saw a net loss of $67.5 billion in AGI and 1,087,351 net tax returns leaving between the years 1992/1993 and 2009/2010—that's more than 60 times Broadway's 2011–2012 revenue. During that same time period, Massachusetts lost $11.8 billion in AGI and nearly 200,000 tax returns. When seeking an explanation for the falloff, there is no way around the fact that New York and Massachusetts rank number one and number eight, respectively, on the Tax Foundation's list of the highest state and local tax burdens (see Table 3.4 in Chapter 3).

While Pennsylvania has fared better than a number of states, it is not immune to the blues that have befallen East Coast states, as evidenced by the $8.5 billion in AGI that Pennsylvania lost between 1992/1993 and 2009/2010, which is more than twice the market value of the Pittsburgh Steelers, Philadelphia Eagles, Pittsburgh Pirates, Philadelphia Phillies, and Philadelphia 76ers combined, making clear to anyone who cares that there is lots of work to be done if Pennsylvania is to remain competitive.

The good news is that, unlike New York, Massachusetts, New Jersey, Michigan, Illinois, and Ohio, Pennsylvania isn't so far in the hole that a turnaround is unachievable. Moreover, Pennsylvania is now led by Governor Tom Corbett, who has a firm grasp of the importance of a sound pro-growth policy, noting in his first State of the State Address, "[Taxes] choke growth. Every credible study on the subject has taught us this: The states that have grown the fastest, attracted the most jobs, have stayed out of the way [of the private sector]. If you tax less, people will see the point in earning more. If you regulate more sensibly, businesses will be able to maneuver in the turns of tight economies."[3]

TABLE 5.1

Net In Returns as a Percentage of Gross Returns
(Returns In + Returns Out)

92/93	93/94	94/95	95/96	96/97	97/98	98/99	99/00	00/01
ID 19.8%	NV 29.4%	NV 24.8%	NV 24.6%	NV 26.7%	NV 21.3%	NV 20.1%	NV 20.1%	NV 19.9%
NV 19.3%	AZ 23.1%	AZ 23.3%	AZ 19.4%	AZ 18.0%	AZ 16.4%	AZ 15.8%	AZ 14.8%	FL 15.6%
CO 18.5%	ID 19.5%	NC 16.8%	NC 16.5%	NC 15.3%	NC 13.5%	CO 13.5%	GA 12.1%	AZ 14.0%
OR 18.4%	GA 18.1%	GA 16.0%	GA 16.4%	FL 15.2%	FL 13.3%	GA 13.3%	FL 11.9%	CO 12.4%
AZ 17.2%	NC 16.6%	OR 15.6%	OR 15.9%	GA 13.4%	GA 13.3%	NC 11.4%	CO 10.6%	GA 8.9%
MT 16.5%	CO 16.2%	TN 15.1%	TN 13.5%	CO 12.5%	CO 11.4%	SC 10.0%	NC 9.9%	NC 8.1%
WA 16.4%	TN 15.5%	ID 14.7%	FL 11.8%	OR 11.6%	SC 10.7%	FL 9.9%	DE 8.0%	NH 7.9%
GA 15.4%	FL 15.0%	CO 14.3%	CO 11.2%	SC 10.3%	OR 7.4%	DE 8.2%	NH 7.8%	OR 6.3%
UT 14.6%	OR 15.0%	FL 13.6%	ID 9.2%	WA 9.6%	TX 7.3%	NH 6.0%	SC 7.1%	DE 5.1%
NC 13.2%	UT 14.7%	MT 11.4%	AR 8.6%	TN 9.3%	TN 6.8%	TN 5.9%	VA 6.6%	WA 4.6%
TN 13.0%	MT 12.1%	AR 11.2%	WA 8.4%	ID 6.9%	DE 6.6%	ID 4.9%	ME 6.6%	ME 4.5%
FL 12.8%	NM 11.7%	WA 9.5%	SC 7.8%	DE 6.5%	WA 6.4%	OR 4.8%	TN 5.4%	TX 4.2%
AR 12.4%	AR 10.7%	UT 8.8%	UT 6.6%	UT 5.7%	ID 4.7%	TX 4.5%	ID 5.1%	SC 4.1%
NM 9.2%	WA 9.2%	NM 7.7%	DE 6.2%	TX 5.1%	NH 4.1%	VA 4.0%	MN 3.4%	VA 4.0%
AL 9.0%	TX 8.3%	DE 6.5%	NH 6.0%	NH 4.4%	KY 2.0%	WA 3.5%	TX 3.4%	ID 3.2%
DE 6.7%	DE 7.6%	MO 5.3%	TX 4.8%	AL 3.9%	AL 1.9%	MN 3.2%	AR 2.3%	MD 3.0%
TX 6.4%	MS 6.6%	SC 5.3%	MO 4.7%	MO 3.2%	VA 1.2%	KY 2.1%	OR 1.9%	TN 2.4%
MN 6.2%	KY 5.5%	NH 5.1%	MT 4.6%	KY 2.7%	AR 0.8%	ME 1.1%	VT 1.9%	RI 2.4%
KY 6.1%	AL 5.3%	TX 4.5%	NM 2.9%	AR 2.2%	ME 0.5%	MO 0.2%	RI 1.8%	CA 1.6%
WV 5.7%	MO 5.2%	MS 4.3%	KY 2.8%	VA 1.9%	OK 0.4%	AR -0.7%	WA 1.0%	MN 1.5%
MO 4.6%	SC 4.7%	KY 3.8%	MN 2.4%	MS 1.5%	MO -0.4%	MS -0.9%	KY 0.9%	VT 0.5%
SC 4.5%	SD 3.9%	AL 2.8%	MS 2.3%	OK 0.7%	KS -0.5%	MD -1.1%	MD 0.9%	MO -0.5%
MS 4.4%	NH 3.4%	VA 1.8%	OK 1.7%	MN -1.6%	UT -1.3%	VT -1.9%	MO 0.3%	KY -0.6%
VA 4.4%	VA 3.0%	MN 1.8%	AL 1.7%	KS -2.2%	CA -1.9%	MA -2.0%	WI -0.5%	AR -1.1%
WI 4.2%	MN 2.9%	IN 1.7%	VT 1.2%	IN -2.3%	MN -2.0%	MT -2.2%	MT -1.0%	DC -1.6%
SD 3.9%	WY 2.7%	SD 1.5%	VA 1.1%	NM -2.4%	MD -2.6%	CA -2.2%	CA -1.4%	HI -2.0%
IN 2.8%	OK 1.1%	VT 0.8%	IN 0.4%	ME -2.9%	MA -2.6%	RI -2.3%	MS -1.7%	WI -3.1%
WY 2.3%	IN 1.0%	WI 0.6%	WI 0.2%	VT -3.2%	VT -3.3%	AL -2.4%	IN -2.8%	AK -3.3%
OK 1.6%	WI 0.2%	NE 0.1%	NE -0.7%	MA -3.5%	ME -3.7%	WI -2.4%	AL -4.0%	MA -3.4%
AK 1.5%	AK 0.1%	OK -0.1%	ME -1.1%	MT -3.5%	IN -4.1%	DC -3.1%	SD -4.0%	MT -3.4%
NH -0.2%	VT 0.1%	WY -0.2%	WV -2.7%	MD -3.5%	AK -4.2%	OK -3.3%	MA -4.2%	UT -5.5%
VT -0.2%	WV -0.2%	MD -1.1%	WY -3.4%	AK -4.1%	NM -4.7%	KS -3.6%	UT -4.3%	AL -5.8%
KS -1.4%	MD -0.7%	WV -1.7%	MD -3.6%	WI -5.2%	MT -4.9%	IN -3.7%	WY -4.5%	OK -5.9%
HI -2.0%	KS -1.7%	KS -3.5%	SD -4.1%	NE -5.8%	WY -5.5%	UT -3.9%	DC -4.7%	SD -5.9%
MD -2.1%	NE -2.5%	LA -3.6%	MA -4.1%	CA -6.5%	WI -5.7%	AK -4.8%	NM -5.4%	WY -6.0%
NE -2.9%	HI -3.3%	ME -4.5%	MO -4.7%	WY -7.1%	WV -6.2%	SD -6.5%	KS -5.6%	IN -6.4%
ND -4.4%	LA -4.7%	ND -4.6%	AK -5.1%	WV -7.8%	RI -7.1%	WV -7.0%	OK -5.7%	MS -6.4%
IA -4.4%	ND -5.5%	MI -5.4%	ND -5.4%	LA -8.9%	LA -8.3%	WY -7.1%	CT -6.5%	NM -6.8%
PA -4.6%	ME -7.0%	IA -5.7%	KS -6.0%	MI -9.0%	DC -8.9%	NM -7.7%	MI -6.6%	CT -7.0%
ME -6.0%	PA -7.6%	OH -6.0%	OH -6.1%	OH -9.4%	NE -9.3%	NE -8.1%	AK -7.4%	NJ -7.2%
OH -6.1%	IA -7.8%	MA -7.2%	IA -6.7%	RI -9.8%	IA -9.6%	CT -8.3%	WV -8.1%	KS -8.1%
LA -9.8%	MA -8.1%	AK -8.6%	LA -7.8%	SD -9.9%	NJ -10.3%	NJ -8.6%	NJ -8.5%	WV -8.3%
IL -10.7%	OH -8.8%	HI -8.8%	PA -9.4%	IA -10.2%	SD -10.6%	MI -8.6%	PA -9.1%	PA -8.9%
NJ -11.3%	NJ -11.2%	PA -9.5%	IL -10.8%	ND -11.5%	OH -10.7%	IA -8.8%	HI -9.5%	MI -10.6%
DC -11.9%	IL -12.0%	NJ -10.5%	HI -11.3%	IL -11.5%	CT -10.9%	OH -9.6%	NE -9.6%	NE -11.0%
RI -12.2%	MI -13.3%	IL -10.8%	NJ -12.1%	HI -12.0%	PA -11.1%	LA -9.8%	OH -10.0%	OH -11.6%
MA -13.4%	DC -13.6%	CT -14.7%	RI -12.1%	DC -12.1%	MI -11.5%	PA -10.0%	IA -10.6%	IL -12.8%
MI -15.2%	RI -15.2%	RI -15.7%	CT -14.6%	IL -13.2%	HI -11.6%	IL -12.1%	IL -13.1%	IA -13.8%
CT -18.0%	CT -17.5%	DC -16.1%	DC -15.6%	CT -13.6%	IL -13.4%	HI -15.1%	LA -13.7%	LA -14.7%
NY -25.3%	NY -26.4%	CA -24.1%	CA -16.8%	PA -13.7%	ND -13.5%	ND -16.2%	ND -16.8%	NY -17.2%
CA -26.1%	CA -29.4%	NY -27.2%	NY -28.0%	NY -27.0%	NY -23.4%	NY -19.0%	NY -17.8%	ND -17.3%

Source: Internal Revenue Service, Laffer Associates.

01/02		02/03		03/04		04/05		05/06		06/07		07/08		08/09		09/10	
FL	17.7%	NV	18.9%	NV	25.1%	AZ	24.3%	AZ	23.3%	SC	17.6%	SC	16.6%	TX	14.5%	TX	11.1%
NV	17.6%	FL	17.2%	FL	23.1%	FL	21.8%	NV	20.0%	NC	16.8%	NC	16.0%	SC	11.0%	DC	9.8%
AZ	14.9%	AZ	15.0%	AZ	19.3%	NV	20.8%	TX	17.6%	NV	15.8%	TX	13.6%	NC	10.6%	CO	8.8%
OR	8.9%	ME	11.6%	DE	10.2%	ID	14.1%	NC	17.4%	AZ	15.8%	CO	10.9%	CO	10.5%	OK	7.6%
ME	8.5%	DE	11.1%	NC	9.9%	NC	12.6%	GA	17.1%	GA	14.3%	OR	10.4%	WY	10.2%	LA	7.5%
DE	8.0%	SC	8.1%	ID	9.8%	SC	12.3%	SC	15.6%	TN	13.1%	AZ	10.2%	WA	8.5%	SC	7.4%
NC	7.3%	ID	7.1%	SC	9.8%	TN	11.4%	ID	14.2%	TX	12.7%	WA	9.5%	DC	8.4%	ND	7.3%
GA	6.8%	OR	6.3%	GA	9.0%	DE	11.2%	OR	13.2%	ID	12.2%	GA	8.6%	OK	8.3%	NC	6.9%
SC	6.2%	VA	5.9%	TN	7.3%	OR	10.1%	TN	12.8%	OR	11.1%	UT	8.5%	OR	7.8%	AK	6.6%
NH	5.9%	GA	5.8%	MT	6.7%	GA	9.3%	FL	12.8%	UT	10.3%	TN	8.0%	LA	7.0%	WV	6.5%
MD	4.8%	TN	5.8%	VA	6.2%	AR	7.9%	AL	11.0%	WY	9.9%	NV	7.8%	TN	6.6%	NM	6.5%
TX	4.8%	NC	5.7%	ME	6.1%	WA	6.2%	WA	10.7%	CO	8.9%	ID	7.6%	WV	5.3%	VA	4.8%
CO	4.7%	MT	4.8%	AR	5.7%	MT	5.5%	AR	10.4%	WA	7.7%	WY	7.1%	AL	5.2%	SD	4.5%
VA	4.2%	NH	4.4%	NM	5.0%	AL	5.1%	DE	8.8%	MT	7.3%	MT	6.2%	AR	4.4%	FL	4.5%
TN	4.2%	NM	3.9%	WA	3.9%	TX	5.1%	CO	8.7%	DE	7.1%	DE	6.2%	AZ	4.0%	KY	4.5%
ID	4.0%	KY	3.8%	HI	3.0%	NM	4.9%	UT	7.0%	LA	6.6%	AL	6.1%	GA	4.0%	TN	4.5%
RI	3.9%	AR	3.6%	AL	2.8%	KY	4.1%	MT	6.5%	AL	6.3%	LA	4.8%	DE	3.9%	AZ	4.4%
WA	3.8%	HI	3.4%	KY	2.7%	VA	4.1%	NM	5.6%	KY	5.8%	AR	4.5%	UT	3.8%	DE	4.4%
NM	3.3%	WV	3.0%	TX	2.7%	CO	2.9%	WY	4.7%	AR	5.3%	KY	4.1%	NM	3.8%	AR	4.4%
WY	2.7%	TX	2.9%	MS	2.4%	HI	2.9%	OK	4.2%	OK	5.1%	SD	3.5%	ND	3.6%	OR	4.3%
KY	1.9%	RI	2.8%	SD	2.4%	MO	1.9%	KY	3.3%	NM	4.9%	WV	2.9%	KY	3.5%	AL	3.2%
AK	1.8%	MD	2.6%	NH	2.2%	ME	1.9%	MO	3.1%	FL	3.0%	OK	2.6%	SD	3.4%	WA	3.2%
VT	1.4%	MO	1.5%	MO	1.4%	UT	1.7%	HI	1.6%	WV	2.5%	DC	1.8%	VA	3.4%	GA	2.5%
WV	1.4%	WA	1.1%	WY	1.3%	NH	1.4%	WV	1.5%	SD	2.0%	MS	0.7%	MT	2.5%	MT	2.4%
HI	1.3%	AL	1.0%	OR	1.1%	WV	1.2%	VA	1.4%	MO	1.9%	NM	0.5%	AK	0.9%	UT	1.2%
MO	0.6%	VT	0.7%	WV	0.2%	MS	0.4%	DC	0.8%	MS	0.8%	VA	0.4%	ID	0.0%	MD	0.9%
AR	0.3%	AK	0.5%	AK	0.2%	OK	−0.3%	SD	0.5%	DC	0.5%	IA	−0.1%	MO	−0.2%	NE	0.5%
OK	−0.1%	MS	−1.1%	CO	−0.4%	SD	−0.3%	NH	0.4%	VA	0.3%	MO	−1.1%	MA	−0.3%	HI	0.2%
MT	−0.2%	OK	−1.4%	MD	−0.9%	WY	−0.4%	AK	−1.3%	ME	0.1%	HI	−1.3%	NV	−0.6%	MO	0.2%
WI	−2.0%	PA	−1.5%	VT	−2.3%	DC	−1.9%	IN	−1.7%	MN	−2.4%	FL	−1.9%	IA	−0.7%	IA	−0.7%
AL	−3.4%	WY	−1.7%	DC	−2.7%	MD	−1.9%	ME	−1.8%	NH	−2.7%	ND	−1.9%	KS	−1.9%	ID	−0.8%
MN	−3.4%	WI	−1.7%	IL	−2.8%	IN	−2.1%	MN	−2.7%	IN	−2.9%	KS	−2.0%	NE	−1.9%	KS	−1.3%
CT	−3.9%	CO	−1.9%	OK	−2.8%	VT	−2.8%	PA	−3.7%	PA	−3.5%	IN	−2.7%	MS	−2.0%	MS	−1.5%
MS	−4.0%	SD	−2.0%	PA	−3.4%	AK	−3.2%	VT	−4.0%	AK	−3.5%	ME	−3.0%	PA	−2.6%	VT	−2.4%
PA	−4.3%	IN	−2.0%	LA	−3.9%	PA	−4.0%	MD	−4.2%	KS	−4.0%	NH	−3.4%	MD	−2.7%	PA	−2.6%
UT	−4.8%	CT	−3.3%	ND	−4.0%	WI	−4.4%	IA	−4.9%	IA	−4.9%	AK	−3.4%	FL	−3.1%	MA	−3.0%
DC	−5.1%	MN	−4.7%	UT	−4.1%	MN	−5.0%	WI	−5.1%	ND	−4.9%	PA	−4.2%	IN	−4.3%	NV	−3.1%
KS	−5.4%	LA	−4.8%	IN	−4.7%	IA	−6.1%	KS	−5.2%	HI	−5.6%	MN	−4.8%	HI	−4.7%	WY	−3.1%
SD	−5.5%	NE	−5.0%	MN	−5.4%	LA	−6.1%	NE	−7.9%	WI	−5.8%	NE	−4.9%	CA	−4.8%	CA	−3.3%
IN	−5.9%	DC	−5.8%	IA	−6.6%	NE	−6.6%	MS	−8.1%	VT	−6.4%	MA	−5.8%	VT	−5.1%	IN	−4.2%
CA	−6.4%	CA	−6.2%	NE	−7.2%	KS	−6.9%	ND	−8.2%	MD	−6.6%	WI	−6.0%	NH	−5.8%	NH	−5.1%
NJ	−6.8%	KS	−6.6%	RI	−7.4%	ND	−9.1%	IL	−9.8%	IL	−7.6%	MD	−6.6%	MN	−6.2%	CT	−8.2%
LA	−7.9%	ND	−6.9%	KS	−8.3%	CT	−9.5%	CT	−10.5%	NE	−7.7%	IL	−7.0%	WI	−6.4%	WI	−8.2%
NE	−9.2%	UT	−7.3%	CA	−9.5%	IL	−12.7%	MA	−14.2%	MA	−11.0%	CA	−7.1%	IL	−7.4%	ME	−8.3%
MA	−9.7%	NJ	−9.0%	CT	−9.7%	NJ	−13.6%	OH	−14.8%	CT	−11.6%	VT	−7.3%	ME	−7.7%	RI	−8.4%
OH	−10.5%	IA	−9.5%	OH	−11.7%	OH	−14.0%	NJ	−15.2%	CA	−14.1%	CT	−9.4%	CT	−8.2%	MN	−8.5%
IA	−11.7%	OH	−9.7%	NJ	−11.8%	RI	−14.4%	CA	−15.9%	OH	−14.3%	NY	−11.4%	NY	−8.8%	NJ	−8.9%
MI	−11.9%	MI	−11.5%	IL	−14.0%	CA	−15.0%	RI	−16.3%	RI	−14.6%	NJ	−11.9%	NJ	−9.0%	NY	−9.8%
ND	−12.8%	MA	−13.4%	MI	−15.1%	MA	−17.5%	NY	−21.3%	NJ	−14.6%	RI	−13.2%	OH	−12.3%	IL	−10.5%
IL	−13.7%	IL	−14.0%	MA	−17.9%	MI	−19.3%	MI	−23.4%	NY	−17.6%	OH	−13.2%	RI	−12.6%	OR	−12.5%
NY	−18.2%	NY	−17.1%	NY	−21.9%	NY	−23.2%	LA	−54.6%	MI	−28.5%	MI	−29.8%	MI	−27.0%	MI	−21.7%

Governor Corbett took some heat for making the tough decision to reduce education funding by $1 billion in 2012, but when chastising him for it, liberals consistently and conveniently left out the fact that included in that sum were federal stimulus dollars that expired when the Governor's term began—a "free money" burden that will be shouldered several times over by generations to come.

Make no mistake: There is no such thing as free money, only smoke and mirrors. Fortunately, Pennsylvania leadership under Governor Corbett is fiscally responsible and on track to operate efficiently within the parameters of a budget that is built upon real numbers generated by hardworking people, every one of whom deserves to live in a state that is committed to growing and prospering and providing new and better opportunities for its residents. And when a state's citizens do well, the state as a whole does well. It makes no sense to balance a state's budget by unbalancing that state's citizens' budgets. The only way for a state to win is if everyone wins.

The sections of this chapter seek to highlight the conversation *How Money Walks* has sparked over the past year, as well as how our work is consistently removing the chains that stunt growth, making forward progress in this game of inches, toward a goal line of nationwide embrace of pro-growth policies, lower taxes, less government interference, and competition among the states that we have proven will only further strengthen the good of the whole.

New Hampshire—Case in Point

History assures us that there will always be defenders of the status quo, folks for whom advancement of any kind is going to be perceived as a threat and be met with vehement, sometimes irrational resistance. "Everything is fine the way it is," they'll insist with a stomp, so fearful are they of progress that any notion of change—particularly if it involves competition—is quickly dismissed, brushed safely under the rug, and covered with a heavy piece of furniture to ensure it never again sees the light of day.

Thankfully, the whole of humanity is composed of, as country singer Miranda Lambert says in her hit song, "All Kinds of Kinds."[4] Accordingly, history also assures us that there will always be pioneers, inventors, explorers, artists, and adventurers—folks who not only shun the status quo but revel in shaking it up.

And that is why there is and always will be conflict between those who want to keep things tightly controlled and seemingly safe, and those who want to test the limits and try new things, which often involves a fair amount of risk.

Somewhere in between the risk-averse and the risk takers lie the reformers, folks who carefully study traditional ways of doing things, test theories for improvements, and put forth recommendations based on factual findings. Yet despite that difference and the fact that reformers are simply trying to improve something or fix what is broken, we're still talking about changing the status quo, and the risk-averse will still try to impede that forward progress.

Such has been the experience of modern-day tax reformers, folks like us who have studied and analyzed tax codes state by state and have solid data to demonstrate beyond a reasonable doubt that Americans are in fact moving at high rates away from high income tax states and into low and no income tax states. This is not a hypothesis, not an idea, not some abstract conclusion. It is a data-driven fact.

And to those who, in the face of all the evidence we provide in this book, still persist in clinging to their one world statist dogma, we reprint here the song George Shultz sang on the occasion of Milton Friedman's 90th birthday:

A fact without a theory is like a ship without a sail.

Is like a boat without a rudder.

Is like a kite without a tail.

A fact without a theory is as sad as sad can be.

But if there's one thing worse in this universe,

it's a theory . . . without a fact.[5]

Nevertheless, there are those who will try to explain away the facts by conjecturing that people are moving in waves to Florida and Texas only because of the weather rather than the tax climate (see our Chapter 8). Among the nine states that currently have no income tax, some are indeed located in more temperate regions for sure, such as Florida and Texas and maybe even Nevada, but others—such as South Dakota, Washington State, Wyoming, Alaska, and New Hampshire—are not (see Table 5.2).

Over the tax/filing years 1992/1993 through 2009/2010, the zero income tax states have gained an amazing 14.2 percent of their 2009/2010 adjusted gross income from the rest of the nation, while the nine highest income tax rate states have lost 8.8 percent of their 2009/2010 adjusted gross income over the same period. Given that so many other factors are also conceivably important, these types of results are powerful.

Critics of tax reform efforts readily dismiss the success stories enjoyed by zero income tax states. They will try to argue that it's not taxes that motivate people; it is the fact that people have been leaving the Northeast and the Rust Belt in favor of the West and South for decades. The fact that the highest-tax states are in the Northeast is merely an inconvenient coincidence in the minds of the deniers. They will argue that income and population losses are inevitable and should just be accepted as part of these long-standing trends, and they shun efforts seeking answers and corresponding adjustments, giving no credence to fact-based conclusions that government policy does in fact matter.

Another way of viewing tax migration and the nine highest and lowest income tax rate states is to look at how many more or less tax filers move into a state relative to the total number of tax returns that move. In Table 5.3 we list the excess percentage of filers who have moved into a state relative to filers who have moved out of that same state out of the total number of tax returns that move, for each and every state for all the tax/file years 1992/1993 through 2009/2010. These states are ranked from the largest percentage of in-migrants down to the largest percentage of out-migrants. We have highlighted the nine highest income tax

	TABLE 5.2

Nine Zero Income Tax States versus Nine Highest Income Tax Rate States (migration of AGI from 1992/1993 through 2009/2010)

PIT Rate Rank	State	18-Year Cumulative Average AGI-Adjusted Net In-Migrant AGI ($000s)	Total AGI of 2009/2010 In-State Filers* ($000s)	18-Year Cumulative Average AGI-Adjusted Net In-Migrant AGI as a Share of Total AGI of 2009/2010 In-State Filers
1	Alaska	−$2,027,189	$16,271,818	−12.5%
2	Florida	$95,779,995	$345,814,899	27.7%
3	Nevada	$18,552,716	$51,533,333	36.0%
4	South Dakota	$783,020	$16,446,613	4.8%
5	Texas	$25,837,426	$446,452,021	5.8%
6	Washington	$13,178,119	$151,838,026	8.7%
7	Wyoming	$1,807,690	$12,632,694	14.3%
8	New Hampshire	$3,772,345	$33,504,596	11.3%
9	Tennessee	$10,759,648	$109,911,657	9.8%
	Sum ↑	$168,443,771	$1,184,405,657	**14.2%**
	Sum ↓	−$178,963,669	$2,037,877,310	**−8.8%**
42	Kentucky	$1,021,366	$73,841,037	1.4%
43	Ohio	−$20,955,875	$226,560,304	−9.2%
44	Maryland	−$9,205,411	$153,466,481	−6.0%
45	Vermont	$948,783	$13,536,384	7.0%
46	New Jersey	−$24,070,129	$249,694,312	−9.6%
47	Oregon	$7,691,752	$71,955,893	10.7%
48	Hawaii	−$1,019,696	$27,122,966	−3.8%
49	New York	−$78,122,819	$448,409,944	−17.4%
50	California	−$55,251,641	$773,289,989	−7.1%

*In-state filers means nonmigrants plus people filing this year who didn't file last year.
Note: The values in this table differ from the values in Table 2.7 of Chapter 2, because the AGI figures have been adjusted by average AGI.

Source: Internal Revenue Service, Laffer Associates.

TABLE 5.3		

Net In-Returns as a Percentage of Gross Migrating Returns (In-Returns + Out-Returns) from 1992/1993 to 2009/2010: Nine Zero Income Tax States (in dark gray) versus Nine Highest Income Tax Rate States (in light gray)

1	NV	18.3%
2	AZ	16.3%
3	NC	12.5%
4	FL	11.9%
5	GA	11.4%
6	CO	9.7%
7	OR	9.5%
8	SC	9.4%
9	TN	8.9%
10	ID	8.7%
11	TX	7.4%
12	DE	7.3%
13	WA	6.8%
14	AR	5.2%
15	MT	4.0%
16	KY	3.3%
17	VA	3.3%
18	UT	2.9%
19	AL	2.8%
20	NM	2.4%
21	NH	2.3%
22	MO	1.8%
23	OK	0.8%
24	WY	0.1%
25	MS	−0.1%
26	ME	−0.3%
27	WV	−0.7%
28	SD	−1.3%
29	MN	−1.4%
30	MD	−1.4%
31	VT	−1.8%
32	AK	−2.1%
33	IN	−2.4%
34	WI	−3.0%

TABLE 5.3 (Continued)		
35	KS	−4.1%
36	HI	−4.2%
37	DC	−4.6%
38	NE	−5.5%
39	PA	−6.3%
40	IA	−6.8%
41	ND	−7.3%
42	LA	−7.4%
43	MA	−7.8%
44	RI	−8.3%
45	CT	−10.3%
46	CA	−10.5%
47	OH	−10.6%
48	NJ	−10.7%
49	IL	−11.4%
50	MI	−15.2%
51	NY	−20.1%

Source: Internal Revenue Service, Laffer Associates.

rate states (light gray) and the nine zero income tax rate states (dark gray). If this doesn't convince you, we've got a bridge to sell you.

New Hampshire, which doesn't levy a personal income tax or a general sales tax, provides a perfect juxtaposition to the other high-tax states in the Northeast. When studying the impact of state government policy, a quick comparison of New Hampshire with Vermont, a neighboring state of almost identical size, is revealing. While New Hampshire levies no personal income tax, Vermont's top personal income tax rate is 8.95 percent, making it the sixth highest in the nation. Even a modest income of $34,500 is taxed at a marginal rate of 6.8 percent in Vermont. Adding to that state's tax burden, Vermont levies a general sales tax of 6 percent, plus a local sales tax of 1 percent in some jurisdictions.

When considering New Hampshire and Vermont, all things save tax codes are pretty much equal, so these two states provide just about the perfect test case for the impact of government tax policy. The difference between these two states that otherwise share so many commonalities

is that Vermont is ranked 13th in the nation in terms of tax burden, according to the Tax Foundation,[6] while New Hampshire is a low-tax
state, ranked 44th in tax burden. Therefore, the difference in economic
performance between these two states can only be attributed to their
respective state tax policies.

Overwhelmingly, the evidence shows that New Hampshire has
outperformed Vermont, as well as other neighboring states. New
Hampshire outperforms Vermont in oh so many ways, including across
six categories of measure, such as passenger air traffic, as logged by the
Transportation Bureau and the Federal Aviation Administration (FAA);
interstate migration patterns, as reported by Atlas Van Lines; income
growth, sourced from the Bureau of Labor Statistics; population growth,
based on U.S. Census Data; income migration, reported by the IRS; and
the relative growth of New Hampshire's tax base versus Vermont's tax
base. These evidential pieces combine to create a clear picture showing that while New Hampshire's growth is not as impressive as that of
Texas, it stacks up impressively against its Northeast neighbors.

The results we cite here are not new. Back in the 1970s, Dartmouth
professor Colin Campbell carried out an incredibly detailed analysis
of New Hampshire and Vermont and came to the same conclusions.[7]
Do you think Vermonters listened? Not on your life. They're the same
as ever.

The Bureau of Transportation Statistics collects extensive data on
various modes of transportation, the most interesting being passenger air
traffic. Air traffic data reflect long-term commitments by municipalities
to build and maintain airports as well as airlines to provide services to
those airports. As a result, decisions to expand air traffic capacity are not
made lightly and are based on credible, long-term trends in the states
where they are documented.

Looking at data for the past 22 years, New Hampshire stands
out among its peers as a success, having experienced explosive
growth in air passenger traffic. In 1990, all Granite State airports
served roughly 264,000 passengers. That same year, Vermont's airports had 308,000 passengers. By 2012, Vermont's passenger traffic

had grown to 619,000 passengers, a jump of over 100 percent, which looks impressive until Vermont is compared to New Hampshire, which experienced staggering growth of more than 1.2 million passengers, translating into growth that exceeded 360 percent, clearly demonstrating that more people are now living in, traveling to, and doing business in New Hampshire than there were in 1990 (see Figure 5.1). So impressive was New Hampshire's growth that it shamed all of its neighboring states. The Granite State's passenger traffic grew by 360 percent, while during the same time period Maine's traffic grew only 81 percent, Connecticut's grew by 15 percent, Massachusetts's grew by 42 percent, Rhode Island's grew by 72 percent, and New York's grew by 50 percent.

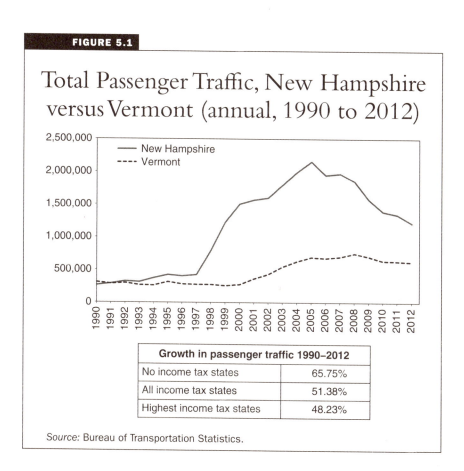

FIGURE 5.1

Total Passenger Traffic, New Hampshire versus Vermont (annual, 1990 to 2012)

Growth in passenger traffic 1990–2012	
No income tax states	65.75%
All income tax states	51.38%
Highest income tax states	48.23%

Source: Bureau of Transportation Statistics.

So we know that low-tax New Hampshire did far, far better than high-tax Vermont, but how did all of the other no income tax states do? Over the period 1990 to 2010, the nine no income tax states saw a combined passenger traffic growth of 66 percent, while the nine states with some of the highest taxes (California, Maine, Maryland, New Jersey, New York, Ohio, Oregon, and Vermont) saw growth of only 48 percent. A stark contrast, indeed.

Another fascinating source of data tracking where people are moving to and from comes from the country's largest moving company, Atlas Van Lines.[8] Every year, Atlas Van Lines tracks the thousands of moves the company does, and calculates a "Traffic Flow Index," based on the percentage of moves into and out of a state. If more than 55 percent of all shipments are going into a given state, that state is classified as a receiving or inbound state. Conversely, if more than 55 percent of all shipments are going out of a given state, that state is classified as an outbound state. If flow into and out of a state is closer to 50/50, that state is classified as balanced. In 2012, Maine, Massachusetts, and Rhode Island fell into the category of balanced, while New York, Vermont, and Connecticut were categorized as outbound states. In all of New England, only New Hampshire was an inbound state.

If the population and income woes of the Northeast are simply due to long-standing migration patterns, as espoused by the skeptics, why is New Hampshire growing through inbound migration? Could it be that a pro-growth state government policy is responsible? To dispel any question about whether New Hampshire's status was a temporary phenomenon, the state has been classified as inbound for the past five years and has never been designated as an outbound state.

Asserting that all population moves of consequence are immutable long-term population migration trends is often an excuse for inaction in the face of failing government policies. It's noteworthy to examine New Hampshire's performance on this measure. We know that the Northeast has been the slowest-growing part of the country over the past decade, with more and more people moving out. Between 2000 and 2010, the Northeast as a whole grew its population by only 3.2 percent, while the South grew by 14.3 percent and the West by 13.8 percent, according to the U.S. Census Bureau.[9] But is the Northeast one big monolith, or are there significant differences among the various states of the Northeast?

Did New Hampshire's pro-growth policies help it to grow faster than its neighbors? You bet they did. Between 2000 and 2010, the Granite State grew its population by 6.5 percent, or more than twice that of the Northeastern region as a whole. Neighboring Vermont grew by only 2.8 percent, while Maine, Massachusetts, and Rhode Island expanded by 4.2 percent, 3.1 percent, and 0.4 percent, respectively (see Figure 5.2). Clearly, there are some larger forces at play here, which are detracting from the growth in the Northeastern region. Yet it is a mistake to conclude that since there are trends working against a state, the government should do nothing to try to alter the situation.

One of the political reasons why the Northeast lags much of the nation—especially the lower Midwest and Southeast—could be the

FIGURE 5.2

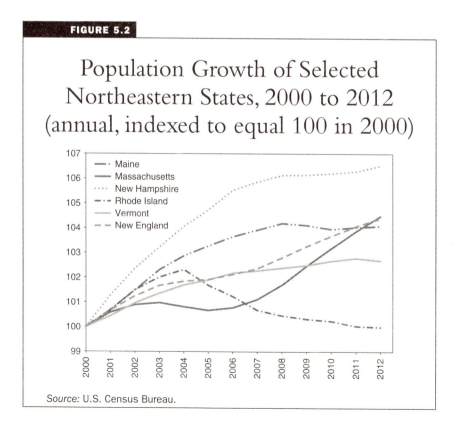

Population Growth of Selected Northeastern States, 2000 to 2012 (annual, indexed to equal 100 in 2000)

Source: U.S. Census Bureau.

TABLE 5.4

Net In-Returns as a Percentage of Gross Returns (In-Returns + Out-Returns) from 1992/1993 to 2009/2010: 23 Right-to-Work States (in gray) versus 27 Forced-Union States + D.C.

#	State	%
1	NV	18.3%
2	AZ	16.3%
3	NC	12.5%
4	FL	11.9%
5	GA	11.4%
6	CO	9.7%
7	OR	9.5%
8	SC	9.4%
9	TN	8.9%
10	ID	8.7%
11	TX	7.4%
12	DE	7.3%
13	WA	6.8%
14	AR	5.2%
15	MT	4.0%
16	KY	3.3%
17	VA	3.3%
18	UT	2.9%
19	AL	2.8%
20	NM	2.4%
21	NH	2.3%
22	MO	1.8%
23	OK	0.8%
24	WY	0.1%
25	MS	−0.1%
26	ME	−0.3%
27	WV	−0.7%
28	SD	−1.3%
29	MN	−1.4%
30	MD	−1.4%
31	VT	−1.8%
32	AK	−2.1%
33	IN	−2.4%
34	WI	−3.0%
35	KS	−4.1%

TABLE 5.4 (Continued)		
36	HI	−4.2%
37	DC	−4.6%
38	NE	−5.5%
39	PA	−6.3%
40	IA	−6.8%
41	ND	−7.3%
42	LA	−7.4%
43	MA	−7.8%
44	RI	−8.3%
45	CT	−10.3%
46	CA	−10.5%
47	OH	−10.6%
48	NJ	−10.7%
49	IL	−11.4%
50	MI	−15.2%
51	NY	−20.1%

Note: Right-to-work status is as of 1/1/2013.
Source: Internal Revenue Service, Laffer Associates.

current right-to work laws. Again using our measures of adjusted gross income and tax filing migration, we list in Table 5.4 the net in-returns as a percentage of gross migrating returns (in-returns plus out-returns) for all states ranked from highest to lowest over the full period 1992/1993 through 2009/2010; the right-to-work states are shaded in gray.

Isn't it astounding how much better the right-to-work states are vis-à-vis the forced-union states? New Hampshire, with all of its other attributes, unfortunately is still a forced-union state. And when you consider only Northeastern states, New York, Connecticut, Rhode Island, and Massachusetts are in the bottom 10 of all states. In fact, there is not one Northeastern state that is a right-to-work state. Of the eight best-performing forced-union states, two are zero income tax states—New Hampshire and Washington.

New Hampshire certainly makes the case that with the right policies a state's performance can improve relative to its neighbors. We see this everywhere in the data. The South has definitely benefited from inbound migration and has done well as a region, but even in the

Southern region of the United States, states with good tax policies have done far better than the region overall. While the Southern region (see Chapter 8) grew by 14.3 percent from 2000 to 2010, zero income tax, pro-growth Texas and Florida grew by 20.6 percent and 17.6 percent, respectively, over the same period. A similar story holds true in the West, which as a region grew a remarkable 13.8 percent from 2000 to 2010. Yet within the Western region, high-tax states such as California grew more slowly (only 10 percent), whereas states with friendlier tax policies expanded much faster, as evidenced by Nevada's 35 percent growth over the same period. Without a doubt, state tax policies matter for relative performance and shouldn't be dismissed as national or regional trends.

We know that New Hampshire has been an outstanding state in terms of air traffic growth and population growth in inbound migration, but what about income growth, especially the growth in taxable income? Data from the IRS Division of Statistics tells the story of which states and counties gained and lost adjusted gross income (AGI). The IRS tracks the migration of people and income based on annual tax return filings and makes these data available for free on its website. These important data provide a clear image of which states gained and which states lost income and taxpayers. States that are gaining taxpayers and income have an easier time balancing their budgets and delivering services, whereas states with shrinking tax bases face cutbacks.

Throughout this book, we rely heavily on the Tax Foundation's measure of total tax burden. The Tax Foundation has done a very careful job in measuring just which of all the taxes collected by a state actually burden the taxpayers of that state. Table 5.5 combines the Tax Foundation's highest and lowest tax burden states and the IRS's adjusted gross income data by state.

While two of the lowest tax burden states, Alaska and Louisiana, have been net losers of total adjusted gross income over the 18-year period 1992/1993 through 2009/2010, and one high tax burden state, Maine, was a net gainer, the pattern is clear. Adjusted gross income is migrating from the high tax burden states and into the low tax burden states.

According to the data from the IRS, New Hampshire had the largest gain of AGI due to migration of all the states in New England (see Table 2.7

TABLE 5.5

Nine Lowest Overall Tax Burden States versus Nine Highest Overall Tax Burden States

Tax Burden Rank	State	18-Year Cumulative Average AGI-Adjusted Net In-Migrant AGI ($000s)	Total AGI of 2009/2010 In-State Filers* ($000s)	18-Year Cumulative Average AGI-Adjusted Net In-Migrant AGI as a Share of Total AGI of 2009/2010 In-State Filers
1	Alaska	−$2,027,189	$16,271,818	−12.5%
2	South Dakota	$783,020	$16,446,613	4.8%
3	Tennessee	$10,759,648	$109,911,657	9.8%
4	Louisiana	−$7,774,866	$77,585,427	−10.0%
5	Wyoming	$1,807,690	$12,632,694	14.3%
6	Texas	$25,837,426	$446,452,021	5.8%
7	New Hampshire	$3,772,345	$33,504,596	11.3%
8	Alabama	$2,685,885	$81,059,302	3.3%
9	Nevada	$18,552,716	$51,533,333	36.0%
	Sum ↑	$54,396,676	$845,397,461	**6.4%**
	Sum ↓	−$186,533,444	$2,056,241,745	**−9.1%**
42	Maine	$1,649,840	$25,768,148	6.4%
43	Massachusetts	−$13,529,722	$179,162,979	−7.6%
44	Minnesota	−$4,335,735	$127,833,471	−3.4%
45	Rhode Island	−$2,091,967	$23,473,916	−8.9%
46	Wisconsin	−$2,204,133	$124,870,434	−1.8%
47	California	−$55,251,641	$773,289,989	−7.1%
48	Connecticut	−$8,577,137	$103,738,552	−8.3%
49	New Jersey	−$24,070,129	$249,694,312	−9.6%
50	New York	−$78,122,819	$448,409,944	−17.4%

*In-state filers means nonmigrants plus people filing this year who didn't file last year.
Note: The values in this table differ from the values in Table 2.7 of Chapter 2, because the AGI figures have been adjusted by average-AGI.

Source: Internal Revenue Service, Laffer Associates.

in Chapter 2). Between tax/file years 1992/1993 and 2009/2010, the Granite State gained $3.2 billion in total AGI, or approximately half a million dollars of AGI per day. By comparison, its neighbors Vermont and Maine gained only $0.77 billion and $1.46 billion, respectively, while Rhode Island, Connecticut, and Massachusetts actually lost $1.75 billion, $7.44 billion, and $11.81 billion, respectively.

Internal Revenue Service migration data closely mirror population growth data: New Hampshire is growing its population and tax base, despite being in a region buffeted by negative demographic trends. New Hampshire's low-tax policies and small government explain the state's superior performance vis-à-vis its neighbors in the region (see Table 5.6). If only it could get the right-to-work issue correct, there's no telling what New Hampshire could do.

While we know that New Hampshire has gained AGI due to migration from other states, the question arises: What about the income growth of people who were already living in the Granite State? Did New Hampshire's tax base grow faster or slower than its neighbors? Using IRS data on total state AGI, we can easily determine that New Hampshire's tax base growth has been the fastest among all New England states, despite not having some of the advantages that other states have. For example, Connecticut's proximity to New York City makes that state a home to many financial service professionals who have seen their incomes grow substantially over the past two decades. Similarly, Massachusetts benefits from having Boston, a city that is home to many large companies and some of the world's most famous universities, yet it

TABLE 5.6

New England: Cumulative AGI Change Due to Migration, 1992/1993 through 2009/2010 (from Table 2.7 in Chapter 2)

New Hampshire	$3.21 billion
Maine	$1.46 billion
Vermont	$0.77 billion
Rhode Island	($1.75 billion)
Connecticut	($7.44 billion)
Massachusetts	($11.81 billion)

too lagged behind New Hampshire's growth in terms of tax base. Could it be coincidence that Connecticut, which is home to the highest taxes in New England—and third-highest in the nation according to the Tax Foundation—experienced the slowest growth in its tax base?[10] Is it a surprise that people and income move to where they are welcomed? In the case of New England, that place is clearly New Hampshire.

Some 40-plus years ago, two-thirds of the New England states were zero income tax states, and boy, were things different back then. New Hampshire was joined by Rhode Island, Maine, and Connecticut as zero income tax states. In fact, just before West Virginia adopted its income tax in 1961, there were 19 states in the United States with no income tax and 31 with an income tax. One state, Alaska, eliminated its income tax since 1960 while 11 states adopted an income tax (see Chapter 1 for a more in-depth analysis of the 11 states to adopt the income tax in the past 50-plus years).

In Table 5.7 we have listed the net in-returns as a percentage of gross migrating returns (in-returns plus out-returns) for all 50 states ranked from highest to lowest over the full tax period for which we have data, 1992/1993 through 2009/2010, and have shaded in gray the performances of the 11 states that have introduced the income tax.

Each and every one of the 11 states that introduced the income tax since 1960 is a net loser of tax returns and in the bottom half of all states. New Hampshire, in contrast, is a net gainer of tax returns and is in the top half of all states. The lesson is pretty basic—if you don't currently have an income tax, do not adopt one.

State policies can mean the difference between a weakening state and a growing, vibrant state that is thriving in the global economy. Yet, as New Hampshire's example demonstrates, state tax policy can have a huge impact in offsetting otherwise negative trends. Despite being located in a section of the country stymied by slow growth, New Hampshire has been able to buck the trend and emerge a winner, attracting people and income. Population growth, income migration, and air traffic growth are just a sampling of the data sets that show how exceptional New Hampshire's performance has been.

TABLE 5.7		
Net In-Returns as a Percentage of Gross Returns (In-Returns + Out-Returns) from 1992/1993 to 2009/2010: 11 States That Introduced the Income Tax over the Past 50-Plus Years		
1	NV	18.3%
2	AZ	16.3%
3	NC	12.5%
4	FL	11.9%
5	GA	11.4%
6	CO	9.7%
7	OR	9.5%
8	SC	9.4%
9	TN	8.9%
10	ID	8.7%
11	TX	7.4%
12	DE	7.3%
13	WA	6.8%
14	AR	5.2%
15	MT	4.0%
16	KY	3.3%
17	VA	3.3%
18	UT	2.9%
19	AL	2.8%
20	NM	2.4%
21	NH	2.3%
22	MO	1.8%
23	OK	0.8%
24	WY	0.1%
25	MS	−0.1%
26	ME	−0.3%
27	WV	−0.7%
28	SD	−1.3%
29	MN	−1.4%
30	MD	−1.4%
31	VT	−1.8%
32	AK	−2.1%
33	IN	−2.4%
34	WI	−3.0%
35	KS	−4.1%

TABLE 5.7 (Continued)		
36	HI	−4.2%
37	DC	−4.6%
38	NE	−5.5%
39	PA	−6.3%
40	IA	−6.8%
41	ND	−7.3%
42	LA	−7.4%
43	MA	−7.8%
44	RI	−8.3%
45	CT	−10.3%
46	CA	−10.5%
47	OH	−10.6%
48	NJ	−10.7%
49	IL	−11.4%
50	MI	−15.2%
51	NY	−20.1%

Source: Internal Revenue Service, Laffer Associates.

Next time someone says that state policy doesn't matter and that wealth migration is simply and solely the result of long-established trends, challenge that person to explain New Hampshire's success.

Top Traders

In this book we focus a lot on the successes of low-tax states, especially the tremendous gains made by Texas and Florida. On the other side of the coin are a lot of stories of failures in high-tax states like California, New York, and Illinois (see Table 2.7 in Chapter 2). While these large states account for the bulk of gains and losses in AGI migration, it is worthwhile to look at the smaller states that round out the picture as well, because these smaller states also demonstrate the fundamental truth that tax policies matter for a state's performance. If it's good economics, it's scalable.

In order to look at income migration but eliminate the factor of state size, we developed a metric that measures the average adjusted gross income of an out-migrant versus the average adjusted gross income of an in-migrant. For each state, we looked at the in-migration and out-migration with each and every other state (a total of 2,550 such pairs). Using data from the IRS Division of Statistics on the income migration between 1992/1993 and 2009/2010, we calculated the average income of those moving from State A to State B and compared it to the average adjusted gross income of people moving from State B to State A. We then calculated the average adjusted gross income of an in-migrant and out-migrant for each state. Finally, we looked at which states had the biggest differences between the average adjusted gross incomes of in-migrants and out-migrants. This metric eliminates the absolute size of the state from consideration and allows us to see which states are doing well—or poorly—even if they are small. States that ranked highly on this metric are on average attracting wealthier, higher-earning citizens from other states, whereas those at the bottom of the ranking are losing their higher-net-worth, higher-earning residents to other states.

In Table 5.8, we list each and every state by its average adjusted gross income of in-migrants relative to out-migrants for the period

TABLE 5.8		
Aggregate of All Returns Filed in the 18 Years 1992/1993 to 2009/2010		
	AGI per Return		
State	**In-AGI per Return ($)**	**Out-AGI per Return ($)**	**Premium of In-AGI per Return over Out-AGI per Return**
FL	$50,068	$37,570	33.3%
MT	$36,327	$29,515	23.1%
WY	$41,047	$33,681	21.9%
SC	$42,681	$35,547	20.1%
VT	$41,572	$35,627	16.7%
ME	$41,624	$35,901	15.9%
NV	$42,565	$36,966	15.1%
NH	$49,695	$43,550	14.1%
SD	$36,568	$32,298	13.2%
ID	$37,368	$33,008	13.2%
AZ	$42,656	$38,232	11.6%
NC	$41,451	$38,551	7.5%
WA	$42,653	$40,141	6.3%

TABLE 5.8 (Continued)		
AR	$34,198	$32,245	6.1%
CO	$43,207	$41,403	4.4%
MS	$32,635	$31,375	4.0%
CT	$65,572	$63,084	3.9%
UT	$39,038	$37,765	3.4%
HI	$35,892	$34,806	3.1%
NM	$35,873	$34,821	3.0%
AL	$37,367	$36,285	3.0%
OR	$37,963	$36,942	2.8%
TN	$38,641	$37,656	2.6%
TX	$43,256	$42,426	2.0%
PA	$46,766	$45,971	1.7%
WV	$33,181	$33,002	0.5%
RI	$43,987	$44,048	−0.1%
WI	$41,797	$42,160	−0.9%
NJ	$56,734	$58,156	−2.4%
CA	$43,644	$45,146	−3.3%
KY	$35,264	$36,478	−3.3%
MI	$41,897	$43,539	−3.8%
IA	$36,088	$37,506	−3.8%
MA	$48,630	$50,657	−4.0%
KS	$38,655	$40,269	−4.0%
VA	$44,997	$47,193	−4.7%
IN	$38,431	$40,387	−4.8%
GA	$40,133	$42,229	−5.0%
DE	$45,974	$48,485	−5.2%
OK	$32,917	$34,841	−5.5%
LA	$33,483	$35,804	−6.5%
NE	$35,489	$38,053	−6.7%
MO	$38,034	$40,989	−7.2%
ND	$29,868	$32,279	−7.5%
OH	$41,170	$44,540	−7.6%
MN	$41,865	$45,865	−8.7%
MD	$44,329	$48,950	−9.4%
IL	$44,408	$49,296	−9.9%
DC	$43,410	$48,396	−10.3%
NY	$44,784	$50,494	−11.3%
AK	$33,159	$37,895	−12.5%

Source: Internal Revenue Service, Laffer Associates.

1992/1993 through 2009/2010. We also list the average AGI for both in-migrants and out-migrants and for all state tax filers.

The results are pretty stark, with states such as New Hampshire, Nevada, and Wyoming near the top of the list. States near the top generally have no state income tax and a very low overall tax burden according to the Tax Foundation.[11] Similarly, near the bottom of our ranking we find Connecticut, Maryland, and New Jersey, each of which has high tax burdens. This is just one more piece of evidence that shows how much state tax policy matters to the behavior of individuals and income migration between states. New Hampshire, Nevada, and Wyoming were ranked 44th, 42nd, and 46th, respectively, in tax burden by the Tax Foundation for 2010 (the most recent available data), which means that their residents paid some of the lowest taxes of any state. On the flip side, Connecticut, Maryland, and New Jersey ranked third, second, and 12th in tax burdens, respectively, putting them near the top of the highest-taxed states in the United States. It is little wonder then that high-income individuals are more likely than not to leave such tax-burdensome locations and migrate to more friendly jurisdictions? Let's look at each state in more detail.

New Hampshire may be a small state in a slow-growing part of the country, yet it consistently outperforms its neighbors. What distinguishes the Granite State from the rest of New England is its remarkably low tax burden and small-government policies. New Hampshire is ranked 44th among all states in tax burden, and the state levies no personal earned income and no general sales tax. As a result, the state has consistently been able to attract residents and has grown its population at twice the rate of the Northeastern region overall. Throughout the 18-year period of 1992/1993 to 2009/2010, the average adjusted gross income of a person moving into New Hampshire was $49,695, compared to $43,550 for the average person leaving the state, a huge difference of more than $6,000. New Hampshire's low-tax status helps explain this trend.

Nevada has seen explosive growth in its population and gross state product over the past 20 years and has been a magnet for wealthy individuals looking to escape from higher-taxed locations, especially

California. Over the past 18 years (1992/1993 to 2009/2010), the average adjusted gross income for a person moving into Nevada was $42,565, which compares favorably with $36,966 for someone going the other way—again a huge difference of nearly $6,000. Nevada's no income or corporate tax and its low state tax burden overall—42nd in the nation—help explain this phenomenon. Nevada provides the perfect companion to New Hampshire—both states enjoyed gains from trading taxpayers with other states; that's to say that on average they received higher-income residents than those leaving the state. Contrary to New Hampshire, Nevada is in the fastest-growing part of the United States, yet just like New Hampshire, Nevada handily beat the region by expanding its population at more than double the Western region's rate.

Rounding out our analysis of the top winners is the state of Wyoming, the smallest state in the United States as measured by population, yet one that is growing rapidly. Wyoming has no personal income tax and ranks 46th in total tax burden, according to the Tax Foundation. Throughout the 18-year period of 1992/1993 to 2009/2010, the average adjusted gross income of a person moving into Wyoming was $41,047 while a person moving out earned on average only $33,681—a staggering difference of well over $7,000 (Table 2.7 in Chapter 2). The state's very low tax burden is clearly attracting wealthy and higher-earning individuals from across the country. If you don't think Wyoming but instead think Jackson Hole, it all becomes clear. This substantial growth comes despite having a harsh climate, which is among the most extreme in the United States, with hot summers and bitterly cold winters. Despite being the smallest state in the United States in population, Wyoming gained over $1.5 billion AGI due to migration—the state's inbound and outbound migrant differential helps explain why.

For every winner there must be a loser, and this brings us to the first of poorly performing states we seek to highlight: Connecticut. The Nutmeg State is among the highest tax burden states in the United States, with a third-place ranking from the Tax Foundation. Not only is Connecticut one of the highest tax burden states, but it's also one of the highest personal income tax rate states, and it is also one of the 11 states that introduced the income tax in the past 50-plus years. And did we mention it's a forced-union state as well? It is. Over the past 18 years (1992/1993 to 2009/2010) Connecticut has lost over $7.4 billion in AGI (Table E3 in Chapter 2). Not only is Connecticut losing its wealthy citizens, but it is penalizing those who stay behind with heavy taxes, making it increasingly difficult for them to justify staying. Even someone with a taxable income of only $10,000 pays a marginal state income tax rate of 5 percent, while the state applies a rate of 6.7 percent to top earners. Combined with high property and sales taxes, it's no wonder those who can leave *are* leaving.

New Jersey makes the biggest loser list as well, with an average outbound migrant adjusted gross income (Table E3 in Chapter 2) of $58,156 versus $56,734 for inbound migrant adjusted gross income during the 18-year period of 1992/1993 to 2009/2010. This loss differential for each taxpayer traded with another state helps explain why New Jersey lost a cumulative $21 billion in AGI between 1992/1993 and 2009/2010. The Garden State has many natural wonders, but ranks second in the nation in tax burden according to the Tax Foundation, outpaced only by its neighbor New York. New Jersey is also a forced-union state and has adopted both an income tax and a sales tax since 1965. Neither the proximity to New York City, a highly skilled workforce, nor the above-average educational achievements by pupils in New Jersey's public schools have been able to keep people and wealth from leaving the Garden State. New Jersey has one of the highest property taxes in the country, not to mention a top state income tax rate of nearly 9 percent (8.97 percent, to be exact). State sales taxes can also easily add up to over 10 percent when you include local taxes. No wonder people in New Jersey ask, "Which exit?"

The recent trade-up in governors from Jon Corzine to Chris Christie is a major ray of hope for New Jersey. Not only did Christie beat Corzine a little over four years ago, but Christie won reelection by a landslide in 2013, showing that maybe, just maybe, the Garden State's residents are ready to accept change.

Maryland, whose Governor O'Malley is one of the highest-ranking tax increasers in the country, is another small-population state that is bleeding wealth to friendlier places. Overall, Maryland lost $7.8 billion in AGI from 1992/1993 to 2009/2010, and consistently loses wealthy individuals to other states. Maryland's average outbound migrant over the 18-year period studied had an average adjusted gross income of $48,950, while the average inbound migrant earned just $44,329, which translates into a crippling loss differential of over $4,600. One factor that helps explain this is the state's high tax burden, ranked 12th in the nation according to the Tax Foundation. While the state's top income tax rate is "only" 5.75 percent, even someone making as little as $3,000 per year is hit with an income tax rate of 4.75 percent. This high rate of taxation of even the working poor helps explain why people are seeking refuge in lower-taxed states.

State tax policy matters, whether your state is big or small. Texas and California (see Chapter 7) may get more attention due to their sheer size and volume of residents and respective wealth moving in and out, but every state government can make a difference by adopting a pro-growth tax policy. Our research shows that even states with small populations can benefit enormously with the right policies and can significantly outperform their regions. While there are always many factors that determine migration and the well-being of a state, having a low tax burden and no state income tax greatly improves the performance of a state's economy, no matter whether it is big or small.

Real-Time Mobility Index

Americans are more mobile than ever, and as demonstrated throughout the past two decades, not at all averse to moving away from states with oppressive income tax climates and into pro-growth states that offer more attractive economic environments that are beneficial to both businesses and individuals alike.

Aiding in the study of these migration trends are different types of publicly available data sets.

Among them, the U.S. Census Bureau's annual surveys track Americans who moved between the states; the Internal Revenue Service tracks taxpayer movement between any two counties or states, as the case may be; and trucking companies, such as United Van Lines, produce annual studies on Americans' residential mobility.

While all of these resources offer essential rearview value, they all suffer from the same weakness: a lack of timeliness. The Census Bureau generally takes three to five years to release its data, while the IRS is just now planning to release tax migration data from 2010–2011, and United Van Lines' reports are big picture, providing very little detail.

As the pace of life is moving faster than ever, there has arisen an immediate need for an up-to-the-minute migration and mobility tool to guide day-to-day decision making so that adjustments can be made in accordance with what's happening today, not just what we know happened last year, or over the past 10 years. To that end, and based on the assumption that mobility in today's world is a commodity, we developed the Real-Time Mobility Index.

In our quest to bring clarity and definition to the picture roughsketched by traditional means, we discovered that analyzing prices quoted by U-Haul on one-way moves between any two cities exposes hidden patterns of American mobility, and that by expanding out that pricing—drilling down to price quotes at the local level—we can reverse-engineer the demand for migration services between various American cities. Thus, we are able to see which cities are enjoying influx migration and which are suffering excessive outbound migration.

For example, if U-Haul experiences a surge in truck rentals originating in New York City and going to Dallas, the price of moving from NYC to Dallas will rise. In contrast, if U-Haul does not book at least as many truck rentals going the other way, the price of moving from Dallas to NYC will decline relative to the inverse price.

The driving determinant behind one-way U-Haul pricing is the simple microeconomics principle of supply and demand. Whenever a person moves from Location A to Location B, the U-Haul truck is deposited at Location B. If traffic moving between the two locations is heavily skewed toward one destination, U-Haul trucks begin to pile up at the more popular location, creating a surplus, while at the same time creating a greater demand for trucks at the city of origin along with the higher prices that naturally accompany scarcity of supply.

Eventually, there may be such a scarcity of trucks at the less desirable location that U-Haul employees may have to drive empty surplus trucks to the depopulating city in order to fulfill demand, a cost passed on to the consumer that only further increases already high prices.

Recognizing the wealth of insight U-Haul pricing reveals, we analyzed more than 200 cities and the associated costs of moving between any two of them, which translates into more than 40,000 city-pairs examined. By comparing the average price of leaving a city versus the average price of arriving at a city, we can derive the relative levels of demand for such services. If droves of people are flocking to a given city, the cost of arriving at that city is high, proving that mobility is just like any other good or service—if demand is high, prices rise accordingly.

By analyzing the relative prices of over 40,000 city-pairs each day, we are able to derive a real-time migration index value for each city and see migration trends as they emerge. By dividing the average in-migration price by the average out-migration price, we derived an index value for each city. An index value of 1 means the price of in-migration and out-migration are the same. Anything above 1 means the price of in-migration is higher than out-migration, while a value below 1 indicates that out-migration is more expensive. As of September 28, 2013, the top 20 inbound cities in the country, according to our Real-Time Mobility Index, were:

Rank ↓	Index Value	City, State
1	1.8018	San Antonio, TX
2	1.7499	Houston, TX
3	1.7393	Pasadena, TX
4	1.7216	Laredo, TX
5	1.7150	Corpus Christi, TX
6	1.7078	Brownsville, TX
7	1.6240	Boise, ID
8	1.5827	Austin, TX

(continued)

Rank ↓	Index Value	City, State
9	1.5608	Tallahassee, FL
10	1.5514	Pocatello, ID
11	1.5498	Mobile, AL
12	1.5265	Fort Worth, TX
13	1.5147	Dallas, TX
14	1.5104	Portland, OR
15	1.5094	Plano, TX
16	1.5076	Garland, TX
17	1.5070	St. Petersburg, FL
18	1.5064	Irving, TX
19	1.5058	Birmingham, AL
20	1.5047	Vancouver, WA

Widely heralded as the most business-friendly state in the Union, it is little surprise that no income tax Texas dominates the list with 12 of the top 20 cities for inbound migration. San Antonio, the top city in our ranking, had an index value of 1.8, which means that on average, it costs 1.8 times as much to move to that city than it does to leave it. On the other side of the coin, the top 20 outbound migration cities in the country were:

Rank ↓	Index Value	City, State
1	0.5565	Yonkers, NY
2	0.5583	Jersey City, NJ
3	0.5656	New York, NY
4	0.5700	Newark, NJ
5	0.5792	Philadelphia, PA
6	0.5963	Springfield, IL
7	0.5970	Scranton, PA
8	0.6061	Bridgeport, CT
9	0.6082	Wilmington, DE
10	0.6134	St. Louis, MO
11	0.6213	Washington, DC
12	0.6294	Baltimore, MD
13	0.6400	Pittsburgh, PA
14	0.6494	Harrisburg, PA
15	0.6721	Los Angeles, CA
16	0.6726	Altoona, PA
17	0.6745	Santa Clarita, CA

Rank ↓	Index Value	City, State
18	0.6750	Lancaster, CA
19	0.6755	Bakersfield, CA
20	0.6765	Rancho Cucamonga, CA

FIGURE 5.3

Real-Time Mobility Index

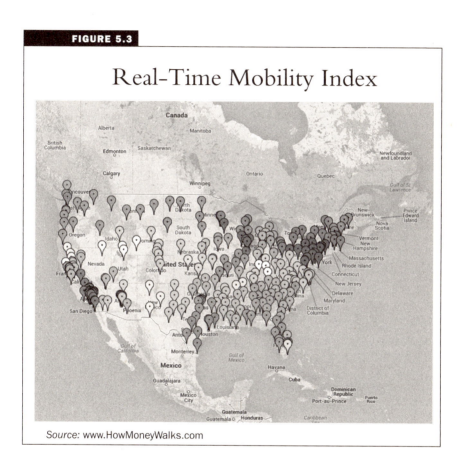

Source: www.HowMoneyWalks.com

Here, the list is more diverse in terms of states, but dominated by high-tax locations like New York, New Jersey, Pennsylvania, and California.

Figure 5.3 presents a compelling visual making the stark case that nationally there is a strong trend of outbound migration away from high-tax states and toward low- and no-tax states. The cluster of pins in the southeast and northwest indicate high inbound migration, while the groupings in the northeast and southwest indicate outbound migration. Pins in states like Utah and New Mexico indicate neutral (index value of approximately 1).

CHAPTER 6

Why Growth Rates Differ

An Econometric Analysis of the Data

The scientific method is a back-and-forth between experiment and theory predicated on the falsifying authority of nature. It allows scientists to make remarkably good predictions about behaviors in new circumstances.

—Philip Ball, *Curiosity*

"The road to serfdom and economic decline is still paved with oppressive taxation, and until that condition is repaired wealth will still hide or melt away."[1]

The purpose of this chapter is simply to provide a different way to view and analyze state performance data in the context of state and local policy actions. As such, this econometric analysis of the 50 states over the past decade is one part of an overall effort to figure out what does and what does not work.

In this chapter, we analyze population growth and gross state product (GSP) growth data as they relate to a series of policy variables such as tax rates, tax burdens, right-to-work laws, and so on.

In our quest to be as thorough as we can be, in this chapter we rely on econometric analysis of the complete time-series cross-sectional data for all 50 states. Our purpose is not so much to develop a comprehensive model of the states as it is to develop as comprehensive an analysis of state economic policies as we can as a guide for current and future state government officials. We can also recognize that as careful as an econometrician can be, mismeasurement of variables, nonlinearity, missing variables, multicollinearity, misspecification of equations, simultaneity bias, and shifts in economic parameters are omnipresent and can bias inferences as to the interpretation of policy results. We can also understand that as useful as least squares regression estimates are for estimating probability distributions, those estimates of probability distributions also presume normal (Gaussian) distributions, which may be a rarity in nature. Therefore, interpretation of the results is far from clear.

Where these econometric analyses are really worth their weight in gold is in conjunction with all of our other tests. Each test and analysis of data has its merits and shortcomings on a stand-alone basis. However, when all of these different ways of comparing and contrasting are put together, the shortcomings can be excised, leaving a massively powerful compilation of data analysis procedures. All together, our data analysis removes almost all doubt as to the effect state and local government policies have on the performance of individual states. It is in this broader context that our econometric analysis of the time-series cross-sectional data should be valued. And without giving away too many secrets of the coming pages, this analysis of the time-series cross-sectional data puts the final nail in the coffin of those who argue that incentives in general, and tax rates, right-to-work, and other supply-side variables, specifically don't matter. They do!

Fortunately for us, we can focus almost exclusively on quantities, not prices. With prices, distributions of the observations may well be of a stable Paretian nature, with a characteristic exponent between one and two, but are more likely to be in the Cauchy range (i.e., characteristic exponent closer to one[2]), rather than in a normal (Gaussian) range where the characteristic exponent more nearly approximates two. For significance tests to be meaningful, the distributions of the observations and the error terms are assumed to be normal. Additionally, the error terms are also assumed to be independent of one another and evenly distributed (homoscedastic) with a fixed degree of dispersion around the mean. If these assumptions of normality are violated, the significance tests lose value (size and power problems).

Moreover, as econometricians, probability distributions presume single one-off tests, not multiple tests with lots and lots of variables, often referred to as data mining. With a simple test, a probability of five in one hundred (a two-tailed t-test of about two standard deviations) that the coefficient is significantly different from zero is a strong statement. However, when 1,000 variables are tested on the same set of observations and those variables are statistically independent from each other, we would randomly expect 50 of these variables to be significantly different from zero at the 5 percent level of significance by chance: hardly a powerful statement. We, and other econometricians, have over the years tested every conceivable variable and in all sorts of different forms. As a result, a new set of correlations, such as the ones we provide, is hardly an appropriate hypothesis test. Beware of any claims of significance and what measures of significance actually mean: *caveat emptor*.

But what we are able to show within the very tight constraints placed upon us by single-equation least squares analysis is whether one variable is correlated with another, just how highly correlated these variables are, and the direction of the correlation. Given the specific characteristics of multiple regressions in a least squares context, we are able to objectively allocate different components of multicollinearity among several variables to the specific variables in question. Given our vision of how state economic policies operate, we have formed a whole set of expectations independent of these specific data sets. For example, it is our expectation that an increase in, say, the tax burden placed on a state will result in slower population growth and slower gross state product growth. Thus, we would expect the coefficient relating tax burden

(TBUR) to population growth (PG) for the time-series cross-sectional analysis for all 50 states over the 10-year time period of 2002–2012 to be both negative and of high correlation value (often referred to as statistically significant). We would also expect the relationship to be reasonable in its dimensions and economically significant as well. If, for example, a one penny increase in the tax burden implied a 10 percent reduction in the state's decadal population growth, we would find such a result unbelievable and we would therefore reject the test itself rather than accept the finding.

Although a common practice suggests that the independent variables should, ideally, be expressed in similar terms to the dependent variable,[3] it is not necessary for variables that change very little over time, such as the tax burden, to follow this practice.

As econometricians, we must also be aware of the presence of heteroscedasticity, or nonconstant variance, in our error terms. In the basic least squares methodology, homoscedasticity, or constant variance, is assumed even though it is rarely valid in practice. For instance, one should not expect the standard deviation to be the same (or constant) for an individual with a predicted income of $100,000 versus an individual with a predicted income of $10,000. With income data, we may expect that the standard deviation is roughly proportional, rather than invariant to income (i.e., higher income levels have higher standard deviations). Although heteroscedasticity in itself will not bias our coefficient estimates, it will bias the standard errors, and as a result, bias the inference drawn from significance tests. Therefore, in our effort to be as econometrically sound as possible, we have asymptotically corrected our least squares analysis for heteroscedasticity using the widely accepted Newey-West standard errors, which also corrects for serial correlation (however, that is less relevant to our data).

As a final point of warning for the reader who yearns to find importance for econometric results, we highlight the Securities and Exchange Commission's requirement for all investment reports of returns: "Past performance is no guarantee of future performance." That statement is about as good as it gets.

List of Variables

With all of these warnings having been written so the reader is well aware of the shortcomings of these econometric tests, let's get on with the measures. Listed here are the variables we are going to examine and their precise definitions.

GSP: *Gross state product,* 2002–2012 growth rate. The growth rate here is not in percentage terms, but instead is the 10-year growth in gross state product from 2002 to 2012, or gross state product in 2012 divided by gross state product in 2002 minus one. For example, Michigan, which was the slowest-growing state, is 0.138, or North Dakota, which was the fastest-growing state, is 1.251. Michigan's growth rate is 0.138, which is equivalent to 13.8 percent, and North Dakota's growth rate is 1.251, or 125.1 percent. Data are from the Bureau of Economic Analysis.

GSPL1: *Gross state product growth lagged one decade,* 1992–2002. For example, Hawaii was the slowest-growing state last decade and is 0.272, or Nevada, which was the fastest-growing state last decade, is 1.326. This is the same variable as GSP, only for 1992–2002. For example, 0.272 is equivalent to a 27.2 percent 10-year growth in gross state product from 1992 to 2002, or gross state product in 2002 divided by gross state product in 1992 minus one. Data are from the Bureau of Economic Analysis.

PG: *Population growth,* 2002–2012 growth rate. Again, the growth rate here is not in percentage terms. For example, Rhode Island = −0.015 or Nevada = 0.269. Here, −0.015 is equivalent to a −1.5 percent 10-year growth in population from 2002 to 2012, or population in 2012 divided by population in 2002 minus one. Data are from the Bureau of Economic Analysis.

PGL1: *Population growth lagged one decade,* 1992–2002 growth rate. For example, West Virginia = −0.001 or Nevada = 0.609. This is the same variable as PG, only for 1992–2002. Here, −0.001 is equivalent to a −0.1 percent 10-year growth in population from 1992 to 2002, or population in 2002 divided by population in 1992 minus one. Data are from the Bureau of Economic Analysis.

TBUR: *Tax burden*, 2010. For example, Alaska = 0.07 or New York = 0.128. Here, 0.07 is equivalent to a 7.0 percent tax burden, which is the percentage of income that taxpayers pay in 2010 in a select group of state and local taxes.[4] Data are from the Tax Foundation.

ALEC: *ALEC-Laffer state competitiveness ranking*, 2013. This is an average of the 15 factors found in the ALEC-Laffer rankings. For example, Utah = 15.1 or Vermont = 35.9. The lower the average of the 15 factors, the better the state's economic outlook. Data are from Laffer Associates and the annual American Legislative Exchange Council 2013 publication *Rich States, Poor States*.

RTW: *Right-to-work*, 1/1/2012. This variable assesses whether a state requires union membership for its employees or whether it is a right-to-work state, as of January 1, 2012 (i.e., it does not include Indiana and Michigan, as their RTW laws were not in place as of 1/1/2012). If the state is a right-to-work state, then RTW is equal to 1, and if the state is not a right-to-work state, then RTW is equal to 0. For example, Colorado = 0 or Nevada = 1. Data are from the National Right to Work Legal Defense Foundation.

OILB: *Production of oil barrels per capita*, 2012. For example, Idaho = 0 or North Dakota = 34.067. OILB is equivalent to the 2012 annual state production of crude oil (measured by thousand barrels per day by the Energy Information Administration) divided by the 2012 state population from the Bureau of Economic Analysis.

PIT: *Top personal income tax rate*, 2013. For example, Nevada = 0 or California = 0.133. Here, 0 is equivalent to a 0.0 percent top personal income tax rate for 2013, which includes local income taxes in the state's largest city and the impact of federal deductibility, if allowed. Data are from Laffer Associates and the annual American Legislative Exchange Council publication *Rich States, Poor States*.

PITP: *Personal income tax progressivity*, 2013. For example, Alabama = −0.002 or California = 0.0374. Here, 0.0374 is equivalent to a 3.74 percent personal income tax progressivity, which is measured as the change in the average tax liability per $100 between income levels of $50,000 and $150,000. Data are from Laffer Associates and the annual American Legislative Exchange Council publication *Rich States, Poor States*.

CIT: *Top corporate income tax rate*, 2013. For example, Nevada = 0 or New York = 0.172. Here, 0 is equivalent to a 0.0 percent top corporate income tax rate for 2013, which includes local taxes and the effect of federal deductibility, if allowed. Data are from Laffer Associates and the annual American Legislative Exchange Council publication *Rich States, Poor States*.

RLT: *Recently legislated tax changes*, 2011–2012. For example, North Dakota = –0.029 or New York = 0.014. Here, –0.029 is equivalent to a –2.9 percent change in a state's tax burden over the 2009 to 2012 period, using static revenue estimates of legislated tax changes per $1,000 of personal income. Data are from Laffer Associates and the annual American Legislative Exchange Council publication *Rich States, Poor States*.

Over the time period 2002–2012, each of these variables is related in one way or another with each of the other variables. In the matrix shown in Table 6.1—the correlation matrix—each variable's correlation (i.e., linear association) with every other variable is presented for the reader's easy reference.

Simply by viewing the correlation matrix, we can harvest a great deal of information. For example, the direction of correlation of each of the policy variables with gross state product growth is as we would

TABLE 6.1

Correlation Matrix

Variables	ALEC	CIT	PIT	PITP	RTW	TBUR	OILB	PGL1	GSP	PG	GSPL1	RLT
ALEC	**1.00**	0.58	0.57	0.53	–0.67	0.60	–0.26	–0.33	–0.34	–0.53	–0.40	0.51
CIT	0.58	**1.00**	0.53	0.26	–0.53	0.61	–0.11	–0.34	–0.31	–0.44	–0.31	0.34
PIT	0.57	0.53	**1.00**	0.73	–0.43	0.73	–0.27	–0.29	–0.33	–0.36	–0.27	0.28
PITP	0.53	0.26	0.73	**1.00**	–0.25	0.46	–0.10	–0.19	–0.13	–0.24	–0.19	0.03
RTW	–0.67	–0.53	–0.43	–0.25	**1.00**	–0.49	0.11	0.32	0.40	0.50	0.34	–0.38
TBUR	0.60	0.61	0.73	0.46	–0.49	**1.00**	–0.30	–0.28	–0.43	–0.47	–0.20	0.40
OILB	–0.26	–0.11	–0.27	–0.10	0.11	–0.30	**1.00**	–0.17	0.71	0.11	–0.21	–0.59
PGL1	–0.33	–0.34	–0.29	–0.19	0.32	–0.28	–0.17	**1.00**	0.06	0.82	0.85	0.23
GSP	–0.34	–0.31	–0.33	–0.13	0.40	–0.43	0.71	0.06	**1.00**	0.44	0.02	–0.45
PG	–0.53	–0.44	–0.36	–0.24	0.50	–0.47	0.11	0.82	0.44	**1.00**	0.64	–0.02
GSPL1	–0.40	–0.31	–0.27	–0.19	0.34	–0.20	–0.21	0.85	0.02	0.64	**1.00**	0.11
RLT	0.51	0.34	0.28	0.03	–0.38	0.40	–0.59	0.23	–0.45	–0.02	0.11	**1.00**

expect. Every single tax variable is negative—meaning above-average taxes are typically associated with below-average gross state product growth—and the oil production per capita variable, the right-to-work variable, and population growth variable are all positive, again as we would expect from economic theory. These results in and of themselves are powerful. If we had chosen 10 random series for a correlation matrix, just to get the a priori theory consistent correct signs for each of the variables would be a one in 1,024 chance.[5] Not too bad for starters. But we're only getting warmed up.

When we view each of the tax variables in conjunction with all of the other tax variables, it is quite reasonable that they are all positively correlated with each other, signifying a common structure of tax policies for each state across all states over the past decade and, of course, a significant amount of overlap in the measurements when it comes to series like the ALEC-Laffer state competitiveness ranking (ALEC) and tax burden (TBUR). It shows that states in general that think having a high personal income tax rate is a good policy also think that a high corporate tax rate is good, high tax burdens are good, and high ALEC scores are also good policy.

Other interesting observations can be made from the statistical relationships reported in the correlation matrix between population growth and its lagged value, and between gross state product growth and its lagged value. With population growth, there appears to be a great deal of momentum where fast-growing states tend to continue to be fast-growing states unless bumped off their paths by shocks in policy variables. Even when fast-growing states are bumped off their paths by shocks in policy variables, it still takes their population numbers a long time to adjust. Such momentum is nowhere to be found for gross state product growth. Gross state product growth is wholly dependent on the here and now, not on the there and then.

The oil variable, OILB, is interesting in that higher taxes, on average, from ALEC, CIT, PIT, and PITP to TBUR, tend to be in states with less oil production per capita, and vice versa. It's possible that high-tax states also discriminate against oil producers as well as other producers and income earners—or maybe the negative correlation is because they have other taxes that are higher because they don't have revenues from oil, or perhaps it's just the capricious behavior of Mother Nature and human ignorance.

When one focuses not solely on the *sign* of the correlation coefficient but on the *size* of the correlation coefficient, things become curiouser and curiouser. But this exercise we'll leave up to the reader.

The two dependent variables we are trying to explain or, if you will, correlate with the other variables across all 50 states are: (1) gross state product growth (GSP) and (2) population growth (PG). And, of course, there always will be a constant term, C, in each and every equation. The period we are covering is from 2002 to 2012. We'll proceed with gross state product growth first.

Gross State Product Growth: Single-Variable Analysis

The first set of tests we have performed are simple linear least squares regressions, where GSP growth is the dependent variable and the single independent variables are OILB, TBUR, CIT, RTW, ALEC, RLT, PIT, PITP, and, finally, GSPL1. The key features of each regression are displayed in Table 6.2. [6]

The first feature to note from equation 9 of the individual univariate regressions is that gross state product growth does not appear to be correlated in any important way with its lagged one-decade gross state product growth. As a result, we will eliminate this variable from any further consideration. We had no preconceived notion about whether there would be an important correlation between gross state product growth and its lagged value, and finding scant evidence of a lag is neither here nor there. It is important to report these results, however, in order to avoid omitted variable bias, which occurs when an explanatory variable is ignored. Omitted variable bias can result in biased estimates, which would render our analysis useless.

By far the most significant variable for gross state product growth (GSP) is shown in equation 1 and is the oil production per capita in the state, OILB. Here the level of importance is an incredible 8.21 *t*-statistic.

TABLE 6.2

Table of Simple Linear Regressions of Gross State Product Growth 2002–2012 on Independent Variables

Equation	Var	Coef	SE*	t-Stat	R^2	F-stat
1	C	0.480	0.023	20.65	0.50	48.49
	OILB	0.022	0.003	8.21		
2	C	1.120	0.152	7.37	0.18	10.80
	TBUR	–6.363	1.495	–4.26		
3	C	0.642	0.064	10.11	0.09	4.98
	CIT	–1.741	0.652	–2.67		
4	C	0.453	0.036	12.67	0.16	9.09
	RTW	0.146	0.058	2.51		
5	C	0.841	0.153	5.50	0.11	6.22
	ALEC	–0.013	0.006	–2.30		
6	C	0.502	0.028	17.98	0.21	12.43
	RLT	–13.110	5.980	–2.19		
7	C	0.619	0.058	10.60	0.11	5.90
	PIT	–1.790	0.854	–2.10		
8	C	0.543	0.045	12.08	0.02	0.80
	PITP	–2.850	2.830	–1.01		
9	C	0.506	0.111	4.55	0.0002	0.0117
	GSPL1	0.015	0.134	0.11		

You won't find many independent correlations where a variable has a t-statistic over 8. If in fact this were a single test and all of the appropriate assumptions held, the chance of this happening randomly would be five in 1,000,000,000,000,000. Oil is most definitely a statistically powerful explanatory variable (in terms of comovement) for a state's overall growth in output. And the coefficient makes sense as well. At $100 per barrel, an increase in oil production of one barrel per person could well translate into a 2.2 percentage point increase in the state's gross state product decadal growth rate, making it an economically powerful explanatory variable. In fact, according to our R^2 results, OILB explains 50 percent of the variation over the 50 states' 10-year growth rates, which is very impressive. This oil variable, OILB, is a clear winner. Oil goes a long way to explain the exceptional growth rates of states like North Dakota, Wyoming, and Alaska. While there may be a lot of oil produced in other larger states, oil's impact will be less because of the size of the state's other productive sectors. That's why OILB is not a huge deal in Texas. Other studies have also obtained results linking oil production to economic growth. Peach and Starbuck use county-level data on New Mexico's oil and gas extraction, and find a "small but positive effect on income, employment, and population."[7] Taking an international approach, Bildirici and Kayikci obtain results that suggest that "oil production has positive effect on the economic growth" of Eurasian countries—in fact, their findings support the notion that there is a "positive bi-directional relationship between oil production and economic growth."[8]

The second most significant variable (i.e., the second highest t-statistic, in absolute value terms) we find is TBUR, or the overall tax burden of the state and is reported in equation 2. Again, the t-statistic for this variable is exceptionally large, and therefore represents a very tight correlation. The variable also makes a lot of economic common sense. What this variable signifies is that an increase in a state's tax burden of one percentage point (say, from 0.08 to 0.09) will reduce that state's decadal growth rate by 6.4 percentage points. While illustrating a very sensitive response, the response is well within reason. On its own, TBUR explains 18 percent of the variation of GSP according to the R^2 result. Engen and Skinner have also obtained results that suggest a negative relationship between the tax burden and economic output; generally, highly taxed countries will experience lower values of marginal productivity of capital as well as a lower output elasticity of labor.[9]

The third variable we examine is in equation 3 and is the relationship between a state's highest corporate income tax rate and that state's gross state product growth. Again, the correlation is negative, as we would expect, and the results reflect a strong correlation, with a t-statistic of -2.67.

The value of the coefficient is also quite reasonable, implying an association whereby a one percentage point higher top corporate tax rate will be associated with a 1.74 percentage point reduction in that state's decadal GSP growth rate. If this correlation were causative—which it probably is, but may not be—then a one percentage point hike in the highest corporate tax rate will, over the decade, reduce state gross product growth rate by 1.74 percentage points. That would be one helluva price for the people to pay for a politician's desire to spend more, and it would, in turn, reduce a lot of other tax revenues from sales taxes, income taxes, property taxes, and yes, maybe even corporate taxes—remember the Laffer curve? Furthermore, this result confirms previous estimations: Lee and Gordon find that "a cut in the corporate tax rate by 10 percentage points will raise the annual growth rate by one to two percentage points," which is a far stronger impact on growth than our estimates suggest.[10] Additionally, this result is documented by other economists, who find that "corporate tax rates are significantly negatively correlated with cross-sectional differences in average economic growth rates"[11] and that "corporate tax rate differentials between states"[12] have led industry toward the South. In fact, in a study by Johansson et al., the results indicate that "corporate taxes are found to be most harmful for growth."[13] At the state level, Benson and Johnson have further confirmed these results, concluding that "this analysis . . . finds a significant negative distributed lag impact of such taxes on capital formation."[14] At the levels of activity found across all states, it is by no means obvious that an increase in a state's highest corporate income tax rate would in fact result in additional public services.

The fourth most significant variable for the gross state product equations is shown in equation 4, and is whether a state is or is not a right-to-work state.

Just becoming a right-to-work state appears to impart a 14.6 percentage point growth advantage over a decade, which is both huge and reasonable. And the variable, RTW, is extremely important, as shown by its t-statistic of over 2.5, as well as by its R^2 value of 16 percent. Wow! We'll have to wait a few years to find out for sure, but Indiana and Michigan may have much brighter futures than even they imagine. The economic importance of this variable at the state level has not been ignored by the literature, either. For instance, Newman obtains results that "lend considerable support to the argument that . . . the extent of unionization and a favorable business climate (enactment of right-to-work laws) have been major factors influencing the redistribution of industry toward the South."[15] Plaut and Pluta also point out that "industry is strongly attracted to states with . . . relatively little union activity."[16]

The fifth most significant variable in equation 5 for gross state product growth is the ALEC variable, which combines all 15 variables used in the ALEC-Laffer publication *Rich States, Poor States*. Once again, the t-statistic reflects an exceptionally strong correlation and the R^2 suggests an important relationship. Where low is good and high is bad, the ALEC score is negatively correlated with gross state product growth.

The next two variables, recently legislated tax changes (RLT) and the highest personal income tax rate (PIT), are also highly important with t-statistics well over 2 and the correlations showing an inverse relationship between a state's prosperity and its highest personal income tax rate. For example, raising a state's highest personal income tax rate by one percentage point will be associated with a reduction of 1.8 percentage points in that state's gross state product growth rate over a 10-year period. What a diabolical trade-off that is. Why do income taxes negatively impact growth? One explanation is that "current tax treatment significantly retards capital accumulation," which reduces the real net rate of return, leading to an "enormous waste of resources" as well as redistributing "a substantial fraction of gross income from labor to capital."[17] This explanation is also suggested by Rabushka, who finds that "high tax rates have frustrated the efficient use of labor and capital and have discouraged entrepreneurship, thus holding down growth."[18] In fact, Prescott finds that the intratemporal tax wedge explains why the United States is more prosperous than France, suggesting that "if France modified its intratemporal tax wedge so that its value was the same as the U.S. value, French welfare in consumption equivalents would increase by 19 percent. Consumption would have to increase by 19 percent now and in all future periods to achieve as large a welfare gain as that resulting from this tax reform."[19] Weinstein offers a different theory: that "indirectly, high personal taxes may be an impediment to business growth since they force up salaries of executive, managerial, and technical personnel."[20] There is also evidence that RLT plays an important role in short-term economic growth; in fact, Romer and Romer find that "tax changes have very large effects on output" such that "an exogenous tax increase of one percent of GDP lowers real GDP by almost 3 percent."[21] These empirical findings are also validated by Engen and Skinner, who report "modest effects, on the order of 0.2 to 0.3 percentage point differences in long-term growth rates in response to a major tax reform," but "nevertheless, even such small effects can have a large cumulative impact on living standards."[22]

While the progressivity of a state's personal income tax structure (PITP) is negatively associated with gross state product growth, the strength of the correlation is such that we should be careful of any undue reliance on this specific test. The mean effect, however, is still projected as negative. However, it has been previously noted by Romans and Subrahmanyam that at the state level, "the degree of progression in the personal tax structure and the proportion of tax revenues flowing into transfer payments . . . are negatively and significantly correlated with growth in state personal income."[23] Poulson and Kaplan provide further evidence (that is also statistically significant) that "greater regressivity had a positive impact on economic growth."[24] In fact, this result has even been demonstrated internationally by Padovano and Galli, who state: "Our analysis of a cross-section time-series panel of 23 OECD countries for 1950s–1980s decades show that high marginal tax rates and tax progressivity are negatively correlated with long-run economic growth . . . these results are consistent with endogenous growth theories and opposite to those of most empirical literature, which relies on measures of effective average tax rates."[25]

Gross State Product Growth: Two-Variable Analysis

Having now looked at the 50-state correlations between gross state product growth and each of the independent variables separately, we now turn to our first set of multiple regressions with two independent variables.

In Table 6.3, we have used oil production in barrels per capita (OILB) in each of the equations because of the insurmountable size of OILB's t-statistic. There's simply no way to understand gross state product growth over the 50 states during this past decade without taking oil production into account. Here in Table 6.3, we have ranked the seven equations using the other seven independent variables plus oil, in descending order of R^2 or F-statistic.

TABLE 6.3

Table of Multiple Two-Variable Linear Regressions of Gross State Product Growth 2002–2012 on Independent Variables

Equation	Var	Coef	SE*	t-Stat	R²	F-stat
1	C	0.430	0.029	15.05	0.61	36.40
	OILB	0.021	0.002	11.14		
	RTW	0.119	0.040	2.98		
2	C	0.577	0.052	11.18	0.56	29.46
	OILB	0.021	0.002	9.19		
	CIT	−1.324	0.560	−2.36		
3	C	0.819	0.109	7.53	0.55	29.27
	OILB	0.020	0.003	5.89		
	TBUR	−3.546	1.103	−3.22		
4	C	0.641	0.115	5.56	0.53	26.32
	OILB	0.021	0.003	7.46		
	ALEC	−0.006	0.004	−1.45		
5	C	0.529	0.043	12.38	0.52	25.83
	OILB	0.021	0.003	6.76		
	PIT	−0.813	0.661	−1.23		
6	C	0.493	0.035	13.97	0.51	24.11
	OILB	0.022	0.003	7.69		
	PITP	−1.354	2.144	−0.63		
7	C	0.480	0.024	20.37	0.50	23.91
	OILB	0.021	0.004	5.35		
	RLT	−1.454	3.535	−0.41		

Combining OILB with RTW is nothing short of awesome. The two variables complement each other enormously. Just look at what happens to the standard error of each of these variables as we move from the simple linear regressions of Table 6.2 to a two-variable multiple regression of Table 6.3. In each case—OILB and RTW—the standard error declines substantially due to a better fit, resulting in higher t-statistics. The actual coefficients also decline, which is to be expected when two regressors are also (positively) correlated with each other. This two-variable regression indicates that the single-variable equation had biased coefficient estimates, since obviously we omitted an important explanatory variable in each single variable regression equation for OILB and RTW. The coefficient for OILB declines by a small amount, while for RTW the coefficient declines by a modest amount, driven by the reduced bias.

Viewing this equation—equation 1 of Table 6.3—at face value, over 60 percent of the variation over the 50 states' 10-year growth rates in gross state product are explained by (actually, correlate with) two variables, which are significantly controlled by state and local government policies. However, the R^2 might be slightly overstated here, as we have a potential outlier problem with North Dakota's OILB data. Excluding North Dakota's OILB observation and then reestimating equation 1 from Table 6.3, we find our R^2 is reduced to 41.1 percent. Nevertheless, the results are still highly significant from our regression that excludes North Dakota's OILB data: the t-statistics for OILB and RTW are 4.1 and 2.95, respectively.

When combined with OILB, equation 2 of Table 6.3, the corporate income tax continues to have a high t-statistic, but slightly smaller than the t-statistic for the simple linear regression. Interestingly, the coefficient for CIT falls in the multiple regression, as does its standard error. OILB's coefficient drops a little from the simple linear equation of Table 6.2, but its standard error drops quite a bit more, providing an even higher t-statistic than OILB had by itself. Again, we have a reduction in the bias that was caused by omitting variables (that were statistically and economically important) in the single-variable regressions for OILB and CIT. Including both OILB and CIT reduces the bias, which changes our coefficient estimate and provides a better fit of the data (i.e., lower standard errors). These variables are highly complementary.

When combined with OILB, the tax burden variable (TBUR) has a far lower coefficient, which more than offsets a slightly lower standard error. TBUR's t-statistic drops from -4.26 to -3.22 as we move from a simple linear regression to a two-variable multiple regression. A t-statistic of -3.22 is still very high. Unfortunately, OILB's t-statistic drops from 8.21 to 5.89 and the equation's R^2 ends up in third place, far behind OILB and RTW, and only slightly behind OILB and CIT. Once again, the inclusion of multiple significant explanatory variables reduces the bias in our estimates, thus reducing the standard error terms.

The four remaining two-variable multiple regressions are quite respectable, but don't rise to the level of importance of the first three two-variable multiple regressions. The coefficients all have the correct signs, and their magnitudes are such that it would be a foolish politician indeed who would ignore their implications for state prosperity.

Gross State Product Growth: Three-Variable Analysis

As a final set of equations for 10-year gross state product growth, we use three variables in a multiple regression framework, as presented in Table 6.4. In each equation, we include oil production in barrels per capita for each state as an independent variable, and then we rotate combinations of two for the three variables right-to-work (RTW), a state's tax burden (TBUR), and finally, a state's highest corporate income tax (CIT).

Two equations from Table 6.4 end up pretty close to a tie: OILB, RTW, and TBUR, and OILB, RTW, and CIT. The third equation OILB, TBUR, and CIT is no slouch by any means, but doesn't rise to the level of the first two equations. However, as we can see from the R^2 values, we do not gain further explanatory power by adding the additional

| TABLE 6.4 | | | | | | |

Table of Multiple Three-Variable Linear Regressions of Gross State Product Growth 2002–2012 on Independent Variables

Equation	Var	Coef	SE*	t-Stat	R^2	F-stat
1	C	0.576	0.105	5.48	0.61	24.43
	OILB	0.020	0.002	9.81		
	RTW	0.103	0.043	2.38		
	TBUR	−1.451	0.951	−1.53		
2	C	0.472	0.072	6.54	0.61	24.30
	OILB	0.021	0.002	11.39		
	RTW	0.103	0.049	2.10		
	CIT	−0.492	0.635	−0.78		
3	C	0.748	0.113	6.62	0.57	20.20
	OILB	0.020	0.003	7.59		
	TBUR	−2.158	1.608	−1.34		
	CIT	−0.844	0.831	−1.02		

regressors. What we can conclude here is that once again, public policy variables are shown to be very important to a state's overall economic health. When combined with our other analyses, the case for caution when it comes to taxes, the benefits of state energy production, and the critical role played by right-to-work is getting stronger and stronger.

Population Growth: Single-Variable Analysis

Population growth (PG) of the 50 states over the past decade warrants a whole different set of considerations than does gross state product growth (GSP). As shown in Table 6.5, population growth (PG) has a very important autoregressive feature that GSP did not have. This decade's population growth for a state is highly dependent on last decade's population growth (PGL1). In fact, the t-statistic is 7.40 and the coefficient is 0.51. What this means is that on average, a state's population growth this decade is, in large part, due to its last decade's growth, while explaining the remaining population growth is up for grabs with policy

TABLE 6.5

Table of Simple Linear Regressions of Population Growth 2002–2012 on Independent Variables

Equation	Var	Coef	SE*	t-Stat	R^2	F-stat
1	C	0.030	0.013	2.32	0.67	98.29
	PGL1	0.507	0.068	7.40		
2	C	0.326	0.071	4.58	0.22	13.53
	TBUR	−2.462	0.661	−3.72		
3	C	0.271	0.061	4.46	0.28	18.28
	ALEC	−0.007	0.002	−3.33		
4	C	0.157	0.032	4.96	0.19	11.54
	CIT	−0.884	0.301	−2.94		
5	C	0.065	0.015	4.28	0.25	15.83
	RTW	0.064	0.025	2.61		
6	C	0.133	0.024	5.46	0.13	7.27
	PIT	−0.694	0.283	−2.45		
7	C	0.110	0.022	4.94	0.06	2.83
	PITP	−1.853	1.073	−1.73		
8	C	0.091	0.018	5.08	0.01	0.62
	OILB	0.001	0.001	1.28		
9	C	0.093	0.018	5.26	0.0005	0.03
	RLT	−0.233	1.115	−0.21		

variables. In words, people take their sweet old time to pack their bags and skedaddle. Population growth (PG) also has another interesting autoregressive feature.

When considering last decade's gross state product growth (GSPL1) as an independent variable to explain PG, the results are statistically significant with a *t*-statistic of 3.53. However, when we run a multivariate regression using GSPL1 and PGL1 to explain PG, we find that GSPL1 loses statistical significance since its t-statistic drops to -0.99 (and its coefficient changes sign). This should not come as a surprise given the presence of multicollinearity, which is evident from the high correlation between GSPL1 and PGL1.

Once we've recovered from the shock of the autoregressive feature of population growth, we're left with a whole set of other policy variables, which are in and of themselves quite interesting.

Skipping around, the most important variable for gross state product growth, OILB, hardly moves the needle for population growth. People, it would seem, don't move for oil, but oil sure as heck makes their state richer. Interesting, no? However, if you exclude outlier observations for OILB, such as North Dakota and (to a lesser extent) Alaska, we find that OILB then becomes statistically significant, with a t-statistic of 2.75. Maybe oil does attract people when it's not packaged in a frozen, featureless terrain. It's sort of like me and tomatoes. The best steak sandwich in the world is ruined by adding one slice of a raw tomato.

TBUR, ALEC, CIT, RTW, and PIT all do very well in correlating with PG (population growth), and each has the expected sign. And even PITP (personal income tax progressivity) does an okay job. The variable RLT (recently legislated tax changes), however, although (like the other independent variables), it does have the expected sign, is only weakly correlated with population growth. Again, we must point out that these single-variable regression estimates will contain some bias due to the fact that we are (intentionally) omitting important variables (i.e., TBUR, ALEC, CIT, RTW, and PIT) from these regressions. Like before, we will include these variables in a multivariate regression—the single-variable regressions are provided in order to help explain the economic underpinnings of our analysis.

From these simple linear regressions on the dependent variable population growth (PG), we can say that every single coefficient has the expected sign and all, save three, coefficients have absolute values of their t-statistics over 2.4, and three coefficients have absolute values of their t-statistics over 3.0. This is nothing short of a miracle. Each of the coefficients when translated into the change in numbers of people as a share of population is, intuitively, in a very reasonable range. For any professional economist, it would be irresponsible to dismiss the importance of taxes and right-to-work on a state's population growth, and any politician who does should have his head or his heart examined. We should not be surprised by these findings, since similar results have been obtained by other studies. For instance, Cebula finds that voters are "attracted by lower state income tax burdens and lower property tax burdens," which confirms the "Tiebout hypothesis that the consumer-voter moves to that area which best satisfies his preferences for public goods."[26] Further confirmation is provided by Gius, who finds that "income taxes have an effect on migration for most races and age groups. Individuals move from states with high income taxes to states with low income taxes."[27] Finally, Clark and Hunter demonstrate that "state income and death taxes display life-cycle effects; working males in their peak earning years are detracted by high income taxes while all migrants aged 55 to 69 avoid counties in states with high inheritance and estate taxes."[28]

Population Growth: Two-Variable Analysis

In Table 6.6 we look at a whole host of two-variable multiple regressions. The first six equations include population growth lagged one decade as one of the independent variables. Population growth lagged one decade was far and away the most important independent variable in the simple linear regressions. The other independent variables tested in these first six equations are ALEC, RTW, TBUR, CIT, PIT, and PITP in descending order.

Looking at the t-statistics and R^2 in these six equations, it is truly impressive how these independent variables work with each other to create a more powerful correlation with population growth (PG), the dependent variable. If we were to interpret the t-statistics in a more traditional probabilistic manner, the first four variables, ALEC, RTW, TBUR, and CIT, would be considered significantly different from zero by a probability well over one chance in 100.

TABLE 6.6						
Table of Multiple Two-Variable Linear Regressions of Population Growth 2002–2012 on Independent Variables						
Equation	Var	Coef	SE*	t-Stat	R^2	F-stat
1	C	0.134	0.032	4.21	0.74	68.33
	PGL1	0.448	0.062	7.26		
	ALEC	−0.004	0.001	−3.88		
2	C	0.022	0.012	1.77	0.73	64.85
	PGL1	0.455	0.063	7.20		
	RTW	0.034	0.011	3.18		
3	C	0.162	0.047	3.44	0.73	64.19
	PGL1	0.463	0.065	7.07		
	TBUR	−1.337	0.426	−3.14		
4	C	0.061	0.020	3.11	0.70	55.41
	PGL1	0.469	0.075	6.25		
	CIT	−0.369	0.141	−2.61		
5	C	0.048	0.019	2.57	0.69	52.10
	PGL1	0.483	0.072	6.71		
	PIT	−0.258	0.177	−1.46		
6	C	0.037	0.016	2.39	0.68	49.89
	PGL1	0.497	0.072	6.96		
	PITP	−0.682	0.536	−1.27		
7	C	0.218	0.059	3.69	0.31	10.76
	RTW	0.046	0.024	1.88		
	TBUR	−1.538	0.531	−2.90		
8	C	0.108	0.029	3.72	0.29	9.76
	RTW	0.048	0.024	1.96		
	CIT	−0.499	0.257	−1.94		
9	C	0.089	0.024	3.73	0.28	8.95
	RTW	0.054	0.024	2.22		
	PIT	−0.347	0.260	−1.33		
10	C	0.075	0.019	3.99	0.26	8.35
	RTW	0.061	0.024	2.52		
	PITP	−0.927	0.909	−1.02		
11	C	0.286	0.060	4.77	0.26	8.16
	TBUR	−1.654	0.600	−2.76		
	CIT	−0.505	0.342	−1.48		
12	C	0.314	0.066	4.74	0.22	6.59
	TBUR	−2.282	0.703	−3.25		

TABLE 6.6						
(Continued)						
	PIT	−0.086	0.324	−0.27		
13	C	0.321	0.068	4.74	0.22	6.57
	TBUR	−2.387	0.641	−3.72		
	PITP	−0.220	1.086	−0.20		
14	C	0.163	0.031	5.21	0.22	6.55
	CIT	−0.699	0.315	−2.22		
	PIT	−0.342	0.241	−1.42		
15	C	0.161	0.032	5.04	0.21	6.29
	CIT	−0.821	0.284	−2.89		
	PITP	−1.025	0.881	−1.16		
16	C	0.133	0.024	5.48	0.13	3.61
	PIT	−0.782	0.322	−2.43		
	PITP	0.487	1.110	0.44		

Even the two personal income tax variables, PIT and PITP, are of the correct (theoretically speaking) sign and of not inconsequential magnitudes. Much like our analysis on GSP, the multivariate regressions for population growth provide better estimates and fits because of the reduced biased caused by omitted variables. Including these important variables changes the coefficient estimates and reduces the standard error terms.

In the 10 two-independent-variable multiple regressions on population growth, we include all variables preselected, save PGL1. These equations are far less powerful in explaining PG than the first six equations but are still quite powerful in their own right. In these following 10 equations it becomes clearer to us that in our search for explanatory power, the variables PIT, PITP, and even CIT probably won't make the cut as separate independent variables because of their correlations with other more powerful independent variables. But don't for a moment conclude from these multiple regressions that either the highest personal income tax rate or the measure of personal income tax progressivity isn't important. What these tests show is the degree of overlap in explaining the variations in population growth (PG) so that the explanations are better allocated to TBUR, ALEC, RTW, and, to a lesser extent, CIT than they are to PIT or PITP. The overlap is still there.

To see what we mean, just look at the standard error of PIT in equation 5 of Table 6.6, which is 0.177, versus the standard error of PIT in equations 9, 12, 14, and 16 of 0.260, 0.324, 0.24, and 0.322, respectively. Such rises in the measured standard errors for the same regressors on the same dependent variable only go to highlight the multicollinearity of PIT with the other regressor variables. The same conclusion of a greatly expanded standard error also applies to the variable PITP, which goes from 0.536 in equation 6 to 0.909, 1.086, 0.88, and finally 1.110 in equations 10, 13, 15, and 16, respectively. Much the same can be written about CIT, which has dropped from a highly significant variable in equation 4 of Table 6.6 to much less significance in equations 8 and 11.

Population Growth: Three-Variable Analysis

In our next attempt at forming a more perfect union of independent variables trying to "explain" population growth, we combine as independent variables PGL1 in each regression with a two-variable combination of TBUR, ALEC, RTW, and CIT (see Table 6.7).

In this competition, CIT drops out as being the variable that consistently has the lowest t score in these multiple regressions. The best equations are equations 1, 2, and 3. Although these three-variable regression equations offer more explanatory power than the two-variable regression equations, the standard error terms for TBUR and RTW increase modestly. However, ALEC's standard error estimates in equations 1 and 3 remain unchanged from the two-variable regression, and CIT's standard error drops in equation 4. From our perspective, there is little doubt that higher-taxed states and forced-union states have naturally lower population growth rates than do lower-taxed and right-to-work states. And the importance of that relationship is truly material.

TABLE 6.7

Table of Multiple Three-Variable Linear Regressions of Population Growth 2002–2012 on Independent Variables

Equation	Var	Coef	SE*	t-Stat	R²	F-stat
1	C	0.178	0.047	3.77	0.76	47.97
	PGL1	0.440	0.063	7.04		
	TBUR	−0.744	0.513	−1.45		
	ALEC	−0.003	0.001	−2.22		
2	C	0.115	0.059	1.94	0.76	47.67
	PGL1	0.440	0.063	6.97		
	RTW	0.024	0.012	1.96		
	TBUR	−0.917	0.524	−1.75		
3	C	0.098	0.046	2.13	0.76	47.36
	PGL1	0.439	0.061	7.17		
	RTW	0.018	0.014	1.23		
	ALEC	−0.003	0.001	−1.94		
4	C	0.036	0.020	1.82	0.74	43.21
	PGL1	0.446	0.066	6.71		
	RTW	0.029	0.012	2.47		
	CIT	−0.154	0.133	−1.15		
5	C	0.156	0.049	3.17	0.73	42.26
	PGL1	0.457	0.069	6.59		
	CIT	−0.108	0.171	−0.63		
	TBUR	−1.180	0.513	−2.30		

Population Growth: Four-Variable Analysis

The final two equations are presented in Table 6.8, where we look at combinations of PGL1, RTW, TBUR, and ALEC as independent variables and PGL1, RTW, TBUR, and CIT as independent variables. The first equation appears a smidgeon better than the second equation, but the differences are there even if they are not overly significant in the grand scheme of things. Although CIT has the "wrong" sign in equation 2 in Table 6.8, its contribution to the overall explanatory power is very low as evidenced by its t–statistic.

| TABLE 6.8 | | | | | | |

Table of Multiple Four-Variable Linear Regressions of Population Growth 2002–2012 on Independent Variables

Equation	Var	Coef	SE*	t-Stat	R^2	F-stat
1	C	0.142	0.062	2.29	0.77	36.69
	PGL1	0.433	0.062	6.95		
	RTW	0.015	0.014	1.09		
	TBUR	−0.664	0.569	−1.17		
	ALEC	−0.002	0.001	−1.26		
2	C	0.115	0.061	1.89	0.76	34.98
	PGL1	0.441	0.063	6.96		
	RTW	0.024	0.012	1.97		
	TBUR	−0.933	0.623	−1.50		
	CIT	0.014	0.171	0.08		

We're going to rely on both of these equations to make the following assertions.

From our econometric analysis, we conclude that the preponderance of evidence over this time period with these variables shows that:

- Population growth has a powerful autoregressive feature that goes a long way in explaining the cross-state variations in population growth.
- RTW, TBUR, and ALEC collectively also contribute mightily to population growth. Their multicollinearity, however, really makes it difficult to separate to what extent each variable by itself, or in concert with PGL1, contributes to explaining the variations in PG.

Conclusions

All in all, we view these econometric results as powerful confirmation that tax rates matter, and matter a lot. We also conclude that whether a state is or is not a right-to-work state also contributes an enormous amount to whether a state experiences population growth.

These econometric results should be used in conjunction with all of the other tests, anecdotes, and examples contained in this book to evaluate the impact state and local government policies have on a state's relative performance.

What we can conclude from the results of this econometric chapter is that there exists powerful evidence to support the facts that higher tax rates, forced unions, and heightened tax burdens inhibit both gross state product growth and population growth. These results fall right in line with the results of our other chapters. No matter how you slice and dice and analyze these data, supply-side state responses to economic policies dominate state performances.

Annotated Econometric Bibliography

Abstracts reprinted with very minor edits for clarity and consistency.

1. **Abuselidze, George. "The Influence of Optimal Tax Burden on Economic Activity and Production Capacity." EconStor Open Access Articles, 2012.**

    That the modern state couldn't exist without taxes is something that doesn't need to be argued to society. It is also acknowledged that tax burden influences not only the budget revenues, but investments, demand and supply, prices, and others. All this has direct as well as indirect influence on the economic activity and production capacity. In the concept of tax burden, the important fact is the connection of tax burden with the economic activity and production capacity. The influence of tax burden on budget tax revenues and production capacity can be realized in two different ways. On the one hand, tax burden influences production technologies' effective usage of resources that accordingly will be depicted on the production capacity, and, on the other hand, the change of tax burden influences budget tax revenues that will be depicted on the economic activity.

2. **Alesina, A., and Dani Rodrik. "Distributive Politics and Economic Growth."** *Quarterly Journal of Economics* **(May 1994).**

We study the relationship between politics and economic growth in a simple model of endogenous growth with distributive conflict among agents endowed with varying capital/labor shares. We establish several results regarding the factor ownership of the median individual and the level of taxation, redistribution, and growth. Policies that maximize growth are optimal only for a government that cares solely about pure "capitalists." The greater the inequality of wealth and income, the higher the rate of taxation and the lower the rate of growth. We present empirical results that show that inequality in land and income ownership is negatively correlated with subsequent economic growth.

3. **Alm, James, and Janet Rogers. "Do State Fiscal Policies Affect State Economic Growth?"** *Public Finance Review* **39, no. 4 (July 2011): 483–526. http://econ.tulane.edu/RePEc/ pdf/tul1107.pdf.**

What factors influence state economic growth? This article uses annual state (and local) data for the years 1947 through 1997 for the 48 contiguous states to estimate the effects of a large number of factors, including taxation and expenditure policies, on state economic growth. A special feature of the empirical work is the use of orthogonal distance regression (ODR) to deal with the likely presence of measurement error in many of the variables. The results indicate that the correlation between state (and state and local) taxation policies is often statistically significant but also quite sensitive to the specific regressor set and time period; in contrast, the effects of expenditure policies are much more consistent.

4. **Barro, R. J. "Determinants of Economic Growth: A Cross-Country Empirical Study." Working Paper 5698, National Bureau of Economic Research, 1996.**

Empirical findings for a panel of around 100 countries from 1960 to 1990 strongly support the general notion of conditional convergence. For a given starting level of real per capita gross domestic product (GDP), the growth rate is enhanced by higher initial schooling and life expectancy, lower fertility, lower government consumption, better maintenance of the rule of law, lower inflation, and improvements in the terms of trade. For given values of these and other variables, growth is negatively related to the initial level of real per capita GDP. Political freedom has only a weak effect on growth but there is some indication of a nonlinear relation. At low levels of political rights, an expansion of these rights stimulates economic growth. However, once a moderate amount of democracy has been attained, a further expansion reduces growth. In contrast to the small effect of democracy on growth, there is a strong positive influence of the standard of living on a country's propensity to experience democracy.

5. **Barro, R. J. "Economic Growth in a Cross Section of Countries." *Quarterly Journal of Economics* 106, no. 2 (1991): 407–443.**

For 98 countries in the period 1960–1985, the growth rate of real per capita GDP is positively related to initial human capital (proxied by 1960 school enrollment rates) and negatively related to the initial (1960) level of real per capita GDP. Countries with higher human capital also have lower fertility rates and higher rates of physical investment to GDP. Growth is inversely related to the share of public investment. Growth rates are positively related to measures of political stability and inversely related to a proxy for market distortions.

6. **Barro, Robert, and Xavier Sala-i-Martin. "Public Finance in Models of Economic Growth." *Review of Economic Studies* 59 (1992): 645–661.**

The recent literature on endogenous economic growth allows for effects of fiscal policy on long-term growth. If the social rate of return on investment exceeds the private return, then tax policies that encourage investment can raise the growth rate and levels of utility. An excess of social return over the private return can reflect learning by doing with spillover effects, the financing of government consumption purchases with an income tax, and monopoly pricing of new types of capital goods. In growth models that incorporate public services, the optimal tax policy hinges on the characteristics of the services. If the public services are publicly provided private goods, which are rival and excludable, or publicly provided public goods, which are nonrival and nonexcludable, then lump-sum taxation is superior to income taxation.

7. Becsi, Z. "Do State and Local Taxes Affect Relative State Growth?" *Economic Review*, March/April 1996.

The South has experienced a remarkable economic awakening over the past 30 years, with Southern states growing at phenomenal rates. At the same time, these states have had, on average, low state and local taxes, and it seems reasonable to infer that tax policies may have contributed to their relative success. However, while policy makers may believe that taxes matter for growth, until recently economic theory suggested otherwise. It was believed that much of long-term growth is determined by automatic forces of convergence, which moved Southern states toward catching up with the rest of the nation. But as theoretical growth models have grown more sophisticated, it has been increasingly recognized that the two explanations for the South's strong showing may not be mutually exclusive.

8. Benson, B., and Ronald Johnson. "The Lagged Impact of State and Local Taxes on Economic Activity and Political Behavior." *Economic Inquiry* 24, no. 3 (1986).

Politicians are frequently characterized as making fiscal decisions based on a shorter time horizon than is required for full taxpayer adjustment, thus generating near-term benefits and relatively high tax rates. This argument requires a negative impact of taxes on economic activity distributed over a relatively long time period. Considerable empirical evidence suggests that state and local taxes do not significantly impact the geographic distribution of economic activity; this analysis, however, finds a significant negative distributed lag impact of such taxes on capital formation.

The approach emphasizes interstate tax competition in formulating the cross-section time-series estimating equation.

9. **Bildirici, M. E., and Fazil Kayikci. "Effects of Oil Production on Economic Growth in Eurasian Countries: Panel ARDL Approach."** *Energy* **49 (2013): 156–161.**

This study aims at analyzing the relationship between oil production and economic growth in major oil-exporting Eurasian countries (Azerbaijan, Kazakhstan, Russian Federation, and Turkmenistan) for the 1993–2010 period. Empirical results reveal that oil production and economic growth are cointegrated for these countries. Furthermore, there is positive bidirectional causality between oil production and economic growth both in the long run and in the short run, which supports the policies about investing in energy infrastructure.

10. **Boskin, M. J. "Taxation, Saving, and the Rate of Interest."** *Journal of Political Economy* **86, no. 2, Part 2: Research in Taxation (April 1978): S3–S27.**

This study presents new estimates of consumption functions based on aggregate U.S. time-series data. The results are striking: A variety of functional forms, estimation methods, and definitions of the real after-tax rate of return invariably lead to the conclusion of a substantial interest elasticity of saving. The implications of this result for the analysis of the efficiency and equity of the current U.S. tax treatment of income from capital are explored. In reducing the real net rate of return, current tax treatment significantly retards capital accumulation. This in turn causes an enormous waste of resources and redistributes a substantial fraction of gross income from labor to capital. Rough estimates of the lost welfare exceed $50 billion per year (a present value close to $1 trillion!) and estimates of the redistribution from labor to capital exceed one-seventh of capital's share of gross income. It also suggests that the usual calculations of tax burdens by income class substantially overestimate both the progressivity of the income tax and the alleged regressivity of consumption taxes.

11. **Canto, V. A., and Robert Webb. "The Effect of State Fiscal Policy on State Relative Economic Performance."** *Southern Economic Journal* **54, no. 1 (July 1987): 186–202.**

The relative performance of different state economies has been a matter of much interest to both policy makers and the public in general. In a neoclassical world where factors are free to move across political boundaries, one would not expect to observe the existence of persistent product price or factor income differentials. Such differentials would disappear either through the trading of goods or factor migration. Yet in seeming violation of neoclassical economic theory, apparent persistent differences in factor incomes have been repeatedly observed among states or regions in the United States. The intent of this paper is to develop and empirically examine a neoclassical model that explicitly incorporates both state and federal fiscal policies in order to explain persistent differences in the levels of market income of the states' economies.

12. **Cebula, R. "Interstate Migration and the Tiebout Hypothesis: An Analysis According to Race, Sex and Age."** *Journal of the American Statistical Association* **69, no. 348 (1974): 876–879.**

This article examines the impact on interstate net migration of differential state and local property tax and transfer policies in the United States by race, sex, and age for 1965–1970. The results offer considerable support to the Tiebout hypothesis that the consumer-voter moves to that area which best satisfies his preferences for public goods. Apparently, differentials in state and local transfer and taxation activities have had an important impact on human migration patterns in the United States over the 1965–1970 period. Thus, Tiebout's arguments cited in Section 1 appear to have at least some validity.

13. **Cebula, R. "Local Government Policies and Migration: An Analysis for SMSA's in the United States, 1965–1970."** *Public Choice* **19 (Fall 1974): 85–93.**

As governmental units exercise their taxing, transfer, and expenditure powers, income redistribution and variations in the levels of burdens and benefits from governmental actions are experienced. Given that there is an immense diversity among Standard Metropolitan Statistical Areas (SMSAs) in the pattern of taxation, transfer, and spending policies, it is natural to ask whether this diversity exercises any major impact over the efficient allocation of our scarce resources. In an attempt to gain insight into the possible economic impact of the diversity of local government policies, this paper focuses upon the sensitivity of human migration to such policies. In particular, the purpose of this paper is to examine the impact, according to race, of local government taxation, income redistribution, and expenditure policies on migration to SMSAs in the United States. The reference time period is 1965–1970. As Tiebout (1956, 418) has argued, the "consumer-voter may be viewed as picking that community which best satisfies his preference pattern for public goods." Presumably, "the consumer-voter moves to that community whose local government best satisfies his set of preferences" (1956, 418). This paper operates within this framework to ascertain whether in fact local government policies have a significant impact on migration. If these policies in fact do prove significant, some very important and very basic economic and political issues may need to be faced. [He finds that state and local tax burdens are inversely related to the amount of in-migration.]

14. **Cebula, R. J. "Migration and the Tiebout–Tullock Hypothesis Revisited."** *American Journal of Economics and Sociology* **68, no. 2 (2009): 541–551.**

This study investigates, using state-level data for the period 2000–2005, the Tiebout hypothesis (as extended by Tullock) of "voting with one's feet." This analysis differs from previous related studies not only in its adoption of more current migration and other data but also in other ways. First, unlike most earlier related studies, it includes a separate measure of the overall cost of living;

second, it examines per pupil (rather than per capita) outlays on public primary and secondary education; and third, in addition to property taxes, it also focuses on per capita state income tax burdens. Inclusion of the last of these variables in the analysis is based on studies that have found the existence of a state income tax to have influenced migration patterns and other studies that have found higher state income tax levels to have resulted in reduced per capita income growth over time. Moreover, including both property tax burdens and income tax burdens broadens the scope of the hypothesis. Strong empirical support for the Tiebout-Tullock hypothesis (as interpreted here) is obtained for the study period.

15. Chirinko, Bob, and Daniel John Wilson. "State Business Taxes and Investment: State-by-State Simulations." *Economic Review of San Francisco Federal Reserve* (2010): 13–28.

This article develops a framework for simulating the effects of state business taxes on state investment and output. Our simulations provide the predicted increase in investment—both in equipment and structures (E&S) and in research and development (R&D)—and the predicted increase in output for a given state resulting from a specified change in one of its three tax policies—the E&S investment tax credit, the R&D tax credit, or the corporate income tax.

16. Clark, D. E., and W. J. Hunter. "The Impact of Economic Opportunity, Amenities, and Fiscal Factors on Age-Specific Migration Rates." *Journal of Regional Science* 21 (1992): 349–365.

Migration models have considered several different categories of determinants, including economic opportunities, amenities, and state and local fiscal factors. Migration has also been shown to depend on the individual's position in the life cycle. This paper represents a first attempt to integrate all three categories of determinants of migration into a life-cycle framework. Empirical findings generated from a countrywide model of white male migration over the period 1970 to 1980 reveal that all three types of determinants are important. Specifically, economic opportunities are most influential for males during their working years. Amenities are also found to follow a life-cycle pattern, with older migrants more attracted to amenable locations than their younger cohorts. Finally, state income and death taxes display life-cycle effects; working males in their peak earning years are detracted by high income taxes while all migrants aged 55 to 69 avoid counties in states with high inheritance and estate taxes.

17. **Dye, T. "Taxing, Spending, and Economic Growth in the American States."** *Journal of Politics* **42, no. 4 (November 1980): 1085–1107.**

What effects, if any, do state taxing and spending policies have on rates of economic development in the states? Do state individual or corporate tax rates or total tax burdens have any identifiable, independent effects on economic growth? Do patterns of state spending for education, highways, welfare, and health, or even the redistributional effects of state taxing and spending, have any identifiable, independent effects on economic growth? Or are economic growth rates solely a product of climate, natural resources, geographic location, existing capital investment, and historical patterns of industrial development? [Dye finds that since newer states have less in the way of organized labor forces and more transportation investment, they tend to have higher economic growth rates relative to older states. He was unable to find an independent linkage between variation in state taxing and variation in economic growth rates; however, he measures economic productivity by the growth in value added by manufacturing.]

18. **Engen, Eric, and Jonathan Skinner. "Taxation and Economic Growth."** *National Tax Journal* **49, no. 4 (December 1996): 617–642.**

Tax reforms are sometimes touted as having strong macroeconomic growth effects. Using three approaches, we consider the impact of a major tax reform—a five percentage point cut in marginal tax rates—on long-term growth rates. The first approach is to examine the historical record of the U.S. economy to evaluate whether tax cuts have been associated with economic growth. The second is to consider the evidence on taxation and growth for a large sample of countries. And finally, we use evidence from micro-level studies of labor supply, investment demand, and productivity growth. Our results suggest modest effects, on the order of 0.2 to 0.3 percentage point differences in growth rates in response to a major tax reform. Nevertheless, even such small effects can have a large cumulative impact on living standards.

19. **Feldstein, M. "Social Security and Saving: The Extended Life Cycle Theory."** *American Economic Review* **66, no. 2, Papers and Proceedings of the Eighty-Eighth Annual Meeting of the American Economic Association (May 1976): 77–86.**

The life cycle model is the central idea in the modern theory of saving because it provides the crucial link between the microeconomics of rational household behavior and the macroeconomics of the rate of saving. The fundamental insight of this theory, that aggregate saving is positive in a growing economy because the younger workers who save are more numerous and have higher earnings than the older retirees who dissave, was presented by Sir Roy Harrod in the second lecture of his famous book, *Towards a Dynamic Economics* (1948). Harrod's description of the household's optimizing behavior, which he notes is an extension of Irving Fisher's (1930) analysis, is remarkably modern and neoclassical for someone who is rightly regarded as one of the great developers of Keynesian economic theory. But it was Franco Modigliani and his collaborators (e.g., 1954, 1957, 1963, and 1966) who developed Harrod's metaphor of "hump saving" into a quantitative theory and began the process of empirical verification that has made the life cycle model a central feature of our current economic understanding. [Feldstein finds that the existence of social security has materially reduced private savings, as people view social security as a substitute for private retirement savings. This is one of the first studies that argued taxation might impair private capital formation.]

20. Gallaway, L., R. Vedder, and Robert Lawson. "Why People Work: An Examination of Interstate Variations in Labor Force Participation." *Journal of Labor Research* 12, no. 1 (Winter 1991).

A casual examination of recent official data describing labor force participation rates by state reveals remarkable variation. For example, in 1985 the participation rate was 52.2 percent in West Virginia and 73 percent in Alaska. The obvious question raised by differences of this magnitude is why they occur. [This study explains interstate variations in the proportion of people who work. On the revenue side, state taxes have an adverse impact on the incidence of work. On the expenditure side, spending on public assistance materially and negatively impacts the proportion of the population age 16 or over who work.]

21. Gius, M. P. "The Effect of Income Taxes on Interstate Migration: An Analysis by Age and Race." *Annals of Regional Science* 46 (2009).

The topic of interstate migration and the effects of taxes on migration have been extensively studied. Prior research has examined not only many possible determinants of migration but also the migrations of various populations, including the elderly, African Americans, and the college educated. The present study attempts to differentiate itself from this prior research by looking at the effect of income taxes on the interstate migration of both whites and African Americans at various ages. Another distinguishing feature of the present study is that it uses data from the NLSY-Geocode, a data set not used previously for this type of study. Results of the present study are similar to the results of prior works; income taxes have an effect on migration for most races and age groups. Individuals move from states with high income taxes to states with low income taxes; these results corroborate the results obtained from the use of aggregate, state-level data. In addition, results of the present study suggest that non-economic factors, such as ties to a particular state and changes in employment status, are also important factors in an individual's migration decision.

22. Gwartney, J., R. Lawson, and Randall Holcombe. "The Size and Functions of Government and Economic Growth." Joint Economic Committee, U.S. Congress, April 1998.

This paper shows that excessively large government has reduced economic growth. These findings present a compelling case that rather than devising new programs to spend any surplus that may emerge from the current [late 1990s] economic expansion, Congress should develop a long-range strategy to reduce the size of government so the country will be able to achieve a more rapid rate of economic growth in the future.

23. Hall, R. "Stabilization Policy and Capital Formation." *American Economic Review* **70, no. 2, Papers and Proceedings of the Ninety-Second Annual Meeting of the American Economic Association (May 1980): 157–163.**

Every recession in the U.S. economy calls forth proposals for remedial stimulus. The government's own expenditures on goods and services can be increased, additional income can be provided to consumers in the hope that they will spend more, new incentives can be provided for investment, and the money stock can be increased. Conventional analysis does not distinguish among these policies with respect to the ratio of their effects on output and inflation. Each can push the economy out of recession and back to full employment at the cost of worsening inflation. All operate along the same Phillips curve. My purpose here is to reconsider the prevailing dogma by examining the possibility of differential effects of stabilization policies operating through capital formation. Expansionary policies either favor investment (monetary expansion and investment incentives) or discourage it (increased government expenditures or consumption). [Hall finds that taxation of productive resources can have potentially debilitating effects on capital formation.]

24. **Helms, L. J. "The Effect of State and Local Taxes on Economic Growth: A Time Series–Cross Section Approach."** *Review of Economics and Statistics* **67, no. 4 (1985): 574–582.**

Results based on pooled time series and cross section data are presented, which indicate that state and local tax increases significantly retard economic growth when the revenue is used to fund transfer payments. However, when the revenue is used instead to finance improved public services, the favorable impact on location and production decisions provided by the enhanced services may more than counterbalance the disincentive effects of the associated taxes.

25. **Johansson, Å., C. Heady, J. Arnold, B. Brys, and L. Vartia. "Tax and Economic Growth." Working Paper 620, OECD Economics Department, 2008.**

This paper investigates the design of tax structures to promote economic growth. It suggests a "tax and growth" ranking of taxes, confirming results from earlier literature but providing a more detailed disaggregation of taxes. Corporate taxes are found to be most harmful for growth, followed by personal income taxes, and then consumption taxes. Recurrent taxes on immovable property appear to have the least impact. A revenue-neutral growth-oriented tax reform would, therefore, be to shift part of the revenue base from income taxes to less distortive taxes such as recurrent taxes on immovable property or consumption. The paper breaks new ground by using data on industrial sectors and individual firms to show how redesigning taxation within each of the broad tax categories could in some cases ensure sizable efficiency gains. For example, reduced rates of corporate tax for small firms do not seem to enhance growth, and high top marginal rates of personal income tax can reduce productivity growth by reducing entrepreneurial activity. While the paper focuses on how taxes affect growth, it recognizes that practical tax reform requires balancing the aims of efficiency, equity, simplicity, and revenue raising.

26. **Landau, D. "Government Expenditure and Economic Growth: A Cross-Country Study."** *Southern Economic Journal* **49, no. 3 (January 1983): 783–792.**

This paper examines the relationship between the share of government consumption expenditure in GDP and the rate of growth of real per capita GDP. The work of the United Nations International Comparison Project has recently made available new estimates for more than 100 countries of both per capita GDP and the share of government consumption. These new estimates are based on direct price comparisons rather than exchange rate conversions. As a result, the statistics for different countries are more comparable and cross-country studies will be more reliable.

27. **Lee, Y., and R. H. Gordon. "Tax Structure and Economic Growth."** *Journal of Public Economics* **89, no. 5–6 (2005): 1027–1043.**

Past theoretical work predicts that higher corporate tax rates should decrease economic growth rates, while the effects of high personal tax rates are less clear. In this paper, we explore how tax policies in fact affect a country's growth rate, using cross-country data during 1970–1997. We find that statutory corporate tax rates are significantly negatively correlated with cross-sectional differences in average economic growth rates, controlling for various other determinants of economic growth, and other standard tax variables. In fixed-effect regressions, we again find that increases in corporate tax rates lead to lower future growth rates within countries. The coefficient estimates suggest that a cut in the corporate tax rate by 10 percentage points will raise the annual growth rate by one to two percentage points.

28. **Levine, Ross. "Stock Markets, Growth, and Policy." Board of Governors of the Federal Reserve System, International Finance Discussion Paper 374, 1990.**

In a model that emphasizes technological progress and human capital creation as essential features of economic development, this paper establishes a theoretical link between the financial system and per capita output growth. . . . Along with recent studies of the role played by financial institutions other than stock markets in promoting growth, this paper contributes to a theoretical foundation on which financial policy recommendations may more confidently rest. The paper finds that direct and indirect taxes [consumption tax, tax on wage earnings, corporate tax, and a capital gains tax] associated with stock market transactions slow real per capita output growth.

29. McLure, C., Jr. "Taxation, Substitution, and Industrial Location." *Journal of Political Economy* **78, no. 1 (January–February 1970): 112–132.**

The threat that high taxes in a region might drive out or repel industry has traditionally worried those responsible for the tax policies of state and local governments in the United States. More recently, the possibility that subsidies might attract industry has led some state and local governments to engage in various forms of subsidization of industry, including tax exemptions, and has given rise to numerous studies of the effects of taxes and subsidies on the location of industry. These studies have used such varied techniques as interviews, econometric analysis, and comparisons of tax liabilities in different states in their attempts to assess the sensitivity of industrial location to tax and subsidy policies. But while these studies have undoubtedly shed some light on this complex question, most of them have been rather ad hoc descriptions of the potentially important determinants of the regional location of industry, including rough estimates of the relative importance of taxes and subsidies. Lacking explicit theoretical foundation, they can be of only limited value in specifying under what conditions, in what manner, and to what extent fiscal variables might be expected to influence industrial location. [The study suggests that production taxes repel capital, and that the precise impact depends on the price elasticity of demand for the produced product. He similarly argues that labor taxes could repel capital even more than capital-based taxes do in certain circumstances. The disincentive effects are largely related to the mobility of the resources and the case of substitutability between capital and labor.]

30. McPhail, Joseph, Peter Orazem, and Rajesh Singh. "The Poverty of States: Do State Tax Policies Affect State Labor Productivity?" Iowa State University Department of Economics, May 2010.

This study demonstrates that in the context of a neoclassical growth model, differences in marginal tax rates on income from capital investment, capital ownership, and consumption will lead to persistent differences in labor productivity across states.

31. Myles, G. D. "Economic Growth and the Role of Taxation." OECD Economics Department Working Paper 713, 2009.

Viewed from an endogenous growth perspective, the link between taxation and growth seems self-evident. Corporate taxation affects the return to innovation and hence must affect the optimal amount of research and development. Personal income taxation reduces the returns to education so must reduce the accumulation of human capital. In simulations of economic growth models the effect of taxation on growth has frequently been demonstrated to be considerable. A clear presumption exists that data on economic activity must reveal a strong correlation between taxation and growth.

32. Newman, R. J. "Migration and Growth in the South." *Review of Economics and Statistics* 65, no. 1 (February 1983): 76–86.

For at least the last two decades [before 1983] the South and Southwest have been the fastest-growing regions in the United States. During this period we have witnessed considerable shifts in the location of economic activity, and, overall, the movement has been decidedly toward the South. Since the early 1960s, when this southern migration began to accelerate, an increasing amount of public attention has been directed to this topic—so much so that it is now popularly referred to as the Sunbelt phenomenon. Numerous explanations have been advanced to account for this rapid growth in the South, but three explanations have persistently evoked an impressive level of debate. First, many have argued that a significant portion of this regional redistribution can be attributed to differentials in state and local taxing policies, in particular the state corporate income tax. These rates vary considerably across states, but even more important is the observation that there have been significant changes in the structure of corporate taxes over the past few decades. [This study finds that corporate income taxes, right-to-work laws, and unionization were factors in the shift of industry to the South.]

33. **Ohanian, L., A. Raffo, and Richard Rogerson. "Long-Term Changes in Labor Supply and Taxes: Evidence from OECD Countries, 1956–2004."** *Journal of Monetary Economics* **55 (2008): 1353–1362.**

We document large differences in trend changes in hours worked across Organisation for Economic Co-operation and Development (OECD) countries between 1956 and 2004. We assess the extent to which these changes are consistent with the intratemporal first-order condition from the neoclassical growth model, augmented with taxes on labor income and consumption expenditures. We find that the model can account for most of the trend changes in hours worked measured in the data. Differences in taxes explain much of the variation in hours worked both over time and across countries.

34. **Ojede, Andrew, and Steven Yamarik. "Tax Policy and State Economic Growth: The Long-Run and Short-Run of It."** *Economic Letters* **116, no. 2 (August 2012): 161–165.**

This paper uses a pooled mean group (PMG) estimator to evaluate the effects of tax policy on state-level growth. We find that property and sales tax rates have negative effects on long-run income growth, while income tax rates have no impact.

35. Padovano, F., and Emma Galli. "Tax Rates and Economic Growth in the OECD Countries (1950–1990)." *Economic Inquiry* 39, no. 1 (January 2001): 44.

This article proposes refined econometric estimates of effective marginal income tax rates for 23 OECD countries from 1951 to 1990. Panel regressions find such measures negatively correlated with economic growth. These results are consistent with endogenous growth theories and opposite to those of most empirical literature, which relies on measures of effective average tax rates. The negative correlation is also robust to consideration of other growth determinants. . . . Our analysis of a cross-section time-series panel of 23 OECD countries for 1950s–1980s decades shows that high marginal tax rates and tax progressivity are negatively correlated with long-run economic growth.

36. Papke, J. A., and Leslie Papke. "Measuring Differential State-Local Tax Liabilities and Their Implications for Business Investment Location." *National Tax Journal*, December 1985.

There is no easy way to answer the question as to whether or not state and local tax differentials make a difference in industrial growth or location. Consider some of the reasons why. From a theoretical standpoint, there are circumstances in which subnational taxation of business enterprises can induce locational shifts. These are related primarily to the competitive conditions in particular types of industry and to the kinds and levels of taxes paid by business. At the same time, a substantial amount of the empirical evidence, particularly of the questionnaire survey type, relating to the importance of taxes in location decisions demonstrates that state local tax differentials have little or no bearing on these decisions. [The authors do eventually show that the business location literature is increasingly showing that taxes do matter, in contrast to earlier studies.]

37. Peach, J., and C. Meghan Starbuck. "Oil and Gas Production and Economic Growth in New Mexico." *Journal of Economic Issues* **45, no. 2 (June 2011).**

This paper examines the relationship between energy production and economic growth in New Mexico using cross section data for the state's 33 counties in Census years 1960, 1970, 1980, 1990, and 2000. The central question is whether or not New Mexico's counties are subject to the resource curse, a phenomenon documented frequently in the literature. Most empirical studies of the resource curse hypothesis have used national or state-level data and a broad definition of natural resources. In contrast, this analysis uses county-level data with a focus on oil and gas extraction. The estimated models suggest that oil and gas extraction in New Mexico counties has had a small but positive effect on income, employment, and population. Similar results were obtained when the model was estimated for 925 counties in 13 energy-producing states for the year 2000.

38. Plaut, T. R., and Joseph Pluta. "Business Climate, Taxes and Expenditures, and State Industrial Growth in the United States." *Southern Economic Journal* **50, no. 1 (July 1983): 99–119.**

Many state and local public officials and businesspeople have placed increasing emphasis on a state's so-called business climate as a central factor in determining its ability to attract industry and promote growth. Exactly what constitutes a good business climate is not entirely clear, but it is usually associated with low state and local taxes, right-to-work laws, little union activity, and a cooperative governmental structure. In the newly emergent Sunbelt/Frostbelt controversy, the relatively good business climate of the Southern states is frequently offered as a major explanation of Sunbelt growth. . . . Despite the vast literature on industrial location, none of the available models use data for all U.S. states to test the relationship between a wide range of both noneconomic and economic factors, including business climate, and multiple measures of industrial growth. Using principal components analysis and a multiple regression model on pooled data for the 48 contiguous states, this paper tests the effect of four groups of variables (accessibility to markets, cost and availability of factors of production, climate and environment, and business climate and state and local taxes and expenditures) on three separate measures of industrial growth (which measure overall, labor-intensive, and capital-intensive growth). Central to the issue is whether regional industrial expansion is more the result of traditional market factors (such as market size and wage rates), newly emergent market factors (such as energy costs), environmental factors, or tax/expenditure and other business climate factors. [Business climate, tax, and expenditure variables as a group are significantly related to state employment and capital stock growth, but not to overall state industrial growth. Again, state growth is measured by manufacturing growth.]

39. Poulson, Barry, and Jules Kaplan. "State Income Taxes and Economic Growth." *Cato Journal* 28, no. 1 (Winter 2008): 53–71.

This article explores the impact of tax policy on economic growth in the states within the framework of an endogenous growth model. Regression analysis is used to estimate the impact of taxes on economic growth in the states from 1964 to 2004. The analysis reveals a significant negative impact of higher marginal tax rates on economic growth. The analysis underscores the importance of controlling for regressivity, convergence, and regional influences in isolating the effect of taxes on economic growth in the states.

40. Prescott, E. C. "Prosperity and Depression: 2002 Richard T. Ely Lecture." Federal Reserve Bank of Minneapolis Research Department, Working Paper 618, 2002.

Prosperity and depression are relative concepts. Today both France and Japan are depressed relative to the United States; equivalently, the United States is prosperous relative to these countries.

I say these countries are depressed relative to the United States because their output per working-age person is 30 percent less than the U.S. level. An interesting and important policy question is: Why are these countries depressed? The answers for these two countries turn out to be very different. The United States is prosperous relative to France because the U.S. intratemporal tax wedge that distorts the trade-off between consumption and leisure is much smaller than the French wedge. I will show that if France modified its intratemporal tax wedge so that its value was the same as the U.S. value, French welfare in consumption equivalents would increase by 19 percent. Consumption would have to increase by 19 percent now and in all future periods to achieve as large a welfare gain as that resulting from this tax reform.

41. Prescott, E. C. "Why Do Americans Work So Much More Than Europeans?" *Federal Reserve Bank of Minneapolis Quarterly Review* 28, no. 1 (2004).

Americans, that is, residents of the United States, work much more than do Europeans. Using labor market statistics from the Organisation for Economic Co-operation and Development (OECD), I find that Americans on a per person aged 15–64 basis work in the market sector 50 percent more than do the French. This was not always the case. In the early 1970s, Americans allocated less time to the market than did the French. The comparisons between Americans and Germans or Italians are the same. Why are there such large differences in labor supply across these countries? Why did the relative labor supplies change so much over time? In this article, I determine the importance of tax rates in accounting for these differences in labor supply for the major advanced industrial countries and find that tax rates alone account for most of them.

42. Rabushka, A. "Taxation, Economic Growth, and Liberty." *Cato Journal* 7, no. 1 (Spring/Summer 1987).

The Third World, often called the less developed countries (LDCs), consists of over 100 nations in Africa, Asia, the Middle East, the Mediterranean, and the western hemisphere. Most of these countries are former British, French, or Dutch colonies that received independence after World War II. Although Central and South American countries were long independent, their failure to sustain economic growth consigns them to the category of Third World economies. A few oil-exporting nations enjoy higher per capita incomes than the majority of non-oil-exporting countries, but even these select nations recently fell on hard times as world oil prices declined. Development specialists paid considerably less attention to taxation than such other aspects of development policy as international transfers, central planning, import-substitution schemes, the role of multinational corporations, and raising expenditure levels. The relationship between taxation and liberty for more than three billion inhabitants of the Third World remains virgin territory. [For several individual countries, the data are consistent with the hypothesis that taxes tend to lower economic growth.]

43. Reed, W. R. "The Determinants of U.S. State Economic Growth: A Less Extreme Bounds Analysis." *Economic Inquiry* **47, no. 4 (October 2009): 685–700.**

This study investigates U.S. state economic growth from 1970 to 1999. I innovate on previous studies by developing a new approach for addressing model uncertainty issues associated with estimating growth equations. My approach borrows from the "extreme bounds analysis" approach of Leamer while also addressing concerns raised by Granger and Uhlig, Sala-i-Martin, and others that not all specifications are equally likely to be true. I then apply this approach to identify robust determinants of state economic growth. My analysis confirms the importance of productivity characteristics of the labor force and industrial composition of a state's economy. I also find that policy variables such as (1) size and structure of government and (2) taxation are robust and economically important determinants of state economic growth. [He finds that increases in the average tax rate results in lower economic growth.]

44. Reed, W. R. "The Robust Relationship between Taxes and U.S. State Income Growth." *National Tax Journal* 61, no. 1 (2008): 57–80.

I estimate the relationship between taxes and income growth using data from 1970 to 1999 and the [48 contiguous] U.S. states. I find that taxes used to fund general expenditures are associated with significant, negative effects on income growth. This finding is generally robust across alternative variable specifications, alternative estimation procedures, and alternative ways of dividing the data into five-year periods, and across different time periods and Bureau of Economic Analysis (BEA) regions, though state-specific estimates vary widely. I also provide an explanation for why previous research has had difficulty identifying this robust relationship.

45. Reynolds, A. "Some International Comparisons of Supply-Side Policy." *Cato Journal* 5, no. 2 (Fall 1985).

Mainstream macroeconomics leaves policy makers wandering through a circular maze of paradoxes. Budget deficits supposedly stimulate private spending, causing inflation, but they crowd out private spending and strengthen the dollar. An increase in public and private borrowing raises interest rates, and higher interest rates reduce borrowing, thus reducing interest rates and raising borrowing.... The task of this paper is half of the Mundell mix— to relate the economic performance of various countries to the microeconomic details of their tax structures. This is not intended to deny the importance of other policy issues such as protectionism, monetary instability, excess regulation, or insecurity of property rights. The basic theme is that the global deterioration of tax policy in the past decade has been most significant in individual income and payroll taxes on both capital and labor. [Nations with high tax rates (from 1979 to 1984) tend to have lower rates of economic growth—there is a Laffer curve effect in countries with excessively high taxation.]

46. Romans, Thomas, and Ganti Subrahmanyam. "State and Local Taxes, Transfers and Regional Economic Growth."

Southern Economic Journal **46, no. 2 (October 1979):
435–444.**

Conflicting sets of evidence exist with respect to the effects of state and local taxes on industry location and regional economic growth in the United States. Survey results of business firms indicate that "high taxes" consistently rank close to or at the top of any list of determinants of industry location. But empirical studies on relative tax burdens have generally concluded that "high taxes do not drive out business," presumably because: (1) Insofar as taxes are higher in one state than another, it may only represent a higher level of public goods production and consumption, and (2) state and local government taxes on business are rather small (relative to total costs and sales) and do not vary greatly (relative to interstate variations in factor and transport costs). Neither firms nor persons have the option of eliminating all state and local taxes through migration. However, two tax issues that may be highly significant to regional economic growth are being ignored or otherwise circumvented by these arguments. The first is the degree of progression in the tax structure. Insofar as tax progression is greater than benefit progression in one locality relative to another, incentives exist for lower- or zero-income individuals to stay or enter and for higher-income individuals to depart. Business may act similarly insofar as the location of firms is dictated by higher-income managerial personnel with personal incentives to locate in low tax progression states. In conclusion, the evidence indicates that it might well behoove state and local governments to consider the effects of egalitarian fiscal policies on their economies. The level of personal taxes does not appear to affect the economic growth rate in either direction, and the level of business taxes is positively correlated with growth. But the degree of progression in the personal tax structure and the proportion of tax revenues flowing into transfer payments (i.e., the redistribution aspects of taxes) are negatively and significantly correlated with growth in state personal income.

47. Romer, C. D., and David H. Romer. "The Macroeconomic Effects of Tax Changes: Estimates Based on a New Measure of Fiscal Shocks." *American Economic Review* **100, no. 3 (June 2010): 763–801.**

This paper investigates the impact of tax changes on economic activity. We use the narrative record, such as presidential speeches and Congressional reports, to identify the size, timing, and principal motivation for all major postwar tax policy actions. This analysis allows us to separate legislated changes into those taken for reasons related to prospective economic conditions and those taken for more exogenous reasons. The behavior of output following these more exogenous changes indicates that tax increases are highly contractionary. The effects are strongly significant, highly robust, and much larger than those obtained using broader measures of tax changes.

48. Scully, G. W. "Optimal Taxation, Economic Growth, and Income Inequality in the United States." National Center for Policy Analysis, Policy Report 316, 2008.

Up to a point, government spending on public goods—such as national defense and protection of property—can raise the economic growth rate. However, as government spending rises, the tendency is to increase spending on nonproductive income transfers—such as subsidy and welfare programs. Research indicates that the high levels of taxation required to pay for such income transfers inhibit economic growth, whereas lower taxes can raise the rate of economic growth.

49. Stokey, Nancy, and Sergio Rebelo. "Growth Effects of Flat-Rate Taxes." *Journal of Political Economy* **103, no. 3 (June 1995).**

This paper presents a quantitative general equilibrium model showing that a revenue-neutral flat tax can permanently boost per capita growth by 0.18 to 0.85 percentage point annually, and that the lower marginal tax rate and the full investment write-off are both important contributors to the increased growth.

50. Vedder, R. "Federal Tax Reform: Lessons from the State." *Cato Journal* **5, no. 2 (Fall 1985).**

Federal tax reform has been a major subject of contemporary debate. Certainly the current system is severely deficient with respect to the trinity of public finance criteria usually applied in evaluating taxes: administrative costs, economic efficiency, and equity. In this article, evidence from the historical experience of state and local governments is examined. Have states with relatively flat-rate income taxes fared better economically than those with highly progressive income taxes similar to the federal tax? The answer, generally, is "yes," adding impetus to the calls for radical federal tax reform. Additional evidence is presented suggesting that "equity" is far less associated with the word "progressivity" in the eyes of the public than conventional political wisdom has it. The notion that support of a radical flat-rate tax would be suicidal politically is also questioned.

51. Vedder, R., and Lowell Gallaway. "Rent-Seeking, Distributional Coalitions, Taxes, Relative Prices and Economic Growth." *Public Choice* **51 (1986): 93–100.**

The 50 U.S. states are an excellent laboratory for evaluating the economic consequences of public policy. While all part of a largely geographically contiguous free trade area with similar customs, commercial laws, language, and foreign policy, each makes some distinctly different public choices that impact on the economic environment. Moreover, the evidence is that there is enormous disparity in the growth experience of the states. For example, from 1970 to 1982, real personal income in some states (e.g., Wyoming) doubled, whereas in others (e.g., New York), it grew hardly at all (less than 1 percent a year). What explains these large differentials? [Change in personal income tax rates and the number of persons receiving Aid for Dependent Children (AFDC) payments adversely impacted economic growth.]

52. Wasylenko, M. "Taxation and Economic Development: The State of the Economic Literature." *New England Economic Review*, March/April 1997.

Those who shape state and local fiscal policy have had a sustained interest in the role that taxation plays in the economic development of states, regions, cities, and special districts or zones. At least 75 studies of employment growth, investment growth, or firm location include an analysis of taxes. Interest in the topic is fueled further when firms complain about the business climate in general or about taxation in particular. State or local policy makers then have the unenviable task of deciphering firms' complaints and deciding whether additional tax incentives and lower taxes represent economic rents or constitute a timely and necessary response to keep firms in place. . . . This review of the literature suggests that taxes have a small, statistically significant effect on interregional location behavior.

53. Wasylenko, M., and Therese McGuire. "Jobs and Taxes: The Effect of Business Climate on States' Employment Growth Rates." *National Tax Journal* 38, no. 4 (December 1985).

An econometric model for total employment growth and for employment growth in six separate industries in states between 1973 and 1980 is specified and estimated. The results indicate that higher wages, utility prices, personal income tax rates, and an increase in the overall level of taxation discourage employment growth in several industries. But factors such as higher state and local spending on education, and per capita income favorably affect job growth. The implications of these findings for employment growth rates in several states are then examined.

54. Weinstein, B. "Tax Incentives for Growth." *Society*, March/April 1977.

There is little evidence to support the significance of state and local government incentives for inducing private investment. Nonetheless, state and local governments apparently believe that they have the means, either through legislative action or by persuasion, to influence the level of economic activity in their region. This belief is evidenced by the fact that tax-free state and local revenue bond financing is offered to industry in 45 states; 29 states offer other types of low-interest loans; 25 states do not collect sales taxes on newly purchased industrial equipment; 38 do not levy inventory taxes on goods in transit; virtually all states have industrial development agencies; and many state and local governments offer tax credits, abatements, and rapid depreciation to encourage new investment in plant and equipment. Why do state and local governments offer these incentives? Presumably the objective is to improve that state's business climate on the assumption that economic development— defined as new investment and job creation—is more likely to occur where the business climate is favorable rather than unfavorable.

55. Yamarik, Steven. "Can Tax Policy Help Explain State-Level Macroeconomic Growth?" *Economic Letters* **62, no. 2 (August 2000): 211–215.**

This paper empirically tests the role of tax distortions in explaining state-level economic growth through the estimation of disaggregated personal income, general sales, and property tax rates. The results show that these disaggregated tax rates generate predictions more consistent with growth theory.

Key Quotes from Econometric Bibliography

Quotes that relate to economic growth variable:

- "The road to serfdom and economic decline is still paved with oppressive taxation, and until that condition is repaired wealth will still hide or melt away."
  —A. Reynolds, "Some International Comparisons of Supply-Side Policy," *Cato Journal* 5, no. 2 (Fall 1985).

- "High tax rates have frustrated the efficient use of labor and capital and have discouraged entrepreneurship, thus holding down growth."

—A. Rabushka, "Taxation, Economic Growth, and Liberty," *Cato Journal* 7, no. 1 (Spring/Summer 1987).

- "Contrary to conventional wisdom, the results of this study lend considerable support to the argument that corporate tax rate differentials between states as well as the extent of unionization and a favorable business climate (enactment of right-to-work laws) have been major factors influencing the redistribution of industry toward the South."

—R. J. Newman, "Migration and Growth in the South," *Review of Economics and Statistics* 65, no. 1 (February 1983): 76–86.

- "[T]ax differentials may be an important location factor. . . . For some types of business enterprises, tax cost differentials will be significant as compared with the differentials in nontax costs."

—J. A. Papke and Leslie Papke, "Measuring Differential State-Local Tax Liabilities and Their Implications for Business Investment Location," *National Tax Journal*, December 1985.

- "Indirectly, high personal taxes may be an impediment to business growth since they force up salaries of executive, managerial, and technical personnel."

—B. Weinstein, "Tax Incentives for Growth," *Society*, March/April 1977.

- "[H]igher wages, utility prices, personal income tax rates, and an increase in the overall level of taxation discourage employment growth in several industries."

—M. Wasylenko and Therese McGuire, "Jobs and Taxes: The Effect of Business Climate on States' Employment Growth Rates," *National Tax Journal* 38, no. 4 (December 1985).

- "Our results suggest modest effects, on the order of 0.2 to 0.3 percentage point differences in growth rates in response to a major tax reform. Nevertheless, even such small effects can have a large cumulative impact on living standards."

—Eric Engen and Jonathan Skinner, "Taxation and Economic Growth," *National Tax Journal* 49, no. 4 (December 1996): 617–642.

- "Results based on pooled time series and cross section data are presented, which indicate that state and local tax increases significantly retard economic growth when the revenue is used to fund transfer payments."

  —L. J. Helms, "The Effect of State and Local Taxes on Economic Growth: A Time Series-Cross Section Approach," *Review of Economics and Statistics* 67, no. 4 (1985): 574–582.

- "Corporate taxes are found to be most harmful for growth, followed by personal income taxes, and then consumption taxes."

  —Å. Johansson, C. Heady, J. Arnold, B. Brys, and L. Vartia, "Tax and Economic Growth," Working Paper 620, OECD Economics Department, 2008.

- "We find that statutory corporate tax rates are significantly negatively correlated with cross-sectional differences in average economic growth rates. . . a cut in the corporate tax rate by 10 percentage points will raise the annual growth rate by one to two percentage points."

  —Y. Lee and R. H. Gordon, "Tax Structure and Economic Growth," *Journal of Public Economics* 89, no. 5–6 (2005): 1027–1043.

- "The paper finds that direct and indirect taxes associated with stock market transactions slow real per capita output growth."

  —Ross Levine, "Stock Markets, Growth, and Policy," Board of Governors of the Federal Reserve System International Finance Discussion Paper 374, 1990.

- "In simulations of economic growth models the effect of taxation on growth has frequently been demonstrated to be considerable."

  —G. D. Myles, "Economic Growth and the Role of Taxation," OECD Economics Department Working Paper 713, 2009.

- "We find that property and sales tax rates have negative effects on long-run income growth, while income tax rates have no impact."

  —Andrew Ojede and Steven Yamarik, "Tax Policy and State Economic Growth: The Long-Run and Short-Run of It," *Economic Letters* 116, no. 2 (August 2012): 161–165.

- "The analysis reveals a significant negative impact of higher marginal tax rates on economic growth."

  —Barry Poulson and Jules Kaplan, "State Income Taxes and Economic Growth," *Cato Journal* 28, no. 1 (Winter 2008): 53–71.

- "[T]he degree of progression in the personal tax structure and the proportion of tax revenues flowing into transfer payments (i.e., the redistribution aspects of taxes) are negatively and significantly correlated with growth in state personal income."

  —Thomas Romans and Ganti Subrahmanyam, "State and Local Taxes, Transfers and Regional Economic Growth," *Southern Economic Journal* 46, no. 2 (October 1979): 435–444.

- "[A] revenue-neutral flat tax can permanently boost per capita growth by 0.18 to 0.85 percentage point annually, and that the lower marginal tax rate and the full investment write-off are both important contributors to the increased growth."

  —Nancy Stokey and Sergio Rebelo, "Growth Effects of Flat-Rate Taxes," *Journal of Political Economy* 103, no. 3 (June 1995).

- "Considerable empirical evidence suggests that state and local taxes do not significantly impact the geographic distribution of economic activity; this analysis, however, finds a significant negative distributed lag impact of such taxes on capital formation."

  —B. Benson and Ronald Johnson, "The Lagged Impact of State and Local Taxes on Economic Activity and Political Behavior," *Economic Inquiry* 24, no. 3 (1986).

- "In reducing the real net rate of return, current tax treatment significantly retards capital accumulation. This in turn causes an enormous waste of resources and redistributes a substantial fraction of gross income from labor to capital."

  —M. J. Boskin, "Taxation, Saving, and the Rate of Interest," *Journal of Political Economy* 86, no. 2, Part 2: Research in Taxation (April 1978): S3–S27.

- "The parameter estimates in my study of U.S. time series data implied that without social security the U.S. capital stock would eventually be some 60 percent higher. . . . The larger capital stock would mean greater productivity, higher real wage rates, and a higher national income."

—M. Feldstein, "Social Security and Saving: The Extended Life Cycle Theory," *American Economic Review* 66, no. 2, Papers and Proceedings of the Eighty-Eighth Annual Meeting of the American Economic Association (May 1976): 77–86.

- "Differences in taxes explain much of the variation in hours worked both over time and across countries."

  —L. Ohanian, A. Raffo, and Richard Rogerson, "Long-Term Changes in Labor Supply and Taxes: Evidence from OECD Countries, 1956–2004," *Journal of Monetary Economics* 55 (2008): 1353–1362.

- "Our analysis of a cross-section time-series panel of 23 OECD countries for 1950s–1980s decades shows that high marginal tax rates and tax progressivity are negatively correlated with long-run economic growth."

  "These results are consistent with endogenous growth theories and opposite to those of most empirical literature, which relies on measures of effective average tax rates."

  —F. Padovano and Emma Galli, "Tax Rates and Economic Growth in the OECD Countries (1950–1990)," *Economic Inquiry* 39, no. 1 (January 2001): 44.

- "I estimate the relationship between taxes and income growth using data from 1970 to 1999 and the [48 contiguous] U.S. states. I find that taxes used to fund general expenditures are associated with significant, negative effects on income growth."

  —W. R. Reed, "The Robust Relationship Between Taxes and U.S. State Income Growth," *National Tax Journal* 61, no. 1 (2008): 57–80.

- "Our results indicate that tax changes have very large effects on output. Our baseline specification implies that an exogenous tax increase of 1 percent of GDP lowers real GDP by almost 3 percent."

—C. D. Romer and David H. Romer, "The Macroeconomic Effects of Tax Changes: Estimates Based on a New Measure of Fiscal Shocks," *American Economic Review* 100, no. 3 (June 2010): 763–801.

- "The results show a strong negative relationship between increases in individual income taxes and the growth in personal income."

"The findings suggest that long-run economic growth would be best served by constraining distributional coalitions, be it through constitutional restraints (e.g., balanced budget amendments, the item veto), statutory changes (e.g., subjecting coalitions like labor unions to the antitrust laws), or some other means (e.g., labor and capital fleeing distributional coalitions, such as in the movement of workers and plants to nonunion areas)."

—R. Vedder and Lowell Gallaway, "Rent-Seeking, Distributional Coalitions, Taxes, Relative Prices and Economic Growth," *Public Choice* 51 (1986): 93–100.

Quotes that relate to population growth variable:

- "The results offer considerable support to the Tiebout hypothesis that the consumer-voter moves to that area which best satisfies his preferences for public goods."

—R. Cebula, "Interstate Migration and the Tiebout Hypothesis: An Analysis According to Race, Sex and Age," *Journal of the American Statistical Association* 69, no. 348 (1974): 876–879.

- "In particular, consumer-voters appear to be attracted by lower state income tax burdens and lower property tax burdens."

—R. J. Cebula, "Migration and the Tiebout-Tullock Hypothesis Revisited," *American Journal of Economics and Sociology* 68, no. 2 (2009): 541–551.

- "[S]tate income and death taxes display life-cycle effects; working males in their peak earning years are detracted by high income taxes while all migrants aged 55 to 69 avoid counties in states with high inheritance and estate taxes."

—D. E. Clark and W. J. Hunter, "The Impact of Economic Opportunity, Amenities, and Fiscal Factors on Age-Specific Migration Rates," *Journal of Regional Science* 21 (1992): 349–365.

- "[I]ncome taxes have an effect on migration for most races and age groups. Individuals move from states with high income taxes to states with low income taxes; these results corroborate the results obtained from the use of aggregate, state-level data."

—M. P. Gius, "The Effect of Income Taxes on Interstate Migration: An Analysis by Age and Race," *Annals of Regional Science* 46 (2009).

CHAPTER 7

Fiscal Parasitic Leakages

Texas versus California*

When experience deviated [from a preexisting scheme of axioms] that made it by definition unworthy of careful scrutiny, for then it obeyed no apparent order.

—Philip Ball, *Curiosity*

O bserving the colorful interchange of words between three-term Texas Governor Rick Perry and three-term California Governor Jerry Brown is entertaining, to say the least.

For our academic friends, the most hilarious comment was made inadvertently by Governor Brown when he, in reference to people coming to California, said that "the British are coming here, so are the French, so are the Russians, so are the Chinese—everybody with half a brain is coming to California."[1]

But for Arthur Laffer and his 12-year-old grandson, the best was yet to come. Dr. Laffer and his grandson both have a keen sense of

---

* Special thanks to Sally Pipes for her edits and comments during the writing of this chapter.

appreciation for public displays of scatological humor, and of this there was no shortage. They could scarcely contain themselves when comments like "looking at our backside"[2] hit the mainstream media.

But beneath all of this slapstick humor is an enormous substrate of the most deadly serious issues of the human condition: poverty versus prosperity.

Millions of people unnecessarily underemployed or unemployed for years and years is hardly a joke. Economic policies that force people to flee their homes in search of a better way of life are not really funny, either. And the vast agglomeration of other issues that almost always accompanies subpar economic performance, such as loss of self-esteem, alcoholism, abusive behavior, lack of respect for others, crime, and poor education, just to name a few, is far from laughable. State capitols are not appropriate sets for *Saturday Night Live*.

This chapter takes a serious look at the economics of two states, Texas and California, over the past decade, in order to highlight the impact that the very different policies of these two states have on their citizens.

A Tale of Two States—A 55-Point Summary

1. A decade ago, Texas accounted for 7.4 percent of total U.S. output, and today it accounts for 9.0 percent. California started this same period at 13.1 percent and ended the period at 12.9 percent of total U.S. output.

2. Population growth in Texas over the past decade was 20.1 percent, fourth highest in the nation, while California's population growth was 9.1 percent, 24th highest.

3. Growth in output, both in aggregate and on a per capita basis, is far higher in Texas than it is in California.

Taxes

4. California is one of the highest-taxed states in the nation, whereas Texas is one of the lowest-taxed states in the nation.

5. State and local tax revenues are growing far faster in Texas than they are in California.

6. Texas has no income or capital gains tax. California has the nation's highest income and capital gains tax rates.

7. California has the third highest workers' compensation costs in the nation ($2.92 per $100 of payroll). Texas is the 13th lowest in this category ($1.60 per $100 of payroll).

8. Even in sales taxes as a percentage of personal income, Texas (2.30 percent) is a good bit lower than California (2.61 percent).

9. Both Texas and California have repealed their state estate taxes.

Migration

10. California has swung from being one of the biggest net in-migration destination states in the nation to being one of the biggest exodus states. Texas's in-migration as of today is the highest in the nation and has, if anything, been increasing.

11. Taxpayers, especially, are moving out of California and into Texas.

12. Renting a U-Haul moving van is far cheaper from Texas to California than from California to Texas (see Table 7.1).

TABLE 7.1

U-Haul Rental Prices between California and Texas

From Texas to California		To California			
		To Sacramento	To San Diego	To Los Angeles	To San Francisco
From Texas	From Austin	$1,260	$1,037	$1,075	$1,259
	From Dallas	$1,336	$1,087	$1,138	$1,335
	From Houston	$1,007	$1,098	$1,140	$1,006
	From San Antonio	$849	$714	$774	$1,069
From California to Texas		**From California**			
		From Sacramento	From San Diego	From Los Angeles	From San Francisco
To Texas	To Austin	$2,087	$2,634	$2,734	$2,159
	To Dallas	$2,035	$2,650	$2,770	$2,108
	To Houston	$2,178	$2,791	$2,898	$2,255
	To San Antonio	$2,037	$2,546	$2,646	$2,108

Source: U-Haul (prices obtained from www.uhaul.com on 2/15/2013 for 26-foot truck rental).

13. Average adjusted gross incomes of people moving out of California and into Texas are consistently much higher than is the average adjusted gross income of taxpayers moving out of Texas and into California.

14. From 2001 to 2012, California dropped from having 55 Fortune 500 companies to 53, a loss of two, while over that same period Texas went from having 45 Fortune 500 companies to 52, a gain of seven.

Poverty

15. Texas has significantly less poverty as a share of its population (16.5 percent) than does California (23.5 percent, the highest in the nation).

16. Texas has the fourth lowest percentage of population on welfare in the nation (0.43 percent), whereas California has the highest percentage of its population on welfare (3.88 percent).

17. California has 30 percent of its population enrolled in Medicaid whereas Texas has 18 percent. The U.S. average is 22 percent.

18. Texas has 15.5 percent of its population on food stamps compared to California's 9.7 percent, but Texas's administrative costs are far less.

Employment

19. Texas's unemployment rate (6.0 percent in December 2013) is much lower than is California's unemployment rate (8.3 percent in December 2013).

20. California has the nation's most powerful public employee unions, while in Texas union membership and power are moderate.

21. Texas is a right-to-work state. California is a forced-union state.

22. Texas has the fastest growth in employment in the nation whereas California ranks 31st.

Oil

23. Texas is doing a far better job in developing its oil reserves than is California.

24. California is estimated to have over 15 billion barrels of shale oil, but regulations and restrictions prevent access to these reserves. California's oil production continues to fall each year, while Texas has ramped up production to levels not seen in 25 years.

25. California is one of a few states that has banned fracking in some areas. Texas encourages fracking.

Debt

26. State and local government debt in Texas is substantially lower than it is in California.

27. Texas's Standard & Poor's (S&P) credit rating (AAA) is far higher than is California's S&P credit rating (A).

Public Services—Employee Inputs

28. California pays its educators 40 percent more per full-time equivalent employee than does Texas.

29. Public welfare employees in California make over $56,000 per year to Texas's $37,000 per annum—a 52 percent premium.

30. California pays its hospital employees 53 percent more than does Texas.

31. California pays its police protection employees 70 percent more than does Texas.

32. California pays highway employees 76 percent more than does Texas.

33. California pays fire protection personnel 86 percent more than does Texas.

34. California pays its corrections employees 93 percent more than does Texas.

35. California pays its state legislators over $95,000 per year. Texas pays its state legislators $7,200 per year.

Public Services—Product Costs

36. California's teachers union has been the single largest contributor to political campaigns in California over the past decade ($212 million), double that of the next largest contributor, also a state government employees union.

37. California's corrections officers are some of the most highly unionized state employees in the nation.

38. California has far and away the most organized and politically active prison guard union in the country. In 2010 alone, this union spent $32 million for political purposes, ranking it the 15th largest political contributor in the state.

39. The annual cost of a prisoner held in Texas is $21,390, or $58.60 a day. In California, the equivalent prisoner costs taxpayers $47,421 per year, or $129.00 per day.

40. California builds one mile of state highway at an average cost of $265,000 while for a mile of highway in Texas the average cost is a little over $88,000, according to the Reason Foundation.

Public Services—Outcomes

41. Texas employs 345 educators for every 10,000 of population, whereas California employs only 231 educators per 10,000 of population. The U.S. average is 286.

42. As measured by the U.S. Department of Education, California student test scores are the fourth worst in the nation, while Texas students' scores are 29th highest out of 50.

43. The California Teachers Association has called 170 strikes since 1975, while Texas teachers are prohibited from striking. In Texas, any teacher who strikes loses his or her license to teach immediately.

44. Of the five mega states—California, Texas, New York, Illinois, and Florida—California, according to the Department of Education, has the lowest educational test scores whereas Texas has the highest.

45. Texas has more hospital employees per 10,000 of population than does California.

46. Texas employs more police protection employees per 10,000 of population than does California (28.9 versus 26.4, respectively).

47. Texas has far more prisoners per 100,000 of population (923 prisoners per 100,000 population) than does California (621 prisoners per 100,000 population).

48. California prisons are currently running at 75 percent over design capacity, while Texas prisons are occupied at about 15 percent below design capacity. California has been ordered by the Supreme Court to reduce its prison population to no more than 137.5 percent of design capacity.

49. Texas has more corrections employees per 10,000 of population than does California (27.7 versus 24.4).

50. Texas has almost 30 percent more highway employees per 10,000 of population than does California.

51. Texas ranked 23rd in the nation in state road conditions, whereas California ranked dead last.

Public Services—Both Inputs and Outcomes

52. Looking solely at classroom teachers in elementary and secondary education, California pays its teachers almost 50 percent more than does Texas, and California employs 40 percent fewer teachers than Texas does per 10,000 of population.

53. For police officers, Texas employs 21 for every 10,000 people whereas California employs only 18. But California pays its police officers a 75 percent premium over Texas police officers.

54. For firefighters, Texas employs 9.2 per 10,000 of population versus California at 7.7 per 10,000. California's firefighters are paid $120,000 per year to Texas's $63,000.

55. California has 74 percent more public welfare employees per 10,000 of population than does Texas, and California pays its welfare workers 52 percent more per worker than does Texas.

The November 2012 Elections in California and Texas

On November 6, 2012, California voters, by a 55 to 45 margin, passed Governor Jerry Brown's Proposition 30, which is a constitutional amendment that raises the state sales tax rate by 25 basis points from 7.25 percent to 7.5 percent. Proposition 30 also raises the highest marginal state income tax rates from 9.3 percent to 10.3 percent for incomes between $250,000 and $300,000, from 9.3 percent to 11.3 percent for incomes between $300,000 and $500,000, from 9.3 percent to 12.3 percent for incomes between

$500,000 and $1 million, and finally from 10.3 percent to 13.3 percent for incomes over $1 million.

The new income tax schedule applies retroactively to all income earned or received since January 1, 2012.

In addition to passing Governor Brown's tax increase, California voters also gave the advocates for big government supermajorities in both houses of the legislature.

Only a few weeks after the election, California's Franchise Tax Board notified taxpayers who had reported a qualified small business stock exclusion or deferral for taxable years beginning on or after January 1, 2008, that, because these provisions are invalid and unenforceable, a Notice of Proposed Assessments will be issued denying the exclusion or deferral.[3] This represents a doubling of the state's capital gains tax for this group of filers, retroactive five years, no less.

The election victory championed by Governor Brown has also set into motion a major effort to eviscerate or repeal Proposition 13, also a constitutional amendment, passed in 1978. California's Prop 13 has limited property tax rates to the lesser of 1 percent of the property's market value or an increase of 2 percent per year. And now there is talk of California setting up an exit fee for anyone who wishes to leave California.

On February 28, 2013, California's Board of Equalization voted 3 to 2 to raise the state gasoline tax by 10 percent from 36 cents to 39.5 cents per gallon effective July 1, 2013. According to the *San Diego Union Tribune*, "The increase is partly due to a $157 million shortfall in gas-tax revenue in fiscal 2012, and also a projection of less consumption by California drivers. . . . [The] American Petroleum Institute [had] listed California's gas taxes as second highest in the nation behind New York. After the July 1 tax increase, however, the 70.1 cents average tax per gallon will lead the nation."[4]

The People Have Spoken

On the same day that California voters spoke so clearly, November 6, 2012, Texas voters sent a majority of moderates and conservatives to the

Texas House of Representatives and Senate. Texas also elected one of the most economically pro-growth U.S. Senators, Ted Cruz, to replace Kay Bailey Hutchison.

Texas has never had an income tax on either earned income or unearned income such as dividends or interest. Texas has no capital gains tax, either. And Texas's state sales tax rate is 6.25 percent.

This chapter attempts to provide an objective assessment of the data without hope or agenda, as if it were Christmas. At Christmas you always tell the truth.

Economic Performance: California, Texas, and the United States

Before we jump into the explicit measures of economic performance, there are a number of everyday observations that should give us a strong clue as to how well California is doing relative to Texas. Quite simply, people "vote with their feet," only nowadays it is with moving vans. Because so many people are trying to leave California for Texas and other destinations and so few people are trying to leave Texas for California, moving van companies have adjusted their prices. In Table 7.1 we have listed the one-way U-Haul prices both ways between four California cities and four Texas cities. It is amazing.

When Dr. Laffer left California for Tennessee, he discovered these data in a very personal way. As Steve Moore and Dr. Laffer wrote in their 2008 paper, "California, Who Are You? Part II":

> [T]housands and thousands more California residents are choosing to leave the state than U.S. residents are choosing to move into California— and it's getting worse. . . . The out-migration flows have become so systemic that the cost to rent a full-sized U-Haul truck to move from Los Angeles to Nashville, Tennessee, is $4,285—more than six times the $557 cost of moving in the opposite direction. Similarly, it costs $4,254 to rent a full-size truck from Los Angeles to Austin, Texas, yet only $407 to complete the reverse trip.[5]

This section provides a high-level yet comprehensive overview of California and Texas over the past decade. After reviewing the U-Haul data, you will not be surprised by the results.

Table 7.2 is fascinating because it contains so much relevant information in a format that facilitates easy comparisons of states. The full 50-state table appears as Table 2.1 in Chapter 2, and allows state-by-state comparisons for the most critical metrics. But our focus in this chapter is not on just any generic bilateral comparison. This chapter focuses on California and Texas. Our hope is to uncover the effects each of these two states' widely divergent policies have had, and, from these results, to infer a more general guide to achieving economic prosperity.

In Table 7.2, looking at Row 1 you can see Texas's population growth, which is the fourth fastest growing among all the states in the nation at 20.1 percent. And by way of comparison, California's population growth is only slightly below the national average and ranks as the 24th fastest growing state in the nation with decadal growth of 9.1 percent. However, when a percentage point comparison is made

Row	Percentage Change, 2002–2012	U.S.*	TX	TX Rank	CA	CA Rank
1	Population	9.3%	20.1%	4	9.1%	24
2	Labor Force Participation Rate	–4.5%	–4.7%	28	–6.0%	35
3	Labor Force	6.9%	16.6%	2	6.6%	24
4	Employment Rate	–2.1%	–0.4%	6	–4.0%	46
5	Employment	4.6%	16.1%	1	2.3%	31
6	Productivity	44.8%	53.8%	10	41.1%	26
7	Gross State Product	51.7%	78.5%	4	44.4%	32
8	Gross State Product per Capita	38.8%	48.6%	10	32.4%	34
	Percentage, December 2012					
9	Unemployment Rate	7.0%	6.2%	16	9.8%	48

TABLE 7.2

* Equal-weighted averages of the 50 states.

solely between California and Texas, the difference in decadal population growth is really quite large, at 11 percent. Texas's population growth
exceeds California's population growth by more than California's population growth exceeds the slowest-growing state in the nation, Rhode
Island at −1.5 percent. If people are voting with their feet, Texas is beating California by a very large amount.

One chart that especially caught our attention was produced by the
U.S. Census Bureau in March 2013 (Figure 7.1). This net migration map
has been reproduced as presented by the U.S. Census Bureau, which chose
these specific time periods. The chart illustrates the enormous change in
population flows into and out of California over the past half century.

FIGURE 7.1

Net Migration between California and Other States, 1955–1960 and 1995–2000

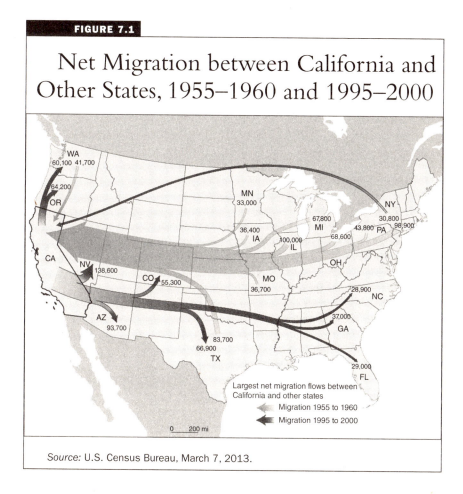

Source: U.S. Census Bureau, March 7, 2013.

The arrowheads reflect the large population flows into California from wherever in the 1955 to 1960 period and the reverse population flows out of California to wherever from 1995 to 2000.

If President Reagan were still alive and could see what Governor Brown has done to California we wonder if he would still joke that "if the Pilgrims had landed in California instead of [at] Plymouth Rock, the East would still be unsettled."

In a recent paper by Tom Gray and Robert Scardamalia,[6] the basic facts of California's radical change in net migration patterns are presented in a very thorough context using multiple sources for data. California has gone from the greatest destination state in the nation in the late 1980s to a state that is currently below the national average in population growth.

Among the many factors Gray and Scardamalia point to are unemployment differentials, significantly different business climates, and relative tax rates. Three observations in particular interested us from their analysis:

1. Foreign migration into California has fallen and is trending downward.
2. The natural increase in California's resident population—births minus deaths—is also falling and will most likely fall further or may even turn negative at some point in the foreseeable future.
3. California's net domestic migration, with but a few exceptions, has been negative since about 1992 and could well be more negative as time goes on.

And, as a consequence of these trends, the authors conclude, "If all these trends continue, California may find itself in a situation similar to that of New York and the states of the midwestern Rust Belt in the last century, which have seen populations stagnate for decades, or even fall."[7]

In a rare display of humor, the authors add, "California is still contributing to the population boom of the southwestern U.S. but now seems to do so mainly by sending residents to neighboring states."[8]

Our view of the changing migration patterns for California focuses primarily on California's changing economic policies.

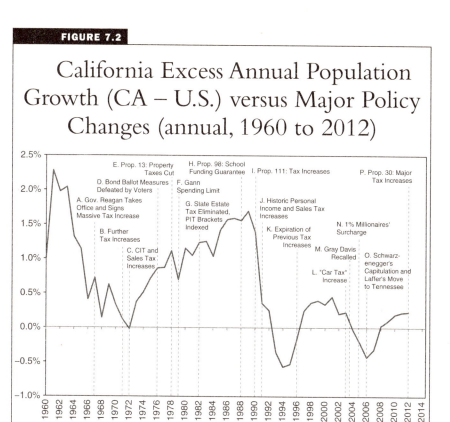

FIGURE 7.2

California Excess Annual Population Growth (CA – U.S.) versus Major Policy Changes (annual, 1960 to 2012)

Source: Bureau of Economic Analysis, Laffer Associates.

In Figure 7.2 we have plotted California's excess population growth (versus average U.S. growth) versus some of California's major economic policy changes.

It is also worthwhile to note that California's migration patterns are not only obvious in migration of people—they are quite clear in the migration of companies as well. Each year, *Fortune* ranks the world's largest companies and publishes the list as the Fortune Global 500. In 2001, 55 Fortune Global 500 companies were headquartered in California, while 45 were headquartered in Texas. It should not surprise you that in the latest 2012 *Fortune* rankings, California is now home to only 53 Global 500 companies, while Texas has added seven over that time period, for a total of 52 Global 500 companies now calling Texas home. Just as people migrate, companies do, too—and much for the same reasons!

As you descend through the rows of Table 7.2, you'll start to see just how stark the performance differentials are between Texas and California. In fact, Texas beats California in every single row of Table 7.2. For a detailed walk-through of each metric that appears in Table 7.2, see Chapter 2. The consequences of differences in economic growth accumulate. In Figure 7.3 we have plotted Texas's gross state product (GSP) as a share of U.S. gross domestic product (GDP) and California's GSP as a share of U.S. GDP over the past 10 years (2002 to 2012). Texas has gone from 7.4 percent of U.S. GDP to 9.0 percent, while California started the decade at 13.1 percent of U.S. GDP and ended at 12.9 percent.

At the end of this past decade, Texas had a lower unemployment rate than did California. When considering state-by-state comparisons, as opposed to international comparisons where populations are considerably less mobile, measures such as unemployment rates are notoriously unreliable as indicators of good economic policies (for more on this

FIGURE 7.3

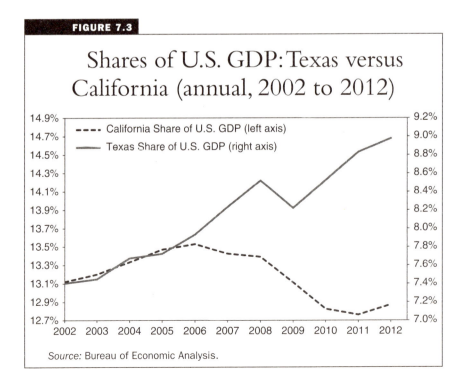

Shares of U.S. GDP: Texas versus California (annual, 2002 to 2012)

Source: Bureau of Economic Analysis.

idea, see Chapter 8). But, if achieved in the correct way—via economic growth rather than contraction—low unemployment rates go a long way to improve a state's quality of life.[9]

When it comes to economic performance, Texas far outperforms California in all the relevant categories. Is it any wonder why people are moving into Texas and out of California?

A Brief Note on Poverty Metrics

Performance is not only about economic growth, although economic growth is the single most important measure of performance. The plight and circumstances of our nation's least fortunate are also a matter of great concern.

In a November 2012 Current Population Report of the Department of Commerce entitled "The Research Supplemental Poverty Measure: 2011,"[10] improved measures of state poverty are presented for each state as an average of the period 2009 to 2011. These improved measures of the incidence of poverty by state include many items that the old measures did not include, such as (1) payroll taxes; (2) in-kind public benefits, such as food stamps; (3) expenses needed to hold a job, such as transportation or child care; (4) medical costs; (5) family situations in addition to family size, such as child support, cohabitation, and so on; and, most important for our purposes, (6) geographic differences in the cost of living.

In Table 7.3, the numbers of people in poverty and their percentage of the respective population are reported for the three-year average (2009–2011) of those in poverty for both Texas and California and the United States as a whole, using this Supplemental Poverty Measure.

TABLE 7.3			
Poverty: United States, California, and Texas (three-year average 2009–2011)			
	United States	**California**	**Texas**
Number of People (000s)	48,423	8,773	4,145
Percentage of Population	15.8%	23.5%	16.5%

Source: U.S. Census Bureau.

Both Texas and California have larger shares of their populations in poverty than does the United States as a whole. California, however, not only has a larger share of its population in poverty than does the United States, but California's share of the population in poverty is virtually 50 percent greater than the U.S. average and is the highest in the entire nation. Texas's share, on the other hand, is only a smidgeon above the U.S. average.

When it comes to alleviating poverty, despair, and unemployment, Texas also outperforms California hands down. Texas not only does a lot better job than California does when it comes to the care and the nurturing of the most prosperous; Texas also treats its least fortunate better than does California. Nevertheless, both states could stand some improvement: California a lot more than Texas.

The Texas Oil Boom and California's Oil Bust: A Clash of Economic Cultures

The greatest irony of the Obama presidency is that the man who pledged in 2008 to "end the tyranny of oil in our generation" has presided over the greatest oil and gas boom in U.S. history. Doubly ironic is that this drilling boom, with oil production up more than 40 percent since 2008, is almost single-handedly keeping the Obama economy afloat. While much attention has been devoted to the astounding oil and gas blitz from the Bakken Shale in North Dakota, the even more impressive surge in production has gone almost unnoticed. It is happening in south and west Texas—the birthplace of the American oil boom 100 years ago—and where the spigots are today operating on full throttle.

Meanwhile, the state just 30 years ago that once rivaled Texas as the nation's biggest oil producer, California, has seen a reversal of fortune, as its oil output continues to fall (see Figure 7.4). This did not happen by accident. It is the culmination of intentional policy choices by these two states, and the hows and whys are worth investigating.

In the wake of historically high oil prices of $80 to $100 a barrel, Texas has capitalized on oil prices by nearly doubling its oil output since 2005. The two richest fields are the Eagle Ford shale formation

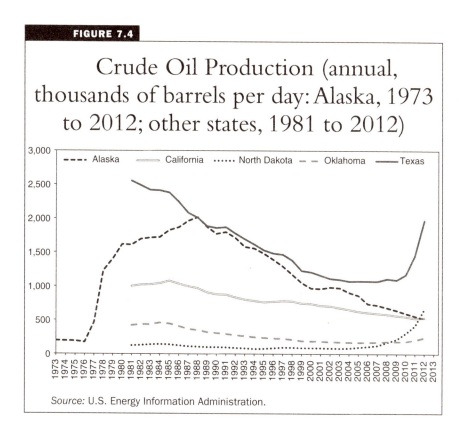

FIGURE 7.4

Crude Oil Production (annual, thousands of barrels per day: Alaska, 1973 to 2012; other states, 1981 to 2012)

Source: U.S. Energy Information Administration.

in south Texas, where production of this black gold is up an astonishing 50 percent in the past year, and the 250-square-mile Permian Basin, one of the richest oil fields on the planet, and which never seems to run dry. The epicenter of the oil revival is Midland-Odessa, one of the fastest-growing metropolitan areas in the country.

Even with the celebrated surge in output in North Dakota, which has moved that state into the number two position in the output of oil, ahead of Alaska and California, Texas produces more oil than the four next biggest-producing states combined. The Lone Star State now produces more than 2 million barrels a day, which generates about $80 billion a year in economic activity. Just the value of this oil production alone surpasses the annual output of all goods and services in 13 individual states. The Texas oil boom is the real and underappreciated economic stimulus in the United States, and its impact on jobs, revenues, and economic production is spectacular.

Now look to the state west of Texas, California, which has been nearly immune to all of these economic forces. Since 1986, California's oil production has fallen by about half, down about 21 percent since 2001 even as the price of oil has skyrocketed. This is *not* because California is running short of oil. To the contrary, California has access to huge reservoirs of oil offshore (about 10 billion barrels, 1 billion of which is in state waters) and even more in the Monterey Shale, which stretches 200 miles south along the coast and inland from San Francisco. The Department of Energy estimates that California has reserves of about 15 billion barrels of oil—which is about double the Bakken Shale in North Dakota. Occidental Petroleum, the big oil player in California, has recently purchased leases from the U.S. Department of the Interior. But the regulatory climate is still hostile to undertake the hundreds of millions of dollars of speculative investments.

Part of the explanation between the oil boom in Texas and the bust in California is deeply rooted in each state's culture. California voters have thumbed their noses at fossil fuels as "dirty energy." The state has passed cap-and-trade climate change legislation that threatens to add substantially to the costs of conventional energy production and refining in the Golden State. The politicians in Sacramento and the Silicon Valley financiers have made huge and mostly wrong multibillion-dollar bets on green energy—especially wind and solar power. Texas has also invested in wind power, generating the most wind energy in the country, but that did not deter the oil bonanza.

While California has frowned upon new drilling innovations, Texas has fully embraced the new technological marvels of horizontal drilling and fracking. These breakthroughs have made old wells profitable to redeploy. The culture of drilling is so ingrained in the business ways of south and west Texas that almost no one in places like Midland ever questioned the wisdom of moving aggressively forward. Meanwhile in California, fracking is viewed as a sinister policy and is even banned in some places—even though fracking is far superior today technologically in cracking through shale rock formations to get at the heavy hydrocarbon gases and liquids stored there for millions of years.

But perhaps California's citizens are starting to see all the jobs and income that they are missing due to their anti-fracking stance. On May 31, 2013, a bill placing a statewide moratorium on fracking in the Golden State failed 37 to 24. The interesting part of the vote is that 12 Democrats were among the 37 votes against the bill, and 18 Democrats abstained. A University of Southern California study estimates that the fracking industry could provide roughly 500,000 jobs to California over the next few years and tens of billions of dollars in state and local tax revenue each year.[11] Now that's an outcome that even the liberals can love.

Another contrast between Texas and California is that almost all the oil in the Lone Star State is on private lands—this is a state where private land ownership is sacrosanct. So farmers and other landholders hope and pray that they are modern-day Jed Clampetts sitting on oil so they can get rich off leasing their land to oil and gas producers.

One of the craziest decisions by the California lawmakers and voters was to impose on the Golden State energy companies a cap-and-trade tax on what they produce. This means, for example, that the cost of refining oil and gas extracted from California is too expensive and inhibits development. In short, Texas loves being an oil-producing state; California hates it.

To Texans, oil is about industrial expansion and jobs, jobs, jobs. Texas has been leading the nation in job creation since the recession ended, and the jobs are in subsidiary industries related to energy production—transportation, high technology, pipe building, light manufacturing, and so on.

How much impact do California's high electrical prices have on manufacturing? Well, the 2012 price for industrial customers in California was 10.8 cents per kilowatt-hour, the seventh highest in the nation. This cost is 88 percent higher than Texas's industrial rate of 5.73 cents.

About $27 billion of electricity was sold in California last year. If California's residential, commercial, and industrial rates were the same as in Texas, California's consumers, businesses, and manufacturing would have saved $10 billion, or about $265 for every Californian.

In the years ahead, this cost gap will get wider as AB 32, California's Global Warming Solutions Act, bites harder in addition to the mandated steep increases in the use of expensive renewable energy.

A couple more observations about energy, the master resource: California imports the most electricity of any state, in effect turning much of the West into an energy colony of California. Other states, even Canadian provinces, are keen to get in on the action—especially if they can sell California electrons and charge more for them if they are "green."

Texans have come to realize another windfall benefit from oil production: It is a cash cow to pay for government services. In 2012, oil and gas royalties, fees, and taxes raised $12 billion in revenue to the state governments. This aids Texas in financing its public services with no state income tax. California charges a 13.3 percent income tax on the richest in the state.

An Overview of Total State and Local Government Revenues—Texas and California

The percentage of GDP of total state and local government revenues from all sources to state and local governments as of 2010 is 21.9 percent for the entire United States, 24.1 percent for California, and 17.1 percent for Texas. If ever a word like *taxaholic* were invented, California would fit the concept to a tee. California has almost 50 percent more state and local revenue relative to the size of its economy than does Texas. California's governments at all levels are huge consumers of revenues. Texas governments are far more sparing with other people's money.

In each and every one of the total revenue components as a share of GSP, California's governmental complex absorbs as much or more than does Texas. This is true pretty much across the board. When it comes to contributions to workers' compensation, social insurance programs such as unemployment compensation, government employee retirement, and sickness and disability, California's revenues as a share of California's GSP are more than two and a half times Texas's share of Texas's GSP. Yikes!

In a later section of this chapter we show just how much good these extra revenues do for the provision of public services in California and Texas.

Texas, California, and the United States: A Comparison of Tax Revenue and Debt Financing

Moving now from population, labor force, and output measures, we cross over into state and local government finances. Just as a state cannot tax its way into prosperity, so too a state cannot balance its budget on the backs of people who are out of work. To run a state the size of Texas or California, state and local governments need tax revenues—lots of tax revenues. To get those tax revenues into the state's coffers, the state needs both a viable tax base that the government can tax and a tax rate to do the heavy lifting. The interesting twist here is that the size of the tax base and the tax rate itself are integrally related to each other.

Here again there is a great deal of readily available information that bears directly on our current topic at hand: state and local taxes. We cannot begin to list all the articles on who is moving from California to Texas, which businesses have decided to expand in California, and so on and so forth. There are also some studies that have been highly touted on millionaire tax returns in California,[12] Maryland,[13] and New Jersey,[14] which are about as useless as studies can be. Such anecdotes are one unreliable way to draw serious conclusions, but there are some widely publicized comprehensive indicators that do make sense and universally point to the conclusions we will reach in this section.

Chapter 5 contains a very detailed use of the Internal Revenue Service's adjusted gross income migration data, but we can't help but highlight a few interesting Texas- and California-specific IRS migration metrics.

For example, for the 18 years of tax returns from 1992/1993 to 2009/2010, the total number of returns moving from Texas to California was 300,310, while the number of returns moving from California to Texas over this same time period was 427,607—quite a difference in favor of Texas. Not only did more filers move from California to Texas than from Texas to California, but the average adjusted gross incomes of the filers moving from California to Texas was considerably larger than the average adjusted gross incomes of filers moving from Texas to California.

In each and every year the surplus of filers moving to Texas from California was positive.

In Table 7.4 we show the net migration of tax returns (in-returns minus out-returns divided by total in- and out-returns) by state by year for the years 1992/1993 through 2009/2010. These states are ranked each year from the highest percentage of in-returns to the lowest percentage of in-returns (largest percentage of out-returns). We have highlighted the annual performances of Texas and California for comparison purposes. The differential is stark, to say the least.

The drastic differences in cost of living between Texas and California are surely part of the reason that so many Californians are moving to Texas. Restrictions on land use are a bane of California. High fees to build on private property. Artificially restricted access to water. Global greenhouse gas rules. Zoning laws. These conspire to make housing, office space, and factories more costly.

How much more costly? The cost of housing in California stood at 176.3 percent of the national average in the last quarter of 2012. Only some of this cost differential is due to the desirability of living in California. Various estimates have pegged the added cost to housing due to restrictive land use regulations of up to 61 percent.

Higher costs for housing drive about two-thirds of the cost of living differences across the country, with California coming in at an overall cost of living of 127 percent of the national average in the fourth quarter of 2012 compared to Texas's 92 percent of the national average.

Cost of living impacts everything, and in California higher costs are largely due to public policy choices: high taxes, burdensome regulations, and a bad lawsuit climate.

Table 7.5 is a distilled version of Table 2.3, highlighting only California and Texas. For a detailed description of each row and metric in Table 7.5, please refer back to Chapter 2.

For Row 1 of Table 7.5, Texas is significantly outperforming California when it comes to economic growth. Row 2 shows Texas cutting taxes as a share of GSP by 5.7 percent over the decade while California raised taxes by 8.1 percent over the decade—no big surprise here.

When it comes to state and local tax revenue (Row 3), however, Texas, even after reducing tax rates, increased tax revenues over the decade by 63.3 percent, ranking Texas number seven in the nation. California, on the other hand, even with its tax rate increase, grew tax revenues by only 54 percent over the decade, putting California in 17th place.

Going from total tax revenues to tax revenues per capita, California beats Texas by increasing tax revenues per capita by 40.9 percent (20th in the nation) to 35.8 percent (28th in the nation), respectively.

To round out Table 7.5 on aggregate state finances, Row 5 shows that Texas at the end of fiscal year 2012 ranked in 20th best fiscal condition in the nation compared to California's 46th best ranking. Texas once again officially outperformed California.

The last row of Table 7.5 lists the S&P ratings of the debt for each state from best to worst. Texas tied for first place along with 13 other states, while California was by itself second from the bottom at 49th place.

Shortly after California passed Proposition 30, a landmark retroactive tax rate increase, Standard & Poor's actually upgraded California's credit rating to A from the lowest rating ever, tied with Illinois at A–. In the same spirit of static analysis, Standard & Poor's also lowered California's credit ratings after the passage of Proposition 13 (1978) and subsequent supply-side tax cuts (1982), only to be forced to raise those ratings back up again once California's growth soared as a result of the tax rate cuts (see Figure 7.5). What is surprising is that, in general, higher taxes are more often than not associated with lower credit ratings, not higher credit ratings.

TABLE 7.4

Net In-Returns as a Percentage of Gross Returns
(In-Returns + Out-Returns)

92/93		93/94		94/95		95/96		96/97		97/98		98/99		99/00		00/01	
ID	19.8%	NV	29.4%	NV	24.8%	NV	24.6%	NV	26.7%	NV	21.3%	NV	20.1%	NV	20.1%	NV	19.9%
NV	19.3%	AZ	23.1%	AZ	23.3%	AZ	19.4%	AZ	18.0%	AZ	16.4%	AZ	15.8%	AZ	14.8%	FL	15.6%
CO	18.5%	ID	19.5%	NC	16.8%	NC	16.5%	NC	15.3%	NC	13.5%	CO	13.5%	GA	12.1%	AZ	14.0%
OR	18.4%	GA	18.1%	GA	16.0%	GA	16.4%	FL	15.2%	FL	13.3%	GA	13.3%	FL	11.9%	CO	12.4%
AZ	17.2%	NC	16.6%	OR	15.6%	OR	15.9%	GA	13.4%	GA	13.3%	NC	11.4%	CO	10.6%	GA	8.9%
MT	16.5%	CO	16.2%	TN	15.1%	TN	13.5%	CO	12.5%	CO	11.4%	SC	10.0%	NC	9.9%	NC	8.1%
WA	16.4%	TN	15.5%	ID	14.7%	FL	11.8%	OR	11.6%	SC	10.7%	FL	9.9%	DE	8.0%	NH	7.9%
GA	15.4%	FL	15.0%	CO	14.3%	CO	11.2%	SC	10.3%	OR	7.4%	DE	8.2%	NH	7.8%	OR	6.3%
UT	14.6%	OR	15.0%	FL	13.6%	ID	9.2%	WA	9.6%	TX	7.3%	NH	6.0%	SC	7.1%	DE	5.1%
NC	13.2%	UT	14.7%	MT	11.4%	AR	8.6%	TN	9.3%	TN	6.8%	TN	5.9%	VA	6.6%	WA	4.6%
TN	13.0%	MT	12.1%	AR	11.2%	WA	8.4%	ID	6.9%	DE	6.6%	ID	4.9%	ME	6.6%	ME	4.5%
FL	12.8%	NM	11.7%	WA	9.5%	SC	7.8%	DE	6.5%	WA	6.4%	OR	4.8%	TN	5.4%	TX	4.2%
AR	12.4%	AR	10.7%	UT	8.8%	UT	6.6%	UT	5.7%	ID	4.7%	TX	4.5%	ID	5.1%	SC	4.1%
NM	9.2%	WA	9.2%	NM	7.7%	DE	6.2%	TX	5.1%	NH	4.1%	VA	4.0%	MN	3.4%	VA	4.0%
AL	9.0%	TX	8.3%	DE	6.5%	NH	6.0%	NH	4.4%	KY	2.0%	WA	3.5%	TX	3.4%	ID	3.2%
DE	6.7%	DE	7.6%	MO	5.3%	TX	4.8%	AL	3.9%	AL	1.9%	MN	3.2%	AR	2.3%	MD	3.0%
TX	6.4%	MS	6.6%	SC	5.3%	MO	4.7%	MO	3.2%	VA	1.2%	KY	2.1%	OR	1.9%	TN	2.4%
MN	6.2%	KY	5.5%	NH	5.1%	MT	4.6%	KY	2.7%	AR	0.8%	ME	1.1%	VT	1.9%	RI	2.4%
KY	6.1%	AL	5.3%	TX	4.5%	NM	2.9%	AR	2.2%	OK	0.4%	MO	0.2%	RI	1.8%	CA	1.6%
WV	5.7%	MO	5.2%	MS	4.3%	KY	2.8%	VA	1.9%	MS	0.5%	AR	-0.7%	WA	1.0%	MN	1.5%
MO	4.6%	SC	4.7%	KY	3.8%	MN	2.4%	MS	1.5%	MO	-0.4%	MS	-0.9%	KY	0.9%	VT	0.5%
SC	4.5%	SD	3.9%	AL	2.8%	MS	2.3%	OK	0.7%	KS	-0.5%	MD	-1.1%	MD	0.9%	MO	-0.5%
MS	4.4%	NH	3.4%	VA	1.8%	OK	1.7%	MN	-1.6%	UT	-1.3%	VT	-1.9%	MO	0.3%	KY	-0.6%
VA	4.4%	VA	3.0%	MN	1.8%	AL	1.7%	KS	-2.2%	CA	-1.9%	MA	-2.0%	WI	-0.5%	AR	-1.1%
WI	4.2%	MN	2.9%	IN	1.7%	VT	1.2%	IN	-2.3%	MN	-2.0%	MT	-2.2%	MT	-1.0%	DC	-1.6%
SD	3.9%	WY	2.7%	SD	1.5%	VA	1.1%	NM	-2.4%	MD	-2.6%	CA	-2.2%	CA	-1.4%	HI	-2.0%
IN	2.8%	OK	1.1%	VT	0.8%	IN	0.4%	ME	-2.9%	MA	-2.6%	RI	-2.3%	MS	-1.7%	WI	-3.1%
WY	2.3%	IN	1.0%	WI	0.6%	WI	0.2%	VT	-3.2%	VT	-3.3%	AL	-2.4%	IN	-2.8%	AK	-3.3%
OK	1.6%	WI	0.2%	NE	0.1%	NE	-0.7%	MA	-3.5%	ME	-3.7%	WI	-2.4%	AL	-4.0%	MA	-3.4%
AK	1.5%	AK	0.1%	OK	-0.1%	ME	-1.1%	MT	-3.8%	IN	-4.1%	DC	-3.1%	SD	-4.0%	MT	-3.4%
NH	-0.2%	VT	0.1%	WY	-0.2%	WV	-2.7%	MD	-3.5%	AK	-4.2%	OK	-3.3%	MA	-4.2%	UT	-5.5%
VT	-0.2%	WV	-0.2%	MD	-1.1%	WY	-3.4%	AK	-4.1%	NM	-4.7%	KS	-3.3%	UT	-4.3%	AL	-5.8%
KS	-1.4%	MD	-0.7%	WV	-1.7%	MD	-3.6%	WI	-5.2%	MT	-4.9%	IN	-3.7%	WY	-4.5%	OK	-5.9%
HI	-2.0%	KS	-1.7%	KS	-3.5%	SD	-4.1%	NE	-5.8%	WY	-5.5%	UT	-3.9%	DC	-4.7%	SD	-5.9%
MD	-2.1%	NE	-2.5%	LA	-3.6%	MA	-4.1%	CA	-6.5%	WI	-5.7%	AK	-4.8%	NM	-5.4%	WY	-6.0%
NE	-2.9%	HI	-3.3%	ME	-4.5%	MI	-4.7%	WY	-7.1%	WV	-6.2%	SD	-6.5%	KS	-5.6%	IN	-6.4%
ND	-4.4%	LA	-4.7%	ND	-4.5%	AK	-5.1%	WV	-7.8%	RI	-7.1%	WV	-7.0%	OK	-5.7%	MS	-6.4%
IA	-4.4%	ND	-5.5%	MI	-5.4%	ND	-5.4%	LA	-8.9%	LA	-8.3%	WY	-7.1%	CT	-6.5%	NM	-6.8%
PA	-4.6%	ME	-7.0%	IA	-5.7%	KS	-6.0%	MI	-9.0%	DC	-8.9%	NM	-7.7%	MI	-6.6%	CT	-7.0%
ME	-6.0%	PA	-7.6%	OH	-6.0%	OH	-6.1%	OH	-9.4%	NE	-9.3%	NE	-8.1%	AK	-7.4%	NJ	-7.2%
OH	-6.1%	IA	-7.8%	MA	-7.2%	IA	-6.7%	RI	-9.8%	IA	-9.6%	CT	-8.3%	WV	-8.1%	KS	-8.1%
LA	-9.8%	MA	-8.1%	AK	-8.6%	LA	-7.8%	SD	-9.9%	NJ	-10.3%	NJ	-8.6%	NJ	-8.5%	WV	-8.3%
IL	-10.7%	OH	-8.8%	HI	-8.8%	PA	-9.4%	IA	-10.2%	SD	-10.6%	MI	-8.6%	PA	-9.1%	PA	-8.9%
NJ	-11.5%	NJ	-11.2%	PA	-9.5%	IL	-10.8%	ND	-11.5%	OH	-10.7%	IA	-8.8%	HI	-9.5%	MI	-10.6%
DC	-11.9%	IL	-12.0%	NJ	-10.5%	HI	-11.3%	NJ	-11.5%	CT	-10.9%	OH	-9.6%	NE	-9.6%	NE	-11.0%
RI	-12.2%	MI	-13.3%	IL	-10.8%	NJ	-12.1%	HI	-12.0%	PA	-11.1%	LA	-9.8%	OH	-10.0%	OH	-11.6%
MA	-13.4%	DC	-13.6%	CT	-14.7%	RI	-12.1%	DC	-12.1%	MI	-11.5%	PA	-10.0%	IA	-10.6%	IL	-12.8%
MI	-15.2%	RI	-15.2%	RI	-15.7%	CT	-14.6%	IL	-13.2%	HI	-11.6%	IL	-12.1%	IL	-13.1%	IA	-13.8%
CT	-18.0%	CT	-17.5%	DC	-16.1%	DC	-15.6%	CT	-13.6%	IL	-13.4%	HI	-15.1%	LA	-13.7%	LA	-14.7%
NY	-25.3%	NY	-26.4%	CA	-24.1%	CA	-16.8%	PA	-13.7%	ND	-13.5%	ND	-16.2%	ND	-16.8%	NY	-17.2%
CA	-26.4%	CA	-29.4%	NY	-27.2%	NY	-28.0%	NY	-27.6%	NY	-23.4%	NY	-19.0%	NY	-17.8%	ND	-17.3%

01/02	02/03	03/04	04/05	05/06	06/07	07/08	08/09	09/10
FL 17.7%	NV 18.9%	NV 25.1%	AZ 24.3%	AZ 23.3%	SC 17.6%	SC 16.6%	TX 14.5%	TX 11.1%
NV 17.6%	FL 17.2%	FL 23.1%	FL 21.8%	NV 20.0%	NC 16.8%	NC 16.0%	SC 11.0%	DC 9.8%
AZ 14.9%	AZ 15.0%	AZ 19.3%	NV 20.8%	TX 17.6%	NV 15.8%	TX 13.6%	NC 10.6%	CO 8.8%
OR 8.9%	ME 11.6%	DE 10.2%	ID 14.1%	NC 17.4%	AZ 15.8%	CO 10.9%	CO 10.5%	OK 7.6%
ME 8.5%	DE 11.1%	NC 9.9%	NC 12.6%	GA 17.1%	GA 14.3%	OR 10.4%	WY 10.2%	LA 7.5%
DE 8.0%	SC 8.1%	ID 9.8%	SC 12.3%	SC 15.6%	TN 13.1%	AZ 10.2%	WA 8.5%	SC 7.4%
NC 7.3%	ID 7.1%	SC 9.8%	TN 11.4%	ID 14.2%	TX 12.7%	WA 9.5%	DC 8.4%	ND 7.3%
GA 6.8%	OR 6.3%	GA 9.0%	DE 11.2%	OR 13.2%	ID 12.2%	GA 8.6%	OK 8.3%	NC 6.9%
SC 6.2%	VA 5.9%	TN 7.3%	OR 10.1%	TN 12.8%	OR 11.1%	UT 8.5%	OR 7.8%	AK 6.6%
NH 5.9%	GA 5.8%	MT 6.7%	GA 9.8%	FL 12.8%	UT 10.3%	TN 8.0%	LA 7.0%	WV 6.5%
MD 4.8%	TN 5.8%	VA 6.2%	AR 7.9%	AL 11.0%	WY 9.9%	NV 7.8%	TN 6.6%	NM 6.5%
TX 4.8%	NC 5.7%	ME 6.1%	WA 6.2%	WA 10.7%	CO 8.9%	ID 7.6%	WV 5.3%	VA 4.8%
CO 4.7%	MT 4.8%	AR 5.7%	MT 5.5%	AR 10.4%	WA 7.7%	WY 7.1%	AL 5.2%	SD 4.5%
VA 4.2%	NH 4.4%	NM 5.0%	AL 5.1%	DE 8.8%	MT 7.3%	MT 6.2%	AR 4.4%	FL 4.5%
TN 4.2%	NM 3.9%	WA 3.9%	TX 5.1%	CO 8.7%	DE 7.1%	DE 6.2%	AZ 4.0%	KY 4.5%
ID 4.2%	KY 3.8%	HI 3.0%	NM 4.9%	UT 7.0%	LA 6.6%	AL 6.1%	GA 4.0%	TN 4.5%
RI 3.9%	AR 3.6%	AL 2.8%	KY 4.1%	MT 6.5%	AL 6.3%	LA 4.8%	DE 3.9%	AZ 4.4%
WA 3.8%	HI 3.4%	KY 2.7%	VA 4.1%	NM 5.6%	KY 5.8%	AR 4.5%	UT 3.8%	DE 4.4%
NM 3.3%	WV 3.0%	TX 2.7%	CO 2.9%	WY 4.7%	AR 5.3%	KY 4.1%	NM 3.8%	AR 4.4%
WY 2.7%	TX 2.9%	MS 2.4%	HI 2.9%	OK 4.2%	OK 5.1%	SD 3.5%	ND 3.6%	OR 4.3%
KY 1.9%	RI 2.8%	SD 2.4%	MO 1.9%	KY 3.3%	NM 4.9%	WV 2.9%	KY 3.5%	AL 3.2%
AK 1.8%	MD 2.6%	NH 2.2%	ME 1.9%	MO 3.1%	FL 3.0%	OK 2.6%	SD 3.4%	WA 3.2%
VT 1.4%	MO 1.5%	MO 1.4%	UT 1.7%	HI 1.6%	WV 2.5%	DC 1.8%	VA 3.4%	GA 2.5%
WV 1.4%	WA 1.1%	WY 1.3%	NH 1.4%	WV 1.5%	SD 2.0%	MS 0.7%	MT 2.5%	MT 2.4%
HI 1.3%	AL 1.0%	OR 1.1%	WV 1.2%	VA 1.4%	MO 1.9%	NM 0.5%	AK 0.9%	UT 1.2%
MO 0.6%	VT 0.7%	WV 0.2%	MS 0.4%	DC 0.8%	MS 0.8%	VA 0.4%	ID 0.0%	MD 0.9%
AR 0.3%	AK 0.5%	AK 0.2%	OK −0.3%	SD 0.5%	DC 0.5%	IA −0.1%	MO −0.2%	NE 0.5%
OK −0.1%	MS −1.1%	CO −0.4%	SD −0.3%	NH 0.4%	VA 0.3%	MO −1.1%	MA −0.3%	HI 0.2%
MT −0.2%	OK −1.4%	MD −0.9%	WY −0.4%	AK −1.3%	ME 0.1%	HI −1.3%	NV −0.6%	MO 0.2%
WI −2.0%	PA −1.5%	VT −2.3%	DC −1.9%	IN −1.7%	MN −2.4%	FL −1.9%	IA −0.7%	IA −0.7%
AL −3.4%	WY −1.7%	DC −2.7%	MD −1.9%	ME −1.8%	NH −2.7%	ND −1.9%	KS −1.9%	ID −0.8%
MN −3.4%	WI −1.7%	WI −2.8%	IN −2.1%	MN −2.9%	KS −2.0%	NE −1.9%	KS −1.3%	KS −1.3%
CT −3.9%	CO −1.9%	OK −2.8%	VT −2.8%	PA −3.7%	PA −3.5%	IN −2.7%	MS −2.0%	MS −1.5%
MS −4.0%	SD −2.0%	PA −3.4%	AK −3.2%	VT −4.0%	AK −3.5%	ME −3.0%	PA −2.6%	VT −2.4%
PA −4.3%	IN −2.0%	LA −3.9%	PA −4.0%	MD −4.2%	KS −4.0%	NH −3.4%	MD −2.7%	PA −2.6%
UT −4.8%	CT −3.3%	ND −4.0%	WI −4.4%	IA −4.9%	IA −4.9%	AK −3.4%	FL −3.1%	MA −3.0%
DC −5.1%	MN −4.7%	UT −4.1%	MN −5.0%	WI −5.1%	ND −4.9%	PA −4.2%	IN −4.3%	NV −3.1%
KS −5.4%	LA −4.8%	IN −4.7%	IA −6.1%	KS −5.2%	HI −5.6%	MN −4.8%	HI −4.7%	WY −3.1%
SD −5.5%	NE −5.0%	MN −5.4%	LA −6.1%	NE −7.9%	WI −5.8%	NE −4.9%	CA −4.8%	CA −3.3%
IN −5.9%	DC −5.8%	IA −6.6%	NE −6.6%	MS −8.1%	VT −6.4%	MA −5.8%	VT −5.1%	IN −4.2%
CA −6.4%	GA −6.2%	NE −7.2%	KS −6.9%	ND −8.2%	MD −6.6%	WI −6.0%	NH −5.8%	NH −5.1%
NJ −6.8%	KS −6.6%	RI −7.4%	ND −9.1%	IL −9.8%	IL −7.6%	MD −6.6%	MN −6.2%	CT −8.2%
LA −7.9%	ND −6.9%	KS −8.3%	CT −9.3%	CT −10.5%	NE −7.7%	IL −7.0%	WI −6.4%	WI −8.2%
NE −9.2%	UT −7.3%	CA −9.5%	IL −12.7%	MA −14.2%	MA −11.0%	CA −7.1%	IL −7.4%	ME −8.3%
MA −9.7%	NJ −9.0%	CT −9.7%	NJ −13.6%	OH −14.8%	CT −11.6%	VT −7.3%	ME −7.7%	RI −8.4%
OH −10.5%	IA −9.5%	OH −11.7%	OH −14.0%	NJ −15.2%	CA −14.1%	CT −9.4%	CT −8.2%	MN −8.5%
IA −11.7%	OH −9.7%	NJ −11.8%	RI −14.4%	CA −15.9%	OH −14.3%	NY −11.4%	NY −8.8%	NJ −8.9%
MI −11.9%	MI −11.5%	IL −14.0%	CA −15.0%	RI −16.3%	RI −14.6%	NJ −11.9%	NJ −9.0%	NY −9.8%
ND −12.8%	MA −13.4%	MI −15.1%	MA −17.5%	NY −21.3%	NJ −14.6%	RI −13.2%	OH −12.3%	IL −10.5%
IL −13.7%	IL −14.0%	MA −17.9%	MI −19.3%	MI −23.4%	NY −17.6%	OH −13.2%	RI −12.6%	OH −12.5%
NY −18.2%	NY −17.1%	NY −21.9%	NY −23.2%	LA −54.6%	MI −28.5%	MI −29.8%	MI −27.0%	MI −21.7%

TABLE 7.5

State Fiscal Health: From Economic Growth to Debt Ratings

Row	Percentage Change, 2001–2011	U.S.*	TX	TX Rank	CA	CA Rank
1	Gross State Product	51.7%	73.2%	4	42.5%	35
2	Total State and Local Tax Revenue as a % of GSP	2.9%	−5.7%	8	8.1%	40
3	Total State and Local Tax Revenue	56.5%	63.3%	7	54.0%	17
4	Total State and Local Tax Revenue per Capita	43.0%	35.8%	28	40.9%	20
	2012					
5	Fiscal Condition Index Score[†]	0.00	−0.18	20	−2.01	46
	Current Rating[†]					
6	General Obligation Credit Rating—S&P	N/A	AAA	1	A	49

* U.S. is equal-weighted averages of the 50 states.
[†] Fiscal Condition Index Score is a ranking from the Mercatus Center. It ranks states according to cash, budget, and long-run and service-level solvency metrics.
[†] Current rating is as of 11/4/2013.

Source: Bureau of Economic Analysis, U.S. Census Bureau, Mercatus Center, Standard & Poor's.

Like Elizabeth Taylor's seventh husband, Standard & Poor's upgrade of California's debt after a massive tax rate increase represents the triumph of hope over experience.

When it comes to the soundness of a state's fiscal circumstances and the generation of tax revenues, Texas outperforms California in each and every category save state and local tax revenue per capita.

Policy Variables Affecting Growth

In the previous sections of this chapter, we have shown beyond a shadow of a doubt that (1) Texas's economy has outperformed California's economy over the past decade, and (2) Texas's government finances have also outperformed California's government finances over the same decade. Now let us see why.

A state's economic performance and, yes, even a state's government finances are subject to powerful external forces outside the control of the state's political apparatus. Oil price increases, for ex-

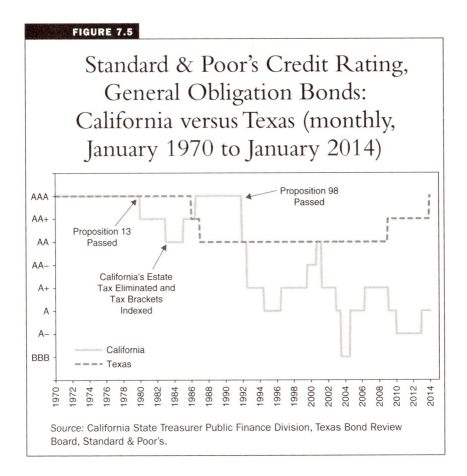

FIGURE 7.5

Standard & Poor's Credit Rating, General Obligation Bonds: California versus Texas (monthly, January 1970 to January 2014)

Source: California State Treasurer Public Finance Division, Texas Bond Review Board, Standard & Poor's.

ample, have benefited zero income tax states such as Wyoming and Alaska beyond their wildest dreams. But oil price increases have also benefited North Dakota and Louisiana, two states that do tax income.

Now we'll turn to look at how California and Texas rank against each other and their 48 competitors according to selected policy variables discussed throughout this book plus a few other measures sprinkled in for good measure.

Right off the bat, Texas has no income tax—either earned or unearned—and no capital gains tax, either. In the category of income taxation, Texas is tied for number one in the nation along with six other states.[15] California, on the other hand, has the highest personal income tax rate in the nation, and that rate applies to capital gains as well as dividends, interest, and other forms of unearned income.

California's personal income tax structure is the single most progressive tax structure in the nation, and Texas, as strange as this may seem without an income tax, is tied for only second place, not first place in this category. It just so happens that Alabama allows federal income taxes to be deducted at the state level, and with that state's statutory tax rate schedule this means that the effective marginal state income tax rate actually goes down the more a taxpayer earns. Go figure! Higher-income people in Alabama progressively pay a smaller portion of their incomes in state income taxes because they pay a larger portion of their incomes in federal income taxes, which are deductible at the state level.

To see just how consequential an income tax can be vis-à-vis economic performance, see Chapter 1 and the first section of Chapter 3.

The California and Texas comparison when it comes to corporate taxes is not much different than it was for personal income taxes. Texas has a very low corporate tax rate with its business franchise tax—from 0.5 percent to 1 percent of taxable margin—that falls on a very broad tax base, making the tax close to the ideal tax for raising revenue while doing the least harm, ranking Texas number four in the nation. California, in contrast, has a very high marginal corporate income tax rate on a narrow tax base. For more on corporate tax rates, see Chapter 3.

California taxes the bejabbers out of successful companies that cost-effectively make desirable products, and does not tax loser companies at all. In fact, even at the state level, California subsidizes a number of loser companies. If you ever get a chance to drive from Palm Springs, California, to Los Angeles, you will pass miles and miles of windmills. Without state and federal subsidies, these windmills would be bankrupt in minutes.

Texas is a right-to-work state, and California is a forced-union state. Whether a state is a right-to-work state or a forced-union state makes a huge difference to a state's prosperity. For specific performance metrics of right-to-work versus forced-union states, see Chapter 4. In fact, even comparing performance metrics of non-right-to-work states without income taxes to right-to-work states *with* income taxes shows that right-to-work legislation makes a material impact on state economic performance.[16] Again, Texas dominates California.

When it comes to the death or estate tax, the two states have a tie. In 1982, California, on the heels of Proposition 13, repealed its estate tax, leaving the state one of 30 states without an estate tax. Texas does not have an estate tax, either.

The existence of a state estate tax can have a shockingly large impact on an admittedly small but highly important segment of a state's population. In Table 7.6 we list the number of federal estate tax returns per 1,000,000 population for Tennessee (which did have an estate tax up to and including 2011), the whole United States, and Florida (which did not have an estate tax), and the average size of each state's taxable estates.[17]

For more on the estate tax, see Chapter 4.

With regard to workers' compensation costs, the seventh most important economic policy variable, Texas ranks 13th lowest in the nation, while California comes in as the third highest workers' compensation

---

TABLE 7.6

Federal Estate Tax Filings in Tennessee, Florida, and the United States: Number of Estate Filings per 1,000,000 Population and Size of Average Estate Filing, 2011

	Estates Filed per 1,000,000 Population	Size of Average Estate*
Tennessee (Separate Estate Tax)†	12.5	$10,626,625
U.S. Average	14.8	$10,464,213
Florida (No Separate Estate Tax)	24.0	$15,771,867

* Gross estate.
† Tennessee passed legislation in 2012 to phase out its estate tax. The exemption amount increases each year through 2015, and the estate tax is fully repealed from 2016 onward.

Source: IRS Statistics of Income Division.

costs in the nation.[18] Adding further insult to actual injury, professional athletes who were never actually based in California but who played a game or two there have been using California's workers' compensation system as a retirement supplement at the end of their careers. For instance, Denver Broncos running back Terrell Davis, a former Super Bowl MVP, played only nine games in California out of an 88-game career. He applied for workers' compensation and received a $199,000 injury settlement on top of his $6.8 million contract and endorsement deals.[19] Or Ernie Conwell, who, according to the *Los Angeles Times*, "won $160,000 plus future medical benefits in California after collecting $181,000 in Louisiana and $195,000 from the NFL. Conwell never played a down for a California team."[20] These policies do not make you want to move your production facilities to California. Once again, Texas wins a clean sweep.

Regarding the minimum wage, California has always had a higher minimum wage than the federal minimum wage, whereas Texas has always stuck with the federal minimum wage. Whatever else you may think of the minimum wage, it surely does increase production costs and reduces a state's competitive position. Just imagine what would happen to a state if it adopted, say, a $100 an hour minimum wage when every other state's minimum wage is below $10 an hour. Texas, which is governed by the federal minimum wage, is tied with 30 other states for the lowest minimum wage in the nation, while California has the eighth highest minimum wage in the nation and thus ranks number 43rd worst in the nation as of 1/1/2013. Texas has it hands down over California.

Measuring the degree to which a state's legal system is business friendly is a tricky business. But using our measure, produced by the U.S. Chamber of Commerce, neither Texas nor California ranks very well among all the states. State judicial systems tend to have a life of their own independent of the political climate elsewhere in a state. But using these rankings, California's courts are significantly less business friendly than are Texas courts. Texas ranks poorly at number 35 out of 50 states, while California once again comes in near the bottom at 47th out of

50 states. Importantly, before Texas reformed its medical malpractice system in 2003, the U.S. Chamber of Commerce ranked Texas's legal system 46th worst in the nation, just behind California at 45th; so Texas has improved, and California has worsened in this category—and that is before the ranking took into account Texas's major loser-pays reform in 2011. This ends up as a nail-biting win for Texas, but a win nonetheless.

In general all taxes are bad, but some are worse than others. Of the bigger taxes, we view that on a dollar-for-dollar revenue basis, a broad-based sales tax does less damage than most other taxes. Property taxes, as currently used by state and local governments, are close to being even with sales taxes.

Yet even when viewing sales taxes, Texas once again outperforms California. Even though Texas has no income tax at all, California has the highest income tax, and Texas has far lower corporate taxes than does California, Texas's sales tax burden still ranks number 24 in the nation, while California's sales tax burden ranks number 33.

Property tax revenues, which we have already mentioned, in Texas as a share of gross state product are quite a bit higher than they are in California. California's unexpected success with property taxes most likely is a direct consequence of its landmark constitutional amendment of June 1978, referred to either as Proposition 13 or as the Jarvis/Gann initiative (see Figure 7.2 earlier in this chapter). This constitutional amendment restricted property taxes on each piece of property in California to never exceed 1 percent of that property's true market value and to never increase by more than 2 percent per year unless the property is sold. When sold, the new basis of a property for tax purposes is the market price at which it sold. In spite of Proposition 13, California's property taxes as a share of personal income are still fairly high in large part because of the enormous historical rise in property values in California relative to the rest of the nation (the numerator) and the recent collapse of California's economy and its personal income (the denominator). California is the winner.

To recap this policy variable section, Texas beats California in personal income tax rates, personal income tax progressivity, corporate income tax rates, right-to-work status, workers' compensation costs, the minimum wage, business-friendly legal system quality, and sales tax burden. Texas and

California tie in the estate tax category, as neither has an estate tax. California's sole win is in the category of property tax burden. On the whole, it's an absolute landslide in favor of Texas and its pro-growth policies.

The Relationship among Taxation, Spending, and the Achievement of Policy Objectives—A Story of Parasitic Leakages

Quite understandably, people, even supposedly knowledgeable experts in state and local finances, use a type of shorthand when they link tax policy to spending objectives. To them, higher tax rates mean more schools, more highways, more police officers, more firefighters, more nurses, and more prison guards. If you extend their logic, higher tax rates lead to equal-percentage increases in tax revenues and, therefore, equal-percentage increases in dollar expenditures, which in turn lead to equal-percentage increases in real resources for state and local governments to provide to the people (i.e., an equal-percentage increase in the provision of public services).

Unfortunately, this shorthand is simply wrong. The relationship, as espoused, between tax rates and state and local provision of public services gets carried too far when tax rate changes, tax revenue changes, dollar government spending changes, and increases in the provision of public services (i.e., real spending changes) are treated as synonyms. They are not.

- Higher tax rates are not synonymous with higher dollar tax revenues.
- Higher dollar tax revenues are not synonymous with higher dollar government spending.
- Higher dollar government spending is most definitely not synonymous with the greater provision of public services.

The leakages here are the equivalent of *parasitic loss*, a term used to describe the diminution of measured horsepower of an automobile when measured at the engine itself and then measured again at the back tires. Not surprisingly, the loss in measured horsepower is quite large when moving from the engine to the back tires. So, too, are the losses in the provision of public services from an increase in tax rates—"parasitic leakages."

Now, it is very true that to have any state and local government spending, real or nominal, there have to be tax revenues, which means there have to be tax rates and tax bases. But going from that statement to a statement that higher tax rates mean an equivalent increase in state and local government services for state residents is simply false.

Proposing higher tax rates is invariably justified on the grounds that there is an increased need for public services—more schools, more schoolteachers, more police officers, more firefighters, more nurses, more prison guards, more libraries, more public welfare, more roads, a cleaner environment, better health standards, and the like. But advocates of higher tax rates ignore the large conceptual leap of faith from higher tax rates to increased public services. And one truth is universal when it comes to tax increases—you never get as much as you thought you would. Beware of "parasitic leakages."

We now come to the final two stages of the state and local government political process, which start with (1) tax rates and tax bases, and then move on to (2) tax revenues, and from there to (3) government spending, and the process ends with (4) provision of public services. The distinction we wish to make is between the total dollars spent by a state's state and local governments (category 3) and the actual provision of public services to state residents (category 4). This distinction is not just at a technical point. There can be a large difference between the dollar amount state and local governments spend on a specific program (such as K–12 public education) and the actual services those programs provide (such as educational test scores)—yet another example of "parasitic leakages."

Intergovernmental Revenues, Federally Mandated Social Services, and State Welfare, Medicaid, and Food Stamp Programs

Intergovernmental revenues represent a large (almost 20 percent nationwide) source of total state and local government revenues. These revenues are remitted to state and local governments to fund a significant portion of some specifically mandated programs for all states. In 2010, these federal funds accounted for 4 percent of California's GSP, or 16 percent of California's state and local government revenues, and 3.7 percent of Texas's GSP, or 22 percent of Texas's state and local government revenues. In spite of the large federal funding of these programs, state and local governments are still required to pay for a consequential portion of the total funding necessary. We will review three such programs.

While welfare, Medicaid, a large portion of unemployment benefits, and food stamps are all partially federally funded and federally mandated state programs, we have generally avoided referring to them when comparing and contrasting all 50 states of the United States. These programs are, after all, applicable to all states. But these programs do have specific state effects, require substantially different state funding across all states, and these effects can vary significantly from state to state. Not only do these federally funded and federally mandated programs have different effects by state, but they also reflect widely divergent characteristics of the states where they are applied. But because the dollars involved are not directly comparable to state and local tax dollars, we discuss each program separately.

Temporary Assistance for Needy Families (TANF)

We start with the program that is officially designated as "welfare," which has the formal handle of Temporary Assistance for Needy Families (TANF). In Table 7.7 we list the percentage of California's, Texas's, and the U.S. average state's population on welfare as of 2011 along with each state's percentage of U.S. population and each state's percentage of U.S. welfare recipients.

Just look at and compare and contrast California and Texas. California has 3.88 percent of its population on welfare, far and away the highest percentage in the nation, whereas Texas has less than one-half of 1 percent on welfare, rating Texas the enviable rank of fourth lowest in the nation. California has over 34 percent of the nation's welfare recipients.

TABLE 7.7			
Welfare Participation, 2011: United States, Texas, and California			
	U.S.	**Texas**	**California**
% of Population on Welfare	1.38%	0.43%	3.88%
Rank	N/A	4	50
Welfare Recipients as a % of 50-State Welfare Recipients	100.00%	2.58%	34.07%
State Population as a % of Total 50-State Population	100.00%	8.26%	12.12%

Being a welfare recipient is defined here as receiving Temporary Assistance for Needy Families (TANF).

Source: BEA (population), U.S. Department of Health and Human Services: Administration for Children and Families.

Not only does California have 34 percent of the nation's welfare recipients, but California state and local governments also employ 18 full-time equivalent (FTE) state and local government welfare workers per 10,000 of population, almost 75 percent more than does Texas at 10.4 full-time equivalent state and local government welfare workers per 10,000 of population (see "Annual Pay per FTE Employee" table later in the chapter).

But now the rub really gets bad. California, on an average salary basis, pays its state and local welfare government employees over 50 percent more per worker than does Texas (again see "Annual Pay" table). Just how does this behavior lead to economic growth and prosperity? Quite simply, it does not.

Medicaid

Medicaid is another federally subsidized, state and local government administered program. And it, too, is very large. In 2010 there were 67 million people enrolled in Medicaid nationwide, and the total bill for Medicaid was $383.5 billion. The federal government paid for 67.8 percent of the total Medicaid bill, and state and local governments paid for 32.2 percent, or $123.5 billion (see Table 7.8). Between 2006 and 2010, total Medicaid payments nationwide went up by almost $85 billion, and enrollment rose by almost seven million people.

TABLE 7.8			
Medicaid: United States, California, and Texas			
	United States	**California**	**Texas**
	2010	**2009**	**2009**
Enrollment (000s)	66,695	11,168	4,488
% of Population	21.6%	30.2%	18.1%
Total Medicaid ($bn)	$383.5	$40.8	$23.0
Medicaid per Recipient ($000s)	$ 5.75	$3.66	$5.12
State Share of Medicaid (%)	32.2%	40.1%	31.7%
State Share of Medicaid ($000s)	$123.5	$16.4	$7.3

Source: Medicaid.gov.

While we do have the total U.S. Medicaid numbers for 2010, we do not have the 2010 numbers separately for California and Texas, or for any of the other states for that matter. On a state-by-state basis we have 2009 numbers. Medicaid enrollment in Texas in 2009 was 4.488 million, or 18 percent of the state's population. California, in contrast, had a total Medicaid enrollment in 2009 of 11.168 million, or 30 percent of its population. California's state and local governments unluckily were held liable for 40 percent of California's total Medicaid bill (the federal government paid the rest) while Texas's state and local governments had only to pay 31.7 percent of its state's total Medicaid bill.

Once again California comes out the biggest loser.

To summarize, in 2009 Texas had a much smaller percentage of its population enrolled in Medicaid than did California (18 percent vs. 30 percent), and Texas had a larger share of its Medicaid expenses paid by the federal government than did California (68.3 percent versus 60 percent).

Supplemental Nutrition Assistance Program (SNAP) Alias Food Stamps

Another federally funded state-administered program is what we used to call food stamps, but it now has the official moniker SNAP. In Table 7.9 we list the U.S. numbers and the California and Texas numbers for this program.

TABLE 7.9			
SNAP, FY 2011: United States, California, and Texas			
	United States	**California**	**Texas**
Number of People (000s)	44,709	3,673	3,977
% of Population	14.4%	9.7%	15.5%
Number of Families (000s)	21,072	1,613	1,608
$ Amount of SNAP Benefits (billions)	$71.81	$6.48	$5.99
Monthly Benefit per Person	$133.85	$147.12	$125.57
Monthly Benefit per Family	$284.00	$335.04	$310.50
Total Administrative Costs (billions)	$6.83	$1.29	$0.54
State Share of Administrative Costs (%)	50.2%	52.3%	47.2%

Source: U.S. Department of Agriculture Food and Nutrition Service.

California pays more per person and per family on food stamps than does either Texas or the United States as a whole. Likewise, state and local governments in California pay a larger share of the administrative costs than does Texas or the average of all states. But where Texas moves way ahead of California is that Texas's administrative costs in aggregate are far lower than are California's administrative costs, in part reflecting the higher costs per employee in California and the expanded administrative efforts in California.

The Provision of Public Services by State and Local Governments

Just how to measure the provision of public services by state and local governments is notoriously difficult and exceptionally important. In most cases, we decided to sidestep output measures of public services and have instead relied upon measures of real inputs such as police personnel per 10,000 population. Where available, we have focused on output measures as well as measures of inputs (i.e., education test scores plus number of educational employees per 10,000 population).

State and local governments all across the United States are employers of a large number of people, many of whom have specific skills and/
or specific duties for which they were hired. State and local governments
also subcontract a large number of projects out to private companies.
The degree to which states outsource the services they provide can vary
quite dramatically from state to state. In California, for example, private
prisons are almost nonexistent, while in Texas 11 percent of all prisoners
are held in privately run facilities.

This section looks solely at specific employees of state and local governments from elected officials on down. The total costs associated with
these services as described in Table 7.10 are the product of the average
(mean) salary and the number of full-time equivalent employees hired.
These data do not include unfunded retirement benefits or unfunded
health benefits.

Table 7.10 lists the current average annual salaries for the governor, state legislators, education employees, hospital employees, police
protection employees, correctional facilities employees, highway employees, fire protection employees, public welfare employees, and other employees. Table 7.10 also lists the annual average pay per full-time
equivalent employee, the number of these full-time equivalent employees per 10,000 population for state and local government employees
combined by function for the United States and both California and
Texas, and the ratio of California to Texas for both the numbers of employees per 10,000 population and their average pay. As a final row, we
have total pay for each function for each state as a share of gross state
product (i.e., average pay times the number of full-time equivalent employees divided by state GSP).

The pattern defined in Table 7.10 is rather interesting. The first
three rows reaffirm what we already know.

Even a cursory overview of this table illustrates the problem to which
we have been alluding throughout this chapter. Annual average salaries
for equivalent categories of state and local government employees vary
considerably across the states. The average annual salary for police protection employees, for example, ranges from $35,442 in Mississippi to

$91,663 in California. On average for all state and local government employees, annual salaries range from $37,022 in Arkansas to $67,524 in California. These types of salary variations make a huge difference to state and local government budgets *and* to the provision of public services.

What is striking, however, is that for all state and local government employees as well as for almost every subcategory, California has the highest average annual salaries in the nation—and that is without consideration of the notorious problem with California's unfunded government employee pension and health benefits.

Average annual pay in Texas, in contrast, is below the U.S. average in every single category of state and local government employees. Salaries have consequences. If the dollar amount of funding is fixed, doubling the price of everything halves the quantity. And California surely has the highest prices when it comes to salaries of government employees.

Take hospitals, for example. The average annual salary for a hospital employee in Texas is $52,699 whereas that same hospital employee in California earns $80,617. For police protection employees, the average annual salary is $91,663 in California and $53,944 in Texas. For correction facilities (i.e., prisons), the average annual salary in Texas is $37,660, and in California it is $72,723. You would think this might be a two-for-one special, and it is. We will cover corrections a little more thoroughly in a few more pages.

We will also cover education much more thoroughly a little later on, but the message is clear even in this summary table. California educational employees have an average annual salary of $61,575 whereas the same group of employees in Texas earns $43,955. Average annual salaries for highway employees in Texas are $42,885 whereas in California they are $75,549. And what does California get for its highly paid highway employees? It gets an average cost of $265,061 to build a mile of highway in California versus $88,539 for a mile of highway in Texas. Is it any wonder why Texas's highways are so much better? The same could be written for bridges as well.

TABLE 7.10

Provision of Public Services: Salaries, FTE Employees, and Total Annual Pay as a Percent of GSP

Annual Pay per FTE Employee, Based on March 2011 Pay

	Governor	State Legislator
CA	$173,987	$95,291*
TX	$150,000	$7,200
CA to TX Ratio	1.16	13.23

	Total	Education Total	Hospitals	Police Protection Total
United States	$51,627	$49,335	$56,246	$63,342
CA	$67,524	$61,575	$80,617	$91,663
TX	$45,022	$43,955	$52,699	$53,944
CA to TX Ratio	1.50	1.40	1.53	1.70

FTE Employees per 10,000 Population, as of March 2011

	Total	Education Total	Hospitals	Police Protection Total
United States	526.0	286.0	31.0	29.7
CA	464.8	231.1	28.0	26.4
TX	564.8	344.6	30.3	28.9
CA to TX Ratio	0.82	0.67	0.92	0.91

Total Annual Pay (mean salaries times FTE employment) as a % of GSP, Based on March 2011 Pay

	Total	Education Total	Hospitals	Police Protection Total
United States	5.38%	2.80%	0.35%	0.37%
CA	6.04%	2.74%	0.44%	0.47%
TX	4.99%	2.97%	0.31%	0.31%
CA to TX Ratio	1.21	0.92	1.39	1.52

Elementary and Secondary Instructional Employees Only:	Annual Pay per FTE Employee	FTE Employees per 10,000 Population	Total Annual Pay as a % of GSP
United States	$52,859	151.4	1.67%
CA	$67,970	110.1	1.44%
TX	$45,700	188.5	1.69%
CA to TX Ratio	1.49	0.58	0.85

Firefighters Only:	Annual Pay per FTE Employee	FTE Employees per 10,000 Population	Total Annual Pay as a % of GSP
United States	$70,093	10.0	0.15%
CA	$119,698	7.7	0.18%
TX	$62,962	9.2	0.11%
CA to TX Ratio	1.90	0.83	1.55

*Note: CA state legislator salary down from $113,098 in 2007.

Source: U.S. Census Bureau, National Conference of State Legislatures, Council of State Government

Corrections	Highways	Fire Protection Total	Public Welfare	Other
$50,253	$49,834	$69,169	$46,336	$52,687
$72,723	$75,549	$114,722	$56,238	$67,146
$37,660	$42,885	$61,813	$36,960	$45,278
1.93	1.76	1.86	1.52	1.48

Corrections	Highways	Fire Protection Total	Public Welfare	Other
23.1	16.5	10.9	16.1	112.7
24.4	10.8	8.6	18.0	117.4
27.7	13.6	10.0	10.4	99.3
0.88	0.79	0.86	1.74	1.18

Corrections	Highways	Fire Protection Total	Public Welfare	Other
0.23%	0.16%	0.15%	0.15%	1.18%
0.34%	0.16%	0.19%	0.20%	1.52%
0.20%	0.11%	0.12%	0.08%	0.88%
1.67	1.37	1.56	2.59	1.72

Police Officers Only:	Annual Pay per FTE Employee	FTE Employees per 10,000 Population	Total Annual Pay as a % of GSP
U.S.	$68,928	22.2	0.32%
CA	$104,729	18.1	0.37%
TX	$59,551	20.9	0.24%
CA to TX Ratio	1.76	0.87	1.50

And when it comes to hospital and fire protection full-time equivalent employees, the answer is still the same. Hospital employees in California earn on average $80,617 per year whereas in Texas they earn $52,699. For fire protection, California full-time equivalent employees pull in $114,722 on average. The corresponding group in Texas earns $61,813. Does it still surprise you why all these cities in California are going broke and Texas is booming?

The last category of full-time equivalent workers we have looked at separately is almost anticlimactic—public welfare employees. Given what you know about welfare from an earlier section and what you know about salaries from this section, you can guess that California pays its welfare employees a lot more and employs a lot more of them. The average public welfare employee in Texas earns $36,960 per year. In California, a corresponding employee earns $56,238. And there you have it—California pays way more than Texas pays. But there is more. Now we get to the actual provision of public services—the number of public employees per 100,000 population.

Whereas in education, hospitals, police protection, corrections, highways, and fire protection Texas employs far more professionals per 10,000 of population than does California, in public welfare the roles are reversed. California employs almost 75 percent more welfare workers per 10,000 population than does Texas. And, of course, as mentioned in the previous paragraph, California pays each of its welfare employees on average over 50 percent more than Texas does. Here is the problem.

In the category of other state and local government employees, California's newfound leadership continues. California pays almost 50 percent more per worker than does Texas, while Texas employs almost 20 percent more workers per 10,000 population than does California.

Whether we like it or not, education, hospitals, police protection, corrections, highways, and fire protection are all government functions that increase output, employment, and general prosperity. These are the areas where Texas far outperforms California.

Welfare and other public services, in contrast, detract from output, employment, and general prosperity but are purported to increase equity and social justice and reduce income disparities. These are the areas where California outspends and outemploys Texas. And to what avail? California has more poverty, unemployment, people in need, and general despair than does Texas. California's highest tax rates create the very destitution that is used as a rationale for more welfare and higher tax rates.

The Performance of State and Local Public Education

From the previous tables you should be able to surmise that it would take a miracle for California to do a better job educating California's K–12 population than Texas does educating its K–12 population. California has 231.1 people in education per 10,000 population whereas Texas has 344.6 people in education per 10,000 population. Texas has 50 percent more people as a share of population working in education than does California.

California's education elite are paid on average $61,575 annually wheras Texas's average salary is $43,955. California's average for a full-time equivalent employee in education is a full 40 percent higher than is the average pay for a similar person in Texas. And to round things out, education is the one major category where Texas actually spends more as a share of state GDP than does California. Unfortunately, as opposed to the hockey competition at the 1980 Winter Olympics at Lake Placid, there is no miracle. California's kids are the big losers.

The National Assessment of Educational Progress (NAEP) is a congressionally authorized project of the National Center for Education Statistics (NCES) within the Institute of Education Sciences of the U.S. Department of Education. NAEP has, over the years, comprehensively and systematically evaluated what American students "know and can do" across all states in math and reading. The project has also evaluated subjects such as science, writing, the arts, civics, economics, geography, and U.S. history, but in a much less systematic way. NAEP carries out these comprehensive tests for fourth graders (nine-year-olds) and eighth graders (13-year-olds) for comparing states at any one moment in time and for assessing long-term trends. These test scores are about as good a measure of the provision of public services as exists.

TABLE 7.11				
Fifty-State Ranking of NAEP Test Scores: **California versus Texas (2003, 2005, 2007, 2009, and 2011)**				
	2011	**2009**	**2007**	**2005**	**2003**
Texas	29	31	26	27	33
California	47	47	48	46	46

Source: U.S. Department of Education: Institute of Education Sciences, Laffer Associates.

Taking the summary statistics compiled by NAEP for each state, we have added the test scores in both math and reading for eighth graders and fourth graders in order to arrive at one summary statistic for a state's educational achievement in any one year. We have then ranked each state for several years from 2003 to 2011 from best (1) to worst (50). Take a look at Table 7.11 and how California fared compared to Texas.

In the summary statistics of Table 7.11, California ranks consistently in the bottom five states in the nation while Texas is around the average of all states and way ahead of California year in and year out.

For fourth graders in reading for the years 1992, 1994, 1998, 2002, 2003, 2005, 2007, 2009, and 2011, Texas outperformed California by a wide margin each and every year. In fact, California was below the national average every single year. Texas's results were mixed when compared to the U.S. average.

When it comes to eighth grade math over a similar sample of 10 specific years from 1990 to 2011, Texas students outperformed California students each and every year by wide and increasing margins over the entire time period. No exceptions.

For the eighth grade reading tests for selected years for which data were available between 1998 and 2011, Texas students again outperformed California students each and every year. In eighth grade science and writing, where tests were performed by NAEP, Texas students were always far superior to California students.

Many forces influence children here in the United States. It is not just state and local government policies that tip the balance. But state and local governments do fund the schools, hire the teachers, set the standards for educational excellence, and set the framework for how teachers as a group are permitted to operate in the broader context of political and social life. The state and local governments' educational system has to be the single most dominant influence on our children's educational achievements.

If it were not so tragic, we would find it extremely funny that California's classroom teachers are the highest-paid classroom teachers in the country, and yet California students rank fifth from the bottom. In 2011, California students were able to test better than their counterparts in only D.C., Mississippi, Louisiana, and New Mexico. Who can argue with a straight face after seeing the example of California that all we need to do is spend more to improve the quality of education?

Teachers in K–12 schools are not just any old randomly selected group of people. They are special in many ways. Because, in part, of their single employer status and because of their significance to society at large, teachers are members of a well-organized workers guild in every state in the nation. This is especially true in California.

The California Teachers Association (CTA) was founded in 1863, has about 325,000 members, and represents all teachers in public schools K–12. The California Faculty Association and the California Community College Association are also affiliated with the CTA.

In politics, the CTA spent about $212 million on political campaigns in the 10-year period from January 1, 2000, to December 31, 2009. This is more than any other union, business, organization, or individual—nearly double that of the California State Council of Service Employees, which came in second.

In 1988, the California Teachers Association was able to get a constitutional amendment passed in California, Proposition 98, which forced the state to spend enormous amounts of the general fund budget on education, and these spending requirements could only be suspended by a two-thirds majority of the legislature. The CTA also has sponsored 170 strikes between 1975 and 2012.

In the NAEP publication on scholastic performance of students in five mega-states—California, Texas, Florida, Illinois, and New York—fourth grade and eighth grade students are evaluated in reading, mathematics, and science during the years 2009 and 2011.[21] The way NAEP reports the results is with three symbols: □ means no significant difference between the state and the nation, ▲ means significantly higher average score than the nation, and last, ▼ means significantly lower average score than the nation. Figure 7.6 presents the results.[22]

California is significantly below the nation in every single one of the six categories for both fourth graders and eighth graders. Florida is significantly below the national average in two categories, significantly above the national average in one category, and tied with the national

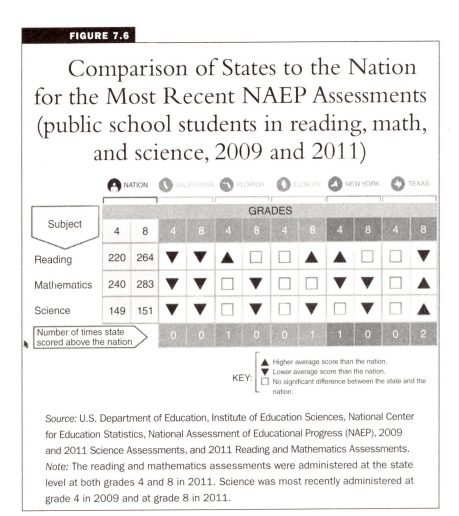

FIGURE 7.6

Comparison of States to the Nation for the Most Recent NAEP Assessments (public school students in reading, math, and science, 2009 and 2011)

Subject	NATION 4	NATION 8	CALIFORNIA 4	CALIFORNIA 8	FLORIDA 4	FLORIDA 8	ILLINOIS 4	ILLINOIS 8	NEW YORK 4	NEW YORK 8	TEXAS 4	TEXAS 8
Reading	220	264	▼	▼	▲	□	□	▲	▲	□	□	▼
Mathematics	240	283	▼	▼	□	▼	□	□	▼	▼	□	▲
Science	149	151	▼	▼	□	▼	□	▼	□	▼	□	▲
Number of times state scored above the nation			0	0	1	0	0	1	1	0	0	2

KEY:
▲ Higher average score than the nation.
▼ Lower average score than the nation.
□ No significant difference between the state and the nation.

Source: U.S. Department of Education, Institute of Education Sciences, National Center for Education Statistics, National Assessment of Educational Progress (NAEP), 2009 and 2011 Science Assessments, and 2011 Reading and Mathematics Assessments.
Note: The reading and mathematics assessments were administered at the state level at both grades 4 and 8 in 2011. Science was most recently administered at grade 4 in 2009 and at grade 8 in 2011.

average in three categories. Illinois is significantly below the national average in one category, significantly above in one category, and tied in four, while New York is above in two, below in two, and tied in two.

Texas is the winner in the mega-states with only one category significantly below the national average, two categories significantly above the national average, and three categories tied.

These results say it all.

Highways: California versus Texas

When it comes to highway spending as a share of state gross product, California has it all over Texas. California spends 37 percent more in total wages and salaries on full-time equivalent employees in highways as a percentage of state GSP than does Texas. But, unfortunately, this dollar advantage does not carry over to improved public highway services. In fact, when it comes to highways, Texas not only offsets its spending shortfall vis-à-vis California, but it flips the spending shortfall and actually provides substantially more highway public services than does California.

In the first place, even though California spends more, as of March 2011 California had 21 percent less state and local full-time equivalent governmental highway employees per 10,000 population than did Texas. Texas's citizens got more personnel attention than California's citizens.

Second, California paid 76 percent more in average salary than did Texas per full-time equivalent highway employee—$75,549 in California versus $42,885 in Texas. But you have not read anything yet.

In a very thorough, well-documented and careful analysis published by the Reason Foundation entitled "19th Annual Report on the Performance of State Highway Systems (1984–2008)," the authors conclude the following:

- The average cost to build one mile of highway in California in 2008 is $265,061, meaning California has the 13th highest cost of highways per mile in the nation; in Texas an equivalent average mile of highway costs $88,539, ranking Texas 48th in cost in the nation. But even more important, it means Texas can build three times as many highway miles than can California for any given amount of dollars.

- A state's road condition is usually measured by special machines that determine the roughness of road surfaces with the smoother roads considered to be in better condition. In ranking the condition of states' rural interstates, Texas ranked 23rd with 0.03 percent poor condition miles of rural road while California ranked 49th, or dead last, with 16.32 percent of rural interstate in poor condition. (Delaware is not included in this ranking because it does not have any rural interstates.) Only California and three other states (New York, New Jersey, and Alaska) reported more than 5 percent poor rural interstate mileage; two-thirds of the poor condition rural interstate mileage in the United States is just in California, Alaska, New York, and Minnesota.

- One performance variable where California ranked better than Texas was in the percentage of deficient bridges, where California ranked 18.88 percent deficient bridges and Texas 19.01 percent. This inverse ranking is likely due to the strict bridge and highway maintenance laws implemented after earthquake damage, particularly after the 1994 Northridge earthquake in which seven major freeway bridges in the area collapsed and 170 were damaged, disrupting traffic in the Ventura–Los Angeles region for weeks following the earthquake.[23] With that being said, Texas was not all that far behind California.

Maintaining a state's highway system has to be about as important a duty as there is for state and local governments. Texas does a far better job than does California. Along these lines, the Reason Foundation released an additional report in February 2013 entitled "Are Highways Crumbling? State Performance Summaries," which evaluates state highway conditions over the past 20 years. Between 1989 and 2008 California's general performance ranked 50th whereas Texas's 20-year general performance ranked 17th.

Prisons: California and Texas

One of the final areas we wish to investigate is also one of the most fascinating areas of state and local governance. Firefighters and police personnel are wonderful heroes possessing both courage and self-sacrifice. Road builders and educators create the future, while politicians and judges occupy positions of enormous personal responsibility and influence. But then we have the prison guards, whose lives are far from glamorous and whose work is often ignored.

Corrections officers in California are paid, on average, 93 percent more per year than are Texas's corrections officers (see Table 7.10). At the same time there are 12 percent fewer corrections officers per 10,000 population in California than there are in Texas. The people of Texas pay less and get more, while the people of California once again pay more and get less. There is still more to this story.

Where the numbers get shocking are the differences in average annual cost per inmate. California's average annual cost per inmate is $47,421, or $129 per day, in 2012, whereas in Texas each inmate's annual cost is $21,390, or $58.60 per day. California spends more than twice as much per prisoner than does Texas.[24] Texas engages in law enforcement less expensively than California. Texas also encourages the use of private incarceration facilities, while California rejects them.

The reason why California does less and spends more harks back to the 1978 Dills Act, which granted the prison guard union—California Correctional Peace Officers Association (CCPOA)—incredible powers to negotiate pay standards and work codes. In 2010, the CCPOA spent a total of $32,452,083 influencing California voters and elected officials.[25] This union was the 15th largest political contributor in California.[26]

Not only does Texas incarcerate more scofflaws per 100,000 population than does California, but Texas does its job far, far less expensively than does California. And on top of all of that, Texas houses its prisoners far more humanely than does California. Just read on.

On May 23, 2011 the U.S. Supreme Court upheld the ruling by a lower three-judge court that the state of California must reduce its prison population to 137.5 percent of design capacity. U.S. Supreme

Court Justice Antonin Scalia called the decision "perhaps the most radical injunction issued by a court in our Nation's history."[27] As of December 31, 2011, California's prison population was at 175 percent of design capacity. Just what will California do with all of these excess prisoners—just let them go? In Texas at the same time the prison population was at approximately 85 percent of design capacity.

Predictably, releasing prisoners has resulted in an increase in crime throughout California. According to the Public Policy Institute of California, there has been a significant increase in property crime (up 7.6 percent in the year after the start of the prisoner releases) in California despite a national-level trend of falling property crime rates.

Conclusion

The differences between California's and Texas's economic policies and performances couldn't be more stark. Texas has a low-tax, business-friendly environment. California has punitively high tax rates and seems to put up every possible barrier to entry for business. How did these two states with so much in common arrive at such different places today? The way we like to put it is that the translation from taxes to the eventual provision of public services suffers from three major "parasitic leakages."

The economic journey starts with tax rates. There is an enormous disconnect between tax rates and tax revenues. Despite California's tax rates being around 65 percent higher than those in Texas, Texas takes in approximately 25 percent less tax revenues than does California—parasitic leakage #1. Not only do higher tax rates cause less economic output, but they also cause people to move to lower tax rate jurisdictions and cause the people who live in the higher-tax location to earn less taxable income. Lawyers, accountants, lobbyists, tax exemptions, exclusions, deductions, and more all create a gap between tax rates and tax revenues. California's higher tax rates also create much of the poverty and deprivations that siphon off government spending. In fact, a significant portion of government spending is required just to offset the damage done by the higher tax rates themselves!

Texas taking in 25 percent less revenue per dollar of GDP than California, however, doesn't translate into 25 percent less spending for Texas. In fact, due to all sorts of waste and inefficiency at California's administrative level, California's actual amount spent per dollar of GDP is approximately equal to Texas's amount of government spending per dollar of GDP—parasitic leakage #2. The reason for this second leakage is the size of the bureaucratic behemoth that is California's state and local government. As of June 2013, there were 380 separate state agencies listed on the State of California's website, including entities such as the Bureau of Electronic and Appliance Repair, Home Furnishings and Thermal Insulation (BEARHFTI) and the Landscape Architects Technical Committee (LATC). Texas takes a much leaner approach to bureaucracy, and it shows when it comes to the translation from tax revenues to government spending.

Finally, we get to the provision of actual services to citizens, which is the ultimate purpose of government, after all. Once again we find California doing a disservice to its citizens—as a result of inflated government employee salaries, unions, regulatory and compliance costs, and more, California's provision of services to its citizens on a per capita basis is around 25 percent less than Texas's provision of services—parasitic loss #3. Take firefighters, for example—Texas employs 9.2 firefighters per 10,000 of population versus California at 7.7 per 10,000, but California's firefighters are paid $120,000 per year to Texas's $63,000. In just about every category of employment, California overpays public employees yet underprovides services to its citizens relative to Texas. About the only important category where California overpays public employees and overprovides services compared to Texas is in the category of public welfare employees. Need we say more?

At the end of the day, California exacts a larger share of its citizens' work output than Texas does and, due to perverse incentives, inefficiency, waste, greed, and corruption, provides far less in terms of public services to its citizens. Texas is welcoming more and more companies, jobs, and people each year, while California is desperately trying to build a wall to keep its companies, jobs, and people from fleeing to greener pastures.

The people have spoken.

CHAPTER 8

Au Contraire, Mon Frère

Criticisms of Our Work—Our Responses

There is no scientific idea so absurd that you cannot find someone with a Ph.D. (indeed often with a Nobel Prize) to support it.

—Philip Ball, *Curiosity*

Conflicts of Interest and Policies

According to Mohamed El-Hodiri, University of Kansas economics professor and senior economist at the Kansas Progress Institute, Kansas is "bleeding for the wrong causes" because "The governor imports Arthur Laffer and pays him big bucks so this unpublished 'expert' can reiterate the commonly accepted theory that cutting the tax rate will increase tax revenue."[1] And this comment from Professor El-Hodiri represents both the depth and the breadth of the criticism we have to deal with on a daily basis in state capitols in this wonderful land of ours.

The ideas and analyses in this book have been disputed by people who, for one reason or another, prefer progressive high-rate taxation and high levels of government spending. At every juncture, and quite contrary to the data, they seem to argue that the higher tax rates are and the more government spending there is, the better. To them we represent an uneducated right-wing fringe biased to serve wealthy, malevolent operatives hell-bent on exploiting the voiceless masses of humanity for their own personal gain. The truth is just the opposite.

State university economists are not required to meet the market test in order to get paid. Their lifestyles are funded by tax dollars at universities that are themselves tax-exempt organizations. These economists provide an endless supply of research studies attempting to poke holes in our arguments. It's a lot easier getting your income from taxes that others are required by law to pay than having to earn what you're paid. All these research economists have to do is convince government employees, contract administrators, and politicians of their worth when these functionaries authorize the payments to the research economists with other people's money not their own. Meeting market standards can be brutal. But how would these research economists know? They wouldn't. Without being consciously aware, these economists are following their own version of "the invisible hand," although in their case it should be called "the invisible handout." It is amazing how incentives operate subliminally to alter the research results of objective academics. These people will rebut arguments they know to be true in order to curry favor with their political benefactors.

Philosophers, government officials, and professors must become actively aware of their assumptions and prejudices in order to overcome them. It's very difficult for government-funded researchers to overcome their own self-interest and be objective.

We, for our part, fully understand why employees of universities and other tax-exempt organizations like high tax rates and generous government spending. Supporting high taxes and exorbitant spending they believe is in their self-interest, and self-interest is the very basis of economics. And, of course, the electorate's self-interest, which we are a part of, is our argument for low-rate, broad-based flat taxes and spending restraint for everyone, not just academics and not just subliminally. The intellect workers of government and quasi-government institutions should live by the rules the rest of us have to follow. If they did, their research results would be very different.

The essence of what we mean here is wholly captured by Upton Sinclair's famous quip: "It is difficult to get a man to understand something, when his salary depends on his not understanding it!"[2] The biggest beneficiaries, at least on a relative basis, of high taxes and generous tax deductions are 501(c)(3) organizations such as universities (Mickey Hepner's and Mohamed El-Hodiri's employers) and tax-exempt foundations (Institute on Taxation and Economic Policy [ITEP]). Tax-exempt operations thrive in high-tax environments. Long live self-interest.

Taxes and Other Supply-Side Policy Variables Don't Affect Population and Gross State Product Growth

Our critics claim that "population trends are decidedly not determined by differences in tax policy between states," and therefore we should "control for population growth."[3] By controlling for population growth, they mean that we should use all of our metrics on a per capita basis. We disagree.

Theory, data, and just plain common sense all point to statewide variations in taxes as a potent factor in people's decisions of where to live and work. Imagine what would happen to population trends if one state had a 100 percent income tax and another state had a 0 percent income tax. We won't even have to use our imagination if Maryland under Governor O'Malley, Illinois under Governor Quinn, Minnesota under Governor Dayton, and California under Governor Brown have their ways.[4]

Population growth differences among the states are precisely the key metrics that tax and other state policies really impact. Ignoring population growth differences among the states when analyzing state economic policies is like doing a study on the causes of lung cancer while ignoring whether people smoke. It just doesn't make any sense. In the exact same sense that smoking causes lung cancer, higher tax rates cause slower population growth and slower economic growth. And migration patterns between states tell a lot about where Americans think prosperity is happening and where it isn't.

But even when principles and theory seem obvious, anecdotes won't settle the arguments, and for this we apologize. Systematic research is the only way to go. The wide range of statistical analyses contained in every chapter of this book should put this counterintuitive critique to bed for good.

One study critical of our research challenges our conclusion that state taxes impact population, job and income growth.[5] The ITEP researchers find that from 2001 to 2010, "residents of high rate income tax states are actually experiencing economic conditions at least as good, if not better, than those living in states lacking a personal income tax." ITEP goes on to reject our findings by writing that "the growth of states lacking an income tax is no more than coincidental."[6] You can't make up quotes like these.

As we have shown extensively in earlier chapters:

- The nine zero income tax states have far higher population growth, labor force growth, employment growth, income growth, and, yes, even tax revenue growth than do the nine highest income tax rate states over the past decade (Chapter 3). And, as if icing on the cake, the nine zero income tax rate states do as well if not better than the highest nine income tax rate states.

- The 11 states with the lowest corporate income tax rates way outperform the 11 highest corporate income tax rate states in terms of population, labor force, employment, and income growth (Chapter 3). They also do a far better job than do their highest-tax counterpart states in providing more and higher-quality public services.

- The zero income tax rate states, when it comes to either population or income growth using a 10-year moving average, have never had a single year over the past half century when they didn't beat the tar out of the equivalent number of the highest income tax rate states (Chapter 3).

- The 11 states that have adopted an income tax over the past 50-plus years have in each and every instance declined as a share of both U.S. population and U.S. income from the date that tax was initiated to the present (see Chapter 1). They have also declined in terms of the quality and volume of the provision of public services.
- Using a time-series cross-section econometric analysis of all 50 states over the past decade shows strong negative correlations between all sorts of tax rates and population growth and growth in gross state product (see Chapter 6).
- IRS tax return data from 1992/1993 to the present show beyond a doubt that tax filers—especially those with high adjusted gross incomes—on balance move out of high-tax states and into low-tax states (see Chapter 5).

In fact, one of our coauthors of this book and his family actually packed up their bags and moved from California to Nashville, Tennessee. Upon arrival, he couldn't help but notice all the other California license plates, which have kept on coming, even up until today. The IRS data of Chapter 5 put exact numbers to this phenomenon. But it's not just people with high incomes who move. People who hope to someday have high incomes also move.

We wonder if these ITEP researchers are just trying to fool with us or if they really believe what they say to be true. Obviously, there are many factors that influence economic growth. But surely if location A lowers its tax rates and location B raises its tax rates, other things being equal, some businesses, some capital, and some people will choose to migrate from B to A (i.e., to where tax rates have fallen and from places where tax rates have risen). Does anyone really disagree with that premise?

In Chapter 7, the effects of high tax rates, excessive regulation, and overspending couldn't be clearer. People and income both move from the high-tax state—California—to the low-tax state—Texas. Not only does Texas way outperform California in all of the regular measures, but it way outperforms California in education, police, highways, fire protection, and prisons. California does have a lot more and much higher paid welfare workers than does Texas, because California needs them.

It was no accident that the auto industry left the highly unionized Midwest for the business-friendly South and that Airbus is opening up its new plant in a more pro-growth low-tax state. In fact, state legislators and governors offer enormous tax-incentive packages to specifically lure businesses to their states because they know businesses, jobs, and people prefer lower taxes. According to a recent Reuters article about the new Volkswagen plant in Chattanooga, Tennessee,

> Volkswagen will receive as much as $707 million of state and local incentives from tax credits over 20 years and property tax breaks over 30 years as well as assistance to pay for worker training, utility infrastructure as well as the donation of the property where the plant sits.[7]

A tax incentive package over $700 million given to an auto company to locate in Tennessee—a zero earned income tax state that also has a low overall tax burden—should serve as proof positive that taxes affect migration and business location decisions.

Therefore, we argue that both population growth and income growth are highly revealing metrics of prosperity. Companies make decisions about where to locate their production facilities, and tax rates affect those decisions. People make the decision whether or not to move, and tax rates affect those decisions. People vote with their feet and generally don't migrate to places where they will be worse off. History shows this to be true over and over. People migrated from East Germany to West Germany, from North Korea to South Korea, from Mexico to the United States, not in search of better weather or accessible suburbs, but because that was where they could find freedom and opportunity and raise their living standard.

A simple question puts the immigration and in-migration issues in perspective: which would you rather have, people lined up on your state's border trying to get in or trying to get out of your state? You know our answer.

Growth Is a Move from North to South, from Clouds to Sunshine, from Cold to Warm

One of our critics inadvertently concedes a broader point that we have made for years that the entrepreneur-hostile Northeast is becoming like Europe and the economic gazelles in the United States are in the laissez-faire South. We have long argued that while tax rates do matter it isn't just tax rates that matter. Government spending matters, the level of regulation matters, and whether the state has a right-to-work law matters a lot, too. Then, of course, there are a lot of nonpolicy factors that matter as well.

The Northeast is losing ground to the South because governments in the Northeast impose much more statist control over their respective state economies. If you have tuberculosis, you may move to Arizona for the favorable climate; if you're a ski enthusiast, you may move to Colorado for easier access to the slopes; if you're an ocean researcher, you may move to Woods Hole, Massachusetts, for the research facilities; but the overriding thrust that pervades the structure of migration is state economics generally and taxes specifically.

The fact that the bureaucratic Northeast is falling further and further behind and the pro-business South is booming should not come as a surprise to anyone and really has little to do with global latitudes. One of the biggest factors behind that phenomenon is that the South, on a whole variety of economic policy variables we have examined, is a region much more receptive to business and worker rights than the high-tax, heavily unionized Northeast. The future is happening in the low-tax South whereas high-tax California, New York, and Illinois are increasingly looking like the Greece of North America. The wonder is why so many politicians still want their states and the country to adopt the tax policies of the loser states, and not the winners.

Another argument used by our critics is that most of the growth we are capturing in our studies is in the southeastern region of the country, and they go on to say that people are moving to states like Florida, Georgia, Tennessee, and Texas solely for the warm weather and the sun, as they flee the cold northeastern states. To paraphrase one study, it is just "coincidental" that the low and no income tax states are in the South and the high income tax states are in the Northeast.[8] Tax rates, they say, don't explain the migration patterns.

There's no doubt that a lot of people move to Florida and Georgia for the nice weather and beaches. These and other reasons are clearly factors that make these states desirable locations. We have even heard that a big factor behind the rise of the South is air-conditioning, and we don't doubt there is more than a kernel of truth to that as well.

One obvious problem with their South/West/sun explanation as a substitute for tax-driven migration, however, is that it doesn't explain why New Hampshire does better than Vermont, or why Nevada does better than its cohorts, or why Tennessee does better than Kentucky. And it sure as heck doesn't explain why one of the states with the nicest weather year-round in the nation, California, is bleeding to death. It doesn't even explain Alaska, South Dakota, and Wyoming. They are hardly warm-weather Southern states. And how about the 11 states that adopted the income tax over the past 50-plus years? Has their weather changed?

People aren't moving out of Buffalo, Detroit, Chicago, Cleveland, and Newark just because it's cold.

Growth Is Predominantly a Matter of Education and Not Taxes and Other Economic Policy Measures

Our state analysis is intended to help advise lawmakers on how to make good choices for their states' residents. State lawmakers cannot, alas, change the weather or where their state is located, or have much of an impact on how much oil they have in the ground; but state lawmakers certainly can change their taxes, how much state and local governments spend, whether their state is a right-to-work state, how many impediments they put in the way of the extraction of oil and natural gas, and how generous their state's welfare system is.

The quality of schools, of course, also matters, as does the state's highway system, but it takes years for those policies to pay dividends.

Cutting taxes can have a near immediate and permanent impact, which is why we have advised Oklahoma, Kansas, and other states to cut their income tax rates if they want the most effective immediate and lasting boost to their states' economies. We strongly believe in good schools, good highways, good hospitals, efficient and fair judicial systems, adequate and comprehensive police protection, good prisons, and good fire protection. What we don't believe is that you can achieve these objectives by overtaxing a state's economy and overpaying public employees.

While education is a complicated and ambiguous measure of growth, let us assure the reader that low-tax, pro-business, high-growth states do just as well if not better in providing quality education than do high-tax, bureaucratic, slow-growth states. Just look at how California, the highest of the high-tax states, gets trounced by Texas, the lowest of the low-tax states, when it comes to Department of Education–measured test scores for fourth and eighth graders (see our Chapters 1 and 7 for more on school test scores and tax rates).

Higher tax rates do not—we repeat, do not—lead to better education, but they do lead to slower growth and more poverty.

Personal Income per Capita and Median Income Growth as Measures of Success Show Taxes Don't Matter

By examining economic variables on a per person basis (i.e., controlling for population growth), some critics try to refute our findings. While looking at anything on a per capita basis makes sense for international comparisons where factors of production and people are relatively immobile, it makes no sense for the various states of the United States. Controlling for population or viewing variables exclusively on a per capita basis is inappropriate and will fool only nonexperts. People, workers, consumers, and income are equally mobile in the United States.

Both population and gross state product (GSP), as studies point out repeatedly, grow much faster in no income tax states than they do in high income tax states. Therefore, when you look at GSP per capita, the numerator and denominator are both growing faster in low-tax states and more slowly in high-tax states, but what you can't know is whether GSP per capita should rise or fall in either high-tax or low-tax states.

Sometimes population will grow faster than the rise in GSP in low-tax states, and at other times it won't. Sometimes population will shrink more slowly than state GSP in high-tax states and sometimes it won't.[9] Thus, exceptionally high per capita income growth can result from high population growth and even higher income growth, or it can result from low income growth and even lower population growth. While these two examples show similar income per capita growth, they are polar opposites when it comes to economic performance.

Given our critics' obsession with per capita metrics, we are surprised they don't examine growth in population per capita. Nevertheless, whatever may happen on a per person basis, low tax rate states attract more people, jobs, and income than do high tax rate states.

The inherent problem with measuring GSP or income on a per capita basis is plainly visible when you examine two states on opposite ends of the growth spectrum: Nevada and West Virginia. First think of Nevada: a zero income tax state, a zero corporate tax state, and a right-to-work state that, over the decade 2001 to 2010, has ranked first in population growth, eighth in GSP growth, eighth in personal income growth, and ninth in nonfarm payroll employment growth. How's that for a rock star state?

Nevada has been a magnet for people, jobs, and output for years, gaining another congressional seat during the 2010 congressional reapportionment. Nevada has also been extremely attractive to foreign immigrants, who usually have incomes below the average of native Nevadans.

Foreign immigration is certainly good for the immigrants, as they are more likely to enjoy higher wages and a higher standard of living. Foreign immigration is also a boon for native Nevadans, who enjoy all the benefits of an inflow of lower-cost, high-quality labor. But, according to our critics' preferred metric, Nevada ranked 48th in per capita personal income growth and 35th in median household income growth from 2001 to 2010.

In contrast, take a state like West Virginia, which one of our critics ranks number one in median household income growth from 2001 to 2010. West Virginia has gone from comprising 0.78 percent of the nation's total personal income in the five years before it introduced a personal income tax in 1961, to comprising only 0.48 percent of the nation's personal income as of 2012. Income has fallen precipitously decade after decade in West Virginia. But then again, so has population. West Virginia's population as a share of the United States over the same period fell from 1.05 percent to 0.59 percent in 2012. We certainly wouldn't consider these metrics of West Virginia the components of a prosperous state. The name West Virginia has been and still is a synonym for poverty and despair. People and jobs and income have been fleeing this high-tax state for a very long time.

But let's really look at ITEP's measure of West Virginia's and Nevada's prosperity in the clear light of day: One point to understand about changes in median income is to recognize that a state's median income is the income of the middle worker, where half of the workers earn more and half of the workers earn less. Median income will rise if low-income workers lose their jobs or leave the state, which is what happened in West Virginia. Median income will fall if a large number of low-income workers find jobs, which is what happened in Nevada. Wouldn't you consider it better if low-income workers found jobs than if low-income workers lost jobs? We would.

West Virginia has experienced the exact opposite of what Nevada has. In West Virginia over the past several decades, able-bodied lower- and middle-class workers and their families have been unable to find work and have left the state for greener pastures elsewhere. Lower-income or no-income people are leaving the state more rapidly than are higher-income people. West Virginia's growth in median income has risen. As the state becomes more and more hollowed out, the last few stubborn above-average-income families still remaining in West Virginia cause the median household income growth to rise. One factor that's changing in West Virginia that does affect the growth in income per capita is the recent development of the Marcellus Shale oil field in towns like Wheeling, which is bringing rapid development as we speak.

It seems that neither Nevadans nor foreign immigrants mind their lackluster per capita ranking given that Nevada continues to attract people, both Americans and foreign immigrants, in droves. Nevada's low median household income growth and low per capita personal income growth are a result of lots of jobs for people at the low rungs of the economic ladder.

One of our most vocal opponents, Professor Mickey Hepner, said, "I don't know about you, but if we have two million more people move to Oklahoma and we are poor as a result, I don't think that's progress. I don't think we're better off."[10] Of course, the problem with Professor Hepner's statement is why would the two million people want to move to Oklahoma in the first place if they became poor as a result? And second, if Oklahomans are as xenophobic as Mickey Hepner, why don't they and he move out? Well, Mickey Hepner hasn't moved out, and a lot of people have moved into Oklahoma. We're going to assume they and he like being there.

And to remove a point of confusion, the people in a state can all be better off even if that state's per capita or median income goes down. If, for example, 50,000 low-income agriculture workers get higher pay by moving into Texas, and Texas's farmers earn more by hiring these high-quality low-pay in-migrants, then everyone is better off and no one is worse off. But the per capita income in Texas may actually go down simply because there are now proportionally more low-income agricultural workers in Texas.

How people who are themselves professionals and who are familiar with this field can make remarks as we reproduce as follows is beyond our ken.

[T]he nine states with "high rate" income taxes have on average seen considerably more economic growth per capita over the last decade than the nine states that fail to levy a broad-based personal income tax. . . .

Four of the nine states without income taxes are actually doing worse
than the average state in regards to economic growth per capita: Texas,
Tennessee, Florida, and Nevada.[11]

The nine highest income tax rate states shrank in population relative
to the nation (6.3 percent growth in population versus the U.S. average of 9.3 percent growth in population over the past decade), while
"the nine states that fail to levy a broad-based personal income tax"
had population growth greater than the national average (14.6 percent
versus 9.3 percent).

And by the way, while it is true that per capita GSP is generally
higher in the high income tax states—like New York, California, and
New Jersey—it is not true that per capita GSP *growth* is generally higher
in those states. We have found that after looking at 40 years' worth of
data, sometimes the no income tax states grow faster in GSP and jobs
per capita, and at other times they don't. For example, in the 2001–2010
period, per capita GSP grew 37.2 percent in the no income tax states,
and just 33.4 percent in the high income tax states. But even when this
measure favors our point of view, it's still inappropriate to use it as an
indicator of good state policies.

Tax Rate Cuts Are Public Service Cuts

Perhaps the universal complaint about cutting tax rates is the resultant
loss of public services. Symmetrically, the universal reason to raise tax
rates is to provide more public services.

In his opposition to a proposal to cut tax rates in Oklahoma, we turn
once again to Professor Mickey Hepner:

> But we could also cut government spending, and this is a concern to
> me. As an educator, I know that what really matters for business voca-
> tion is the ability of us to train the workforce, the ability of us to pro-
> vide the necessary services that the companies need. It's hard for me
> to imagine a successful economy that's populated with unhealthy,
> uneducated individuals who often have to travel down dirt roads
> populated with criminals.[12]

What Professor Hepner is doing here and elsewhere is to assume tax rate reductions lead to public service reductions and then to assert this as fact: that tax rate cuts are public service cuts. To "assume" something and then declare it as "fact" is not terribly academic, or at least it shouldn't be. Well, it's not fact; far from it. Tax rate cuts are not cuts in public services.

Tax cuts are definitely not always or even usually linked with public service cuts. As often as not, in the tax and spending ranges in which states currently find themselves, a cut in tax rates will provide the resources to improve public services, and the additional economic growth will reduce the need for many public services such as food stamps or unemployment benefits.

In the first place, a cut in tax rates will lead to more jobs and higher incomes, thereby reducing the need for welfare, unemployment benefits, and income supplements. Higher growth will also mean that tax revenues will fall less than expected and may even rise.

People will choose more work over nonwork; people will choose staying in the state rather than leaving; people will select producing income over sheltering income. A tax cut sets into motion all sorts of positive reactions in a state that make everyone—including the beneficiaries of public services—better off. Of course, government needs revenues to provide public services, but there are dumb ways and smart ways to tax, and overtaxing can be just as bad as undertaxing.

One of the surprising findings of this book is that more often than not increases in tax rates have led to reductions in the provision of public services relative to the states that don't raise tax rates. Examples are contained in Chapters 1 and 7.

Linking any and all tax cuts to spending cuts is just plain wrong. One of the most disgusting acts lawmakers can and do commit is to enact policies that create the very poverty and despair they then use as an excuse to call for more programs and more spending and higher taxation. This vicious cycle is all too common—think Detroit or Chicago.

Other Factors Affect Population Growth (Oil, Sunshine, Accessible Suburbs, Etc.), and Therefore Taxes, Right-to-Work Laws, and Other Supply-Side Variables Don't

If not taxes or public services or right-to-work policy or retrievable oil reserves, our question to our critics is: What does account for differences in state population growth rates and growth rates in output?

Some of their explanations caught us quite by surprise. For example, one reason given is that population growth is higher in no income tax states because no income tax states are in the South and the West, which are areas of the country with higher birthrates and Hispanic immigration—as if Hispanics are somehow different from other Americans. And, if these reasons aren't enough for a quizzical look, how about "accessible suburbs"[13] as a reason for population growth? But in our critics' explanation of population growth there's no mention of taxes, spending, right-to-work policy, or welfare generosity. Ostensibly they must not think that these policy variables matter.

To quote one of our critics, "demographers have identified a large number of reasons for the population growth occurring in the South and West that are completely unrelated to these states' tax structures. Lower population density and more accessible suburbs are important factors, as are higher birth rates, Hispanic immigration, and even warmer weather."[14] Of course, we all know that taxes are not alone in explaining migration patterns among states, but let's be serious. The reasons our critics give for population growth are the academic equivalent of "the dog ate my homework." If our critics would only look a little further, they would find a lot of academic sources that suggest taxes, regulations, right-to-work policy, and other variables we employ are relevant if not dominant.

In Chapter 6, we report on some 50 or more academic studies from professors at Harvard, Yale, the University of Chicago, and so on in the most prestigious journals such as the *American Economic Review*, the *Journal of Political Economy*, and many others that document the precise statistical relationships between the policy variables we outline and growth in population and output. We're reminded of an old phrase, that facts have a stubborn insistence that ultimately unseats cozy certainties.

Just because people move for reasons other than taxes does not mean that they don't move for taxes as well.

Our critics say we don't even take account of "oil and sunshine." In all of our work, we have specifically taken into account all sorts of other factors including "oil" and, yes, even "sunshine." As shown in Chapter 3, if the revenues of the two zero income tax states with the highest severance taxes are eliminated from the comparison of zero income tax states with all states and the highest tax states, the seven remaining no income tax rate states are still way ahead of the U.S. average and even further ahead of the highest income tax rate states in growth of income, employment, and population. And even in times past when there was an oil bust and oil prices fell, the zero income tax states, including the oil states, outperformed the nation and the highest-tax states.

But of course oil and sunshine do matter. North Dakota's economy is booming today, not so much because of its tax code, but because it has massive amounts of new natural gas and oil operations. But one issue here is that North Dakota allows the exploitation of its oil reserves. California, which has huge reserves of oil and natural gas, has a government that makes the exploitation of California's oil reserves difficult. Public policies make a difference even when a state is endowed with natural resources.

One feature of North Dakota's performance is especially interesting to us. Oil has driven North Dakota to be the fastest-growing state in the nation when it comes to gross state product. However, North Dakota's population growth over the past decade has been far from stellar—ranking 22nd highest in the nation in spite of having the number one GSP growth of any state over that same time period.[15] Perhaps it is North Dakota's state income tax that creates the discrepancy.

Our rebuttals to our critics' oil comments notwithstanding, our detractors still persist in arguing that no income tax states tend to be energy-rich states—like Alaska, Texas, and Wyoming—and that this is the real reason no income tax states are doing well. If true, then our critics should explain the performances of New Mexico, Oklahoma, Montana, West Virginia, and Louisiana, each of which has proportionally more oil severance tax revenue than Texas or Nevada or Florida. For a more in-depth discussion of the effects of oil severance taxes on state performance, see Chapter 3.

What our critics also miss in their focus on oil and sunshine are what we have found to be other important growth factors: Right-to-work states way outperform closed-shop or forced-union states, and estate and corporate taxes and overregulation also negatively affect growth.[16] These factors are about as straightforward and commonsense as anything can be, and yet our critics never mention them even though they have been shown over and over again to be key factors in determining growth.

Correlations between Tax Rates and Growth Reflect a Simultaneous Equation Bias (Reverse Causation); That Is, Growth Causes Tax Cuts, Not the Reverse

An unintentionally humorous argument put forth by critics of our work is that people move from one place to another just for the helluvit, and, of course, they take their incomes with them. This is exactly what ITEP argues.[17] And then, sensing the coming prosperity, the states' legislatures and governors cut their states' tax rates. Thus, it really is future prosperity that causes current tax cuts, not the reverse.[18] And this, they argue, is why we find a "spurious correlation" between growth rates and taxes. In technical econometric terminology, this mutual causation is called a simultaneous equation bias.

In the words of Mickey Hepner, "the relationship is presumed to be changes in taxes lead to or determine the change in income levels, but in reality what we saw in the 1980s was just the opposite. . . . Again, it's not the tax cuts that led to the growth, it's the growth that led to the tax cuts." Hepner goes on to say that "this is why a number of state economists have looked at this study [an Arduin, Laffer & Moore Econometrics study of Oklahoma[19]] . . . and say this is not reliable in pointing the

way for Oklahoma's future. In fact, I don't know of a single state economist that has supported and endorsed this [tax cut] plan."[20]

Mickey Hepner's comments imply that during bad times government raises tax rates and during good times they cut tax rates. Not
only is this contrary to the logic of any school of economics we've ever
seen—you can't tax an economy into prosperity—but it's also contrary
to the facts. At the national level, President Reagan cut tax rates in the
heart of a recession/depression. President Kennedy cut tax rates in the
worst period of a recession. President Harding also cut tax rates at
the bottom of an economic cycle. In all three cases, prosperity like we
have rarely seen ensued.

And even on the state level, we have seen many examples of states
that cut taxes during tough times and grew their economies. The best
examples of the past 35 years may be Michigan and California. Michigan
was in a mini-depression in the early 1990s, and even in the midst of
this economic crisis then-Governor John Engler cut tax rates more than
at any time in the history of Michigan. The economy of this Rust Belt
state boomed as a result for most of the 1990s and even at one point
had an unemployment rate below the national average (hard to believe
today).

After John Engler left office, his successor, Jennifer Granholm, raised
taxes, and the long and deep slide that Michigan is experiencing now
began anew.

California passed its famous Proposition 13 in June 1978 in the
midst of a deep downturn. Proposition 13, which in static terms reduced
property taxes in California by some 60 percent with no offsets, led to a
12-year boom in California never to be achieved again.

The same was true in New Jersey. The New Jersey economy was
in collapse in the early 1990s after James Florio raised taxes. Governor
Christine Todd Whitman cut tax rates by more than 20 percent, and
New Jersey went through a mini-boom and had a budget surplus. And
then along came Jon Corzine. Beelzebub smiled.

And as far as raising tax rates? On the national level, it was only
Hoover and Roosevelt who raised tax rates in a Depression, and you

can see how that worked out. President Obama is trying his level best to follow in Hoover's and Roosevelt's footsteps. When President Clinton raised income tax rates, we were well into a boom.

To Hepner and others, passage of Proposition 13 in California in 1978 would have to have been the direct consequence of a vision of the 1980s future prosperity by the state's clairvoyant voters and then followed on by optimistic Governor Jerry Brown. Today, California is led by a pessimistic Governor Jerry Brown, and the state's cyclopean politicians foresee their own state's demise and thus raise taxes. The next thing they'll tell us is that having a baby causes sex nine months earlier.

But the real simultaneous equation bias our critics never mention exists at the very core of their faulty logic of looking at the growth in median income or in income per capita. Both income and population depend on taxes. But by combining both income and population in a ratio of income per capita, the true correlations are made to disappear—spuriously.

Endogeneity arises when an independent variable is related to the error term from a regression analysis, which is problematic as it introduces bias to the coefficient estimate. Simultaneity is a specific type of endogeneity that occurs when "one or more of the explanatory variables is *jointly determined* with the dependent variable, typically through an equilibrium mechanism."[21] To illustrate, consider the supply and demand for a product, where the price represented in the supply equation is set by the demand for the product given the cost of production. In contrast, the price represented in the demand equation results from the consumers' response to the price of the product. In equilibrium, these two equations are necessarily equated to one another, resulting in an equilibrium price and equilibrium quantity. However, as Alfred Marshall pointed out, the intersection of supply and demand is like scissors—one cannot tell which equation determines price, much like one cannot tell which scissor blade cuts a sheet of paper.[22] Therefore, when collecting price and quantity data, what is observed are the equilibrium values, which makes the choice of the dependent variables arbitrary. This in turn renders efforts to describe the determination of equilibrium price and quantity as flawed. For example, consider the market for labor, where average wages affect the hours of work, but the hours of work are affected by average wages—in other words, average wages are determined simultaneously by supply and demand forces. The data on average wages reflect the equilibrium values, assuming that the labor market clears, of course, leading one to be unable to tell whether the observations are from the supply side or the demand side.

If gross domestic product (GDP) per capita is used as a proxy for average wages, then changes in the overall value of the GDP per capita variable can be attributed to either changes in GDP (i.e., income) or changes in population. Assume GDP per capita rises—that could be attributed to an increase in overall GDP (i.e., income) with either no change or a smaller change in population, or be because population has declined as a result of individuals moving (and income has not yet relocated). Therefore, when estimating whether employment growth influences GDP per capita growth, issues of simultaneity pose a problem since it is not clear if employment is determining population changes, or if population is determining employment changes.[23] Or, in other words, the question becomes whether jobs follow people or people follow jobs.[24] Given this interdependency, employment growth and income growth are then also plagued by simultaneity.[25] In order to reduce this bias, we consider population growth, GDP growth, and employment growth, rather than using per capita measures.

There Are High-Tax States That Outperform Low-Tax States; Therefore the Supply-Side Theory Is Wrong

There is every reason in economics to consider tax and tax rate differences among states as valid considerations when studying economic performance differences among states. Economics is, after all is said and done, the study of incentives, and taxes surely are an incentive.

People don't work or save to pay taxes. They work and save to have an after-tax income and an after-tax return on their savings. On a conceptual level at least, it makes all the sense in the world that people take into account state differences in taxes on income and savings when they choose the state where they live and work and pay taxes.

Likewise, businesses don't locate their production facilities in order to pay taxes. They locate their production facilities to make an after-tax return for their shareholders. Again, there is every reason on Earth to suspect that state differences in taxes will affect business location decisions.

To take the smoking/cancer analogy to taxes/economic growth a step further, in cancer studies, researchers were able to relate smoking to lung cancer in study after study. The correlations were strong and consistent. Populations of people who smoked for longer periods of time had a greater likelihood of developing lung cancer than did people who smoked for shorter periods of time. For those who once smoked and who now don't smoke, the probability of developing lung cancer depends on how long it has been since the ex-smoker last smoked. The number of cigarettes smoked affects the probability of contracting lung cancer.

Symmetrically, the longer a tax has been in place, the more damage it is likely to do. The larger that tax is, the greater the expected damage as well. And finally, the more difficult it is to avoid that tax, the greater will be the prospective damage.

It's important to remember that not every long-term heavy smoker of unfiltered cigarettes contracts cancer. Far from it. While in mathematics a counterexample is sufficient to disprove a theorem, a counterexample when it comes to probabilities and likelihood functions is to be expected. The relationship between smoking and cancer is one of likelihood, not one of certainty. The same type of likelihood relationship exists between tax rates and economic growth.

Not every tax cut increases economic growth, but cutting tax rates should raise the likelihood of higher economic growth. Showing an example where higher tax rates are associated with higher growth doesn't discredit the theory that tax rate increases reduce the likelihood of higher growth. But consistent repeated cases of an association between higher tax rates and higher growth would be sufficient to discredit the theory.

In some cases associations can be very intense where, say, taxes and economic growth move very closely together with few anomalies and in other cases the associations can be loose with a lot of unexplained variations in the correlation of the two series. These differences in closeness of the correlation are measured by what is called an equation's R^2 or percent of variation explained.

The specificity of the correlations is also important. For example, in lung cancer studies, researchers found results that make intuitive sense. The crude logic as to why lung cancer is caused by smoking is that tars from the smoke embed themselves in the smoker's lungs. Smoking tends to affect those areas most where the smoke actually comes into contact with the body most. Thus one tends to find the incidence of lung cancer, throat cancer, mouth cancer, and lip cancer greater in smokers than in nonsmokers. All the areas where the smoke touches the body are the same areas where the cancer is presumed to occur and also where it does occur. The analogy with taxation and growth is amazing. Specific taxes have specific effects as well as general effects. State estate taxes affect the migration patterns of wealthy people. County sales taxes in California affect where Californians buy goods. Internet exemptions from sales taxes also affect Internet sales relative to brick-and-mortar sales. Corporate profit taxes in Detroit drove corporations to move their headquarters. And so the story goes.

Even with state tax rates being the enormously powerful drivers of growth that they are, it only stands to reason that other factors also matter and that some of the highest income tax states will, from time to time by chance or due to other factors—such as an energy or an agricultural boom or bust, or increases in military spending, which benefit states like California and Virginia—outperform some of the zero income tax states, just as some lifetime smokers will outlive some nonsmokers. But if you were a betting person, you would quickly figure out that nonsmokers, on average, are a helluva lot healthier than are smokers, and zero income tax states are far more likely to achieve prosperity than are high-tax states. It's as simple as that.

Given the statistical and theoretical tour de force of our results, a dedicated state official would never shackle the state citizenry with high income tax rates, just as a responsible parent would never encourage a child to smoke.

The fact that cannot be refuted is that the no income tax states, on average, have had higher and, in some cases, substantially higher growth rates in population, employment, tax revenues, and gross state product (GSP) over the past 10 years and over the past half century than the highest income tax states. It's indisputable.

The Oklahoma Argument against Tax Cuts

> [W]e see that the Oklahoma economy is already doing pretty well. In fact, we are doing better than most of the states that don't have a personal income tax. . . . Since 2000, Oklahoma's per capita personal income has grown at the seventh fastest pace in the nation, faster than seven of the nine states that lack a personal income tax. . . . So, I am concerned that eliminating the income tax won't generate the payoffs that the proponents are claiming that it will generate.[26]

In his analysis of Oklahoma's recent prosperity, Professor Mickey Hepner and his academic colleagues in Oklahoma don't give any credit to Oklahoma's major income tax rate cuts from 2005 to 2009 or the adoption of right-to-work legislation by Oklahoma in 2001.[27] And yet they all, to a person, use Oklahoma's recent period of economic prosperity as a reason not to cut tax rates rather than as proof of what tax rate cuts can do. And we bet that each one of our current detractors supported the tax cuts and the right-to-work legislation at the time. Surprised? We're not. You should reread the first section of this chapter. Our critics to a person are union members in a closed shop being paid from tax dollars working in a tax-exempt organization. That's what professors are.

For the whole period 1997 through 2004, prior to Oklahoma's income tax rate cut, Oklahoma's gross state product grew 43 percent versus U.S. growth of 43 percent. After Oklahoma's income tax rate cut, from 2004 to 2012, Oklahoma's GSP grew by 43 percent versus U.S. growth of 32 percent. Coincidental? We don't think so. Tax cuts help.

But now let's take Hepner's chosen mortal combatant for Oklahoma—Texas. Hepner states:

> And I can tell you with great glee and with great joy, that by all three of
> those metrics, per capita growth in the state economy, per capita personal
> income growth, median household growth, we are thumping Texas and
> it's not even close.[28]

The real record from 1997 through 2012 is presented in Figure 8.1.
As shown in Figure 8.1, Texas outperformed Oklahoma in the
1997–2004 period by 50 percent to 43 percent. Over the period 2004
through 2008—after Oklahoma's tax cut—Oklahoma outperformed
Texas 36 percent to 34 percent. Then in the 2008–2012 period, Texas
once again outperformed Oklahoma by 16 percent to 5 percent. From
this evidence, Oklahoma badly needs another tax cut.

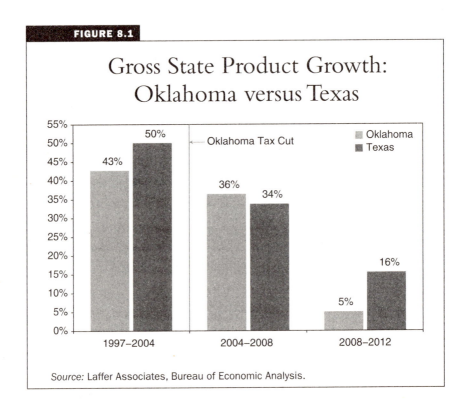

FIGURE 8.1

Gross State Product Growth: Oklahoma versus Texas

Source: Laffer Associates, Bureau of Economic Analysis.

Using IRS data from U.S. income tax returns for the six years 2005 through 2010, 2,217 more tax filers moved from Oklahoma to Texas than from Texas to Oklahoma, and the average adjusted gross income of the filers who moved from Oklahoma to Texas was $3,455 higher than the average adjusted gross income of filers who moved from Texas to Oklahoma (see Table 8.1).

So we're not really sure what Professor Hepner means when he says that "we are thumping Texas and it's not even close."[29] He goes on to say even more:

> In short, we don't have to be more like Texas to beat them, we are already doing that. In fact we are doing it so badly I often wonder why they are not trying to be more like us, because the lessons are showing that we are outperforming them.[30]

Upon reflection we would ask Mickey Hepner, if income tax rates shouldn't be cut or eliminated, just how high should they go? Why not replace all other taxes with higher income taxes? Then perhaps he could have his dream of one remaining tax-dodging rich Sooner where the streets and schools are empty.

TABLE 8.1
IRS State-to-State Migration Data: Oklahoma versus Texas*

	Sum, 2005–2010		2005–2010
	Aggregate Adjusted Gross Income ($000,000s)	# of Returns Filed	Average Adjusted Gross Income per Filer
Filers in Texas Who Previously Filed in Oklahoma	$2,695.29	58,302	$46,229.79
Filers in Oklahoma Who Previously Filed in Texas	$2,399.02	56,085	$42,774.66
Net Difference	**$ 296.27**	**2,217**	**$ 3,455.12**

* One year's worth of IRS migration data is created by matching individual tax returns from one year with the next year. For example, the first year in the sums, 2005, comes from filers' 2004 returns matched with those same filers' 2005 returns.

Source: Internal Revenue Service, Laffer Associates.

Other than being steadfastly opposed to any reduction in either state spending or income taxes, what do Mickey Hepner and the others have to offer?

Income Distribution Becomes More Even with Progressive High-Rate Tax Codes

Our critics frequently point out that the progressive state income tax takes from those who can most afford to pay taxes, and that any cut in the income tax would "shift the tax burden away from the highest earning people . . . to more on the backs of the lower-income and middle-class families."[31] This argument used by Professor Hepner and all opponents of income tax cuts is called the Robin Hood effect.

But as we have tried to explain, progressive income taxes don't redistribute income; they redistribute people. Progressive income taxes are also directed at employers, who are the very people who hire lower- and middle-income people. By targeting employers, progressive taxes also hurt employees. You can't love jobs and hate job creators.

But most importantly, the income tax literally protects the wealthiest among us and prohibits the poorest members of our society from ever becoming wealthy. Wealthy people don't pay the type of taxes on their wealth that would redistribute income. Warren Buffett, for example, may be worth nearly $60 billion,[32] which is mostly in the form of unrealized capital gains that have never been and never will be taxed.[33] At least three of Buffett's children and Bill and Melinda Gates own separate charitable foundations, to which Warren Buffett contributes tax free. Using the Congressional Budget Office's (CBO's) definition of income, in 2010 Buffett had comprehensive income of close to $12 billion yet reported paying taxes of a little less than $7 million on reported adjusted gross income of a smidgeon under $40 million. His effective tax rate was about $6/_{100}$ths of 1 percent ($7 million ÷ $12 billion = 0.0006) versus the 17.4 percent he claims to have paid ($7 million ÷ $40 million).[34]

The ITEPs, Mickey Hepners, and El-Hodiris of this world don't ever suggest taxing the Warren Buffetts at a low-rate flat tax on a comprehensive definition of income, including increases in unrealized capital gains and charitable contributions to his children's and his rich friends' foundations, but instead argue for higher tax rates on the income Warren Buffett doesn't report. The hypocrisy knows no bounds.

And then there are the special tax shelters and avoidance schemes that are accessible only by the wealthiest members of society—the very people targeted by gift and estate taxes. Elaborate tax-avoidance schemes like charitable lead annuity trusts (also known as Jackie O. trusts), family limited partnerships, grantor retained annuity trusts, and dozens more schemes all allow the ultrawealthy to avoid all sorts of taxes that are unavoidable for a typical family. Just as an example, the Walton Family Foundation, of Walmart fame, is funded by 21 different Walton family trusts that will over a period of time facilitate the transfer of billions of dollars in a totally tax-free manner.[35] It just goes on and on.

Again, our detractors would seem to prefer high tax rates that no one pays over low tax rates for one and all that yield sufficient revenues to provide needed public services.

Much more visible examples of loophole exploitation—and in this case, ones that are in constant use by lawmakers everywhere—are the enormous tax-incentive packages awarded to corporations by states trying to keep businesses from leaving. We gave a great example of these types of tax breaks earlier in this chapter. That example was of the tax breaks Volkswagen received from the state of Tennessee. Let's also take Illinois as an example, where sky-high tax rates and overregulation not only have repelled potential in-migrants, but also have caused an exodus of jobs, companies, and people out of the state. In 2011, Illinois Governor Pat Quinn signed legislation giving tax credits to keep Sears and CME Group—both threatening to leave unless awarded special tax breaks—in Illinois. According to the *Chicago Tribune*, combined tax credits for the two companies will amount to $371 million a year of lost revenue to the state of Illinois.[36] High tax rates sure are great if you don't have to pay them!

And when it comes to the poor, the minorities, and the disadvantaged, incentives matter as much as they do for anyone else. Taxing rich people and giving the money to poor people will increase the number of poor people and reduce the number of rich people. The dream in America has never been to make the rich poorer. It has always been to make the poor richer. To help the poor, the only sustainable answer is economic growth. The best form of welfare is a good, high-paying job, and the best tax for creating jobs is a low-rate flat tax. And progressive income taxes, forced unions, death taxes, and other anti-growth policies stop growth and create the very poverty they profess to cure.

But just in case you still aren't on board, just look at the increase in per capita personal income and gross state product per capita over the past 10 years for the nine highest and lowest income tax states, the nine highest and lowest tax burden states, and the 11 highest and lowest corporate income tax rate states, shown in Table 8.2. It would seem that those who wish to redistribute income have succeeded, only they have redistributed income from the poor to the rich! The so-called Robin Hood effect, in truth, turns out to be the "reverse Robin Hood effect."

TABLE 8.2

State per Capita Metrics Grouped by Policy

Grouped by Personal Income Tax Rates	2013 Top Marginal Personal Income Tax Rate	% Change, 2002–2012 PI per Capita	GSP per Capita
9 Zero PIT States	0.0%	41.6%	41.4%
50-State Average	5.7%	40.7%	38.8%
9 Highest PIT States	10.2%	39.6%	37.6%

Grouped by Corporate Income Tax Rates	2013 Top Marginal Corporate Income Tax Rate	% Change, 2002–2012 PI per Capita	GSP per Capita
11 Lowest CIT States	3.4%	48.0%	48.5%
50-State Average	7.2%	40.7%	38.8%
11 Highest CIT States	11.1%	39.2%	39.7%

Grouped by Tax Burden	2010 Tax Burden as a Share of Personal Income	% Change, 2002–2012 PI per Capita	GSP per Capita
9 Lowest Tax Burden States	7.8%	44.3%	46.2%
50-State Average	9.5%	40.7%	38.8%
9 Highest Tax Burden States	11.3%	39.0%	33.9%

Source: Bureau of Economic Analysis, Laffer Associates.

The Probity of the ALEC-Laffer Measures Is Nonexistent; Therefore Their Policy Prescriptions Are Wrong

In this section we simply reproduce a part of the excellent report by Eric Fruits, PhD, and Randall Pozdena, PhD, entitled "Tax Myths Debunked."[37]

A recent example is the critique of the ALEC-Laffer state policy rankings in *Rich States, Poor States* by Peter Fisher of the Iowa Policy Project. It has the provocative title, "The Doctor Is Out to Lunch"[38] (this is a direct reference to Dr. Laffer). It has been widely disseminated by a network of progressive organizations and friends in the liberal press.

Fisher's findings that the ALEC-Laffer state rankings bear no relationship to state economic health is contrary to the data. But, once again, it is the oversimplification of the analysis that leads him to the wrong conclusion. He fails to recognize that the *Rich States, Poor States* analysis consists of rankings, not predictions of growth rates. Hence, the obvious appropriate comparison is between ALEC-Laffer policy rankings and rankings of state economic performance. Fisher could have done this very simply by using well-known, consistent measures of comparative state performance.

We present the analysis Fisher easily could have done in the following discussion.

The Federal Reserve Bank of Philadelphia has prepared comparable indexes of state economic health (for all months since 1979).[39] Because the indexes are single measures (comprised of multiple factors[40]), they are easily ranked.

Those rankings can then be compared with ALEC-Laffer rankings of the pro-market policy postures by the 50 states.

Figure 8.2 and Table 8.3 present the results. They demonstrate clearly that, contrary to Fisher and his progressive colleagues, there is a positive relationship between the ALEC-Laffer rankings and state economic health rankings. Figure 8.2 shows the association graphically between the policy rankings presented in the 2008 *Rich States, Poor States* publication and the actual performance of the 50 states in 2008, 2009, 2010, 2011, and 2012 (as of June).[41] The positive association is obvious from the graphic.

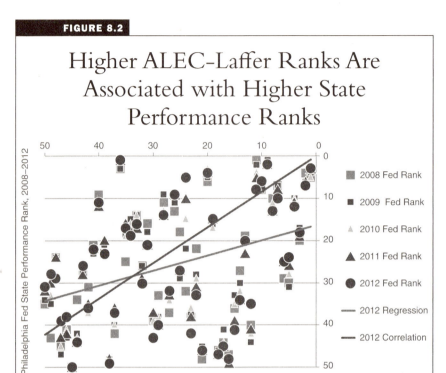

FIGURE 8.2

Higher ALEC-Laffer Ranks Are Associated with Higher State Performance Ranks

Source: E. Fruits and R. Pozdena, "Tax Myths Debunked," American Legislative Exchange Council, February 2013, www.alec.org/docs/Tax_Myths.pdf.

TABLE 8.3

The Correlation of ALEC-Laffer State Policy Ranks and State Economic Performance

| | ALEC-Laffer State Policy Rank Year | | | | |
	2008	2009	2010	2011	2012
Spearman Rank Order Correlation: ALEC-Laffer Ranks vs. FRB-State Performance Ranks					
Contemporaneous	38.9%	40.7%	28.7%	26.4%	27.1%
1 Year Ahead	39.6%	38.6%	27.5%	27.4%	
2 Years Ahead	37.2%	37.0%	27.0%		
3 Years Ahead	35.8%	36.7%			
4 Years Ahead	35.7%				

Source: E. Fruits and R. Pozdena, "Tax Myths Debunked," American Legislative Exchange Council, February 2013, www.alec.org/docs/Tax_Myths.pdf.

Table 8.3 performs a more statistically sophisticated test, measuring a special type of correlation when one is studying ranks (the so-called Spearman rank correlation). This properly measures the correlation between the ALEC-Laffer state policy rankings and the Philadelphia Federal Reserve's state performance rankings.[42] In this case, the correlation is presented for years contemporaneous with the *Rich States, Poor States* publication as well as one, two, three, and four years afterward (to the extent the future years have occurred).

The findings are completely contrary to Fisher:

- There is a distinctly positive relationship between the *Rich States, Poor States* economic outlook rankings and current and subsequent state economic health.

- The formal correlation is not perfect (i.e., it is not equal to 100 percent) because there are other factors that affect a state's economic prospects. All economists would concede this obvious point.

However, the ALEC-Laffer rankings alone have a 25 to 40 percent correlation with state performance rankings. This is a very high percentage for a single variable considering the multiplicity of idiosyncratic factors that affect growth in each state—resource endowments, access to transportation, ports and other marketplaces, and so on.

We encourage all policy makers to read the professional literature on the effects of public policy factors, such as tax rates and right-to-work policy, and not fall prey to flawed demonstrations. Earlier in this paper, we further debunked the notion that factors like tax rates don't matter. We never though otherwise.

Federal Tax Rates Are More Important Than State Tax Rates, and Therefore State Tax Rates Don't Matter

Our critics also say that federal tax rates, because they are so much higher than state tax rates, matter far more than state tax rates. And, for some purposes, this may well be true. You would have to hunt far and wide to find someone more opposed to higher tax rates than we are.

But just because federal tax rates matter more than state tax rates for the whole U.S. economy, this doesn't mean state tax rates don't matter. In fact, conceding that federal tax rates matter guarantees that state tax rates also matter. Taxes are taxes, after all.

Based on economics, an important reason why the income tax should be eliminated rather than eliminating other taxes is that the income tax directly impacts the marginal or incremental incentive to work and innovate. No other major state tax has anything like the marginal impact an income tax has. On a dollar-for-dollar basis, the income tax is far and away the most deleterious tax to output, employment, and production of the major taxes.

While federal tax codes are generally quite similar in all 50 states, state and local tax codes can be substantially different from state to state.[43] Therefore, if someone is going to move from one state to another for tax reasons, it seems clear that state and local taxes should be the deciding factor. It is one heckuva lot easier for a business or family to move from one state to another than from one country to another.[44]

The Wealthy Used Public Resources, and They—Not Others—Should Pay for Those Public Resources; We Need More Progressive Taxes, Not Less

During our debate, Professor Hepner made one of the most curious arguments we had ever heard. It wasn't more than two months after Professor Hepner made his argument that President Obama took his words almost verbatim for his own. Here's what Professor Hepner said:

> [T]he wealthy don't become wealthy on their own. They became wealthy as part of a system, as a part of a country that supported and educates its populace, that provides roads, that allows commerce to take place, that supports the infrastructure of the city, the state and this nation.[45]

And then Professor Hepner goes on to say that the wealthy owe their success to government and should therefore pay higher tax rates than those who aren't wealthy.

The first logical fallacy with Hepner's inference from an obviously correct observation is that government didn't provide the "system" of resources; the taxpayers and the private sector did. Henry Ford invented the automobile before there were public roads for cars.

The second fallacy is that everyone had an equal chance to use all of the resources our society provided. Those resources that were provided by our society were provided for everyone—those people who used them well *and* those people who didn't use them well. As a result, there is no reason why those who used our publicly available resources well should be required to pay proportionally more than those people who didn't use our publicly available resources as well.

And this then leads to the third fallacy of making those who use our publicly available resources well pay disproportionately more. Taxing the people who benefited the most from using our publicly available resources at higher tax rates will only assure less aggregate wealth and progress for future generations (i.e., less publicly available resources in the future). Incentives matter.

When Is Enough Evidence Enough? If the Facts Were Reversed, We Would Concede

We ask ourselves, is there any amount of disconfirming data that would ever cause our critics to change their minds? We're reminded of the quote from the late logician Bertrand Russell:

> Persecution is used in theology, not in arithmetic, because in arithmetic there is knowledge, but in theology there is only opinion. So whenever you find yourself getting angry about a difference of opinion, be on your guard; you will probably find, on examination, that your belief is getting beyond what the evidence warrants.[46]

If each of the 11 states that adopted progressive income taxes increased its growth rate relative to the rest of the nation, we would be left-wing converts applying to ITEP or the University of Central Oklahoma's College of Business for jobs.

We really wonder just what type of evidence it would take to convince our critics of their wayward ways and then to join forces with us. For us, if the nine zero income tax states consistently underperformed the nine highest income tax states, the very foundation of our beliefs would be shaken.

If taxpayers were migrating on balance from low-tax states to high-tax states and their adjusted gross incomes were higher than the incomes of those who moved from high-tax states to low-tax states, we would be waving a white flag.

If our econometric findings revealed higher tax rates were significantly correlated with faster population growth and greater prosperity, we would raise both hands and shout, "We surrender!"

If California growth rates were accelerating as Governor Jerry Brown enacts each tax increase while Texas's prosperity was collapsing around Governor Rick Perry's low-tax, low-regulation, free-enterprise policies, we would be begging for mercy from our detractors while lying prostrate on the ground.

With all of our evidence and documentation, our critics should no longer believe the views they previously held on the effect of state taxes on growth. One reason our critics want the federal government to give tens of billions of dollars to states for hiring teachers and firefighters and for building roads, rather than states raising and spending the money themselves, is that they know that states are precluded economically on competitiveness grounds from raising their own taxes significantly. Some of our critics derisively call this the "race to the bottom." But why would there be a tax-cutting race to the bottom if taxes don't affect behavior and migration?

There is nothing that deceives our critics more easily than their confidence in their own judgment divorced from reasoning. The potential for self-deception is always great; that is why we have "piled on" with every possible way to check, double-check, test, and double-test our hypotheses. We wish our critics would join with us in testing their beliefs.

In fact, even Christina Romer, former Chair of President Obama's Council of Economic Advisers, acknowledged in her academic work as recently as 2010 that tax rates have profound impacts on economic growth outcomes, writing, "In short, tax increases appear to have a very large, sustained, and highly significant negative impact on output"; at another point, "The persistence of the effects is suggestive of supply effects"; and later, that "tax cuts have very large and persistent positive output effects"; and again, "In all cases, the effect of tax changes on output remains large and highly statistically significant."[47] Why can't our critics understand these findings?

Or consider another example: Our critics have been arguing for a long time—and so have retailers—that Internet sales should be taxed. They argue that people will buy products on the Internet if doing so will enable them to avoid sales taxes. Wait, if taxes don't affect behavior, why should it matter whether remote sales are or are not sales tax exempt? And states have tried to persuade the federal government to require all states to tax Internet purchases so that the states that do impose those taxes are not losing firms and sales to states that do not.

Why do high-tax states like New York, California, Illinois, New Jersey, and others spend so much tax-enforcement money trying to find out whether high-income residents spend 183 days in Florida or Tennessee to avoid income taxes? If income taxes don't matter, why would people try to pretend they live in zero income tax states? We all know people who will not set foot in California or New York for more than 182 days of the year to avoid the tax levy. Northerners even have a name for those people who spend just enough time in Florida in order not to pay income taxes. They're called "snowbirds."

Not only do the state data confirm our view of the world of the 50 states, but the relationships between country growth rates and country economic policies also confirm our worldwide view. Time series of countries and time series of states show the same results. And then there are the studies of specific states and specific taxes, again confirming our view. What more do we have to do to demonstrate the most basic tenet of economics? You can't tax a state into prosperity, nor can a poor person spend himself or herself into wealth. If you tax rich people and give the money to poor people, sooner or later you'll have lots and lots of poor people and no rich people. This really isn't that hard to understand.

We are willing to change our hypotheses if quantitative observations of the real world—especially human behavior related to policy actions—did not accommodate. Why aren't our critics willing to change if they are shown to be wrong?

Perhaps we first need to put universities and public policy groups on the tax rolls like everyone else by getting rid of the 501(c)(3) exemptions. And then we should no longer subsidize professors by showering them with tax dollars and instead require them to earn the money they are paid like all the rest of us. If they don't play the game, they shouldn't be allowed to make the rules.

Notes

Prologue

1. Colin D. Campbell and Rosemary G. Campbell, "A Comparative Study of the Fiscal Systems of New Hampshire and Vermont, 1940–1974," Wheelabrator Foundation, 1976.

2. Philip Ball, *Curiosity: How Science Became Interested in Everything* (Chicago: University of Chicago Press, 2012).

3. Thomas R. Dye, "The Economic Impact of the Adoption of a State Income Tax in New Hampshire," National Taxpayers Union Foundation, October 1999, http://heartland.org/sites/all/modules/custom/heartland_migration/files/pdfs/6926.pdf.

4. Thanks to Professor James Blumstein, University Professor of Constitutional Law and Health Law at Vanderbilt University, for his review and suggestions concerning the Commerce Clause and Privileges and Immunities Clause of the Constitution.

5. Arthur B. Laffer, Stephen Moore, and Jonathan Williams, "Tax Reform to Fix California's Economy," in *Rich States, Poor States*, 6th ed. (Arlington, VA: American Legislative Exchange Council, 2013), www.alec.org/publications/rich-states-poor-states.

6. For more on the nuances and problems with using per capita metrics, see Chapter 8.

7. Eric Fruits and Randall Pozdena, "Tax Myths Debunked," American Legislative Exchange Council, February 2013, www.alec.org/docs/Tax_Myths.pdf.

Chapter 1 The Fall from Grace

1. Data on state and local tax revenue are as of 2011 due to data re-lease lag.

2. Professor Mickey Hepner is dean of the College of Business at the University of Central Oklahoma in Edmond, Oklahoma. This quote was taken from Dean Hepner's comments at the State Chamber of Oklahoma's "Tax Policy Forum," held on May 9, 2012. The forum was set up as a debate between Dean Hepner and Dr. Arthur Laffer. The debate is available for viewing at the following web address: http://youtu.be/uMnKdMHxYTU.

3. See note 2.

4. The numbers presented in Table 1.1 are rounded figures. To be as precise as possible in the text, we have calculated percentage change figures from the unrounded figures.

5. These words were taken from New York City Mayor Michael Bloomberg's August 6, 2013 address to a group of citizens in New York. A full transcript is available here: www.nyc.gov/portal/site/nycgov/menuitem.c0935b9a57bb4ef3daf2f1c701c789a0/index.jsp?pageID=mayor_press_release&catID=1194&doc_name=http%3A%2F%2Fwww.nyc.gov%2Fhtml%2Fom%2Fhtml%2F2013b%2Fpr269-13.html&cc=unused1978&rc=1194&ndi=1.

Chapter 2 Economic Metrics

1. For a more extensive analysis of major policy variables and their associated performance outcomes, see Arthur B. Laffer and Wayne Winegarden, "Eureka!," Pacific Research Institute, 2012.

2. These combinations in fact are the products of 1 plus the percentage change in each column minus 1. Think of them as the sums of each column and you won't be too far off.

3. See note 2.

4. See note 2.

5. See note 2.

6. See note 2.

7. See note 2.

8. Sarah Arnett, "State Fiscal Condition: Ranking the 50 States," Mercatus Center, George Mason University, Working Paper, January 2014, http://mercatus.org/publication/state-fiscal-condition-ranking-50-states.

9. Arthur B. Laffer, Stephen Moore, and Jonathan Williams, *Rich States, Poor States*, 6th ed. (Arlington, VA: American Legislative Exchange Council), www.alec.org/publications/rich-states-poor-states.

10. Emily Gross, "U.S. Population Migration Data: Strengths and Limitations," Statistics of Income Division, Internal Revenue Service, www.irs.gov/file_source/pub/irs-soi/99gross_update.doc.

11. Ibid.

Chapter 3 The Nine Members of the Fellowship of the Ring to Balance Out the Nine Nazgûl

1. The Nazgûl, also known as the Ringwraiths, are nine evil ghosts who fight the nine members of the fellowship of the ring in J. R. R. Tolkien's *The Lord of the Rings*.

2. By 10-year growth rates, we mean, for instance, 2002–2012. While 2002–2012 is 11 years of data, it is 10 years of growth between those years of data.

3. We have decided to use equal-weighted averages for these purposes. Weighting the averages by another measure (perhaps by GSP or by population) creates its own set of problems. For example, imagine looking at population-weighted average performance metrics for the zero income tax group of states if Texas and Wyoming were the only zero income tax states. No matter what happens in Wyoming, its tiny weight will prevent any real impact on the average.

4. The nine states with no personal earned income tax are Alaska, Florida, Nevada, New Hampshire, South Dakota, Tennessee, Texas, Washington, and Wyoming. Tennessee and New Hampshire tax dividend and interest income only. Greater detail is available on request.

5. We use "real" data in Figure 3.3 because the high rates of inflation in the late 1970s to early 1980s led to rapid growth in nominal personal income. When the nominal growth rates are plotted, it is very difficult to see the differences between the categories because the levels are so high. By deflating the nominal values to "real" series, the differences between state categories are plain to see. All personal income values were deflated using the same GDP implicit price deflator series.

6. In Table 3.4, tax burden as a share of personal income is calculated by the Tax Foundation. It is based on data from the Census Bureau's State and Local Government Finances data set, but makes several modifications in order to take into account certain factors, such as taxes paid to other states, that are not accounted for in unadjusted Census figures. For more information, visit: http://taxfoundation .org/tax-topics/tax-burdens.

Chapter 4 Piling On

1. Henry George, *Progress and Poverty* (New York: Appleton, 1879), Chapter 17, www.henrygeorge.org/madsen.

2. Ibid.

3. More information about right-to-work laws can be found at the following web address: www.nrtw.org/b/rtw_faq.htm.

4. For those readers who aren't familiar with these two characters, Bo Schembechler was the coach of the University of Michigan's football team, and Woody Hayes was the coach of Ohio State's football team. Their rivalry, known as the Ten Year War, lasted from 1969 to 1978 and remains one of the most famous and bitter rivalries in college football history.

Chapter 5 Give unto Caesar

1. Keith Richards, quoted in a *Fortune* magazine article: Andy Serwer, "Inside the Rolling Stones Inc.," *Fortune*, September 30, 2002, http://money.cnn.com/magazines/fortune/fortune_archive /2002/09/30/329302/.

2. Travis H. Brown, *How Money Walks* (St. Louis, MO: Author, 2013), www.howmoneywalks.com.

3. Read the full text of Governor Corbett's address here: http://articles.philly.com/2011-03-08/news/28668900_1_budget-address-first-budget-tree.

4. Miranda Lambert, "All Kinds of Kinds," *Four the Record*, 2013.

5. As printed in Robert L. Pollock's interview with Secretary Shultz in: Robert L. Pollock, "George Shultz: Memo to Romney—Expand the Pie," *The Wall Street Journal*, July 13, 2012, http://online.wsj.com/news/articles/SB10001424052702303740704577523541037952090.

6. Tax Foundation, http://taxfoundation.org/article/state-and-local-tax-burdens-all-states-one-year-1977-2010.

7. See the Prologue for a more detailed description of Professor Campbell's contributions to state economics.

8. Atlas Van Lines, www.atlasvanlines.com/migration-patterns/pdf/2012_Migration_Patterns.pdf.

9. U.S. Census Bureau, www.census.gov/popest/data/intercensal/state/state2010.html.

10. Tax Foundation, http://taxfoundation.org/article/state-and-local-tax-burdens-all-states-one-year-1977-2010.

11. Ibid.

Chapter 6 Why Growth Rates Differ: An Econometric Analysis of the Data

1. A. Reynolds, "Some International Comparisons of Supply-Side Policy," *Cato Journal* 5, no. 2 (Fall 1985).

2. However, the Cauchy shape also relies heavily on another parameter, beta, to be close to zero.

3. That is, since GSP is the proportional change in population between 2002 and 2012, TBUR should be measured as, for instance, some sort of average of the decadal tax burden.

4. Tax burden as a share of personal income is calculated by the Tax Foundation. It is based on data from the Census Bureau's

State and Local Government Finances data set, but makes several modifications in order to take into account certain factors, such as taxes paid to other states, that are not accounted for in unadjusted Census figures. For more information, visit: http://taxfoundation .org/tax-topics/tax-burdens.

5. Or, more formally, $\dfrac{1}{2^{10}}$.

6. Note that in Table 6.2 and for the following tables in this chapter, SE$\star$ denotes that the standard errors have been corrected for heteroscedasticity and serial autocorrelation (HAC).

7. J. Peach and C. Meghan Starbuck, "Oil and Gas Production and Economic Growth in New Mexico," *Journal of Economic Issues* 45, no. 2 (June 2011).

8. M. E. Bildirici and Fazil Kayikci, "Effects of Oil Production on Economic Growth in Eurasian Countries: Panel ARDL Approach," *Energy* 49 (2013): 156–161.

9. Eric Engen and Jonathan Skinner, "Taxation and Economic Growth," *National Tax Journal* 49, no. 4 (December 1996): 617–642.

10. Y. Lee and R. H. Gordon, "Tax Structure and Economic Growth," *Journal of Public Economics* 89, no. 5–6 (2005): 1027–1043.

11. Ibid.

12. R. J. Newman, "Migration and Growth in the South," *Review of Economics and Statistics* 65, no. 1 (February 1983): 76–86.

13. Å. Johansson, C. Heady, J. Arnold, B. Brys, and L. Vartia, "Tax and Economic Growth." Working Paper 620, OECD Economics Department, 2008.

14. B. Benson and Ronald Johnson, "The Lagged Impact of State and Local Taxes on Economic Activity and Political Behavior," *Economic Inquiry* 24, no. 3 (1986).

15. Newman, "Migration and Growth in the South."

16. T. R. Plaut and Joseph Pluta, "Business Climate, Taxes and Expenditures, and State Industrial Growth in the United States," *Southern Economic Journal* 50, no. 1 (July 1983): 99–119.

17. M. J. Boskin, "Taxation, Saving, and the Rate of Interest," *Journal of Political Economy* 86, no. 2, Part 2: Research in Taxation (April 1978): S3–S27.

18. A. Rabushka, "Taxation, Economic Growth, and Liberty," *Cato Journal* 7, no. 1 (Spring/Summer 1987).

19. E. C. Prescott, "Prosperity and Depression: 2002 Richard T. Ely Lecture," Federal Reserve Bank of Minneapolis Research Department, Working Paper 618, 2002.

20. B. Weinstein, "Tax Incentives for Growth," *Society*, March/April 1977.

21. C. D. Romer and David H. Romer, "The Macroeconomic Effects of Tax Changes: Estimates Based on a New Measure of Fiscal Shocks," *American Economic Review* 100, no. 3 (June 2010): 763–801.

22. Eric Engen and Jonathan Skinner, "Taxation and Economic Growth," *National Tax Journal* 49, no. 4 (December 1996): 617–642.

23. Thomas Romans and Ganti Subrahmanyam, "State and Local Taxes, Transfers and Regional Economic Growth," *Southern Economic Journal* 46, no. 2 (October 1979): 435–444.

24. Barry Poulson and Jules Kaplan, "State Income Taxes and Economic Growth," *Cato Journal* 28, no. 1 (Winter 2008): 53–71.

25. F. Padovano and Emma Galli, "Tax Rates and Economic Growth in the OECD Countries (1950–1990)," *Economic Inquiry* 39, no. 1 (January 2001): 44.

26. R. Cebula, "Interstate Migration and the Tiebout Hypothesis: An Analysis According to Race, Sex and Age," *Journal of the American Statistical Association* 69, no. 348 (1974): 876–879; R. J. Cebula, "Migration and the Tiebout-Tullock Hypothesis Revisited," *American Journal of Economics and Sociology* 68, no. 2 (2009): 541–551.

27. M. P. Gius, "The Effect of Income Taxes on Interstate Migration: An Analysis by Age and Race," *Annals of Regional Science*, 2009.

28. D. E. Clark and W. J. Hunter, "The Impact of Economic Opportunity, Amenities, and Fiscal Factors on Age-Specific Migration Rates," *Journal of Regional Science* 21 (1992): 349–365.

Chapter 7 Fiscal Parasitic Leakages: Texas versus California

1. As reported in the *Los Angeles Times* PolitiCal blog: Laura Nelson, "Gov. Jerry Brown: 'Texas, Come on Over,'" February 2, 2013.
2. Ben Boychuk, "A Mighty Wind," *City Journal*, February 19, 2013.
3. "FTB Notice 2012-03," State of California Franchise Tax Board, December 21, 2012.
4. Jonathan Horn, "It's Official: Gas Tax Going Up," *San Diego Union Tribune*, March 1, 2013.
5. Arthur B. Laffer and Stephen Moore, "California, Who Are You? Part II," Laffer Associates, January 18, 2008.
6. Tom Gray and Robert Scardamalia, "The Great California Exodus: A Closer Look," Manhattan Institute, Civic Report 71, September 2012.
7. Ibid., 4.
8. Ibid., 5.
9. Average income per capita is what it says it is—a state's total income divided by the state's population. Income per capita can therefore rise because exceptional economic growth even exceeds exceptional population growth, as is the case with Texas. But there is also a second way average income per capita can increase rapidly, and that occurs when the economy collapses at a slower rate than the population flees, which is the case of West Virginia. Even though both Texas and West Virginia have rapid growth in average incomes per capita, they mean very different things.

On the flip side, some economies have rapid population growth as a result of good economic conditions, but even though their economies also grow rapidly, they do not grow rapidly enough to make average income per capita rise exceptionally rapidly, which is the case of Nevada. Even though Nevada's average income per capita growth is low, Nevada is still a big winner. People are moving into Nevada in droves.

With the unemployment rate, the same ambiguous principle is at work. The labor force can grow faster than jobs or vice versa.

10. Kathleen Short, "The Research Supplemental Poverty Measure: 2011," Current Population Reports P60-244, November 2012.

11. "Fracturing in California," *The Wall Street Journal*, June 8, 2013.

12. Charles Varner and Cristobal Young, "Millionaire Migration in California: The Impact of Top Tax Rates," Working Paper, 2012.

13. "Where Have All of Maryland's Millionaires Gone? Nowhere— They're Probably Just Not Millionaires Anymore," Institute on Taxation and Economic Policy, May 29, 2009.

14. Cristobal Young and Charles Varner, "Millionaire Migration and State Taxation of Top Incomes: Evidence from a Natural Experiment," *National Tax Journal* 64 (June 2011): 255–284.

15. Remember that, while there are nine states that do not tax earned income, two (New Hampshire and Tennessee) of the nine zero earned income tax states do tax so-called unearned income, which primarily consists of interest and dividend income.

16. For more on this topic, see Arthur B. Laffer and Stephen Moore, "Boeing and the Union Berlin Wall," *The Wall Street Journal*, May 13, 2011.

17. Arthur B. Laffer and Wayne H. Winegarden, "The Economic Consequences of Tennessee's Gift and Estate Tax," Laffer Center and Beacon Center of Tennessee, March 2012.

18. Data on workers' compensation costs are from the Oregon Department of Consumer & Business Services' 2012 Workers' Compensation Index report.

19. Marc Lifsher, "Athletes Cash In on California's Workers' Comp," *Los Angeles Times*, February 23, 2013.

20. "Pro Athletes Who Shop for Workers' Comp," *Los Angeles Times*, May 6, 2013.

21. "Mega-States," National Center for Education Statistics, U.S. Department of Education.

22. NAEP results for other subject areas and grade levels were either not available for all states or only available for one or two years, which would prohibit us from creating a composite state score for more than those available years.

23. "Northridge Earthquake 10-Year Retrospective," Risk Management Solutions, 2004.

24. Christian Henrichson and Ruth Delany, "The Price of Prisons: What Incarceration Costs Taxpayers," Vera Institute of Justice, February 29, 2012.

25. Sam Stanton, David Siders, and Denny Walsh, "Legal War Ahead on California Bid to End Federal Prison Controls," *Sacramento Bee*, 2013.

26. "Big Money Talks: California's Billion Dollar Club," California Fair Political Practices Commission, March 2010.

27. "California's Prison Break," *The Wall Street Journal*, December 18, 2013.

Chapter 8 Au Contraire, Mon Frère

1. Mohamed El-Hodiri, "Kansas Is Bleeding for the Wrong Causes," *Wichita Eagle*, May 10, 2013, www.kansas.com/2013/05/10/2796605/mohamed-el-hodiri-kansas-is-bleeding.html.

2. Upton Sinclair, *I, Candidate for Governor: And How I Got Licked* (Berkeley: University of California Press, 1935), 109.

3. "States with 'High Rate' Income Taxes Are Still Outperforming No-Tax States," Institute on Taxation and Economic Policy, February 2013, www.itep.org/pdf/lafferhighrate.pdf.

4. B. Smith, "The Great Minnesota Exodus Tax Acts of 2013," *St. Paul Pioneer Press*, December 27, 2013, http://ads.twincities.com/st-paul-mn/communication/newspaper/smith-robert/2013-12-27-811679-paid-advertisement-the-great-minnesota-exodus-tax-acts-of-2013-analysis-they-merely-re-distribute-population-as-for-businesses-let-s-not-kill-the-geese-that-lay-the-golden-eggs-the-warehouse-tax-does-not-bode-well-for-the-minnesota-busine.

5. "'High Rate' Income Tax States Are Outperforming No-Tax States," Institute on Taxation and Economic Policy, February 2012, www.itepnet.org/pdf/junkeconomics.pdf.

6. Ibid.

7. Bernie Woodall, "Tennessee Legislator Believes Governor Offered VW Deal to Keep UAW Out," Reuters, September 12, 2013, www.reuters.com/article/2013/09/12/us-autos-vw-tennessee-idUSBRE98B1BW20130912.

8. "'High Rate' Income Tax States Are Outperforming No-Tax States."

9. For more on this topic, see Chapter 1.

10. Mickey Hepner is a University of Central Oklahoma faculty member and dean of the College of Business. Hepner's remarks are from the State Chamber of Oklahoma's "Tax Policy Forum" on May 9, 2012. Watch the debate here: https://www.youtube.com/watch?v=uMnKdMHxYTU&feature=youtu.be

11. "States with 'High Rate' Income Taxes Are Still Outperforming No-Tax States."

12. See note 10.

13. "'High Rate' Income Tax States Are Outperforming No-Tax States."

14. Ibid.

15. "The past decade" is 2002–2012.

16. Arthur B. Laffer and Wayne H. Winegarden, "The Economic Consequences of Tennessee's Gift and Estate Tax," Laffer Center for Supply-Side Economics and Beacon Center of Tennessee, March 2012, www.laffercenter.com/2012/03/economic-consequences-tennessees-gift-estate-tax/.

17. Here's what they wrote: "Since a larger population brings with it more demand, it's only natural that states experiencing the fastest population growth would also experience more growth in the total number of jobs and total amount of economic output."

18. In academic circles, this phenomenon of a future event causing a current event is called the fallacy of *post hoc, ergo propter hoc.*

19. "Eliminating the State Income Tax in Oklahoma: An Economic Assessment," Arduin, Laffer & Moore Econometrics and Oklahoma Council of Public Affairs, November 2011, http://heartland.org/sites/default/files/OCPA_ALME_Income_Tax_FINAL.pdf.

20. See note 10.

21. Jeffrey Wooldridge, *Introductory Econometrics*, 4th ed. (Mason, OH: South-Western Cengage Learning, 2009), 546.

22. Alfred Marshall, *Principles of Economics*, 8th ed. (London: Macmillan, 1920).

23. D. Clark and C. Murphy, "Countywide Employment and Population Growth: An Analysis of the 1980s," *Journal of Regional Science* 36 (1996): 235–256.

24. G. Gebremariam, T. Gebremedhin, and P. Schaeffer, "Analysis of County Employment and Income Growth in Appalachia: A Spatial Simultaneous-Equations Approach," *Empirical Economics* 38 (2010): 23–45.

25. Ibid.

26. See note 10.

27. Oklahoma cut personal income tax rates starting in 2005 from a high of 7 percent in 2004 to 5.25 percent in 2013.

28. See note 10.

29. See note 10.

30. See note 10.

31. See note 10.

32. As of the 2013 Forbes 400 ranking of America's wealthiest people, Warren Buffett's wealth is estimated to be $58.5 billion. www .forbes.com/forbes-400/list/.

33. For more on Warren Buffett and taxation, see: Arthur B. Laffer, "Warren Buffett's Call for Higher Taxes on the Rich," Laffer Associates, January 3, 2012. Summarized in Arthur B. Laffer, "Class Warfare and the Buffett Rule," *The Wall Street Journal*, January 11, 2012.

34. See Arthur B. Laffer, "Class Warfare and the Buffett Rule," *The Wall Street Journal*, January 11, 2012, http://online.wsj.com/news/ articles/SB10001424052970203462304577138961587258988.

35. Zachary R. Mider, "How Wal-Mart's Waltons Maintain Their Billionaire Fortune," Bloomberg, September 11, 2013, www .bloomberg.com/news/2013-09-12/how-wal-mart-s-waltons- maintain-their-billionaire-fortune-taxes.html.

36. Kathy Bergen, "Quinn Signs Sears-CME Tax Breaks into Law," *Chicago Tribune*, December 16, 2011, http://articles.chicagotribune .com/2011-12-16/business/chi-quinn-signs-searscme-tax-breaks-into-law-20111216_1_cme-and-cboe-sears-cme-employee-income-taxes.

37. Eric Fruits and Randall Pozdena, "Tax Myths Debunked," American Legislative Exchange Council, February 2013, www .alec.org/docs/Tax_Myths.pdf.

38. Peter Fisher, "The Doctor Is Out to Lunch: ALEC's Recommendations Wrong Prescription for State Prosperity Iowa Policy Project," Iowa Policy Project, July 24, 2012, www.iowapolicyproject .org/2012Research/120724-rsps.html.

39. Specifically, the Federal Reserve Bank of Philadelphia produces a monthly index for each of the 50 states. The indexes combine four state-level indicators to summarize current economic conditions in a single statistic. The four state-level variables in each index are nonfarm payroll employment, average hours worked in manufacturing, the unemployment rate, and real wage and salary disbursements (inflation-adjusted). Nonfarm payroll employment, the unemployment rate, average hours worked in manufacturing, and the consumer price index are obtained from the Bureau of Labor Statistics. Wages and salary disbursements (a component of personal income) and gross domestic product by state can be obtained from the Bureau of Economic Analysis. The methodology employed by the Philadelphia Fed ensures consistent measurement across the 50 states, so the state indexes are comparable to one another.

40. Theodore M. Crone and Alan Clayton-Matthews, "Consistent Economic Indexes for the 50 States," *Review of Economics and Statistics* 87 (2005): 593–603.

41. Data on state indexes retrieved September 2012 from: www .philadelphiafed.org/research-and-data/regional-economy/ indexes/coincident/coincident-historical.xls. The data used are the monthly June indexes for all states, to permit analysis for the years 2008 through 2012, and are ranked by the authors (Fruits and Pozdena).

42. Given the simplicity of the ALEC-Laffer state ranks (as an un-weighted average of its component rankings), this is an impressive correlation.

43. Not surprisingly, federal taxes can vary across states even when the federal tax codes don't change. The alternative minimum tax (AMT) is much more impactful in high-tax states because state tax payments are a "preferred deduction" and therefore not allowed in the calculation of the AMT tax base. There is at least one state that allows federal taxes as a state deduction, and federal taxes allow state tax deductions if the filer itemizes.

44. For some people, federal taxes have become so onerous that they have renounced their citizenship specifically for tax reasons. It has become an issue of national concern of late about wealthy Americans who are renouncing their citizenship and moving abroad for tax reasons. In this light, ITEP's contention that no one moves from one state to another for tax reasons is a stretch, to say the least.

45. See note 10.

46. Bertrand Russell, *Unpopular Essays* (New York: Simon & Schuster, 1950).

47. Christina D. Romer and David H. Romer, "The Macroeconomic Effects of Tax Changes: Estimates Based on a New Measure of Fiscal Shocks," *American Economic Review* 100 (June 2010), http://emlab.berkeley.edu/users/dromer/papers/RomerandRomerAER-June2010.pdf.

Bibliography

For further research into the factors affecting economic growth, see the following:

Abuselidze, G. "The Influence of Optimal Tax Burden on Economic Activity and Production Capacity." EconStore Open Access Articles, 2012. http://econpapers.repec.org/article/zbwespost/76882.html.

Adams, J. R. "New York Moves to the Supply-Side." Laffer Associates, April 8, 1981.

Alesina, A., and S. Ardagna. "Tales of Fiscal Adjustments." *Economic Policy* 27 (October 1998): 489–545.

Alesina, A., S. Ardagna, R. Perotti, and F. Schiantarelli. "Fiscal Policy, Profits, and Investment." *American Economic Review* 92, no. 3 (June 2002): 571–589.

Alesina, A., and R. Perotti. "Fiscal Expansions and Adjustments in OECD Countries." *Economic Policy* 21 (1995): 207–247.

Alesina, A., R. Perotti, and J. Tavares. "The Political Economy of Fiscal Adjustments." Brookings Institution, Papers on Economic Activity, Spring 1998.

Alesina, A., and D. Rodrik. "Distributive Politics and Economic Growth." *Quarterly Journal of Economics* 109, no. 2 (May 1994): 465–490.

Alm, J., and J. Rogers. "Do State Fiscal Policies Affect State Economic Growth?" *Public Finance Review* 39, no. 4, 483–526, July 2011. Link to working paper version: http://econ.tulane.edu/RePEc/pdf/tul1107.pdf.

Altig, D., A. J. Auerbach, L. J. Smetters, A. Kent, and J. Walliser. "Simulating Fundamental Tax Reform in the United States." *American Economic Review* 91, no. 3 (2001): 574–595.

Americans for Fair Taxation. "Replacing the U.S. Federal Tax System with a Retail Sales Tax—Macroeconomic and Distributional Impacts." Americans for Fair Taxation, December 1996.

Ardagna, S. "Fiscal Stabilizations: When Do They Work and Why?" *European Economic Review* 48, no. 5 (October 2004): 1047–1074.

Arduin, Laffer and Moore Econometrics. "Eliminating the State Income Tax in Oklahoma: An Economic Assessment." OCPA, November 2011.

Arduin, Laffer and Moore Econometrics. "Enhancing Texas' Economic Growth through Tax Reform: Repealing Property Taxes and Replacing the Revenues with a Revised Sales Tax." Texas Policy Foundation, 2009.

Atkinson, A., and A. Leigh. "Understanding the Distribution of Top Incomes in Five Anglo-Saxon Countries over the Twentieth Century." IZA Discussion Paper 4937, May 2010.

Auerbach, A. J. "Capital Gains Taxation in the United States." Brookings Institution, Papers on Economic Activity, no. 2 (1988): 595–631.

Auerbach, A. J. "Tax Reform, Capital Allocation, Efficiency and Growth." Unpublished, December 21, 1995.

Auten, G., and R. Carroll. "The Effect of Income Taxes on Household Behavior." *Review of Economics and Statistics* 81, no. 4 (1999): 681–693.

Auten, G., H. Sieg, and C. Clotfelter. "Charitable Giving, Income, and Taxes: An Analysis of Panel Data." *American Economic Review* 92, no. 1 (2002): 371–382.

Ball, Philip. *Curiosity: How Science Became Interested in Everything*. Chicago: University of Chicago Press, 2012.

Bankman, J. "Who Should Bear Tax Compliance Costs?" Working Paper, Berkeley Program in Law and Economics, University of California, Berkeley, 2003. www.escholarship.org/uc/item/2tt3c5dr.

Barro, R. J. "Determinants of Economic Growth: A Cross-Country Empirical Study." National Bureau of Economic Research, No. 5698, 1996. www.iedm.org/uploaded/pdf/robertjbarro.pdf.

Barro, R. J. "Economic Growth in a Cross Section of Countries." *Quarterly Journal of Economics* 106, no. 2 (May 1991).

Barro, R. J., and X. Sala-i-Martin. "Convergence." *Journal of Political Economy* 100, no. 2 (1992): 223–251. www.jstor.org/discover/10.2307/2138606?uid=3739912&uid=2129&uid=2&uid=70&uid=4&uid=3739256&sid=21103343115223.

Barro, R. J., and X. Sala-i-Martin. "Public Finance in Models of Economic Growth." *Review of Economic Studies* 59 (1992): 645–661.

Bartik, T. J. *Who Benefits from State and Local Economic Development Policies?* Kalamazoo, MI: W.E. Upjohn Institute, 1991.

Bartlett, B. "The Futility of Raising Tax Rates." Cato Institute Policy Analysis, no. 192, April 8, 1993. http://heartland.org/sites/all/modules/custom/heartland_migration/files/pdfs/5313.pdf and http://heartland.org/sites/all/modules/custom/heartland_migration/files/pdfs/5314.pdf.

Baumol, W. J. "Macroeconomics of Unbalanced Growth: The Anatomy of Urban Crisis." *American Economic Review* 57, no. 3 (1967): 415–426.

Baumol, W. J., R. E. Litan, and C. J. Schramm. *Good Capitalism, Bad Capitalism, and the Economics of Growth and Prosperity.* New Haven, CT: Yale University Press, 2007.

Beach, W. W. "The Case for Repealing the Estate Tax." Heritage Foundation, Backgrounder 1091, 35298.

Becsi, Z. "Do State and Local Taxes Affect Relative State Growth?" *Economic Review,* March/April 1996. https://www.frbatlanta.org/filelegacydocs/ACFD5.pdf.

Benson, B. L., and R. Johnson. "The Lagged Impact of State and Local Taxes on Economic Activity and Political Behavior." *Economic Inquiry* 24, no. 3 (1986): 389–401.

Bildirici, M. E., and F. Kayikci. "Effects of Oil Production on Economic Growth in Eurasian Countries: Panel ARDL Approach." *Energy* 49 (January 2013): 156–161.

Block, S. "A Taxing Challenge: Even Experts Can't Agree When Preparing a Sample Tax Return." *USA Today,* 39167. www.usatoday.com/money/perfi/taxes/2007-03-25-tax-preparers-hypothetical_N.html.

Blomquist, S., and H. Selin. "Hourly Wage Rate and Taxable Labor Income Responsiveness to Changes in Marginal Tax Rates." Uppsala
University Working Paper, 2009.

Blundell, R., and T. Macurdy. "Labor Supply: A Review of Alterna-
tive Approaches." Institute for Fiscal Studies, Working Paper Series
W98/18, 1999. http://aysps.gsu.edu/isp/files/SESSION_VII_
LABOUR_SUPPLY_A_REVIEW_OF_ALTERNATIVE_
APPROACHES.pdf.

Boeri, T., M. Burda, and F. Kramarz, eds. *Working Hours and Job Sharing
in the EU and USA: Are Europeans Lazy? Or Americans Crazy?* New
York: Oxford University Press, 2008.

Boskin, M. "A Framework for the Tax Reform Debate." U.S. House of
Representatives, June 6, 1995.

Boskin, M. "Taxation, Saving, and the Rate of Interest." *Journal of Political
Economy* 86, no. 2, Part 2: Research in Taxation (April 1978): S3–S27.

Boskin, M., G. G. Cian, and H. W. Watts, eds. *The Economics of the Labor
Supply in Income, Maintenance and Labor Supply.* Chicago: Rand
McNally, 1973.

Broadbent, B., and K. Daly. "Limiting the Fall-Out from Fiscal
Adjustment." Goldman Sachs, Global Economics Paper 195, 2010.

Brostek, M. "Tax Compliance: Multiple Approaches Are Needed to
Reduce the Tax Gap." Tax Issues Strategic Issues Team, Government
Accountability Office, GAO-07-391T, 2007.

Brueckner, J., and L. Saavedra. "Do Local Governments Engage in
Strategic Property-Tax Competition?" *National Tax Journal* 54
(2001): 203–229.

Brumbaugh, D. L., G. A. Essenwein, and J. G. Gravelle. "Overview of the
Federal Tax System." CRS Report for Congress, RL32808, March
10, 2005.

Buchholz, T. G., and R. W. Hahn. "Does a State's Legal Framework Affect
Its Economy?" U.S. Chamber of Commerce, November 13, 2002.

Burkhauser, R., J. Larrimore, and K. Simon. "A 'Second Opinion' on the
Economic Health of the American Middle Class." NBER Working
Paper 17164, 2011.

Burman, L. E., K. Clausing, and J. O'Hare. "Tax Reform and Realizations of Capital Gains in 1986." *National Tax Journal* 47, no. 1 (1994): 1–18.

Burman, L. E., and W. C. Randolph. "Measuring Permanent Responses to Capital-Gains Tax Changes in Panel Data." *American Economic Review* 84, no. 4 (September 1994): 794–809.

California Business Roundtable. "Twelfth Annual Business Climate Survey." California Business Roundtable, January 2002.

California Chamber of Commerce. "Survey: Migration Out of State Growing." California Chamber of Commerce, February 27, 2003.

Canto, V. A., and R. I. Webb. "The Effect of State Fiscal Policy on State Relative Economic Performance." *Southern Economic Journal* 54, no. 1 (July 1987).

Carroll, R., and D. Joulfaian. "Tax Rates, Taxpayer Behavior, and the 1993 Tax Act." U.S. Department of the Treasury, Office of Tax Analysis Working Paper, 1998.

Cebula, R. J. "Interstate Migration and the Tiebout Hypothesis: An Analysis According to Race, Sex and Age." *Journal of the American Statistical Association* 69, no. 348 (December 1974): 876–879. www.jstor.org/discover/10.2307/2286156?uid=3739912&uid=2129&uid=2&uid=70&uid=4&uid=3739256&sid=21103342323413.

Cebula, R. J. "Local Government Policies and Migration: An Analysis for SMSA's in the United States, 1965–1970." *Public Choice* 19, no. 3 (November 17, 1974): 85–93. http://mpra.ub.uni-muenchen.de/50068/.

Cebula, R. J. "Migration and the Tiebout-Tullock Hypothesis Revisited." *American Journal of Economics and Sociology* 68, no. 2 (2009): 541–551. www.ppge.ufrgs.br/GIACOMO/arquivos/eco02268/cebula-2009.pdf.

Cebula, R. J. "A Survey of the Literature on Migration-Impact of State and Local Government Policies." *Public Finance/Finances Publiques* 34, no. 1 (1979): 69–84.

Checherita, C., and P. Rother. "The Impact of High and Growing Debt on Economic Growth: An Empirical Investigation for the Euro Area." ECB Working Paper 1237, August 2010.

Chirinko, B., and D. J. Wilson. "State Business Taxes and Investment: State-by-State Simulations." *Economic Review* of San Francisco Federal Reserve (April 2010): 13–28. http://ideas.repec.org/a/fip/fedfer/y2010p13-28.html.

Clark, D. E., and W. J. Hunter. "The Impact of Economic Opportunity, Amenities, and Fiscal Factors on Age-Specific Migration Rates." *Journal of Regional Science* 3, no. 3 (1992): 349–365.

Clotfelter, C., and R. Schmalbeck. "The Impact of Fundamental Tax Reform on Nonprofit Organizations." In *Economic Effects of Fundamental Reform*, edited by Henry Aaron and William Gale, 211–246. Washington, DC: Brookings Institution Press, 1996.

Cobb, C. W., and P. H. Douglas. "A Theory of Production." *American Economic Review* (March 1928): 139–165.

Congressional Budget Office. "Labor Supply and Taxes." U.S. Congress: Congressional Budget Office, January 1996.

Coors, A. C., and A. B. Laffer. "Tax Trouble in Gotham City." Laffer Associates, May 6, 2003.

Coors, A. C., A. B. Laffer, and M. Miles. "Dividends: Stop the Discrimination." Laffer Associates, December 16, 2002.

Cournede, B., and F. Gonand. "Restoring Fiscal Sustainability in the Euro Area: Raise Taxes or Curb Spending?" OECD Economics Department Working Paper 520, 2006.

Cox, W., and E. J. McMahon. "Empire State Exodus: The Mass Migration of New Yorkers to Other States." Empire Center for New York Policy, 2009.

Crone, T. M., and A. Clayton-Matthews. "Consistent Economic Indexes for the 50 States." *Review of Economics and Statistics* 87 (2005): 593–603.

Dowding, K., and P. John. "Tiebout: A Survey of the Empirical Literature." *Urban Studies* 31 (1994): 767–797.

Dye, T. R. "The Economic Impact of the Adoption of a State Income Tax in New Hampshire." National Taxpayers Union Federation, October 1, 1999. http://heartland.org/sites/all/modules/custom/heartland_migration/files/pdfs/6926.pdf.

Dye, T. R. "Taxing, Spending, and Economic Growth in the American States." *Journal of Politics* 42, no. 4 (November 1980): 1085–1107.

Edwards, C. "Income Tax Rife with Complexity and inefficiency." Cato Institute Tax & Budget Bulletin 33, April 2006.

Edwards, C. "Options for Tax Reform." Cato Institute Policy Analysis, no. 536, February 24, 2005.

Engen, E., J. Gravelle, and K. Smetters. "Dynamic Tax Models: Why They Do the Things They Do." *National Tax Journal* 50, no. 3 (1997): 657–682.

Engen, E., and J. Skinner. "Taxation and Economic Growth." *National Tax Journal* 49, no. 4 (December 1996): 617–642.

Feenberg, D. R., and J. M. Poterba. "Income Inequality and the Incomes of Very High-Income Taxpayers: Evidence from Tax Returns." In *Tax Policy and the Economy*, Vol. 7, edited by J. M. Poterba, 145–177. Cambridge, MA: MIT Press, 1993.

Feldman, N., and P. Katuscak. "Effects of Predictable Tax Liability Variation on Household Labor Income." Charles University Center for Economic Research and Graduate Education, 2012. https://www.cerge-ei.cz/pdf/wp/Wp454.pdf.

Feldstein, M. "Tax Avoidance and the Deadweight Loss of the Income Tax." *Review of Economics and Statistics* 81, no. 4 (1999): 674–680. www.jstor.org/discover/10.2307/2646716?uid=3739912&uid=2129&uid=2&uid=70&uid=4&uid=3739256&sid=21103343548453.

Fleisher, M. P. "Why I'm Not Hiring." *The Wall Street Journal*, August 9, 2010.

Forman, J. "Simplification for Low Income Taxpayers." Joint Committee on Taxation: Study of the Overall State of the Federal Tax System, 2001.

Fox, W. F., H. W. Herzog, and A. M. Schlottman. "Metropolitan Fiscal Structure and Migration." *Journal of Regional Science* 29, no. 4 (1989): 523–536.

Fruits, E., and R. Pozdena. "Tax Myths Debunked." American Legislative Exchange Council, February 2013. www.alec.org/docs/Tax_Myths.pdf.

Fullerton, D. "Comment on 'High-Income Families and the Tax Changes of the 1980s: The Anatomy of Behavioral Response.'" In

Empirical Foundations of Household Taxation, edited by Martin Feldstein and James Poterba, 189–192. Chicago: University of Chicago Press, 1996.

Gale, W. G., and J. Holtzblatt. "The Role of Administrative Factors in Tax Reform: Simplicity, Compliance and Enforcement." Brookings Institution, 2000. www.brookings.edu/views/papers/gale/20001201.pdf.

Gallaway, L., R.Vedder, and R. Lawson. "Why People Work: An Examination of Interstate Variations in Labor Force Participation." *Journal of Labor Research* 12, no. 1 (Winter 1991).

Garrett, T. "U.S. Income Inequality: It's Not So Bad." Federal Reserve Bank of St. Louis, Spring 2010. www.stlouisfed.org/publications/itv/articles/?id=1920.

Genetski, R. J., and L. Ludlow. "The Impact of State and Local Taxes on Economic Growth: 1963–1980." *Harris Economics*, December 17, 1982. http://heartland.org/sites/all/modules/custom/heartland_migration/files/pdfs/15673.pdf.

Genetski, R. J., and J. W. Skorburg. "The Impact of State & Local Taxes on Economic Growth: 1975–1987." Chicago Association of Commerce and Industry. http://heartland.org/policy-documents/impact-state-local-taxes-economic-growth-1975-1987.

Gentry, W. H., and R. C. Hubbard. "The Effects of Progressive Income Taxation on Job Turnover." *Journal of Public Economics* 88, no. 11 (2004): 2301–2322.

Ghatak, S., P. Levine, and S. Price. "Migration Theories and Evidence: An Assessment." *Journal of Economic Surveys* 10 (1996): 159–198.

Giavazzi, F., and M. Pagano. "Can Severe Fiscal Contractions Be Expansionary? Tales of Two Small European Countries." In *NBER Macroeconomics Annual*, 95–122. Cambridge, MA: MIT Press, 1990.

Giavazzi, F., and M. Pagano. "Non-Keynesian Effects of Fiscal Policy Changes: International Evidence and the Swedish Experience." *Swedish Economic Policy Review* 3, no. 1 (Spring 1990): 67–112.

Giertz, S. "The Elasticity of Taxable Income: Influences on Economic Efficiency and Tax Revenues, and Implications for Tax Policy." In

Tax Policy Lessons from the 2000s, edited by Alan Viard, 101–136. Washington, DC: AEI Press, 2009.

Giertz, S. "The Elasticity of Taxable Income during the 1990s: New Estimates and Sensitivity Analyses." *Southern Economic Journal* 77, no. 2 (October 2010): 406–433.

Giertz, S. "The Elasticity of Taxable Income over the 1980s and 1990s." *National Tax Journal* 60, no. 4 (2007): 743–768.

Giertz, S. "Panel Data Techniques and the Elasticity of Taxable Income." Congressional Budget Office, Working Paper 2008-11, 2008.

Giertz, S. "Recent Literature on Taxable-Income Elasticities." Congressional Budget Office, Technical Paper 2004-16, 2004.

Gillen, A., and R. K. Vedder. "North Carolina's Higher Education System: Success or Failure?" Center for College Affordability and Productivity, February 2008. www.epi.soe.vt.edu/perspectives/policy_news/pdf/NCReport0508.pdf.

Gius, M. "The Effect of Income Taxes on Interstate Migration: An Analysis by Age and Race." *Annals of Regional Science* 46 (October 29, 2009): 205–218.

Government Accountability Office. "Tax Policy: Summary of Estimates of the Costs of the Federal Tax System." Government Accountability Office, GAO-05-878, 2005.

Greenwood, M. J. "Human Migration: Theory, Models, and Empirical Studies." *Journal of Regional Science* 25 (1985): 521–544.

Guihard, S., M. Kennedy, E. Wurzel, and C. Andre. "What Promotes Fiscal Consolidation: OECD Country Experience." OECD Economics Department, Working Paper 553, 2007.

Guyton, J. L., J. F. O'Hare, M. P. Stavrianos, and E. J. Toder. "Estimating the Compliance Costs of the U.S. Individual Income Tax." Paper presented at the 2003 National Tax Association Spring Symposium, 2003.

Gwarney, J., R. Lawson, and R. Holcombe. "The Size and Functions of Government and Economic Growth." Joint Economic Committee, U.S. Congress, April 1998.

Hagen, J. V., and R. Strauch. "Fiscal Consolidations: Quality, Economic Conditions and Success." *Public Choice* 109, no. 3–4 (2001): 327–346.

Harberger, A. "Taxation, Resource Allocation, and Welfare." In *The Role of Direct and Indirect Taxes in the Federal Revenue System*, edited by John Due, 25–75. Princeton, NJ: Princeton University Press, 1964.

Heckman, J. J., L. Lochner, and C. Taber. "Tax Policy and Human-Capital Formation." *American Economic Review* 88, no. 2 (1998): 293–297.

Heim, B. "The Effect of Recent Tax Changes on Taxable Income: Evidence from a New Panel of Tax Returns." *Journal of Policy Analysis and Management* 9, no. 1 (2009): 147–163.

Heim, B. "The Elasticity of Taxable Income: Evidence from a New Panel of Tax Returns." U.S. Department of the Treasury, Office of Tax Analysis Working Paper, 2007.

Heller, W., as cited by B. Bartlett. "'Testimony before the Joint Economic Committee of Congress, 1977' as cited in *National Review*." *National Review*, October 27, 1978.

Helms, L. J. "The Effect of State and Local Taxes on Economic Growth: A Time Series–Cross Section Approach." *Review of Economics and Statistics* 67, no. 4 (November 1985): 574–582. www.jstor.org/discover/10.2307/1924801?uid=3739912&uid=2129&uid=2&uid=70&uid=4&uid=3739256&sid=21103342323413.

IRS. "2008 Annual Report to Congress." *National Taxpayer Advocate*, December 31, 2008.

IRS. "2009 Annual Report to Congress." *National Taxpayer Advocate*, December 31, 2009.

Johansson, Å., C. Heady, J. Arnold, B. Brys, and L. Vartia. "Tax and Economic Growth." OECD Economics Department, Working Paper 620, 2008. www.oecd.org/tax/tax-policy/41000592.pdf.

Joines, D. H. "The Kennedy Tax Cut: An Application of the Ellipse." A.B. Laffer Associates, September 25, 1980.

Joint Committee on Taxation, Staff. *Study of the Overall State of the Federal Tax System and Recommendations for Simplification, Pursuant to Section 8022(3)(B) of the Internal Revenue Code of 1986. Vol. 3, Academic Papers Submitted to the Joint Committee on Taxation.* Washington, DC: U.S. Government Printing Office, April 2001.

Jorgenson, D. W. "Accounting for Growth in the Information Age." Working Paper, 2001.

Jorgenson, D. W. "The Economic Impact of Fundamental Tax Reform." Committee on Ways and Means, U.S. House of Representatives, June 6, 1995.

Kadlec, C. W., and A. B. Laffer. "A General Equilibrium View of the U.S. Economy." A.B. Laffer Associates, December 14, 1979.

Kadlec, C. W., and A. B. Laffer. "The Jarvis-Gann Tax Cut Proposal: An Adoption of the Laffer Curve." A.B. Laffer Associates, June 1978.

Karemera, D., et al. "A Gravity Model Analysis of International Migration to North America." *Applied Economics, Taylor and Francis Journals* 21, no. 13, 1745–1755, October 2000.

Keating, D. "A Taxing Trend: The Rise in Complexity, Forms, and Paperwork Burdens." *National Taxpayer's Union* 127, April 15, 2010.

Keating, R. J. "Small Business Survival Index 2010." Small Business Survival Committee, 2010.

Kimball, M. S., and M. D. Shapiro. "Labor Supply: Are the Income and Substitution Effects Both Large or Both Small?" National Bureau of Economic Research, Working Paper, May 16, 2003.

Kirchgässner, G., and W. Pommerehne. "Tax Harmonization and Tax Competition in the European Union: Lessons from Switzerland." *Journal of Public Economics* 60 (1996): 351–371.

Kneller, R., and F. Misch. "What Does Ex-Post Evidence Tell Us about the Output Effects of Future Tax Reforms?" Center for European Economic Research, Discussion Paper 11-029, 2011. http://ftp.zew.de/pub/zew-docs/dp/dp11029.pdf

Koenig, E. F., and G. W. Huffman. "The Dynamic Impact of Fundamental Tax Reform Part 1: The Basic Model." *Federal Reserve Bank of Dallas Economic Review*, First Quarter.

Kohn, R., R. Vedder, and R. Cebula. "Determinants of Interstate Migration, by Race, 1965–1970." *Annals of Regional Science* 7, no. 1 (1973): 100–112. http://mpra.ub.uni-muenchen.de/52311/.

Kotlikoff, L. J. "The Economic Impact of Replacing Federal Income Taxes with a Sales Tax." Cato Institute Policy Analysis, no. 193, April 15, 1993.

Kubik, J. "The Incidence of the Personal Income Taxation: Evidence from the Tax Reform Act of 1986." *Journal of Public Economics* 88, no. 7–8 (2004): 1567–1588.

Laffer, A. B. "California Dreaming." A.B. Laffer Associates, June 25, 1991.

Laffer, A. B. "The California Flat Tax Proposal Tax Amendment." Laffer Associates, October 20, 1995.

Laffer, A. B. "A California Tax Update." A.B. Laffer Associates, 29308.

Laffer, A. B. "California, Who Are You?" Laffer Associates, February 17, 2006.

Laffer, A. B. "The Complete Flat Tax." A.B. Laffer Associates, 1984.

Laffer, A. B. "The Complete Flat Tax 1992 Style." A.B. Laffer Associates, 1992.

Laffer, A. B. "The Ellipse: An Explication of the Laffer Curve in a Two Factor Model." A.B. Laffer Associates, 29410.

Laffer, A. B. "A Flat Rate Tax for California State and Local Governments: Presentation to the California Commission on Tax Policy." Laffer Associates, April 28, 2003.

Laffer, A. B. "Flat Taxism: Western Europe Under Fire." Laffer Associates, February 12, 2004.

Laffer, A. B. "The Great California Tax Experiment: From Karl Marx to Adam Smith and Back Again." A.B. Laffer Associates, May 28, 1993.

Laffer, A. B. "How to Mark Dubya a Winner: The Flat Tax." *The Wall Street Journal*, May 31, 2001.

Laffer, A. B. "Is the California Tax Revolt Over? An Analysis of California's Proposition 111." A.B. Laffer Associates, 33010.

Laffer, A. B. "Jack Kemp Letter." Laffer Associates, October 17, 1995.

Laffer, A. B. "The Only Answer: A California Flat Tax." Laffer Associates, October 2, 2003.

Laffer, A. B. "A Proposal for California Complete Flat Tax." A.B. Laffer Associates, 1990.

Laffer, A. B. "Proposition 13: The Tax Terminator." Laffer Associates, June 27, 2003.

Laffer, A. B. "Russia's 12-Step Recovery Starts with the Flat Tax." Laffer Associates, June 6, 2002.

Laffer, A. B. "Will Gray Davis Survive?" Laffer Associates, August 6, 2003.

Laffer, A. B., and D. Arduin. "Pro-Growth Tax Reform and E-Fairness." Laffer Associates and Let Freedom Ring, July 2013. www .standwithmainstreet.com/ArtLafferStudy.pdf.

Laffer, A. B., and C. S. Hammond. "Either California's Housing Prices Are Going to Fall or California's In for One Helluva Rise in Personal Income." Laffer Associates December 28, 1990.

Laffer, A. B., and T. Jeffrey. "California in the Crosshairs." Laffer Associates, May 21, 2003.

Laffer, A. B., and M. Laffer. "A Study of California's Housing Prices." Laffer Associates, November 19, 1998.

Laffer, A. B., P. Marcal, and M. McNary. "Rosa Californica." Laffer Associates, January 28, 1993.

Laffer, A. B., M. McNary, and L. Vitanza. "California D.P. (During Pete)." A.B. Laffer Associates, June 8, 1994.

Laffer, A. B., and S. Moore. "California, Who Are You? Part II." Laffer Associates, January 18, 2008.

Laffer, A. B., and S. Moore. "Taxes Really Do Matter: Look at the States." Laffer Center for Supply-Side Economics, September 2012. www.laffercenter.com/wp-content/uploads/2012/09/2012-09-TaxesDoMatterLookAtStates-LafferCenter-Laffer-Moore.pdf.

Laffer, A. B., S. Moore, and J. Williams. "Tax Reform to Fix California's Economy." In *Rich States, Poor States*, 6th ed. Arlington, VA: American Legislative Exchange Council, 2013. www.alec.org/ publications/rich-states-poor-states/.

Laffer, A. B., and J. Thomson. "Tax Amnesty: A Win/Win for All." Laffer Associates, May 12, 2003.

Laffer, A. B., and W. H. Winegarden. "The Economic Consequences of Tennessee's Gift and Estate Tax." Laffer Center for Supply-Side Economics and Beacon Center of Tennessee, March 2012. www .beacontn.org/wp-content/uploads/The-Economic-Consequences-of-Tennessees-Gift-Estate-Tax.pdf.

Laffer, A. B., W. H. Winegarden, and D. Arduin. "Competitive States 2010: Texas vs. California, Economic Growth Prospects for the 21st Century." Texas Public Policy Foundation, October 10, 2010.

Laffer, A. B., W. H. Winegarden, D. Arduin, and I. McDonough. "The Economic Impact of Federal Spending on State Economic Performance: A Texas Perspective." Texas Public Policy Foundation, April 1, 2009.

Laffer, A. B., W. H. Winegarden, and J. Childs. "The Economic Burden Caused by Tax Code Complexity." Laffer Center for Supply-Side Economics, April 14, 2011.

Landau, D. L. "Government Expenditure and Economic Growth: A Cross-Country Study." *Southern Economic Journal* 49, no. 3 (January 1983): 783–792. www.jstor.org/discover/10.2307/105871 6?uid=3739912&uid=2129&uid=2&uid=70&uid=4&uid=373925 6&sid=21103342008853.

Lawrence, L. "Individual Taxpayer Response to Tax Cuts: 1982–1984, with Implications for the Revenue Maximizing Tax Rate." *Journal of Public Economics* 33, no. 2 (1987): 173–206. http://piketty.pse.ens.fr/files/Lindsey1987.pdf.

Lazear, E. P. "Productivity and Wages." *Business Economics* 41, no. 4 (October 2006): 39–45.

Lee, Y., and R. H. Gordon. "Tax Structure and Economic Growth." *Journal of Public Economics* 89, no. 5–6 (2005): 1027–1043.

Legislative Analyst's Office. "California's Tax System: A Primer." California Legislative Analyst's Office, January 2001.

Liebig, T. *A New Phenomenon—The International Competition for Highly-Skilled Migrants and Its Consequences for Germany.* Stuttgart/Berne/Vienna: Haupt, 2004.

Liebig, T., P. A. Puhani, and A. Sousa-Poza. "Taxation and Internal Migration: Evidence from the Swiss Census Using Community-Level Variation in Income Tax Rates." IZA Discussion Paper 2374, Institute for the Study of Labor, 2006. www.iza.org/en/webcontent/publications/papers/viewAbstract?dp_id=2374.

Looney, A., and M. Singhal. "The Effect of Anticipated Tax Changes on Intertemporal Labor Supply and the Realization of Taxable Income." National Bureau of Economic Research, Working Paper 12417, 2006. www.nber.org/papers/w12417.

Macurdy, T. "An Empirical Model of Labor Supply in a Life-Cycle Setting." *Journal of Political Economy* 89, no. 6 (1981): 1059–1085.

Mahroum, S. "Europe and the Immigration of Highly-Skilled Labor." *International Migration* 39 (2001): 27–43.

Mankiw, G. N., and M. Weinzierl. "Dynamic Scoring: A Back-of-the-Envelope Guide." *Journal of Public Economics* 90, no. 8–9 (September 2006):1415–1433.www.sciencedirect.com/science/article/pii/S0047272705001738.

Massey, D., J. Arango, G. Hugo, A. Kouaouci, and E. Taylor. "Theories of International Migration: A Review and Appraisal." *Population and Development Review* 19 (1993): 431–466.

McDermott, J., and R. Westcott. "An Empirical Analysis of Fiscal Adjustments." *IMF Staff Papers* 43, no. 4 (1996): 723–753.

McLure, C., Jr. "Taxation, Substitution, and Industrial Location." *Journal of Political Economy* 78, no. 1 (January/February 1970): 112–132.

McPhail, J., P. Orazem, and R. Singh. "The Poverty of States: Do State Tax Policies Affect State Labor Productivity?" Iowa State University Department of Economics, May 2010.

McQuillan, L., and H. Abramyan. "U.S. Tort Liability Index: 2010 Report." Pacific Research Institute, 2010.

Mieszowki, P., and G. Zodrow. "Taxation and the Tiebout Model: The Differential Effects of Head Taxes, Taxes on Land Rents, and Property Taxes." *Journal of Economic Literature* 27 (1989): 1098–1146.

Minarik, J. "The Tax Shares Boomlet." *Tax Notes* 23 (1984): 1218–1220.

Mirrlees, J. "An Exploration in the Theory of Optimum Income Taxation." *Review of Economic Studies* 38, no. 2 (1971): 175–208.

Mitchell, D. J. "The Impact of Government Spending on Economic Growth." Heritage Foundation, Backgrounder 1831, March 15, 2005.

Mueller, D. C. *Public Choice III*, Cambridge University Press, 2003.

Mullen, J. K., and M. Williams. "Marginal Tax Rates and State Economic Growth." *Regional Science and Urban Economics* 24, no. 6 (1994): 687–705.

Munnell, A. H. "How Does Public Infrastructure Affect Regional Economic Performance?" *New England Economic Review* (1990): 11–12.

Munnell, A. H. "Lessons from the Income Maintenance Experiments."
Federal Reserve Bank of Boston Conference Series 30, 1987.

Munnell, A. H. "Policy Watch: Infrastructure Investment and Economic
Growth." *Journal of Economic Perspectives* 6, no. 4 (1992): 189–198.

Myles, G. D. "Economic Growth and the Role of Taxation." OECD
Economics Department, No. 713, 2009.

Navratil, J. "The Tax Reform Act of 1986: New Evidence on Individual
Taxpayer Behavior from Panel Tax Return Data." In *Essays on the
Impact of Marginal Tax Rate Reductions on the Reporting of Taxable
Income on Individual Tax Returns*, Chapter 3. Doctoral dissertation,
Harvard University, 1995.

Nellen, A. "Simplification of the EITC through Structure Changes."
Joint Committee on Taxation: Study of the Overall State of the Federal Tax System, 2001.

Newman, R. J. "Migration and Growth in the South." *Review of Economics and Statistics* 65, no. 1 (February 1983): 76–86.

Oates, W. "The Effects of Property Taxes and Local Public Spending
on Property Values: An Empirical Study of Tax Capitalisation and
Tiebout Hypothesis." *Journal of Political Economy* 77 (1969): 951–971.

Office of Economic Analysis, State of Oregon. "Oregon Economic and
Revenue Forecast," vol. 29, no. 4, 2009.

Ohanian, L., A. Raffo, and R. Rogerson. "Long-Term Changes in Labor
Supply and Taxes: Evidence from OECD Countries, 1956–2004."
Journal of Monetary Economics 55, no. 8 (November 2008): 1353–1362.

Ojede, A., and S. Yamarik. "Tax Policy and State Economic Growth: The
Long-Run and Short-Run of It." *Economic Letters* 116, no. 2 (August
2012): 161–165.

Organization for Economic Cooperation and Development.
"International Mobility of the Highly Skilled." Paris: OECD, 2002.

Padovano, F., and E. Galli. "Tax Rates and Economic Growth in
the OECD Countries (1950–1990)." *Economic Inquiry* 39, no. 1
(January 2001): 44–57. http://pirate.shu.edu/~rotthoku/Prague/
Tax%20Rates%20and%20Economic%20Growth%20in%20the%20
OECD%20Countries.pdf.

Papke, J. A., and L. Papke. "Measuring Differential State-Local Liabilities and Their Implications for Business Investment Location." *National Tax Journal*, December 1985.

Parcell, A. "Income Shifting in Responses to Higher Tax Rates: The Effects of OBRA 93." Washington, D.C.: Office of Tax Analysis, U.S. Department of the Treasury, 1995.

Peach, J., and C. M. Starbuck. "Oil and Gas Production and Economic Growth in New Mexico." *Journal of Economic Issues* 45, no. 2, (June 2011).

Pew Center of the States. "Beyond California: States in Fiscal Peril." Pew Charitable Trusts, November 2009. www.pewtrusts.org/uploadedFiles/wwwpewtrustsorg/Reports/State_policy/BeyondCalifornia%281%29.pdf.

Plaut, T. R., and J. Pluta. "Business Climate, Taxes and Expenditures, and State Industrial Growth in the United States." *Southern Economic Journal* 50, no. 1 (July 1983): 99–119.

Plosser, C. I. "The Search for Growth." In *Policies for Long-Run Economic Growth*. Kansas City, MO: Federal Reserve Bank of Kansas City, 1992.

Plotkin, J., and A. C. Coors. "The AMT: Another Reason to Hate April 15th." Laffer Associates, February 7, 2005.

Poulson, B., and J. Kaplan. "State Income Taxes and Economic Growth." *Cato Journal* 28, no. 1 (Winter 2008): 53–71.

Prescott, E. C. "Prosperity and Depression: 2002 Richard T. Ely Lecture." Federal Reserve Minneapolis Research Department, Working Paper 618; *American Economic Review* 92, no. 2 (May 2002): 1–15.

Rabushka, A. "Taxation, Economic Growth and Liberty." *Cato Journal* 7, no. 1 (Spring/Summer 1987).

Rabushka, A. "Ten Myths about Higher Taxes." Hoover Institution Essays in Public Policy, 1993. http://heartland.org/sites/all/modules/custom/heartland_migration/files/pdfs/5463.pdf and http://heartland.org/sites/all/modules/custom/heartland_migration/files/pdfs/5464.pdf.

Randolph, R. "Dynamic Income, Progressive Taxes, and the Timing of Charitable Contributions." *Journal of Political Economy* 103, no. 4 (1995): 709–738.

Razin, A., E. Sadka, and P. Swagel. "Tax Burden and Migration: A Political Economy Theory and Evidence." *Journal of Public Economics* 85 (2002): 167–190.

Rector, R., and R. S. Hederman Jr. "Two Americas: One Rich, One Poor? Understanding Income Inequality in the United States." Heritage Foundation, Backgrounder, No. 1791, 2004. www.heritage .org/research/reports/2004/08/two-americas-one-rich-one-poor-understanding-income-inequality-in-the-united-states.

Reed, W. R. "The Determinants of U.S. State Economic Growth: A Less Extreme Bounds Analysis." *Economic Inquiry* 47, no. 4 (October 2009): 685–700.

Reed, W. R. "The Robust Relationship between Taxes and U.S. State Income Growth." *National Tax Journal* 61, no. 1 (2008): 57–80.

Reed, W. R., and C. L. Rogers. "Tax Burden and the Mismeasurement of State Tax Policy." *Public Finance Review* 34, no. 4 (2006): 404–426.

Reed, W. R., and C. L. Rogers. "Tax Cuts and Employment in New Jersey: Lessons from a Regional Analysis." *Public Finance Review* 32, no. 3 (2004): 269–291.

Report of the President's Advisory Panel on Federal Tax Reform, "Simple, Fair, and Pro-Growth: Proposals to Fix America's Tax System." President's Advisory Panel on Tax Reform, 2005. www .taxpolicycenter.org/taxtopics/upload/tax-panel-2.pdf.

Reynolds, A. "Some International Comparisons of Supply-Side Policy." *Cato Journal* 5, no. 2 (Fall 1985).

Romans, T., and G. Subrahmanyam. "State and Local Taxes, Transfers and Regional Economic Growth." *Southern Economic Journal* 46, no. 2 (October 1979): 435–444.

Romer, C. D., and D. H. Romer. "The Macroeconomic Effects of Tax Changes: Estimates Based on a New Measure of Fiscal Shocks." *American Economic Review* 100, no. 3 (June 2010): 763–801.

Sammartino, F., and D. Weiner. "Recent Evidence on Taxpayers' Response to the Rate Increases in the 1990s." *National Tax Journal* 50, no. 3 (1997): 683–705.

Schön, W., ed. *Tax Competition in Europe.* Amsterdam: International Bureau of Fiscal Determination, 2003.

Scully, G. W. "Optimal Taxation, Economic Growth and Income Inequality in the United States." National Center for Policy Analysis, Policy Report 316, September 2008.

Showalter, M. H., and N. K. Thurston. "Taxes and Labor Supply of High-Income Physicians." *Journal of Public Economics* 66, no. 1 (1997): 73–97.

Singleton, P. "The Effect of Taxes on Taxable Earnings: Evidence from the 2001–2004 U.S. Federal Tax Acts." Syracuse University, Working Paper Series, 2007.

Sjaastad, L. "The Costs and Returns of Human Migration." *Journal of Political Economy* 70 (1962): 80–93.

Stark, O. *The Migration of Labor.* Cambridge, MA: Basil Blackwell, 1991.

Stathopoulos, P. "DOR Targets Delinquent Taxpayers to Attack Budget Woes." *State Tax Notes, Tax Analysts,* October 6, 2003.

Stokey, N., and S. Rebelo. "Growth Effects of Flat-Rate Taxes." *Journal of Political Economy* 103, no. 3 (June 1995).

Sullivan, M. "Practical Aspects of Dynamic Revenue Estimation." Heritage Center for Data Analysis Report, June 14, 2004.

Tavares, J. "Does Right or Left Matter? Cabinets, Credibility and Fiscal Adjustments." *Journal of Public Economics* 88 (2004): 2447–2468.

Tax Division of American Institute of Certified Public Accountants. "Guiding Principles for Tax Simplification." American Institute of Certified Public Accountants, 2002. www.aicpa.org/interestareas/tax/resources/taxlegislationpolicy/advocacy/downloadabledocuments/tpcs%202%20-%20principles%20for%20tax%20simplification.pdf.

Taylor, H., D. Krane, and A. Cottreau. "U.S. Chamber of Commerce State Liability Systems Ranking Study." Harris Interactive, January 11, 2002.

Tiebout, C. "A Pure Theory of Local Expenditures." *Journal of Political Economy* 64 (1956): 416–424.

U.S. Treasury Department. "Income Mobility in the U.S. from 1996 to 2005." Washington, DC: Internal Revenue Service, 2007.

U.S. Treasury Department. "Statistics of Income: Individual Income Tax Returns." Washington, DC: Internal Revenue Service, annual since 1916.

Vedder, R. K. "Economic Impact of Government Spending: A 50-State Analysis." National Center for Policy Analysis, Report 178, April 1993. www.ncpa.org/pdfs/st178.pdf.

Vedder, R. K. "The Effect of Taxes on Economic Growth: What the Research Tells Us." Texas Public Policy Foundation, 2002.

Vedder, R. K. "Federal Tax Reform: Lessons from the State." *Cato Journal* 5, no. 2 (Fall 1985).

Vedder, R. K. "The Impact of State and Local Taxes on Economic Growth: What the Research Shows." Commonwealth Foundation, May 1990.

Vedder, R. K. "Money for Nothing?: An Analysis of the Oregon Quality Education Model." Cascade Policy Institute, 2000.

Vedder, R. K. "Right-to-Work Laws: Liberty, Prosperity and Quality of Life." *Cato Journal* 30, no. 1 (2010).

Vedder, R. K. "Taxation and Immigration." Taxpayers Network, 2003. www.taxpayersnetwork.org/_Rainbow/Documents/Taxation%20 and%20Migration.pdf.

Vedder, R. K. "Taxation and Migration: Do Tax Decisions of State and Local Government Officials Impact on the Movement of People?" Taxpayers Network, March 2003.

Vedder, R. K., and M. Denhart. "Texas' Higher Education System: Success or Failure?" Texas Public Policy Foundation, 2008.

Vedder, R. K., M. Denhart, and J. Robe. "Right-to-Work and Indiana's Economic Future." 2011.

Vedder, R. K., and L. Galloway. "The Economic Impact of Washington's Minimum Wage Law." Ohio University, 2003. http://biz.npri.org/ minimum/WAMinWageStudy.pdf.

Vedder, R. K., and L. Galloway. "Rent-Seeking, Distributional Coalitions, Taxes, Relative Prices and Economic Growth." *Public Choice* 51 (1986): 93–100.

Vedder, R. K., and J. Hall. "Effective, Efficient, Fair: Paying for Public Education in Texas." Texas Public Policy Foundation, 2004.

Wanniski, J. "An Authentic Guide to Supply-Side Economics." A.B. Laffer Associates, May 2, 1980.

Wasylenko, M., and T. McGuire. "Taxation and Economic Development: The State of the Economic Literature." *National Tax Journal* 38, no. 4 (December 1985). http://surface.syr.edu/cgi/viewcontent.cgi?article=1001&context=ecn.

Weber, C. "Obtaining a Consistent Estimate of Taxable Income Using Difference-in-Differences." University of Michigan, Working Paper, 2010.

Weinstein, B. L. "Tax Incentives for Growth." *Society* 14, no. 3 (1977): 73–75.

Westbury, B. "Growth Grade for Diamond and Saez—Solid, and Well-Earned F." Four Percent Growth Project, May 1, 2012. www.bushcenter.org/economic-growth/4-growth-project.

Wilson, J. "Theories of Tax Competition." *National Tax Journal* 52 (1999): 269–304.

Yamarik, S. "Can Tax Policy Help Explain State-Level Macroeconomic Growth?" *Economic Letters* 62, no. 2 (August 2000): 211–215.

Young, L., and R. H. Gordon. "Tax Structure and Economic Growth." *Journal of Public Economics* 89, no. 5–6 (2005): 1027–1043. www.sba.muohio.edu/davisgk/growth%20readings/17.pdf.

Acknowledgments

The authors had a lot of help in bringing this book to fruition. And for this help they are truly grateful.

First and foremost, Nicholas Drinkwater has to be singled out as the *primum primorum* of those to whom we owe so much. In every aspect of the research, organization, and writing, this book simply would not have been possible without him.

We would also like to say thank you to our friends, colleagues, and family members for all they have done to edit, comment, support, and critique the themes and ideas presented in this book. We would especially like to thank Kelly Sarka, as well as Paul Abelkop, James Blumstein, Mark Broach, John Burke, Chuck DeVore, Rachael Hamilton, Rowena Itchon, Nick Jordan, Marc Miles, Kenneth Petersen, Sally Pipes, Brooke Rollins, Carol Roth, Ford Scudder, Lucas Tomicki, Horacio Valeiras, Collette Wheeler, and Drew Zinder.

We also owe a large debt of gratitude to Tom Smith, who has enabled us to create a website, www.savetaxesbymoving.com, to display just how stark the differences are between personal income tax rates from one state or locality to another and just how much these differences in taxes can add to (or subtract from) one's wealth over time.

Finally, we would like to thank the entire team at John Wiley & Sons for all of their hard work in publishing this book, especially in such a short time frame.

About the Authors

Arthur B. Laffer, PhD, is the founder and chairman of Laffer Associates, an economic research and consulting firm. Dr. Laffer is best known for the Laffer curve, a diagrammatic representation of the relationship between tax rates and tax revenues. His work has been credited with triggering a worldwide tax-cutting movement in the 1980s, earning him the distinction in many publications as the father of supply-side economics. One of his earliest successes in shaping public policy was his involvement in Proposition 13, the groundbreaking California initiative that drastically cut property taxes in the state in 1978. A member of President Reagan's Economic Policy Advisory Board for both of Reagan's terms, Dr. Laffer also served as the first Chief Economist of the Office of Management and Budget (OMB) under George Shultz and advised Prime Minister Margaret Thatcher on fiscal policy in the United Kingdom during the 1980s. He has been a faculty member at the University of Chicago, University of Southern California, and Pepperdine University. Dr. Laffer received a BA in economics from Yale University and an MBA and a PhD in economics from Stanford University.

Stephen Moore is Chief Economist at the Heritage Foundation. He served as a member of the *Wall Street Journal's* editorial board from 2005 to 2014. Moore was also the founder and president of The Club for Growth and is the author of a number of books, including *Return to Prosperity*. He has also served as a senior economist on the Congressional Joint Economic Committee and as a senior economics fellow at the Cato Institute, where he published dozens of studies on federal and state tax and budget policy. Moore graduated from the University of Illinois and holds a master's degree in economics from George Mason University.

Rex Sinquefield, often referred to as one of the world's leading financial gurus, now spends most of his time and resources dedicated to philanthropic causes. Raised in Saint Vincent Orphanage in St. Louis, Missouri, Sinquefield earned a business degree from Saint Louis University and an MBA from the University of Chicago, studying under Eugene Fama, the father of efficient markets. He went on to develop some of the nation's first index funds, and, along with associate David Booth, formed Dimensional Fund Advisors in 1981, which today oversees more than $350 billion in global assets. After retiring in 2005, Sinquefield returned to his much-loved state of Missouri, where he cofounded and serves as president of the not-for-profit organization the Show-Me Institute, the state's only free-market think tank. Rex and Dr. Jeanne Sinquefield also have become some of Missouri's most important philanthropists; they founded the Chess Club and Scholastic Center of Saint Louis, relocated to St. Louis the World Chess Hall of Fame, and fund the Mizzou New Music Initiative.

Travis H. Brown is the author of *How Money Walks* and a regular contributor to *Fox and Friends* as well as Forbes.com, and has appeared on various radio and television broadcasts such as Bloomberg News, Fox Business Network, CNBC, Newsmax.com, NPR, and CSPAN. Publications including *U.S. News & World Report*, the *Atlanta Journal Constitution*, and the *Dallas Morning News* have cited Brown's work when reporting on taxes and the economy. An issue advocate who has worked across 35 states throughout the past 20 years, Brown frequently advises governors, state think tanks, and national civic organizations with his data-driven strategies. His company, Pelopidas, LLC, is based in both St. Louis, Missouri, and Naples, Florida. Brown holds undergraduate degrees in both agricultural economics and political science from the University of Missouri–Columbia and an MBA from Washington University in St. Louis. Dedicated to giving back to his community, Brown sits on the board of directors for Wings of Hope and the Saint Louis Science Center.

Index

Abuselidze, George, 159

Adjusted Gross Income (AGI), 23,
43, 45, 52, 99, 101, 116, 118,
121, 124–127

Aid For Dependent Children
(AFDC), 184

Alabama, 73, 138, 220

Alaska
forced-union state, 56, 96
highways, 241
non-income tax state, 2, 119
oil production, 24, 88, 93, 143,
152, 209, 219, 260
population growth, 30
sales tax burden, 116, 137
taxation policy, 67
weather explanation, 106,
116, 252
work participation, 169

ALEC–Laffer policy prescription
is wrong (argument),
273–275

ALEC–Laffer state economic
competitive index, 76–80

ALEC-Laffer State Rankings,
37–39

Alesina, A., 159

All Kinds of Kinds (Lambert), 105

Alm, James, 160

American Economic Review,
168–171, 183, 191

*American Journal of Economics and
Sociology*, 165–166, 191

American Legislative Exchange
Council (ALEC)
criteria, 23, 39
publications, 145
ranking, 54, 77, 80, 87, 138,
140, 273, 275
State Economic
Competitiveness Index, 76

American Petroleum
Institute, 200

Annals of Regional Science,
169–170, 192

Arizona, 100, 251

Arkansas, 234

Arnett, Sarah, 36